A BRIEF HISTORY OF
INDIA

Alain Daniélou

Translated from the French by Kenneth Hurry

Inner Traditions
Rochester, Vermont

Inner Traditions International
One Park Street
Rochester, Vermont 05767
www.InnerTraditions.com

A Brief History of India was first published in French under the title *L'Histoire de l'Inde* by Fayard, 1971. It was subsequently published in Italian under the title *Storia dell'India* by Astrolabio/Ubaldini, 1984. English text and translation copyright © 2003 by Alain Daniélou.

LIBRARY OF CONGRESS CATALOGING-IN-PUBLICATION DATA

Daniélou. Alain.
    [Histoire de l'Inde. English]
    A brief history of India / Alain Daniélou ; translated from the French by
Kenneth Hurry
        p. cm.
    Originally published: Paris : Fayard, 1971.
    ISBN 0-89281-923-5 (hardcover)
        1. India—History. 2. India—Civilization. I. Title.
DS436.D2613 2003
954—dc21

                                                        2002038707

Printed and bound in the United States at Lake Book Manufacturing, Inc.

10 9 8 7 6 5 4 3 2 1

Text design and layout by Virginia Scott Bowman
This book was typeset in Garamond with BeLucian as the display typeface

Contents

Preface

The various languages of India contain very few chronicles that can be actually considered historical, except for relatively recent periods. However—owing to its situation, social system, and the continuity of its civilization—India is itself a sort of history museum, with its separate departments preserving the cultures, races, languages, and religions that have come into contact over its vast territory, without ever mixing together or destroying each other. No invader has ever entirely eliminated the culture of the more ancient peoples, and new beliefs and knowledge have never supplanted the beliefs and knowledge of former times.

In this strange country, we may even today encounter Stone Age peoples—mariners who sew their boats together because they are unfamiliar with the use of metals, civilizations whose technology has remained at what we usually term prehistoric levels—and yet these civilizations have preserved their languages, customs, traditions, philosophy, and religion down to our own time. The mysterious and ancient Dravidian civilization exists side by side with the other evolutionary levels of the great Indo-Aryan civilization that came from the north. In India the latter became the Sanskrit culture that coexists today with considerable vestiges of Iranian, Greek, Scythian, Parthian, Chinese, Tibetan, Mongolian, Persian, Arab, and European influences. In India too we find ancient forms of Judaism, survivals of primitive Christianity, and Parsis who found refuge from an Islamized Iran.

The inexperienced observer is surprised by this profusion of races, languages, and different customs, and finds it difficult to unravel the threads of this tangled maze. At the same time, a more profound study makes it easy to place each group and every aspect of life in its original context. Recognizing the tiny cultural islands surviving from periods almost forgotten elsewhere but which have been miraculously preserved in India can occasionally throw an astonishing light on the history of other parts of the world.

If we wish to understand India and utilize the facts, we must approach it using different methods from those we might employ for another country. This is because the history of India is not merely a chronology—a series of accounts of battles, conquests, and palace revolutions. It rests only momentarily on dynastic lists that appear ephemeral beside the permanence of its institutions. India's history is too long and too vast for the events of any particular period to play a definitive role, and Hindus have never given much importance to passing events. The history of India—with its discoveries in the fields of science, arts, technology, social structures, religions, and philosophical concepts—is the history of humankind, of our own human nature.

In its distant past, India was not an isolated country, as it has sometimes been in more recent centuries. The significant factors in India's history—such as major invasions, the expansion of successive civilizations, and the efforts of the human mind to discover the inner nature of the world—have often come from the same sources that have forged the history of other peoples, and give us a glimpse of what our own prehistory may have been like. At times, the history of India takes us from the isles of Oceania to the shores of the Atlantic. Owing to a curious phenomenon of the Indian spirit, the various currents meeting on Indian soil—instead of destroying or replacing each other—become fixed on their arrival in this magic land. They remain unchanging, side by side, in an extraordinarily eternal environment, where evolution appears to have halted and where events belonging to civilizations elsewhere separated by thousands of years appear to be almost contemporary.

The details of many of the views on India's ancient history adopted in the first section of this study are still disputed today, although on the whole they are in line with the views of historians who have sought a general idea of the human adventure. We must not forget that the concept of dividing the history of the various peoples into compartments arose at a time when the Western world refused to believe in humankind's antiquity. At the end of the eighteenth century, "very few scholars including geologists were prepared to accept that the world was much older than 4,004 BC according to the interpretation of the Old Testament."[1] Even at the end of the nineteenth century, the theosophist Bishop Lightfoot, following Kepler, calculated—apparently without covering himself with ridicule—that the world had been created at 9 A.M. on 23 October 4004 B.C.E. My own uncle, the curé of Saint-Pierre-de-Chaillot, affirmed at the beginning of the twentieth century that "since God is almighty, there was nothing to stop him from creating the world with corpses in it," to explain away prehistorical discoveries in apparent contrast to the articles of faith, which today have been prudently forgotten.

The conclusions reached by geology, archaeology, and prehistorical studies have not so far managed to correct our historical concepts inherited from the nineteenth century. Even though such concepts are built on erroneous data and on absolutely unjustifiable short-term evolutionary conceptions, they have been considered as established fact, in the name of which all Indian documents that contradict these theories have been rejected as works of fantasy. We should now take them up again. At no level—whether religious, linguistic, artistic, or philosophic—has there been any perceptible evolution developing from elementary primitive forms during the few thousands of years that we deem "historical." History that does not take into account the heritage of older civilizations more or less purposely forgotten will never be more than fiction with a falsely scientific basis.

According to H. D. Sankalia, "What was once believed to be prehistory has now come into the range of history. Thus both in Egypt and Mesopotamia history commences around 3,000 B.C. So it will be in India . . . when the Indus script is deciphered.[2] Hence the period prior to 3,000 B.C. and up to about 5,000 B.C. may be called Protohistory. For during

---

1. H. D. Sankalia, *Prehistory and Protohistory of India and Pakistan* (Bombay, 1962).

2. The script of the cities of the Indus was deciphered in 1969 by Danish scholars.

this interval of 2,000 years or so, . . . many of the essentials of the historical period were being formulated or taking shape."[3]

India provides us with the most surprising documents about this protohistorical period and previous periods—literary and archaeological documents, as well as living documents, miraculously preserved—through which we can relive forgotten ages and comprehend the origin and nature of our beliefs, rites, institutions, and languages, the invention of which is often arbitrarily attributed to much later periods and civilizations. As a result, the latter are given an unmerited importance, providing a wholly unjustifiable and puerile image of the barbarity and ignorance of earlier periods.

The history of India covers so vast a period of time that it is impossible to provide a complete picture. I have consequently sought to focus on certain salient points as being characteristic of various eras, while merely indicating events or periods which are seemingly less significant.

---

3. H. D. Sankalia, *Prehistory and Protohistory of India and Pakistan,* xv.

PART ONE

Origins

1
The First Civilization: The Proto-Australoids

The study of the first peoples of India reveals that technology and civilization are not always synonymous. Human beings, living under extremely simple material conditions, have actually developed the social institutions, and the religious, philosophical, and artistic concepts that are the very foundation of modern civilizations, often to such a level of refinement and with such an intuition of the realities of the visible and invisible world that our own conceptions may in comparison appear infantile and really "primitive." The introduction of writing was preceded by vast periods of civilization, reflection, and knowledge transmitted by oral tradition. The resultant beliefs, social systems, and knowledge are still being transmitted, writing having merely fixed certain aspects at a given period. The Hebrew prophets and Vedic sages belonged to civilizations of a kind we currently term prehistoric, with extremely organized and efficacious systems of oral transmission. This is why oral transmission is the only means deemed valid by Brahmans with regard to the Vedic hymns, the most ancient of which are the work of poets and sages who knew nothing of writing. The sacred nature of oral transmission has survived, even though some texts were written more than four thousand years ago. Great importance is attributed to oral tradition among all peoples, including Westerners, and the Celts in particular. Even today, the words of consecration in the Catholic Church are only considered "efficacious" if they are transmitted orally. A study of those populations that, in India, have refused the usage of writing, agricultural developments, and any change in their social institutions and beliefs is essential before measuring the very relative contribution made by more recent civilizations.

The limits of what we call human are not always easy to determine. Before the appearance of Homo sapiens, Indian fauna was distinguished by a great abundance of anthropoids (discovered in excavations at Shivalik, and elsewhere). A few excavations, performed on a rather chance basis, have revealed that from the remotest ages, going back more than fifty thousand years, there have been a great variety of civilizations that we term prehistoric, classified according to the kind of tools they employed. In other countries, only chipped or polished flint has survived the destruction of time and invaders. In India, however, some of these civilizations have continued down to our own times. By studying the primitive populations that have survived in India, we can probably obtain a reasonably precise picture of how particular groups of human beings lived in what we call the Stone Age, along with their customs and beliefs.

In the upper valley of the Indus, five glacier cycles can be identified. As elsewhere in the world, these mark changes in the climate, inevitably accompanied by vast movements of populations. At the end of the second glacier cycle, double-edged flint tools of the Chellean-Acheulean type are found, while after the third cycle we encounter an industry of quartzite pebbles with a single cutting edge, finished on both sides, of the kind known as Sohan. The first kind is also found in the Krishna and Godavari valleys in southern India, and the second at Narmada in central India. In central India geometric microliths and bone tools have also been discovered. The Khasi tribes in Assam still continue to make microliths. At a general cultural level, including their way of life and social structure, there is no reason to consider that these tribes differ very greatly from the peoples who lived in India over fifty thousand years ago. The funerary urns and hematite cliff paintings of the oldest prehistoric strata are hardly any different from those produced today.

Along the entire southeast coast of India, we also find populations of fishermen whose boats—often very large—are built without using metals of any kind. Their timbers are skillfully shaped and bent by fire; holes are then bored, also using fire, and they are "sewn" together with the aid of towropes. Such boats are probably identical to those used by prehistoric navigators on their long sea trips, thus explaining how the most ancient peoples of India spread so widely, eastward to Malaysia, the Sunda Islands, Melanesia, Australia, Easter Island, and the coast of Chile, and, in the other direction, to Madagascar, Socotra (an island in the Indian Ocean), Arabia, Egypt, and Mesopotamia.

Iron technology in India must have reached a very high level of perfection very early. Even today, no one knows what technology was used to produce the iron pillars with worked capitals (erected during the Maurya period in the third century B.C.E.) that still defy time and rust. Iron is the first metal to appear in excavations in various regions, particularly in Bellari in central India. Some scholars have therefore concluded that the use of iron originated in India, although no such generalization should be made on the basis of the very meager data available. Iron was known to the Hittites 1500 years before the Christian Era. In the Ganges valley, the use of iron predates the eighth century B.C.E. In some parts of the world, one metal may have been preferred to another for practical reasons, as well as on religious grounds, since magical properties were attributed to certain metals, iron in particular. The discovery of metallurgical technologies has not necessarily followed the same path everywhere. India apparently never had a Bronze Age, but jumped directly from polished stone to iron.

Among the proto-Australoid peoples who are the heirs of this early culture, iron—rather than gold, copper, or bronze—plays a ritual and sacred role. Rings of iron, or sometimes of iron and copper, are exchanged by brides and grooms. Young brides wear bracelets of pure iron, made from freshly mined ore, processed in the tribe's small earthenware blast furnaces. Such blast furnaces are constructed as a column of brick clay about three feet high and sixteen inches wide. They are fueled by wood charcoal and fanned by two buffalo-skin bellows. Using ropes and counterweights, the upper skin of the bellows is lifted to allow the air to enter. Standing on the skin, a young boy then blocks the air inlet with his heel and, with the force of his weight, sends the air rushing through the mouth of the bellows into the blast furnace. Jumping from one bellows to another, he manages to keep up a sufficient supply of air. The heat of the furnace thus melts the iron, or softens it enough so that it can be struck into the shape of arrowheads or small jewels. Arrowhead factories of this kind can still be found among very isolated tribes living in the forests of central India. Furthermore, the traditions of such tribes are unchanged at a social, religious, and ethical level, with no influence of note from any of the other populations of the Indian continent.

The social system of the proto-Australoid peoples—the most ancient in the whole of India—comprises small groups forming tribes, each having its own area of forest that serves as its hunting territory. Agriculture is deemed immoral, an outrage to the earth that is wounded thereby, and a fall from grace for those who practice it. The economy of these surviving populations is based on hunting and territorial rights. If a group is deprived of its ancestral lands, it rapidly declines and disappears, since these extraordinarily stable peoples adapt with great difficulty to new ways of life. This probably explains the remarkable permanence of their customs, language, and institutions. The social system of these peoples is based on matriarchy, and they are ruled and governed by an old woman. This kind of organization can also be found among certain more developed cultures that have a proto-Australoid origin, such as in Kerala in southern India. Polyandry is very widespread and springs from the matriarchal system; the woman is either free to choose, or she marries a man and his brothers (as among the Khasis). This kind of polyandry is also common in Tibet. It is mentioned in the great epic poem, the *Mahabharata*, whose chief heroes are the five Pandava brothers and their common wife, Draupadi. Although the Pandavas probably belonged to the later Dravidian civilization, it is as always possible to see the influence of the country's more ancient culture on the institutions of subsequent civilizations. Such survivals can be found even among the most modern civilizations of Europe and Asia.

The first inhabitants whose non-assimilated survivors still exist in India spoke and continue to speak Munda languages, a linguistic group whose origins have not been clearly established. They are directly linked to the most ancient strata of the population in Burma, Malaysia, and Indochina, and include the Vaddas of Sri Lanka, the Talas of the Celebes, the Batins of Sumatra, and the Aboriginal peoples of Australia. The Munda language group is "the most widely diffused on earth. It has been traced from Easter Island off the coast of South America in the east to Madagascar in the west, and from New Zealand in the south to the Punjab in the north."[1] Toward the West, successive invasions have obliterated the ethnic and linguistic traces of this first civilization, but certain signs and survivals in customs, music, rites, and so on, lead to the surmise that it may have stretched—as in the case of subsequent civilizations—as far as the Mediterranean basin and Africa. Among the peoples mentioned by ancient writers are the Minavars (fishermen), from whom came the Mina (fish), a people whose name is found as far away as Egypt. Striking similarities between the culture of the Munda peoples and that of the Pygmies could lead to the assumption that the Pygmies are a distant branch of this great ethnic and cultural group, driven out of Europe by the northerners, then from northern Africa by the negroid Africans and the Arabs.

In India these ancient peoples were driven back by successive invaders—first the Dravidians, then the northerners—and withdrew into the forests and mountains, where they still lead a simple and poetic life. It would be wrong, however, to consider that such peoples are savages. Their social, ethical, and religious concepts and the richness of their languages bear witness to a long history, which must formerly have been kinder to them. To this group belong the Mom-Khmers of Cambodia, and the flowering of the monuments of Angkor testifies to their aptitude for developing high forms of civilization. In India some of these ancient proto-Australoid peoples mixed with the invaders and form one of the

---

1. J. B. Bory, S. A. Cook, and F. E. Adcock, *The Cambridge History of India*, vol. I, Indian ed. (Delhi, 1963), 43.

racial components of the population. Other groups of Proto-Australoids rejected such a racial, religious, social, and cultural mix and are still almost intact, forming one of the world's most ancient cultures, which functions nowadays at a relatively rudimentary level.

Many ethnic groups in India have preserved the social traits of these ancient peoples as well as the Munda languages. The main ones are: the Santals, who at present number around three million; the Gonds, mentioned by Ptolemy under the name of *Gondaloi*; the Bhils, who are probably the ancient Villavars or "bow-drawers;" the *kui-*, *kolami-* and *kondhi*-speaking peoples of central India and Orissa; the populations of the Nicobar islands in the Gulf of Bengal; and the Khasis of Assam. The Vaddas of Sri Lanka also belong to the same culture. According to legend, they belonged to the Naga (snake) clan. Sri Lanka was even called the isle of the Naga (Naga-dvipa); the Nagas are mentioned in many Indian legends as semi-divine beings of enormous wealth. The Abhiras, today known as the Ahirs, have also preserved many of their customs, but have lost the language of their forefathers. Taken as a whole, the non-assimilated Munda tribes, whom the Hindus call Adivasi (the first inhabitants), still number over forty million individuals.

The Munda languages are particularly rich in vowels and semi-consonants, and utilize prefixes, suffixes, and infixes, which denote singularity, duality, or plurality. A distinction is also made between "animate" and "inanimate,"though not between masculine and feminine. Juxtaposed nouns are used instead of adjectives, and act as attributive adjectives. A few studies have been made of Munda languages, but it appears that no search has been made for any survivals of these very ancient languages in the Near East, Europe, and Africa (except for Madagascar). In the field of music, on the other hand, related forms seem to exist not only in Malaysia, Polynesia, and Australia, but also among the mountain dwellers of Asia and Europe and in central Africa. There are striking similarities between certain popular yodeling songs from the Caucasus and the Tyrol, songs of the Pygmies, and those of the Gonds in India.

Among the Munda peoples we find no dietary restrictions, no social taboos, none of the religious or moral conceptions that are characteristic of the Hindus. At the same time, we often find in popular Hinduism—as in many other countries—some traces of the beliefs, rites, and practices of that great prehistoric civilization from which we all may well descend. However, the only authentic "witnesses" of this civilization seem to be the Munda peoples of India and a few "primitive" tribes in Malaysia and Australia. We know too little of Africa, with its multiple languages and its religious, ritual, and philosophic concepts, to be able to discern the various currents that have contributed to the formation of the ancient African civilizations, of which, as often as not, only inextricably muddled vestiges still remain.

The religion of these early inhabitants of the Indian subcontinent is based on animistic beliefs, owing to which the people are always alert and attentive to the supposed needs of the hostile spirit world. Their religious practices turn on omens and propitiatory rites, of which vestiges still remain among almost all peoples in the form of gestures used to ward off bad luck. In the religion of the proto-Australoid peoples, such gestures and rites are a constant preoccupation and have an impact on every action. The *Yakshas*—spirits dwelling in certain trees or animals—must be honored to ensure their benevolence. The tree known as *Karam* or *Karama* plays a very important role. The king and queen of the Karam are particularly powerful spirits. Karam branches are essential in every ceremony. In order to obtain them, however, the forest has to be searched for a tree that is willing to give its branches and allows them to be cut.

Karam dances also play an important role, taking place either around the trees or on the *akhra*, village dance floor. The words and tunes that accompany the dances are usually of a very archaic nature. Only the dance—by its magical power of exorcism—can create an atmosphere of true security, which is why the dance floor is located in the very center of the village organization. In actual fact, it plays the role of a temple, a place for communication with the spirits. Throughout the world, similar structures—possible reminders of this early culture—can be found, such as the Temple of Heaven in Beijing, which is also just a platform. Among the pre-Celtic remains in the British Isles and in Brittany, we find the tree-cult and the social and magical importance of the dance. Pliny mentions the presence of a branch of the sacred tree at all Druidic rites. A Tamil novel of the third century, the *Shilappadikaram*,[2] gives a remarkable description of the dance-floor in a village of Ahira dairy workers, as well as the propitiatory performance of the dance at the moment the hero is threatened by major tragedies. Such dances—and the spirit in which they are performed—are no different from those of the Gonds or the Ahira nowadays, and are reflected in the dances of the *Tarantellati* in Apulia, southern Italy. The solidarity of community life is reflected in these festivals and rejoicings, in which the dances and the Karam in particular play an essential role. The psychological role of community dances in creating a feeling of refuge and an area of safety is a universal inheritance from animistic cultures, and is not unconnected with the dances performed by some modern Western youth.

Another practice of noteworthy value was the use of obscene words and gestures to ward off ill-omened influences. Obscenities were indispensable during certain festivals and especially at weddings. Survivals can be found throughout lower-class India: pottery covered with erotic pictures painted in bright colors, is used to carry wedding presents; erotic dances are seen as essential to a couple's future happiness, as well as during the seed-sowing and spring festivals. Vestiges of these traditions can be found in our own carnivals; the obscene gestures are used to ward off bad luck in southern Italy and in other Mediterranean countries.

Animals also play a familiar and almost human part. The crow is deemed wise, because it knows medicinal herbs. Its behavior has to be observed, and provides omens. The idea of consulting omens through bird-flight or the entrails of animals—which was so widespread throughout the ancient world—certainly belongs to the concepts of this early civilization. The tales in Kipling's *Jungle Book* come from the oral literature of the Mundas, as do the Sanskrit fables of the *Panchatantra* that in turn inspired Aesop and La Fontaine.

In another aspect of Mudra culture, magic practices often require the

---

2. Ilango Adigal, *Le Roman de l'Anneau (Shilappadikaram)*, trans. Alain Daniélou, 2nd ed. (Paris, 1981).

tribe or individual to be identified with an animal. At weddings, among the Baigas in particular, the bride's father, brother, or paternal uncle is possessed by the tiger-god and seizes upon a kid; he then kills it with his teeth and drinks its blood.

Research started in the middle of the twentieth century has shown the importance and high cultural level of these peoples, who once lived— as they still do—in the center of the Indian subcontinent, but are unknown to archaeology. It is only through references to the journeys made—in about the sixth century B.C.E.—by the Buddha and Mahavira, in order to preach the good news, that we know of the existence of the sixteen powerful republics (*samgha*) that stretched between Ujjain in the southern part of Rajputana (now Rajasthan), and Mithila in Bihar. From the texts annexed to the Vedas, and the *Puranas*, we know there were powerful states—some belonging to the Munda culture, as they still do today—in the regions we call Assam, the Uttar Pradesh, Madhya Pradesh, Rajasthan, Maharashtra (Vidarbha), Gujarat (Saurashtra), and in the south as far as Kanyakumari.

2

The Second Civilization: The Dravidians

THE PRE-ARYAN WORLD

In a very remote period, a dolichocephalic (long-headed) people with a bronzed complexion and straight black hair appeared in India beside the Munda peoples. It is assumed that this people must have had a foreign origin, although they had already spread throughout India by the fourth millennium B.C.E. Who were these people and where did they come from? The civilization that, in India, spoke agglutinative languages belonging to the Dravidian family seems to be a branch of a civilization—sometimes known as "Mediterranean"—that stretched from Spain to the Ganges prior to the third millennium B.C.E.[1]

Several historians have spoken of a great civilization whose traces can be found from India to southern Europe, starting from the sixth millennium before our era. "We must now realize that an early culture of this kind once extended from the Mediterranean to the Ganges valley, and that the whole of the Ancient East has behind it this common inheritance."[2] "It has been established beyond a possibility of doubt that India

---

1. Alain Daniélou, *Shiva and Dionysus* (Vermont, 1984).

2. A. K. Coomaraswamy, *History of Indian and Indonesian Art* (London, 1927), 5.

played a part in that early complex which shaped the civilized world before the advent of the Greeks."[3] "The Dravidians are a branch of the Mediterranean race. Such is the opinion of modern anthropologists. Accordingly there must exist some relationship between the Dravidians of India and the other branches of the great Mediterranean race, the Iberians of Spain, the Ligurians, the Palasgians, the Etruscans, the Libyans, the Minoans of Crete, the Cyprians, the Egyptians, the Hittites and the Sumerians. It is therefore not strange that some of the signs of the Mohenjo Daro script should have some resemblance to the signs of the scripts of these nations."[4] It has also been noted that "there is a common early Asiatic art, which has left its uttermost ripple marks alike on the shores of Hellas, the extreme west of Ireland, Etruria, Phoenicia, Egypt, India and China. All that belongs to this phase of art is the common inheritance of Europe and Asia."[5]

According to Elliot Smith, the Egyptians of the pre-dynastic period also belonged to the Mediterranean race. In Stoessinger's view, the sixty skulls found in Egyptian pre-dynastic burials are dolichocephalic and are identical to those found in India. To the same race belonged the Libyans and the Berbers who, according to Jéquier, occupied the whole Mediterranean basin prior to the Aryan invasion. This race was neither Aryan nor Semitic. It was an immense stratum of population, which played a basic role in the birth of all the great civilizations from India to the extreme West, but which is not the aboriginal stratum and probably did not originate in India, although it became established there at a very early period. However, "there can be little doubt that Dravidian languages were actually flourishing in the western regions of northern India at the period when languages of the Indo-European type were introduced by the Aryan invasions."[6]

From an ethnic point of view, the Indian branch of these ancient

---

3. H. Frankfort, "The Indus Civilisation and the Near East," *Annual Bibliography of Indian Archaeology* 7 (Leyden, n.d.), 12.

4. H. Heras, S.J., *Studies in Proto-Indo-Mediterranean Culture* (Bombay, 1953), 63.

5. A. K. Coomaraswamy, *History of Indian and Indonesian Art*, 14.

6. J. B. Bory, S. A. Cook, and F. E. Adcock, *The Cambridge History of India*, vol. I, 37.

peoples of Dravidian culture included the populations of the Indus and
Ganges basins as a whole, as well as those of central India. The southern
peoples, who alone speak Dravidian languages today, are, on the other
hand, greatly mixed with the older aboriginal peoples—the Mundas,
Negritos, and others, with the contribution of African and Madagascan
elements. They are not representative of the ancient Dravidian type. At
the same time, the Brahmans of the south, imported from the north during a relatively recent period and taken as Aryans, are as often as not pure
Mediterranean-Gangetic types, that is, ancient Dravidian.

Today, the Indians of the north speak mainly Indo-European languages. However, the northern Aryan racial element has been almost
completely dissolved among the local—and far more numerous—populations. The very white Indians of the north are often Parths or Scyths
who arrived much later; they were assimilated by Hinduism and—in
many cases—by Islam later on. As in other countries, linguistic divisions
in India do not necessarily correspond to racial or ethnic divisions. The
populations that speak a certain language today are not the ones that
spoke that language originally, except in the case of very isolated groups,
such as the primitive tribes still speaking the Munda languages that may
well be their original tongue. Other languages have sometimes been
transferred to different populations. Four main forms of Dravidian languages survive today in the south of the peninsula: Tamil, Telugu,
Kanada, and Malayalam. The Kurukh and Oraon of Orissa are also
archaic Dravidian languages, and there is also a Dravidian enclave—
Brahui in Baluchistan—close to the Iranian border. From a racial point
of view, the Brahui-speaking populations are now Turko-Iranian. This is
not indicative, however, inasmuch as they have assimilated neighboring
traits, and are not exclusive with regard to marriage.

The term *Dravidian* comes from the ethnic noun *Dravida, Dramida,*
or *Dramila* (Pali: *Damila*), from which the modern adjective *Tamil*
derives.[7] The name *Termilai*—given by Herodotus to the ancient inhabitants of Greece—is probably the same as *Dramila*. The Dravidian lan-

7. J. B. Bory, S. A. Cook, and F. E. Adcock, *The Cambridge History of India*, vol. I, 537.

guages are related to Georgian and Peuhl and—according to certain writers—to Sumerian. Sumer was thus merely a branch of this early Indo-
Mediterranean civilization. The ancestors of the Egyptians—who were
aware of their oriental origin—must have come from India too, passing
through Socotra and the south of Arabia. Attempts have been made to
derive the pre-Celtic word *Druid* from *Dravida* and, similarly, the name
of the Minoans of Crete from Mina (the fish-people). Such a relationship
is not altogether unlikely, if a great Indo-Mediterranean civilization really
did exist. From an ethnic point of view, there is no doubt that the ancient
Gangetic peoples, apart from the Mundas, are of the same strain as those
of the Mediterranean during the protohistoric period.

In the northwest of India, and as far as Gujarat, Aryan invasions
effaced the Dravidians, both racially and linguistically. Among the
Marathas, the language disappeared but not the ethnic traits. The same
happened to the Kalingas (of present day Orissa), except in the south,
where Telugu is still spoken. As a whole, the Gangetic population has preserved its Dravidian traits, even though it has been entirely Aryanized
linguistically.

The introduction of "cerebral"[8] consonants—characteristic of
Dravidian languages and non-existent in Indo-European languages—
into the Indo-Aryan languages of India proves with some degree of certainty that the general language of India prior to the Aryan invasion was
Dravidian. The same influence can be seen in the grammatical structure
of Hindi, which preserves a Dravidian substrate despite its almost entirely
Aryanized vocabulary. The relationship of non-Indo-European languages
to Dravidian languages outside India has not been clearly established,
although little research has been done on it.[9] Suggestions have been made
concerning Basque (western Iberians), Georgian (eastern Iberians),
Sumerian, and even Turkish. Sumerian and Hurrian (a language of ancient
Mesopotamia, Syria, and Asia Minor) seem to be the languages most
directly related to Dravidian.

---

8. Sounds made with the tongue on the palate rather than on the back of the teeth.

9. J. B. Bory, S. A. Cook, and F. E. Adcock, *The Cambridge History of India.*

THE INDUS CIVILIZATION

When the sand-buried ruins of what we now call the Indus Civilization were discovered at the end of the nineteenth century, a new horizon opened on the origins of India's history, as also on that of the Near East and the West. These ruins, covering a considerable area of which only a tiny part has been explored, reveal the existence—between the third and second millennium B.C.E.—of one of the most developed and refined civilizations of the ancient world. Little by little it became clear that this civilization was not limited to the Indus valley; it stretched as far as the Ganges valley and along the coast toward modern Mumbai (Bombay). Mohenjo Daro—the best preserved of the towns of this civilization—is uniquely modern, with its grid of streets, its balconied houses, its bathrooms, jewels, engraved seals, system of writing, and so on. Such a city is the result of a very long-lived culture, and some of its features explain aspects that have remained obscure in the history of other countries.

Many factors lead one to believe that Heras's still contested theory concerning the Indian origin of the ancient Mediterranean civilization—or at least of the existence of a common civilization, the first of the great civilizations to leave monumental remains and developed systems of writing—will in the near future become an undoubted historical fact. The Chogha Mish civilization in Iran, which flourished from the fifth to the third millennium B.C.E., is visibly related to that of the Indus and of Sumer. In the most ancient villages of the Ganges valley where modern archaeologists have been able to make excavations, pottery has been found of the same kind as that of Iran. Using carbon 14, the University of Pennsylvania has been able to date the finds to about 2000 years B.C.E.[10] Sumerian art and writing are clearly related to the art and writing of Mohenjo Daro and Harappa. The area covered by the Sumerian civilization is very small, however, compared to the immense territory and vast cities of northern India. "If the Sumerians, as is generally supposed, represent an intrusive element in Mesopotamia, then the possibility

---

10. H. D. Sankalia, Prehistory and Protohistory of India and Pakistan, 201.

is clearly suggested of India proving ultimately to be the cradle of their civilization, which in its turn lay at the root of the Babylonian, Assyrian, and Western Asiatic cultures generally.[11]

The most ancient documents of the Sumerians—who appear to have been a Mediterranean race—go back to 4000 B.C.E.[12] "There is no doubt that the Indus must have been one of the oldest centers of human civilization, and it seems natural to consider that the strange non-Semitic and non-Aryan people who came from the east to civilise the west was of Indian origin, particularly when we see to what point the Sumerians looked like Indians in appearance."[13]

The Egyptians attributed an eastern origin to their culture, stating that they had come from the East by sea, from the land of "Punt" (southern Arabia). Maritime communications and trading from the mouths of the Indus to the south of Arabia and as far as the Egyptian coast—very important during the early period of Egypt—had always existed. The fact that the Egyptians had built a canal from the Nile to the Red Sea implies a considerable volume of trade toward the south and east. The center of sea trade between India and the Mediterranean appears to have been the south of Arabia and Socotra (probably the Egyptian Paa-enka), the Greek Dioscorida, called Sukhadara dvipa (the Happy Isle) by the Indians.[14]

The geographical sections of the *Puranas* (Ancient Chronicles of India) mention Mecca among the holy places, under the name of Makheshvara, together with its black stone as an emblem of the god Shiva. The *Periplus of the Erythraean Sea,* written in the first century C.E., tells of the founding of the city of Endaemon, or modern Aden: "In the early days of the city when the voyage was not yet made from India to Egypt, and when they did not dare to sail from Egypt to the ports across the ocean (those of India), but all came together at this place, it received

---

11. A. K. Coomaraswamy, *History of Indian and Indonesian Art,* 5.

12. George A. Barton, *Semitic and Hamitic Origins Social and Religious* (Philadelphia, 1934), 39.

13. H. R. Hall, *The Ancient History of the Near East* (London, 1913), 174.

14. H. Heras, S. J., *Studies in Proto-Indo-Mediterranean Culture,* 359.

the cargoes from both countries." The *Periplus* indicates that Endaemon had been founded by Indian merchants, the Minas, whom Strabo calls Minaeans. Pliny speaks of the Minaeans as the most ancient of trading peoples and mentions relations between the Minaeans and King Minos of Crete. The prophet Ezekiel relates that their trading expeditions reached as far as the Phoenician city of Tyre.[15]

The first Minoan period appears to belong to the third millennium B.C.E. We find Minaei in Yemen, Minya in Boeotia and in northern Greece. Herodotus reminds us that the chief of the ancient inhabitants of Athens, who came from Crete, was named Pandion, a name that is typical of Dravidian royal families (see below). According to Sergi, "the Egyptians and all other Hamitic peoples came out of Asia," while according to Haddon, "at the beginning of history, some Asians came to Egypt, first from the south, eventually bringing with them bronze and probably also the plough and wheat."

In the seventh century St. Isidore made a summary in his *Encyclopaedia* of knowledge derived from ancient Greek and Latin authors, many of whose works have now disappeared. He also speaks of "Ethiopians" in his *Etymologiarium* (IX.2.128): "They came in ancient times from the River Indus, established themselves in Egypt between the Nile and the sea, towards the south, in the equatorial regions. They became three nations: the Hesperians to the west, the Garamantes in Tripolitania, and the Indians in the east. ["The Hesperians" are the ancient inhabitants of Spain; "Garamantes" can be connected to Karama ("city" in Dravidian); and "the Indians" refers to the inhabitants of Ethiopia, who were also mistaken in ancient literature for the inhabitants of India.]"[16]

Between the sixth and the first millennium B.C.E., relations between India and the Near East are evident. Precious stones—amazonite—coming from Nilgiri in southern India have been found at Ur prior to the Jemdet Nasr period (3000 B.C.E.). Indian seals have been found in Bahrain and in

---

15. *Ibid.*, 441.

16. *Ibid.*, 401.

Mesopotamia in pre-Sargonic levels (2500 B.C.E.).[17] Traces of Indian cotton have also been found, and there are archaeological indications of sea trade with India in the Larsa period (2170 to 1950 B.C.E.). The beams of the Temple of the Moon, at Ur of the Chaldees, and those of the palace of Nebuchadnezzar (sixth century B.C.E.) were of teak and cedar wood coming from Malabar in southern India.

"Apart from the existence of teak in the ruins of Mugheir Ur . . . an ancient Babylonian list of clothing mentions *sindhu* [of the Indus] or muslin, the *sadin* of the Old Testament, the *sindon* of the Greeks. Similarly the Tamil *arisi*, 'rice' had become the Greek *orydsa*, mentioned by Theophrastus and Arrian. Monkeys are also mentioned in the Bible as *kophim*, a word which is akin to the Egyptian *gofe* and to the Greek *kebos* or *kepos*. [T]he Sanskrit *kapi* [also] comes from the Dravidian. . . . No other is the origin of the biblical *tukkim*, 'peacocks,' which may be connected with the Greek *taos*, 'peacock,' both deriving from the Dravidian *toka* or *tokai*. It is also admitted the Egyptian *eb*, 'elephant,' and the Greek *el-ephas* come from the Dravidian *ipa*."[18] Also, the Hebrew term for sandalwood is *almug*, close to the Tamil *valgu*, whereas the Greek *santalon* comes from the Sanskrit *chandana*.

In Baluchistan the levels of the pre-Mohenjo Daro civilization—in which pottery of the Mesopotamian type is found—date back to 3400 or 3200 B.C.E.[19] "A great variety of motifs [in Indian art] antedating the age of Hellenistic influence present a Western Asiatic appearance, suggesting parallels in Sumerian, Hittite, Assyrian, Mykenean, Cretan, Trojan, Lykian, Phoenician, Achaemenid and Scythian cultures."[20] The ancient terracotta sarcophagi at the "prehistoric" sites of southern India are of the Mesopotamian type, as are the structures of certain types of boats still in use. The pottery and objects of the Dravidian era in India are identical to similar objects found in eastern Asia and in Europe. It appears certain

---

17. Louis Renou and Jean Filliozat, *L'Inde Classique*, t. I, (Paris, 1953), 122.

18. *Ibid.*, 7.

19. *Ibid.*, 123.

20. A.K. Coomaraswamy, *History of Indian and Indonesian Art*, 11.

that the large flat stone constructions known as dolmens belong to the Dravidian civilization and that the word *dolmen* itself comes from *Dramila* (Dravidian).[21] The skulls found at the Spanish dolmens are dolichocephalic, pre-Celtic, and of the same type as Dravido-Indian skulls. There is therefore every reason to consider that the great Neolithic Indo-Mediterranean culture has to do with the Dravidians, whatever their original homeland.

In the tradition of the Indian *Puranas* numerous myths and legends are found that are also known in Mesopotamia. One of these legendary stories is the one about the Flood that has come to us from the Sumerians, through Babylon. A Hurrian fragment referring to it was found at Boghazköy. This story is one of the basic myths of the pre-Aryan tradition in India. The hero of the Flood is called Manu. Manu comes from the Dravidian root *man*, which means "clay." Manu is "the man of clay," like Adam, meaning mankind in general, of whom he is the progenitor. Manu's surname is Satya Vrata, a name probably connected with *vratya*, the term used to mention the Dravidians in the Atharva Veda and the Panchavimsha Brahmana.[22] Among the institutions belonging to the great fundamental culture of the pre-Aryan world of India and Europe is probably that of royalty, as opposed to tribal organization. The *Mahabharata*, the Matsya Purana, and the Bhagavata Purana call Manu "king and prophet" (Rishi). He was adept in Yoga. The Bhagavata Purana calls him "king of Dravida." In the Indian version of the Flood, a fish guided the ark. There is a very important cult at Madurai in southern India that is connected with the Mina (fish) and the Goddess Minakshi (fish-eyed), the tutelary deities of the Mina, the fish-people, who are one of the main Dravidian clans.

According to Mortimer Wheeler,[23] the Indus civilization stretched southward at least to the estuaries of the Narmada and the Tapti. This is the Gujarat region, which seems to have been known in Mesopotamia

---

21. *Ibid.*, 6.

22. H. Heras, S. J., *Studies in Proto-Indo-Mediterranean Culture*, 44.

23. Sir R. E. Mortimer Wheeler, "The Civilisation of the Indus," *Antiquity* XXXII (1958): 246.

and Egypt by the name of Meluhha. According to Leemans, "it would be strange for the name of the country where the Indus civilization was found not to be known in Mesopotamia when, according to archaeological evidence, relations must have been frequent in the Akkad and Our III periods. No other name than that of Meluhha can be envisaged."[24] At the same time, according to Basham, it was the Gujarat region that longest maintained its independence from the Aryans who only penetrated there starting from the Shatapatha Brahmana period (about 1000 years before our era).

In India the main Indian centers of this pre-Aryan culture, of which important sites have survived, are—besides Mohenjo Daro and the other known but unexplored cities of the Indus—the city of Harappa and several less important centers. The city of Benares (Varanasi) certainly dates from this period, but the very summary excavations made up to now have not reached levels earlier than the Maurya period (third century B.C.E.), even though building levels continue to a great depth. At the time when the Buddha was preaching his first sermon at Sarnath, a suburb of Varanasi, the city was already considered the oldest in the world. The dates given by the *Puranas* place the foundation of Varanasi earlier than the sixth millennium. The Harappa civilization is the last—and also the most refined—stage of a long cultural development, the center of which was not necessarily the Indus valley, although it is in this region and in Baluchistan (Kulli culture) that climatic and geographical conditions have best preserved the archaeological remains.

Kalinga (Orissa) long remained a center of the ancient Dravidian culture, until it was crushed by the Maurya Emperor Ashoka around 264 B.C.E. Pliny calls the Kalinga capital "Pertalis." The area is still one of the centers of ancient Shaivism, whose priests, even today, are not Brahmans. A Dravidian language, Telugu, is still spoken by part of the population, which has maintained its pure Dravidian racial features. "The chief opponents of Aryan progress . . . were the Dravidian races, who had covered the country with a network of strongly centralized and well established

---

24. W. F. Leemans, *Foreign Trade in the Old Babylonian Period* (Leyden, 1928), 164.

governments . . . [which had] . . . made India a great exporting country. . . . [They] . . . had founded and maintained a flourishing inland and foreign trade long before the advent of the Aryans. . . ."[25] The Dravidians—whom the Vedas call Dasa or Dasyu—are represented in Aryan texts as amazing peoples possessed of the devil, famous for their science, their institutions, and the splendor of their cities.

The Aryan conquest put an end to the Mohenjo Daro civilization. This did not happen in a day, or even in a century, entailing a long process of the destruction and assimilation of a highly developed urban civilization by hordes of barbarian shepherds and warriors from the north. This phenomenon is not peculiar to India and involved the ravaging of the whole of the Near East and the eastern end of the Mediterranean. Only Egypt, due to its marginal geographical position, seems to have escaped these invasions, and its monuments show a continuity that is not found elsewhere. In India the Aryans lived in villages of huts that have left no traces. After the destruction of the Dravidian cities (Puras), no important monuments of stone or brick can be found prior to the fifth century B.C.E.

The ancient peoples were gradually subdued and reduced to slavery *(dasa)* by the Aryans. The Dravidians kept their language only in their former southern colonies, nowadays known as Dravidian country. However, as in the case of the Greeks, the conquerors assimilated little by little the culture of the conquered peoples. One of the Dravidian dynasties of the south, the Pandyas of Madura, belonged to an ancient tribe called Marar. At the beginning of our own era, its descendants considered themselves the heirs of the Pandavas of the Mahabharata.[26] The grammarian Panini (fourth century B.C.E.) acknowledged this relationship. The Chola kings of Coromandel belonged to the tribe of the Tiraiyar, and the Chera dynasty of Malabar to the Vanavar tribe, who may be the "monkey-people" (Vanara) of the Ramayana. Strabo mentions an

---

25. H. Heras, S. J., *Studies in Proto-Indo-Mediterranean Culture,* 6.

26. Ilango Adigal, *Le Roman de l'Anneau (Shilappadikaram),* trans. Alain Daniélou, 2nd ed. (Paris, 1981), 192.

embassy from Augustus in about 22 B.C.E. to a king "Pandion." At that time, an important Roman city existed close to modern Pondicherry.

Megasthenes recalls the legend in which Heracles (the god-hero Krishna in the *Mahabharata*) set up his daughter (or wife) Pandaia as sovereign of the southern countries, "there where the pearls are taken from the sea." The Heracles of Megasthenes is undeniably Krishna. The often-proposed identification of Heracles with Shiva is untenable from the point of view of Indian mythology, particularly the idea that Shiva could have a daughter. Krishna's city, Mathura, lies in the north of India. The creation of a Mathura (Madura) in the south is probably linked to the establishment of a Pandava in one of the southern colonies.

Up to the beginning of the Christian Era, the influence of Aryan culture was little felt in southern India. A few groups of Brahmans had acquired a certain position in literature and religion, but played no role in daily life. There was no caste system. The pre-Aryan religions—ancient Shaivism and Jainism—were still the main ones. Buddhism, as a kind of reformed Hinduism, inspired by Jainism, had also made an important place for itself.

ARCHAEOLOGICAL AND LITERARY SOURCES

What do we know about the Indus civilization? The principal documents furnished by archaeology are—besides objects of everyday use—engraved seals bearing images and written characters. Although the script, of which several different readings have been proposed, has not been definitively deciphered, some conclusions can be drawn about religion and culture. However, we may find many facts, mixed with mythological elements, in the ancient historical works of the Hindus—the *Puranas* (Ancient Chronicles) and the *Itihasas* (Legendary Accounts)—referring with certainty to a very ancient civilization that can only be the great Dravidian civilization. A critical study of these texts, either transcribed from oral tradition or translated at a later date into Sanskrit from forgotten languages, makes it possible to gather a great deal of data on protohistorical India.

No literary document concerning the ancient Dravidian civilization exists today in its original form. The ancient poems in the Tamil language, forming what is known as the first Sangam (Poets' Club), are probably much later than the Vedic period, although according to Tamil tradition they are very ancient indeed. We do possess, however, other sources of information that are important, though secondhand. We must not forget that the Vedic Indians were illiterate, which was certainly not the case of the inhabitants of India previous to them.[27] It was therefore inevitable that the development of Aryan culture should be almost entirely founded on the historical, religious, and scientific literature of their predecessors. Part of this literature survived the persecutions of many centuries, thanks to oral transmission. History and religion were kept alive by a special clerical class, similar to the Celtic bards. These depositories of sacred literature were known as *Sutas*. The *Vayu Purana* (I, 31–32) explains the role of the Suta. "The suta's duty, as understood by men of property in former times, was to preserve the genealogies of the gods, sages, prophets, and the most glorious kings, as well as the traditions of great men." The Magadhas were another kind of bard, and all the *Purana*s agree in attributing the bardic institution to the "first king," Prithu, who gave his name to the earth (Prithivi).

Each development of Sanskrit thought has drawn on pre-Sanskrit sources. Late Vedic literature (1000 B.C.E.) provides many details of the elements of ritual, philosophy, and religion that come from this ancient culture. Its influence can also be found in the arts and sciences, medicine, astronomy, and mathematics. Our greatest interest will, however, lie in the *Purana*s whose subject matter refers almost entirely to pre-Aryan history, cosmology, and religion. In a phenomenon peculiar to India, texts, narratives, rites, and techniques that had remained hidden for centuries suddenly reappear quite ordinarily in life and culture at various periods, as though nothing had happened. The *Purana*s were translated into Sanskrit at a relatively late period, when the ancient Shaivite religion had been totally assimilated by Brahmanism. It is not

---

27. H. D. Sankalia, *Prehistory and Protohistory of India and Pakistan,* 271.

known from which language the *Purana*s were translated, but it was certainly an ancient Dravidian language, probably different from Tamil. There are, however, Tamil versions that in some cases are older than the Sanskrit ones. Orally-transmitted *Purana*s also exist in several Indian tongues among the Shaivite populations who are nowadays considered to be of lower caste.

The *Purana*s are vast works somewhat like the Bible, containing genealogies—of kings as well as dynasties of sages—going back to the sixth millennium B.C.E., together with information about wars, towns, customs, law, science, and the arts. There are eighteen main *Purana*s and eighteen secondary ones, some of which are of considerable bulk. The *Skanda Purana* alone has twenty volumes. Almost none of this literature has been translated into European languages, and it has been the subject of very little critical study. Some of the *Purana*s have not even been printed in their entirety. As far as the *Purana*s that belong to the oral tradition are concerned, we know next to nothing about them.

Besides the *Purana*s, there also survive two great epic poems, the *Itihasas* (Legendary Accounts), called the *Mahabharata* and the *Ramayana*, both of which refer to events that occurred before or at the start of the Aryan invasions. Although they have been rewritten and adapted in Sanskrit, they too contain highly important information about pre-Vedic India. The *Mahabharata* alone comprises eighteen books. Its current form is considered to be a summary of a still larger work, traces of which can be found in the various oral versions or existing manuscripts.

The few studies made on the texts of the *Purana*s and *Itihasas* for the purpose of seeking information about pre-Aryan India have given interesting results, among which the works of Pargiter and Heras must be mentioned. However, most of the critical work required to separate the original elements from later additions still remains to be done—and the task is immense. The *Purana*s contain numerous references to countries and civilizations outside India, located throughout the seven continents (*sapta-dvipa*).

The texts of the *Purana*s were later adapted to make them conform to the theological conceptions of the Aryans, who considered the Vedas as revealed texts representing the original source of all knowledge and all religion. Such adaptations, however, had little effect on the body of information contained in the *Puranas*. The extreme antiquity of these texts was recognized; the fact that Parashara, the narrator of the *Vishnu Purana,* is deemed to be the grandson of the sage Vashishtha, who composed the seventh chapter of the Rig Veda, is probably merely a justification for including these texts—so profoundly non-Aryan in spirit—among the sacred literature of the Hindus. According to the Atharva Veda, Parashara was a contemporary of Parikshit, the famous king of the Aryan Kurus. The Atharva Veda (XI, 8, 7) speaks of "those who know the *Puranas*" as another way of saying "a scholar."

Unlike the Vedas—the prerogative of a very limited priestly class—the *Puranas* were and have remained the basis of popular religious literature for all Indians except for the Mundas. They represent the ancient tradition, common to all the Indian peoples, that survived the Aryan invasion and eventually assimilated it. Some of the *Puranas* in their present form belonged to everyday literature in the fourth century B.C.E. Megasthenes quotes certain elements from them. In his *Artha Shastra* (fourth century B.C.E.), Kautilya advises the princes to read them. "These are the same *Puranas* that have existed since Vedic times . . . the contents of which are found almost exactly in the ancient parts of the existing *Puranas.*"[28]

The *Puranas* gradually incorporated later elements from various cultures, including the Aryan culture, which is perfectly in accord with their character as historical books to which new chapters were ceaselessly added. This is why the great commentator of the Vedas, Sayana, mentions the history of Pururava and the nymph Urvasi as a typical example of the *Purana* literature. These two—who are mentioned in the Rig Veda (X, 95)—are considered to be the ancestors of the great race of the Ailas, the Aryans.[29]

There are six Shaivite *Puranas,* known as the *Matsya, Kurma, Linga, Shiva, Skanda,* and *Agni.* Six *Puranas* are dedicated to Brahma the

28. S. D. Gyani, *Agni Purana, A Study* (Varanasi, 1964), 28–29.
29. F. E. Pargiter, *Ancient Indian Historical Tradition* (Delhi, 1922), 38.

Creator and are called the *Brahmananda, Brahmavaivarta, Markandeya, Bhavishya, Vamana,* and *Brahma.* A further six are known as the *Vaishnavite Puranas,* and relate to divine heroes who are assimilated as incarnations of Vishnu. These are the *Vishnu, Narada, Bhagavata, Garuda, Padma,* and *Varaha Puranas.* The *Upa-Puranas* (secondary *Puranas*) form a collection, which is more or less the same as that of the main *Puranas.*

As a rule, each *Purana* covers five topics:

1. The creation of the world
2. The cosmic cycles and successive creations and annihilations of worlds
3. The genealogies of the gods and prophets
4. The "great epochs" of humankind and cycles of evolution periodically returning to the point of departure
5. The history of the royal dynasties

The narrative that gives a particularly interesting view of the pre-Aryan world is the *Ramayana.* This narrative, of which several shorter versions are given in the *Puranas,* was based on ancient sources, drawn up in the form of a long epic poem in Sanskrit by a sage called Valmiki, whose Yogic power allowed him to "see" the events of this distant past. The period in which it was drawn up is uncertain, though very ancient. The *Ramayana* was later incorporated among the sacred books of the Hindus. Although the Valmiki version was adapted in order not to offend the concepts of Aryanized Brahmanism, none of the chief elements of the narration allow it to be dated within the Aryan period. The *Ramayana* is assuredly an adaptation of very ancient non-Sanskrit texts.

According to the genealogies of the *Puranas,* as also according to tradition, Rama, the hero of the *Ramayana,* lived at least five centuries (Pargiter) before Krishna who took part in the great war of the *Mahabharata.* Like Krishna, Rama is a dark-skinned prince. Hindu chronology places the Mahabharata war at about 3000 years before our era, and places Rama at about 3500 B.C.E. Western chronology proposes 2000 B.C.E. At the time of the Ramayana, many sites, such as the confluence of the Ganges and the Jumna, were still covered by forest, whereas in the *Mahabharata* they are the sites of major cities.

The *Ramayana* is the story of a prince of Ayodhya (to the north of Varanasi), called Rama, who, as the result of the intrigues of one of his father's young wives, goes into exile in the forest. His wife, Sita, is kidnapped by Ravana, the king of Lanka (Sri Lanka). *Rama* means "charming" and the hero is the prototype of the "Prince Charming" of European legend. With the aid of the army of monkeys (the aboriginal Munda tribes), Rama conquers Lanka and rescus Sita.

We shall speak elsewhere of Krishna—the other divine hero of the ancient Dravidians—and of the great epic poem called the *Mahabharata*, since the "great war" which is its main theme symbolizes the one between the Dravidians and the Aryan conquerors.

DRAVIDIAN RELIGIONS

The religion of the Indus civilization included the cults of the Mother and of Shiva—of which phallic emblems similar to those used today are found, as well as images in Yoga posture. It should be remembered that in Hinduism, Yoga is a discipline created by Shiva and that its philosophy and technique have maintained a strictly Shaivite character that tends to sublimate and utilize sexual energies for spiritual and magical ends. Here we are dealing with religious forms and practices wholly unknown to the Vedas and the Aryans. The word *shiva* merely means "favorable." This adjective is used to avoid pronouncing the god's magical name, a name that appears to have been *An* in ancient Dravidian (and may have been the origin of the cult of St. Anne in Brittany).

According to the *Puranas*, it was toward the sixth millennium B.C.E. that the god Shiva manifested himself in India and taught men religion, philosophy, and the arts and sciences. Shaivism remained the dominant religion in India until the arrival of the Aryans, who violently attacked the Shiva cult and phallus worship in particular. Gradually, however,

Shaivism—which continued to be the religion of the people—was integrated into Brahmanic religion, of which it now forms an essential aspect. In fact, in the concepts known today as Hindu, the contribution of ancient pre-Aryan philosophy is much more important than that of the Vedic Aryans.

The religion known as Shaivism in India seems to have expanded immensely in Indo-Mediterranean protohistory and, under different forms, played a major role in the ancient world. The myth of Osiris in Egypt, for example, is a variation on one of the stories of Shiva described in the *Puranas*. The Egyptians, moreover, considered that Osiris had come from India riding on a bull, the vehicle of Shiva. The ithyphallic god Min was also considered to be of Asian origin.

The cults of Dionysus in Greece and of Bacchus in Latin countries are also branches of Shaivism. Furthermore, the Greeks speak of India as the sacred homeland of Dionysus, and the historians of Alexander identified the Indian Shiva with Dionysus and mention the histories and dates of the *Puranas* as referring to Dionysus. We also know that Alexander's Greeks came into contact with Indian Shaivites in the town of Nysa, close to modern Djelalabad in the Kabul valley. Homer also speaks of this center of Dionysian worship. He mentions Lykurgos the Edonian who "formerly furiously pursued the nurses of Dionysus at the holy mountain of Nysa." In actual fact this is a mythological account concerning Shiva's son, Skanda, and the seven nurses. Skanda (god of beauty and war) and Shiva are often mistaken for each other in the traditions of the Middle East, Greece, and Rome. In his *Guide to Geography* Ptolemy calls the town of Nysa both Nagara (the town) and Dionysopolis. The god's Greek name, Dio-nysos, appears to mean the "god of Nysa," the name being derived from the center of his cult.

The Edonians were a Thracian people, living on the banks of the River Strymon. Their customs were also bacchanalian. Megasthenes, speaking of philosophers, tells us that some of them who live in the mountains are worshippers of Dionysus. As proof that the god lived among them they cite the fact that the vine grows wild only in their country, and that neither ivy, nor laurel, nor myrtle, nor box, nor other evergreen plants exist beyond the

Euphrates, except in gardens where they need a lot of care. The vine, which is native to India, must thus have been a contribution of the ancient Indo-Mediterranean civilization to the Western world.

In Hindu texts Shiva is shown as a lustful, naked adolescent, wandering through the primeval forest and seducing the wives of ascetics. His emblem is the phallus. His feasts are orgiastic. Although he is the god of procreative forces, Shiva is also the priest who teaches how to master them and transform them into intellectual and spiritual powers. He is the inventor of Yoga and its extraordinary methods of physical and mental control.

The invention of the arts, and music in particular, is also attributed to Shiva. He is the central figure of pre-Aryan Dravidian religion in India and in all its branches in the Near East and around the Mediterranean, as far as pre-Celtic Europe. Although—due to the scarcity of documentation—the importance of this great fundamental religion in the formation of later religions has been largely under-estimated, it was almost universal. The body of its tradition has been preserved down to our own times only in India. However, anyone familiar with Shaivite rites, symbols, and festivals would easily recognize evident survivals in the rituals of the major religions, as well as in the customs of all peoples, whether Breton "pardons," Druidic rites, legendary narratives, carnivals, or popular dances, rites, and superstitions. Most of the Dionysian rites described by the Greek authors still exist today in India. The dithyramb, with its ecstatic dances, is still today called the *kirtana* (song of glory). The name of Bacchus, common to both the god and his followers, the Bacchants, certainly derives from the term *bhakta* (participant), and is still employed to designate the adepts of divine love who sing and dance to the point of ecstasy.

Side by side with the basic rites of Shaivism—still performed in the temples of India—there are associated rites known as "Tantric rites," in which magical and erotic aspects predominate. Among such aspects, we must mention the god's presence at the funeral pyre and the use he makes of the ashes of the dead; the practice of inebriation, which helps to create mystical conditions; and orgiastic and lewd rites. The ancient sects practicing these forms of Shaivism—such as the Pashupata, Kapalika, Kalamukha, and others—were frequently condemned by a puritan Brahmanism, just as the rites of Dionysus-Bacchus were condemned by the Christians. The cult of the female principle is also practiced by such sects, who also employ intoxication and sexual relations as a means of spiritual realization.

Among these Tantric cults—very important in India although always secret in character—the Dionysian religion continues in the same form it had in antiquity. A considerable sacred literature, known as the *Tantra*s and the *Agama*s (few of which have ever been published), belongs to those Shaivite sects that worship the phallus and to those that venerate the female principle. These sects also practice human sacrifice, and it is their custom for the worshipper to offer his head as a sacrifice to the Goddess Kali, Shiva's wife. Numerous representations of such sacrifices can be found in temples of southern India belonging to the Pallava and Chola periods. They are also mentioned in the *Shilappadikaram*.

Hindu thought, starting from the Upanishads (the most ancient philosophical, cosmological, and moral works of the literature attached to the Vedas), took a great part of its inspiration from ancient Shaivite philosophy. The texts mention sages, spiritual masters of the *Asura*s (the Titans, anti-gods, or gods of the enemy), whose teachings were adopted by the Aryans. Yoga became an essential element in Brahmanic teaching. The relations between Dionysus and the Titans in Orphic writings, the Titans' destruction by Zeus, the god of the Aryans, and the rebirth of Dionysus among the "new men," are a transparent narrative of a proven historical fact. Hinduism as we know it, together with Indian philosophy, are largely adaptations and continuations of pre-Aryan Shaivism, the main religion of the peoples who established the Indus civilization. Its traces can easily be found in Greece, Egypt, and Rome, and throughout the Christian world.

Apart from Shaivism, another highly important religion is found in ancient India: Jainism. "Unlike Buddhism, the Jain Church has its own prehistory: The Master, whose teaching is reproduced by the canon, Mahavira, is described as the last of a series of prophets or patriarchs, whose origins are lost in an unfathomable past."[30] Jainism is a moralistic and atheistic religion, since it deems that direct intervention of the supernatural or by the gods plays no role in the life of humankind. One improves oneself through one's actions during the course of one's life and, at death, one is reborn in another body. This cycle continues until, after numerous lives, one attains perfection and dissolves in the Absolute. Jainism does not deny the possibility of one or more transcendent beings, but it denies that humans can have any contact with such beings or obtain any proof of their existence. It is consequently entirely useless and futile to worry about the supernatural world. From Jainism comes the theory of *karma* and reincarnation, as well as that of non-violence, which prescribes that the supreme virtue is not to make any living being suffer, not even the smallest insect. Pious Jains can still today be seen wearing a white linen mask, for fear of swallowing an insect, walking carefully lest they crush an ant. Vegetarianism resulting from non-violence is also, in India, of Jain origin. The virtue of total nudity, purifications, and frequent ablutions are also Jain ideas, as well as suicide through fasting and the ideal of the monastic life.

The Artha Shastra—the major work on political arts written by Kautilya about 300 B.C.E.—describes the duties of a Jain monk: "He must control the organs of the senses, detach himself from worldly things and communication with mankind. He must beg for his food, live in the forest without remaining for any length of time in one spot. He must keep himself scrupulously clean, both within and without, abstain from harming living beings, be sincere, chaste, without envy, good, and patient." These rules can be found almost word for word in many Jain texts. Similar rules were adopted by Buddhist monks and by wandering Brahmanic ascetics.

It appears that Jain missionaries frequently visited the Near East, Greece, and Egypt, both before and after the beginning of the Christian Era, and Jain thought certainly played a role in the concepts of the Essenes and the early Christians. Jainism's greatest influence, however, was on Buddhism—a religion born in the fifth century B.C.E. as a reform

---

30. Louis Renou and Jean Filliozat, *L'Inde Classique*, t. II, 628.

of Hinduism. In revolt against the hierarchy, rites, and sacrifices of Vedic Brahmanism, Buddhism was profoundly inspired by the moral concepts and practices of Jainism. Mahavira and Gautama Buddha were contemporaries and both were disciples of an ascetic named Gosala.

It is likely that the naked sages of India—known in Greece and throughout the ancient world—were Jains. At the outset of the Christian Era, the populace of India belonged to one of the four major religions: Brahmanism, Shaivism, Jainism, and Buddhism. These four religions were close together during the historical period and lived in relative harmony, as can be seen from the *Shilappadikaram*, the Tamil novel of the third century C.E., mentioned earlier. However, whereas Buddhism gradually declined in India, Jainism still has many followers today.

Many historians of the nineteenth century were greatly attracted by Buddhism and wished to see it as the source of a certain current of religious thought. They consequently asserted that the last Jain prophet, Mahavira (559–487 or 468 B.C.E.), was the founder of Jainism and that the long list of his predecessors was a fiction invented afterward. This theory does not stand up to serious study. The historical reality of Parshvadeva—the Jain prophet who preceded Mahavira by two-and-a-half centuries—is now recognized. There is no real reason to doubt Jain tradition with its twenty-four prophets, or *tirthamkaras*, according to which the origins of Jainism go back several millennia, thus making it one of the great currents of Indo-Mediterranean religious thought, reflected in the most ancient currents of thought of both West and East.

According to Jain texts, the founder of Jainism was a king called Rishabha who renounced his throne after transferring power to his son Bharata. Bharata became the first of the "Sovereigns of the Universe" (*chakravartin*) and gave his name to the Indian subcontinent. Rishabha and Bharata are to be found among the most ancient characters mentioned by the *Purana*s. These historical characters, who pre-date the Mahabharata war, can only belong to the pre-Aryan civilization. Information about the first twenty prophets or *tirthamkaras* (ferrymen of the ford) who followed Rishabha Deva is very limited, and comes from the Jain *Lives of the Saints*. The nineteenth prophet, Malli, appears to have been a woman. The twenty-second prophet, Arishkanemi, is a contemporary of Krishna and the *Mahabharata* epic thought to have been of the Aryan conquest of India.

When serious study has been performed on the historical data of the *Puranas* (similar to what has been done with the Bible), the historical reality of the traditions narrated by these vast works will no longer be put in doubt. "An old text among the sacred lore of the Buddhists mentions sixty-three different philosophical schools—probably all of them non-Brahman—existing at the time of Buddha, and there are passages in Jain literature exhibiting a far larger number of such heretical doctrines. . . . We may therefore suggest that revolts against the Brahman doctrines date from a much more remote age than the time of Gautama Buddha . . . and Vardhamana Mahavira, the founder or rather reformer of the Jain church.[31]

There is a vast literature about Parshva, the last-but-one of the Jain prophets, who died two hundred and fifty years before Mahavira and thus lived in the eighth century B.C.E.[32] The Jain Kalpasutra—written by the pontiff Bhadrabahu in the fourth century B.C.E.—tells us that Parshva was a nobleman belonging to the warrior caste (Kshatriya), not to that of the Brahmans. He was son of King Ashvasena of Varanasi and his wife Vama. There is no king of this name in the Brahmanic genealogies, only a king of the Naga (snakes). This indication may be interesting, because the title *Kshatriya* was often given to royal families of Dravidian descent. This is still the case today for certain royal families, such as the Vijayanagar, who are certainly of Dravidian origin and only marry with other non-Aryan families, but have falsified their genealogy to be officially considered Kshatriya Rajputs, and thus Aryans.

Parshva lived for thirty years in the splendor of the royal palaces and married. Subsequently, he renounced the world and became a monk. He spent eighty-four days in meditation, at the end of which he attained enlightenment. He became a prophet and lived a life of perfect saintliness. At the age of one hundred, he attained liberation, *nirvana*, on the summit

---

31. J. B. Bory, S. A. Cook, and F. E. Adcock, *The Cambridge History of India,* vol. I, 134.

32. James Hastings and Louis A. Gray, *Encyclopaedia of Religion and Ethics,* vol. I (Edinburgh, 1953–1959), 202.

of Mount Sammeta, surrounded by his disciples. Mount Sammeta—today called Parshvanatha—is a steep hill located in Bihar, between Varanasi and Calcutta, and continues to be one of the important centers of Jainism.

Parshva's doctrine was a continuation of that of his predecessors, requiring four vows: "Not to destroy life, not to lie, not to steal, not to have possessions." Chastity was not part of his program, but was introduced by Mahavira. Moreover, Parshva allowed his disciples to wear two pieces of raiment. Complete nudity—which seems to have been the ancient rule—was reestablished by Mahavira, causing a schism. The community divided into "white-clothed Jains" *(shvetambara)* and "Jains clothed with space" *(digambara),* meaning naked. It was Keshin, a strict adherent of Parshva's doctrine, who opposed Mahavira and founded the dissident sect.

The life and teachings of Mahavira are known through numerous texts, particularly the Acharanga and the Kalpasutra. Mahavira is said to have been begotten by a Brahman, Rishabhadatta, with his wife Devananda at Kundapura, a district of Vaishali in Bihar. The gods transferred the embryo to the womb of a princess of Magadha, called Trishala, wife of Prince Siddhartha and related to King Bimbisara. This transfer is clearly borrowed from the Krishna legend. Further marvelous events accompanied the birth of the future *tirthamkara.*

Like Parshva, Mahavira was raised in princely pomp, cultivating the arts and sciences, and married the noble Yashoda, with whom he had a daughter. At the age of twenty-eight, he lost his parents, renounced the world, and left his family with the permission of his elder brother. He wore a monk's robe and at first lived in a park close to his native city. After thirteen months, he abandoned clothing and led the wandering life of mendicant monk for twelve years. He then became the disciple of an ascetic of lowly birth called Gosala, also the master of Gautama, who became the Buddha. After meditating for two days, preceded by lengthy mortifications, he received enlightenment beneath a tree, close to a village, and became omniscient, that is, *jina* (conqueror). Mahavira continued his wandering life and died near Patna at the age of seventy-two while reciting sacred texts. The date of his death is uncertain. "The dynastic list of the Jains . . . tells us that Chandragupta, the Sandrakottos of the Greeks, began his reign . . . in 313 B.C.E., . . . and Hemachandra states that at this time 155 years had elapsed since the death of Mahavira, which would thus have occurred in 468 B.C.E.[33] Such a date cannot be far from the truth.

During the last thirty years of his life, Mahavira visited all the great cities of Bihar, especially the kingdoms of Magadha, Anga, and Videha. He frequently met King Bimbisara and his son Ajatashatru. He made many conversions among the members of high society. He had frequent discussions with Buddhists. These conversations are reported in Buddhist texts, but not by the Jains. This is because initially Buddhism was not a major religion compared to Jainism, which was very powerful and ancient. Mahavira recommended total nudity, the severest of disciplines, and suicide by inanition as the best ways of attaining "liberation." He separated from Gosala and the two became mortal enemies. Gosala was the reformer of the Ajivika sect, which has left no written document. Of the eleven priests or school leaders appointed by Mahavira, only one— Sudharman—outlived him.

The Jain canon contains some highly interesting elements concerning ancient history. Some of the historical works exist in Sanskrit versions dating back originally to about the third century B.C.E. They have, however, been re-shaped and updated as late as the tenth century. We know nothing about any texts earlier than the Sanskrit ones. However, the immense libraries of the Jain monasteries have never been explored, and ancient manuscripts in Dravidian languages, particularly in ancient Kanada, could provide very important documents on certain aspects of the history of Indian thought, very probably going back to the earliest periods of the pre-Aryan civilization.

SOUTHERN INDIA, LAST REFUGE OF THE DRAVIDIAN WORLD

Southern India, which seems to have been originally a colony of the northern Dravidian civilization, served the latter as a refuge at the time

---

33. J. B. Bory, S. A. Cook, and F. E. Adcock, *The Cambridge History of India,* vol. I, 139.

when the northern invaders were ravaging the fertile plains of the Indus and the Ganges. The protection afforded by the Deccan plateau, together with its distance, allowed the Dravidian culture to maintain its integrity, from many points of view, down to our own times. Indeed, southern India is still a culturally and even politically independent country. Any domination by the northern empires was always temporary and rather nominal. Archaeology indicates that the southern kingdoms had direct trade relations with Egypt, Babylon, Arabia, and Palestine, as early as the second millennium B.C.E. and probably well before that. Since most ancient times, the institutions of the southern kingdoms had the benefit of stability and continuity that northern India never knew after the Aryan invasions. The cloth used to wrap Egyptian mummies is dyed with indigo from southern India. We have already seen that the teak employed in buildings at Babylon came from Malabar, in modern Kerala. According to the Bible, King Solomon imported ivory, monkeys, and peacocks from southern India. Many of the terms employed in ancient Mediterranean languages derive from Tamil.

While the northern plains underwent periodic ravages and the domination of invaders, the south maintained its independence through the ages, together with a very high level of civilization. During the first century B.C.E., trade with Rome was considerable, mainly consisting of pepper, pearls, and precious stones. The cities were very cosmopolitan. The kings employed Greek and Roman soldiers. There was a major Roman colony in the region of Pondicherry. The south also remained faithful to the ancient pre-Aryan religions: animist, Shaivite, or Jain. Brahmanism managed to penetrate only superficially, and only during the first centuries of the Christian Era, at the same time as Buddhism, Christianity, and Judaism. Brahmanic concepts were a mere superstructure added to the customs of a traditional society that kept its ancient cults and, to a large extent, polyandry and matriarchy. The caste system, too, remained a mere superstructure, with imported Brahmans and a few pariahs kept at a distance from society, although there are a few traces of other castes.

The Tamil kingdoms stretched from Kanyakumari in the south to the Tirupathi mountains in the north. They were, and remained, divided into three regions, governed from protohistorical times by three dynasties, the Chola, Pandya, and Chera. The Tamils claim that their culture is very ancient, as borne out by the literature of the poetic academies, the Sangams. The creation of the first Sangam is attributed to the non-Aryan sage Agastya, who is said to have lived at Madura (Madurai) and was later accepted into the pantheon of Vedic sages. According to tradition, the first Sangam developed under the successive patronage of eighty-nine Pandya kings. It included five hundred and forty-nine poets and is said to have lasted 4440 years. The works of the first Sangam were destroyed when Madura was overwhelmed by the sea. Later on, the second Sangam was established, counting one thousand seven hundred poets and lasting 3700 years. After the disappearance of the second Sangam, a third was established under the patronage of forty-nine Pandya kings and lasted 1850 years. In actual fact, the only works still existing are those of the third Sangam, which ended at the beginning of the Christian Era. Besides this literature, there exists a grammar of the Tamil language, the *Tolkappiyam,* that today is usually dated around the second century B.C.E. It is believed that the two famous surviving Tamil verse novels—the *Shilappadikaram* and *Manimekhalai*—must have been written toward the second and third centuries of our era.

The dates attributed to the various Sangams have often been treated as pure fiction, but for no valid reason. Humankind did not begin a few centuries—or even a few millennia—ago. The arts and poetry certainly existed in the remotest periods of prehistory. The fact that certain traditions have preserved a memory of them is not in itself surprising. The most ancient languages appear at a remarkable stage of development and perfection. The "scientific prudence" that consists of denying anything for which no tangible archaeological evidence is available sometimes totally falsifies the perspective used to envisage the origins of "historical" civilizations. Even if the Sangams never existed, those remote times certainly included both kingdoms and poets. Why is it strange that tradition should guard some memory of them, however summary it may be?

The Sangam religion was originally ancient Shaivism, which has remained predominant, especially the cults of Shiva and Murugan (or

Skanda), Shiva's son. Little by little the cult of Vishnu also took an important place, and has been linked to the cult of the pre-Aryan divine heroes who are accepted in the Brahmanic pantheon: Rama, Krishna, and Balarama. Women occupy an important place in Dravidian society and take an active part in literary and artistic life. The matriarchal system—in which all family property belongs to the wife and the daughter inherits from her mother—is still practiced today in Kerala. Even in royal families, the throne passes from mother to daughter, and the king is merely a consort. This practice is deemed to be the only effective way of guaranteeing the transmission of royal blood. According to the ancient Indian dictum—"When a father says, 'This is my son,' it is a matter of faith; when a mother says it, it is based on knowledge"—social institutions should be based on realities, not on belief.

The three Tamil monarchies, considered to be of immemorial antiquity, are mentioned for the first time in Indian archaeological documents in the edicts of Ashoka (274–232 B.C.E.).[34] The Pandya kingdom occupied the extreme south, comprising the modern districts of Kanyakumari, Tirunevelli, Ramnad, and Madura. Madura was the capital. The Chera kingdom, to the west, corresponds to modern Kerala. Its capital was Vanji. The Chola kingdom to the east included the plain and mouth of the Cauvery and the plain stretching between two rivers, both of which are called by the name of Vellar. Its capital was Urayur. During the reign of Nedunjelian, the Pandyas conquered Coorg and Mangalore, to the North of Kerala. The Cholas, under Karikala (about 190 C.E.), acquired a position of predominance that they maintained until about 550.

---

34. Throughout the book, the dates given after the names of sovereigns are those of their reign.

3

The Third Civilization:
The Aryans

THE AILAS

The Vedic Aryans were not the first northern people to descend on India. Round-skulled skeletons of a Celtic type have been found which pre-date them. The Aryan tribes were nomadic tribes of large blue-eyed men, dolichocephalous, related to the Iranians, the Achaeans, Celts, Ligurians, and other Germanic peoples who gradually invaded western Asia and Europe. The Indo-Aryan racial type exists in Kashmir, in the Punjab between the Indus and the latitude of Ambala (76° 46' E), and in Rajasthan. The men are tall of stature, fair-skinned, dark-eyed, with a plentiful beard, and long-headed, with a straight and prominent but not particularly long nose. The region now occupied by peoples of this type forms the eastern part of the vast territory colonized by the Aryans in the earliest historical period, that of the Rig Veda.[1] These regions have since been greatly re-Aryanized by Scythian and Parthian invasions.

According to the *Puranas*, the land was originally occupied by five races *(vamsha)*, all descended from a common ancestor called Yayati.

---

1. *The Cambridge History of India*, (London and Delhi: Cambridge University Press, 1963) vol. I, 38.

According to Pargiter, the Vedic Indians called the Aryan race "Aila." *Arya*, meaning "noble," is only an adjective.[2] The peoples speaking the Munda language were called "Saudyumna." The peoples called "Manva" were the Dravidians, who occupied the rest of India. The language of the Indian Aryans, Vedic Sanskrit, is the oldest of the languages known as Indo-European, of which written documents and spoken forms exist. It belongs to the same linguistic family as Greek, Latin, Breton, Lithuanian, Persian, and the Germanic languages. As a result of successive invasions, this group of languages gradually replaced the Dravidian basis of the Indo-Mediterranean languages, to which ancient Tamil, Sumerian, Georgian, Cretan, Etruscan, Egyptian, Tuareg, Basque, Albanian, Peuhl, and others all belong.

Climatic changes were probably responsible for driving the Aryan pastoralists from their original homeland in Russia and central Asia. According to *The Cambridge History of India*, "Over large tracts of Asia the climate has changed within the historical period. The rainfall has diminished or ceased; and once fruitful lands have been converted into impassable deserts. Both Iran and Turkestan, the two reservoirs from which the streams of migration flowed into the Indus valley, have been affected by this desiccation of the land. [Turkestan], a region which once formed a means of communication not only between China and India, but also between China and Europe, has now become an almost insuperable barrier. The same causes have tended to separate India from Iran."[3]

The separation of the Vedic Aryans and the Iranians took place prior to 2800 B.C.E. Starting from this period, the former began emigrating progressively to modern Afghanistan and the northwest of the Indian subcontinent (modern Pakistan). According to Hindu chronology, the separation between the Iranians and the Vedic Aryans took place almost one thousand years earlier. "The Indo-Aryans came from Bactria, over the passes of the Hindu Kush into S. Afghanistan, and thence by the valleys of the Kabul river, the Kurram and the Gumal rivers—all of them rivers well known to

2. F. E. Pargiter, *Ancient Indian Historical Tradition*, chap. XXV, 295.

3. J. B. Bory, S. A. Cook, and F. E. Adcock, *The Cambridge History of India*, vol. I, 34–35.

the poets of the Rigveda—into the N.W. Frontier Province and the Punjab. In the age of the Rigveda they formed five peoples, each consisting of a number of tribes in which the women were of the same race as their husbands. . . . We may be certain, therefore, that the invasions were no mere incursions of armies, but gradual progressive movements of whole tribes, such as would have been impossible at a later date, when climatic causes had transformed the physical conditions of the country."[4]

The Aryans' descent upon India was progressive and very probably similar to the Mongol and Muslim invasions that, centuries later, transformed Indian civilization in exactly the same way, destroying the great cultural centers and monuments and imposing the language of a rather primitive invader on peoples who were more culturally developed. The Aryan conquest was not always smooth. According to the Rig Veda (VII, 18, 33 and 83), the sage Vishvamitra himself led the Bharatas on an expedition against the enemy, but was defeated.

"In the age of the Rigveda the Aryans had not broken through the barrier [constituted by the country that separates the Indus valley from that of the Ganges], although the Jumna is mentioned in a hymn (VII, 18, 19), in such a way as to indicate that a battle had been won on its banks. It was only at some later date that the country between the Upper Jumna and Ganges and the district of Delhi were occupied. A record of this occupation has been preserved in some ancient verses quoted in the Shatapatha Brahmana (XIII, 5, 4, 11-14), which refer to the triumphs celebrated by Bharata Dauhshanti after his victories on the Jumna and Ganges, and to the extent of his conquests. In their new home the Bharatas, who were settled in the country of the Sarasvati at the times of the Rigveda (see III, 23, 4), were merged in the Kurus; and their whole territory . . . became famous in history under the name of Kurukshetra—'the Field of the Kurus.'[5]

---

4. *Ibid.*, 39.

5. *Ibid.*, 41–42.

The disaster represented by the Aryan conquest can easily be imagined by taking stock of the fact that there is in India no monument built dating from the period between the end of Mohenjo Daro and the Buddhist era (fifth century B.C.E.). As presented in the hymns of the Rig Veda, the Aryan occupants were intellectually and materially rather undeveloped nomads. Their language, religion, and social institutions were of the Indo-European type, like those of the ancient Persians of the *Avesta* and the Greeks of Homer's poems. They were unskilled in the arts and metalworking. At the start, Aryan colonization was, from many points of view, similar to the Inca Empire which was colonized by the illiterate and fanatical Spanish adventurers. The whole population was reduced to slavery (*dasa*), without any sort of civil rights.

In the Purusha-sukla—belonging to the later hymns of the Rig Veda—we find the first mention of a status being granted to slaves and the employment of the term *Shudra*, as applied to slaves, considered to be a fourth caste in the hierarchy of the Aryan state. The term *Shudra* probably comes from the name of a non-Aryan people reduced to slavery that the Aryans had started to recognize as having human status. They could no longer be killed at will, but were not allowed to better their condition on pain of the severest punishments. This state of affairs has lasted practically down to our own times.

Classical Sanskrit—as well as all the languages of northern India, formerly known as the Prakrits—derives from Vedic, the language of the Aryan tribes. The main Prakrits spoken today are Hindi, Bengali, Gujarati, Marathi, Punjabi, and Sindhi, all of which are related to Sanskrit, but with different contributions and admixtures from the previous languages of India.

The enslavement of the vanquished but culturally more developed Munda and Dravidian peoples could not but influence the Aryan language itself. Besides the introduction of writing and the set of "cerebral" letters, Sanskrit and all the languages of India contain a great number of words and forms that bear no relation to the vocabulary and structure of Indo-European languages. The extraordinary development of Sanskrit as a literary language, as well as the Aryans' political and cultural domination, led to the abandoning and loss of almost all the works written in other languages. Some ancient poetical and literary works have survived, but only in the Tamil language, and they are unfortunately very few in number and of uncertain date.

The Vedic Indians were carnivorous. They cooked meat in earthenware or metal pots or spit-roasted it. As with the Homeric Greeks, "the slaughter of oxen was always in some degree a sacrificial act, and one specially appropriate for the entertainment of guests, as the second name of the heroic Divodasa Atithigva, 'the slayer of oxen for guests,' and as the practice of slaying oxen at the wedding festival abundantly show." *The Cambridge History of India* goes on to say that "there is no inconsistency between this eating of flesh and the growing sanctity of the cow, which bears already in the Rigveda the epithet *aghnya*—'not to be killed.' If this interpretation of the term is correct, it is merely a proof of the high value attached to that useful animal, the source of the milk which meant so much both for secular and sacred use to the Vedic Indians."[6]

In actual fact, however, the sacredness of the bull—Shiva's vehicle—and later on of the cow, are of Dravidian origin. The sacred bull is represented many times on seals from Mohenjo Daro. The sacred nature of the cow and vegetarianism were notions that were completely foreign to the Aryans; they were borrowed from the ancient Shaivite and Jain Dravidians. Even today, the idea that virtuous living is connected to vegetarianism (an idea that comes from Jainism) and respect for life (the life of the cow in particular—an idea that comes from Shaivism), is so deeply anchored in the popular concept of good and evil, that even Christians or Muslims who wish to influence the Indian masses are obliged to practice, or pretend to practice, these "virtues."

The intoxicating drink of the Vedic Aryans was called *soma*. It is rather difficult nowadays to determine its nature, because the same name has probably been attached to different beverages at different periods. "It is difficult to resist the impression that the Soma was at first a popular drink in the home whence the Vedic Indians entered India, and that in

6. J. B. Bory, S. A. Cook, and F. E. Adcock, *The Cambridge History of India*, vol. I, 90–91.

India itself they found no plant which precisely coincided with that whence the Soma had first been produced, and so were compelled to resort to substitutes. . . . The popular drink was evidently *sura*, which seems to have been distilled from grain. It was extremely intoxicating and the priests regarded it with disapproval."[7] Wine made from wild grapes was a drink utilized by Dionysian Shaivites. According to the descriptions of its preparation given in the Vedas, the *soma* used in India was an unfermented drink, made of Indian hemp or hashish. This drink is still today a ritual and sacred drink, called *bhang*. It is the most important of the ancient beverages sacred to Shiva. These drinks were, of course, adopted by the Aryans, who no longer had access to the plants needed for their ancestral beverage. *Bhang* has a very special effect. It makes one's perceptions more intense and facilitates mental concentration. For this reason, it is employed by Yogis. When the Greeks speak of the "wine" used by the Indian followers of Dionysus-Shiva, they are most probably alluding not only to grape wine, but also to *bhang*, of which tasty drinks are made that cause a very strange state of harmless intoxication.

The music of the nomadic Aryans does not appear to have been very developed, but they rapidly adopted autochthonous instruments. The Vedas mention percussion instruments, stringed instruments, and flutes. In the kingdom of the dead where the god Yama reigns, the sound of the flute is heard. Drums were used to frighten the enemy in battle. Hymns were chanted.

THE GREAT MAHABHARATA WAR

After a long period of disasters—limited to the regions occupied by the Aryans—a rising of the Dravidian princes allowed them to reestablish some kind of balance and to acquire a place in the hierarchy, at least for the nobility of the sword. This nobility was the origin of most of the Kshatriya caste (warrior princes), always opposed to the Brahman caste (priests), who represented the purely Aryan element. The whole religious

---

7. *Ibid.,* 91.

tradition of the Kshatriyas has been preserved, parallel to the Vedic tradition preserved by the Brahmans, and this warrior caste gave rise to the major reformers, such as Mahavira and Gautama Buddha.

The revolt of the Dravidians against the Aryans is reported, in symbolic form, in the narration of the great war of the *Mahabharata*. In this vast epic the opposing armies are commanded by two families: the "sons of Pandu" (Pandava) and the "sons of Kuru" (Kaurava). Pandu is the ancestor claimed by the Dravidian dynasties, the Pandyas, up to the first centuries of our own era, mentioned by Tamil literature from the south of India. The Pandavas are dark-skinned Dravidian kings who practice polyandry. As related above, the five Pandu brothers have a single wife, Draupadi. The Sanskrit version of the Mahabharata gives many explanations to excuse their polyandry, a custom borrowed by the Dravidians from the Mundas that certainly required no apology in pre-Aryan society. The counselor of the Pandavas is the hero Krishna, who later on becomes a god. Black-skinned, wise, and prudent, he is the one who obtains victory, establishes peace, and takes up supreme royalty.

The adversaries of the Pandavas are the sons of Kuru—represented as schemers and traitors without morals—who had seized power and against whom the Pandavas had to foment revolt. *Kuru* is the name of the Aryans' original homeland among the northern steppes, to the north of the Hindu Kush. In its northern reaches, night and day last six months. Called "northern Kuru" (Uttara Kuru), it is frequently mentioned in Sanskrit literature as the home of the ancient sages, the Aryans' ancestors.

It appears that by the time of the Mahabharata war, the Aryans had already largely assimilated the ancient Dravidian civilization, and the Dravidians the Aryan institutions. The conflict was social, rather than cultural. The victory of the Dravidian Pandavas reestablished a certain balance, thanks to which the Brahmanic civilization was able to develop rites, sciences, and arts which were in theory Vedic, but in practice borrowed from Dravidian tradition in all fields of thought. The fact that the victory of the "good" Dravidian Pandavas against the "bad" northern Kauravas was considered normal is a further indication of how far Dravidian tradition had been assimilated.

According to Western historians, the Mahabharata war—the decisive battle of which took place at Kurukshetra close to modern Delhi—dates back to the years 1500 to 1000 B.C.E. This appears debatable, however, since the conditions of India described in the poem are not at all likely only a few centuries before the birth of Buddha. For example, "Parikshit is celebrated as a king of the Kurus in the . . . Atharvaveda: according to the [*Mahabharata*], he was appointed king of [the Kurus] more than thirty-six years after the great war."[8] Therefore, a date substantially earlier than 1500 B.C.E. is more likely.

According to Indian tradition, the Mahabharata war took place about 3000 B.C.E. It marks the beginning of the fourth age of the world, *Kali Yuga* (Dark Age or Age of Conflicts). *Kali* means "quarrel;" *Yuga* means "era" or "age." In relation to religious ceremonies, initiations, and so on, the era of the Kali Yuga still runs today; 1980 C.E. corresponds to the year 5082 of the Kali Yuga. Thus, "that the war between the Kurus and the Pandus is historical and that it took place in ancient times cannot be doubted, however much its story has been overloaded with legend, and however late may be the form in which it has been handed down."[9]

The traditional history of the war belongs to the non-Aryan literary tradition. It was many centuries before the tale of the Dravidians' victory over the Aryans was accepted in Brahmanic religious literature and, more especially, before its real meaning was forgotten. Unlike the texts of Shaivism, it was only incorporated into the Brahmanic tradition at a relatively late period, when the fusion of the two cultures was complete. It is not mentioned in the *Brahmanas* or the *Sutras*. Authorship is, however, attributed to the sage Vyasa, who is also supposed to have written the final text of the Vedas. Indeed, the origin of this traditional history is non-Aryan. It must have been translated and rewritten in Sanskrit at a relatively ancient period. The original text has certainly been re-edited since then and contains many additions. The poem as a whole, however,

---

8. *Ibid.,* 273.

9. *Ibid.,* 274.

certainly depicts a historical event, one that is mentioned rather briefly in the *Puranas* and in the Veda commentaries.

The current version of the *Mahabharata*, or one very close to it, existed in Sanskrit prior to the fifth century B.C.E. Its name is mentioned by Panini (fourth century B.C.E.). The *Mahabhashya*—by the grammarian Patanjali (second century B.C.E.)—makes allusion to its characters and the style of the work. Greek references to an Indian Homer, and sundry inscriptions, indicate that the ancient Dravidian heritage had been entirely assimilated and adapted for employment in Indo-Aryan legendary history.

The celebrated *Bhagavad Gita*—one of the texts inserted into the *Mahabharata* at a later date—is a long teaching discourse given by the divine hero Krishna to the Pandava, Arjuna, who is ready to withdraw from his duty as a soldier in order to avoid the horrors of war. According to Professor Gode, this treatise is borrowed from ancient Samkhya philosophy and has been recast to conform to the concepts of later Vedanta philosophy.

In its present form, the *Mahabharata* is a mine of information about every subject, mixing elements from ancient history with later data. As it stands, the poem comprises eighteen books and two hundred and fifty thousand lines. The principal peoples of India and the great cities of antiquity are mentioned in the *Mahabharata,* and detailed dynastic lists of the royal families that reigned after the war are provided by the *Puranas*, particularly for the Purus, the Ikshvakus, and the kings of Magadha.

Like Rama, the hero of the *Ramayana* epic, the god-hero Krishna—who plays such a central role in the *Mahabharata*—is one of the legendary heroes of the Dravidian civilization. The Greeks identified him with Heracles. His story takes up considerable space in the *Puranas* and is reflected in the myths of all later religions, Christianity in particular. Krishna was the son of a princess in the time of King Kamsa, who had been forewarned that he would be killed by a child still to be born. In order to save Krishna from the king's orders to kill all the newborn children, he was transferred before his birth to the womb of a shepherdess, who became his "adoptive" mother. Raised among the shepherds, his love affairs with his half-sister Radha and with the shepherdesses of Vraja are still today recalled with emotion. Eventually he killed King Kamsa, became king, and aided the Pandavas with his counsels. The body of his adventures and loves is poetically related in one of the later *Puranas*, the *Bhagavata Purana*.

Both Krishna and Rama were adopted by Brahmanism, in the form of incarnations of Vishnu. The development of devotional mysticism, or *bhakti* (the cult of divine love envisaged in its romantic and sensual aspect) among cults like Buddhism, which drew on essentially anti-Brahmanic Dravidian elements, should be mentioned. Much later on, this aspect was greatly promoted by the poet Jayadeva in his famous work the *Gita Govinda*, which hinges totally on popular traditional cults associated with the names of Krishna and Rama. This conception of mystical love, presented as a mixture of poetry, music, dance, ecstasy, and detachment, is, as its name indicates, the direct heir of the Shaivite *bhakta* tradition.

VEDIC RELIGION

The Vedic religion, brought by the Aryans from Turkestan and the plains of Russia, is related to the Persian religion, as well as to the religions of Greece and northern Europe. The Vedic gods personified the forces of nature—the Sky (Dyaus), the Sun (Surya), the Moon (Chandra), Fire (Agni), the Wind (Vayu), and so on—as well as knightly virtues such as Friendship (Mitra), Honor (Aryamana), Justice (Shakra), and Knowledge (Vishnu). One of the features of Vedic mythology is that of grouping the gods in pairs, in particular Mitra and Varuna, and the twin gods, the Ashvins. There are also groups of divine beings, such as the Maruts (a troupe of young delinquent and temperamental gods), Adityas (sovereign principals), and Vasus (universal laws). The male element predominates in the Vedic pantheon, as in Aryan society, and goddesses are but pale reflections of their husbands, except Aurora (Ushas) and the Earth (Prithivi).

The center of the Vedic cult is the hearth—the altar in the center of the family dwelling—where the fire is fed with offerings. This fire must never go out. This feature of Vedic religion must be a survivor from a remote era, in a northern environment, in which fire was captured and domesticated by an ancient race, the Ribhu, who thus transformed human life. If the sacred fire went out, it was deemed a bad omen: the god has left the house. In ancient times, and in a cold environment, the loss of fire in the hearth could clearly have serious consequences for family safety and unity. In most Indo-European languages, the term *hearth* has thus remained the symbol of the family home.

The destiny of the dead in the ancient Vedic religion is unclear. We know that they dwelled in a dark place where they conversed with Yama, king of the infernal world. We also know that they were buried; the current custom of burning the dead is perhaps due to the Indian climate. Human sacrifice does not appear to have been practiced in the early period of Vedic religion. However, the concept that life after death must reflect the world of the living gave rise to the custom of burying—and later on burning—widows together with their husbands.

The Aryans' sacred texts are called the Vedas, a word formed from the root *vid*, meaning "to know." Initially they were transmitted orally and were probably not written down until the Aryans had learned the use of writing from contact with the earlier populations of India. There are four Vedas—the Rig, the Yajur, the Sama, and the Atharva. They are collections of hymns used during rites, addressed to various divinities. The names of the authors of many of these hymns are known, but the texts themselves are considered to be of divine inspiration and are deemed to be a summary of all the knowledge revealed by the gods to human beings. The first three Vedas are manuals of hymns used by the three main classes of priests present at the sacrificial rites, the *yajña*s.

The most ancient of the Vedas is the Rig Veda. The hymns it contains were primarily composed shortly after the arrival of the Aryans in northwest India, although some of these hymns may have already existed when the Aryans were still living in central Asia. In any case, they retain a memory of their northern environment and its long winter nights. Many of the hymns make allusion to kings, and especially to the Indian peoples' fierce resistance to the invaders. The ancient inhabitants of India are mentioned as dark-skinned demons, living in marvelous cities.

The Yajur Veda is divided into two parts, the white Yajur and the black Yajur. It was composed after the Rig Veda and contains many pre-Aryan elements. The Sama Veda, a collection of chanted hymns, contains very few that are proper to it, most being chanted versions of the hymns of the Rig Veda and the Yajur Veda. Musical notation for these hymns existed from a very early date. Since the hymns are taught by complex oral methods—making any change in the text or intonation almost impossible—the tradition of Vedic chant has been preserved down to our own times without any major alterations or modernization of the language. The Atharva Veda is very different from the other three. It deals mainly with ritual elements borrowed from the indigenous religions, and is characteristic of the Aryans' assimilation of ancient Indian culture.

The AtharvaVeda is "a heterogeneous collection of the most popular spells current among the masses, and its most salient teaching is sorcery. . . . These features indicate that these songs began with and embody the ancient beliefs and practices of the peoples whom the Ailas [Aryans] subjugated, so that naturally the spirit which breathes therein is that of a prehistoric age."[10] Here we find a phenomenon that is characteristic of Indian history. The texts that in their current version appear to be the latest are often the most ancient from the point of view of their content.

When the Aryans invaded northern India, they encountered a highly developed urban civilization that astounded them. After centuries of combat, during which the institutions and beliefs of the ancient populations of India were held to be diabolical, magical, and evil, the Aryans gradually absorbed the customs and ideas of the conquered peoples. At a religious and philosophical level, the Aryans adopted the gods, and more especially the ideas, cosmology, and metaphysics of the ancient Indians. The Vedic religion absorbed, incorporated, and preserved the forms and rites of other cults. Instead of destroying them, it adapted them to its own needs. It borrowed so much from the Dravidians and other indigenous

---

10. F. E. Pargiter, *Ancient Indian Historical Tradition,* 319.

populations of India that it is very difficult to unravel the ancient Aryan elements from the others.[11] The very institution of priesthood, the figure of the Brahman himself, was not, according to Pargiter, an Aryan institution.[12] The conception of the "priest" was borrowed from the Daityas, Danavas, and Asuras—various names given to non-Aryans—who had been represented as having a demonic character. The indigenous influence also gave rise to the philosophical texts known as the Upanishads that demonstrate an almost complete fusion of Aryan and pre-Aryan thought. In the later texts of the Vedas and in the Upanishads, many of the sages mentioned are ancient prophets or philosophers of the indigenous Asuras, "the black men," earlier represented as demons, to whom the same status was now given as to the Aryan prophets.

Born from a fusion of Vedism and pre-Aryan religions, Brahmanism spread rapidly as a formalistic religion centered on increasingly complex rites. The great sacrifices became a very important part of Indian life, an expression of which can be found in the texts called *Brahmanas*. The *ashvamedha* or horse sacrifice—a rite that kings had to perform—developed into a series of ceremonies employing thousands of priests for months and swallowing the greater part of state revenues. Sacrifices sometimes became hecatombs. Priestly power dominated the whole of social life. By the end of the prehistorical Aryan era, life became an interminable ritual enterprise and prohibitions of all kinds paralyzed human relations.

---

11. Sarvapalli Radhakrishnan, *Eastern Religions and Western Thought* (London, 1940), 308.

12. F. E. Pargiter, *Ancient Indian Historical Tradition*, 306.

PART TWO

The Beginnings
of History

4

The Sources

Writing was known and widely employed before the Aryan era. This fact plays an important role in explaining the nature of later historical texts, since the beginnings of Sanskrit literature do not—as previously believed—represent a written culture developed by the Aryans among populations that were still relatively primitive. Sanskrit is a language of northern origin that developed thanks to a system of writing learned by the Aryans in India from their Dravidian predecessors. This meant, first, that the literature belonging to the invaders' oral tradition could be transcribed, and second, that a vast amount of existing written literature could be translated and adapted into their tongue.

The fact that a historical narration, an ancient genealogy, a philosophical concept, or an astronomic theory should appear in Sanskrit at a relatively late date does not mean that the ideas or facts to which they refer are of the same age. It was not a matter of recovering an oral tradition, but of transcribing in a new language a written document that was often of great antiquity. This peculiarity explains the phenomenon of the creation of classical Sanskrit, an artificial language invented to replace the more ancient non-Aryan literary languages.

The text of the Rig Veda—a remarkable document about Aryan life, society, and religion—has been preserved with the utmost care, even though the Aryans were illiterate at the time when the first hymns were composed. These poems, together with their laws, customs, mythology, and so on, were thus transmitted by oral tradition until the time when the Aryans learned the art of writing from the conquered peoples. But even then, a prejudice in favor of the oral tradition hindered the transcription of sacred texts. The same happened in other branches of the Indo-European family. The Druids never accepted that the principles of their teaching should be transmitted through written documents. It is therefore very difficult to date the Vedic hymns, from the point of view both of their composition and of their transcription. *The Cambridge History of India* (vol. I, 99–100) suggests between 1200 and 1000 B.C.E. for the transcription of the *Chhandra*s, the first Vedic hymns, and from 1000 to 800 B.C.E. for the period of the *Mantra*s and the last of the Vedic hymns.

The Vedas were followed by the *Brahmana*s, important works explaining the nature and form of ritual. They also include theological and philosophical descriptions and commentaries. They have been recast many times and appear on the whole to have been composed between the tenth and seventh centuries B.C.E., although *The Cambridge History of India* gives 800 to 600 B.C.E. for their composition and 600 to 200 B.C.E. for that of the literature of the *Sutras*. Such dates would appear too conservative, however, taking into account that the great grammarians of classical Sanskrit—Yaska and Panini—lived respectively in the sixth and fourth century B.C.E. By the time of the Buddha, Vedic literature was as archaic as the Bible is for us. "Scientific" elegance, unfortunately, always requires historical events to be dated as late as possible, often leading to absurd results. Recent prehistorical discoveries and more especially carbon 14 dating were needed to make it possible to date certain ancient events more reasonably.

As far as the Aryan tribes' advance into India is concerned, ethnological data agrees entirely with the historical indications given in the literature. "In the Rigveda Aryan communities have scarcely advanced beyond the country of the river Sarasvati (Sirhind), which for ever afterwards was remembered with especial veneration as Brahmavarta, 'the Holy Land'. In the *Brahmana*s the center of religious activity has been transferred to the adjacent country of the south-east, i.e. the upper portion of the doab between the Jumna and the Ganges, and the Muttra district of the United Provinces. This was Brahmarishidesha—'the Country of the Holy Sages.' Here it was that the hymns of the Rigveda, which were composed in the Northwest . . . (VIII, 24, 27) were collected and arranged; and here it was that the religious and social system which we call Brahmanism assumed its final form—a form which, in its religious aspect, is a compromise between Aryan and more primitive Indian ideas, and, in its social aspect, the result of the contact of different races.[1]

The Aryan contribution was not very great from a point of view of civilization, but this strong and active race from the north adopted—after fighting it—the civilization of the conquered, giving it a new and vigorous orientation. The Aryans' religious and social conceptions overturned the ancient world of India, as those of its Muslim and then European invaders were later to do. Their main contribution was the Sanskrit language, which was to become—like Greek elsewhere—one of the most important, if not the most important, of languages from a cultural point of view.

SANSKRIT AS A LANGUAGE

Ancient pre-Aryan writing is related to Sumerian script, while the most ancient Sanskrit script—Brahmi—derives from the Phoenician. "Brahmi has been traced back to the Phoenician type of writing represented by the inscription in which Mesha, King of Moab (c. 850 B.C.E.), records his successful revolt against the kingdom of Israel. It was probably brought into India through Mesopotamia, as a result of the early commerce by sea between Babylon and the ports of western India. It is the parent of all the modern Indian alphabets.[2] Brahmi was developed by the grammarians to form a complete phonetic script with fifty-two letters that could also be combined and are based on all the possibilities of articulation of the vocal organs. Consequently, it is capable of expressing the phonemes of all lan-

---

1. J. B. Bory, S. A. Cook, and F. E. Adcock, *The Cambridge History of India*, vol. I, 41.

2. *Ibid.*, 55.

guages, which has always been a basic problem in India. The various Indian scripts are all built on the same phonetic divisions: only the shape of the letters differs. The most widespread of these scripts—Devanagari—is today employed for Sanskrit and the principal languages of the north of India.

Another script appeared in India toward the sixth century B.C.E. The script is called Kharoshthi and derives from Aramaic, the official government language of the whole Persian Empire. At the time when northwest India fell under Persian domination, Aramaic was imposed on Gandhara and the Indian provinces. An inscription in Aramaic has been found at Taxila. In later Indian inscriptions, starting from the third century B.C.E., the alphabet was adapted to include the supplementary sounds needed to express the Indian languages, although it retained traces of its Semitic origin in its right to left direction and by an imperfect representation of vowels. This is the reason why it was eventually replaced by Brahmi, which is much more complete and easy to use. In its most developed form, Kharoshthi is found in Chinese Turkestan, toward the third century C.E., following the expansion of the Kushana Empire. There too, as in India, it was in the end replaced by Brahmi. It was not until the Muslim invasions that another Semitic alphabet was imposed on India—Persian—also not well suited to the phonemes of Indian languages.

Vedic—the language spoken by the nomadic Aryans—was solid and complex, but without any features that distinguished it from other Indo-European languages. It developed as a result of contacts with the various languages of India, and many new concepts and words were incorporated. The various *Prakrit*s, or "natural languages," such as Pali, Maharashtri, and Magadhi arose through such contacts. From them in turn India's modern languages such as Hindi, Bengali, Gujarati, and Marathi have descended.

The creation of Sanskrit, the "refined" language, was a prodigious work on a grand scale. Grammarians and semanticists of genius undertook to create a perfect language, artificial and permanent, belonging to no one, that was to become the language of the entire culture. Sanskrit is built on a basis of Vedic and the Prakrits, but has a much more complex grammar, established according to a rigorous logic. It has an immense vocabulary and a very adaptable grammar, so that words can be grouped together to express any nuance of an idea, and verb forms can be found to cover any possibility of tense, such as future intentional in the past, present continuing into the future, and so on. Furthermore, Sanskrit possesses a wealth of abstract nouns, technical and philosophical terms, unknown in any other language. Modern Indian scholars of Sanskrit culture have often remarked that many of the new concepts of nuclear physics or modern psychology are easy for them to grasp, since they correspond exactly to familiar notions of Sanskrit terminology.

Such a rich vocabulary often makes it difficult to translate philosophical, technical, cosmological, and other Sanskrit texts into other languages. While we have to make shift with three words with a badly defined meaning to express the notion I-me-self, Sanskrit has more than thirty distinct words. These have to be translated using expressions such as "sense of self," "notion of self," "self-consciousness," "universal self," "individual self," "self-perception," "individual soul," "entity represented by the word *I,*" and so on. The result is, of course, confusing, whereas the Sanskrit text is perfectly clear and simple. Sanskrit was codified at a relatively remote period by several grammarians whose writings have been almost totally lost. A summary was made of them toward the sixth century B.C.E. by the grammarian Yaska, then again in the fourth century by the grammarian Panini, whose monumental work remains as the basis of Sanskrit down to our own days. This grammar was then developed by the philosopher Patanjali in the second century B.C.E., in his "Great Commentary," the *Mahabhashya.* Later on, toward the seventh century C.E., another grammarian-philosopher, Bhartrihari, regrouped all previous ideas in his *Vakyapadiya,* developing a whole theory of language from the point of view of semantics, psychology, and symbolism. It is one of the most remarkable works that has ever been written on the nature of the human phenomenon of language.

The creation of Sanskrit was the greatest accomplishment of the Aryan world in India. Many texts, originally belonging to other Indian languages, were translated or adapted into Sanskrit, while most of those that were not, disappeared. An immense scientific, religious, philosophical, and dramatic literature was developed, a great part of which still exists, but is nowadays often inaccessible, left lying in manuscript form in innumerable badly-classified libraries.

In the very limited domain of Sanskrit musical theory, there are over one thousand works, still in the form of unpublished manuscripts. In other fields such as medicine, astronomy, geography, history, and philosophy, a vast number of works remains to be explored. Their rediscovery could one day change many of our notions about the history and civilization of the world, since only Sanskrit literature has developed continuously, without interruption, down to our own times. It was only relatively recently that the brutal Muslim conquest, followed by European colonization, interrupted the course of its development. But those invasions left few linguistic traces, since the prestige of Sanskrit was too great. Even Persian—the official language of the Muslim Empire for four centuries—left very few traces except for Urdu, a Persianized form of Hindi, spoken by the Muslims of India and Pakistan. The same happened to English, still a common language in India, which has, however, never reached the population as a whole, or produced any noteworthy literary work. It can consequently never replace Sanskrit and its derivatives as an instrument of culture and communication, whatever its advantages at the international and interprovincial level.

HISTORICAL WORKS

The Hindus have always been interested in historical events, to the extent that the events themselves become an example, a lesson. A historical event is considered rather like the subject of a theater play with a moral. To make the example more striking, facts, words, and actions belonging to other persons are wrapped around one character, as probably occurred in the case of the Christian Gospels.

The twelfth century *Raja Tarangini* is the first of the historical chronicles in Sanskrit dealing with history in the sense that we give to the word today. This vast work, drawn from the *Purana*s, gives the history of the various dynasties from the beginning of the Kali Yuga that, according to the author, began in 3102 B.C.E., at the time of the Mahabharata war. This date—with an approximation of a few years—is the one given by all Indian sources, but has been questioned by Western historians, with no cogent proof. After the *Raja Tarangini*, other historical chronicles appeared, first in Sanskrit and later in other Indian languages.

Besides the vast literature of the *Puranas*, however, many other texts provide important historical data. One of the principal ones is the *Artha Shastra*, a treatise on the political arts, written in the third century B.C.E. Numerous treatises on ritual, symbolism, astronomy, medicine, and geography also occasionally provide interesting data, the names of kings, comments on geographical divisions and social conditions, various contacts with other nations, and so on. The *Shilappadikaram* gives much information about the dynasties reigning up to the third century C.E., and their contacts with other kingdoms such as those of the Greeks.

FOREIGN SOURCES

Egyptian texts make mention of Indian divinities. Hittite sources mention India. The inscriptions of Darius, king of Persia, mention the Punjab as a satrapy (province). Before annexing the west of India, Darius had had the course of the Indus explored by Skylax, around 517 B.C.E. Skylax's log book is lost to us, but was used by Hecataeus of Miletus. We also have a fragment of *Indika* by Ktesias, a physician of the school of Cnidos, who lived for seventeen years at the court of Artaxerxes Memnon, King of Persia, starting from 416 B.C.E. Herodotus mentions major historical events, mixed with legends. But it was the historians of the period of Alexander the Great who gave the Western world the first solid facts about India.

Megasthenes—sent to Chandragupta as ambassador several times by Seleukos Nicator, King of Syria, between 302 and 297 B.C.E.—is the source most used by Greek historians. Considerable fragments of his work, *Indika*, have been preserved, in particular by Strabo. The *Periplus of the Erythraean Sea*, dating from the first century C.E., is an anonymous guide for travelers and merchants, but like Ptolemy's *Geography*, it is only incidentally interested in history. Among Latin documents, Trogus Pompeius, a Gaul, wrote a history of the world between 28 and 14 B.C.E., a summary of which was preserved by Justin (second century), containing interesting data concerning the relations of Seleucid Syria with India. Pliny and Strabo provide information about political conditions in India. There is also a Roman road map of the fourth century that includes India.

Staring from the fourth century C.E., Chinese sources contribute important documents about India, through which, in particular, we know about the Scythian invasion. The monk Fa Hsien visited India between 399 and 414 and has left a work of some forty chapters. The most important Chinese visitor to India was Hiuen Tsang, between 629 and 645. He produced a magnificent work, which has been translated into numerous languages. Other Chinese travelers have also left the impressions of their travels. Starting from the seventh century, the Tibetans too produced a considerable literature about India.

5

Buddhism and the Empire of Magadha

BUDDHISM

Gautama, or Siddhartha, known as the Buddha (the Enlightened One), belonged to a princely family. He was born at Lumbinivana, in the south of Nepal, in 563 B.C.E. His teaching, and especially the propagation of his doctrine, has sometimes been seen as an attempt by the royal (Kshatriya) power to free itself from the domination of the sacerdotal (Brahman) caste and to unite both spiritual and temporal power in the same hands. Such may not have been the views of Gautama himself, since he was essentially a religious reformer. It is certain, however, that this new religion was a political godsend to the princes, who wanted to escape from the power of the Brahmans, and that the encouragement received by Buddhism and its rapid diffusion were the result of political calculation.

Gautama reacted violently against ritualistic Brahmanism, and against the inhuman nature of its sacrifices and prohibitions. The kings supported the new religion that freed them from the priestly empire and relieved them of the enormous expenditure caused by the major sacrifices. Buddhism also became a powerful tool of cultural influence and the main vehicle of India's colonial expansion. Thanks to Buddhism, Indian influence spread to Burma, Indochina, Indonesia, Tibet, and Mongolia, and even to China and Japan. Toward the West, the influence of Buddhism was less, although it certainly played a role in the religious movements that troubled the Near East, Egypt, and Greece in the centuries prior to the birth of Christianity. Its influence is also easily recognized in the elaboration of primitive Christian doctrine. The life of Buddha, under the alias of St. Josaphat, has even been incorporated in the Christian *Lives of the Saints.*

In India itself Buddhism seems never to have reached the masses, who were always conservative and attached to their rites, mysteries, and customs. Furthermore, after more than a millennium, the major Hindu philosophers organized a counteroffensive and, in scholarly contests, attacked the very principles of Buddhist philosophy. In the face of this attack, Buddhism disintegrated and disappeared completely from the Indian subcontinent, only surviving in outlying areas such as Nepal, Sri Lanka, Burma, Tibet, and Indochina, as well as in China and Japan.

In many of these countries, however, and in Tibet especially, Buddhism absorbed numerous elements from previous religions, particularly the Shaivite cult and the cult of the female principle, or Shakti. It became known as the "Great Vehicle" (Mahayana), as opposed to original Buddhism, or "Little Vehicle" (Hinayana). Tibetan Buddhism, with its magical rites and gods, hardly retains anything of original Buddhism except names and formulas.

Starting from the fifth century B.C.E., the rise and development of Buddhism brought about a new conception of history. It is from this time onward that we find texts that can properly be termed historical. The ancient Hindus saw in human events a manifestation of the divine, and did not separate mythology from legend and history. With Buddhism, religion and history become tangible realities. The Buddha's successors are carefully labeled. The kings who protected the new doctrine were deified, beginning the first great inversion of religious concepts that was to affect most later religions. The gods were no longer abstract principles, manifested throughout creation, but were deified human beings. Gods and saints became historical characters. History, even when falsified, became chronological, a conception of historical reality that continues down to our own times.

The most ancient Buddhist documents of a historical nature that have been preserved come from the island of Sri Lanka. They are in the Pali language and refer to the island's ancient history, the life of the Buddha, and the development of the Buddhist community. The *Dipavamsha (History of the Island)*, based on even more ancient documents, dates from the fifth century C.E. The *Mahavamsha (Great History)* only reached its final edition toward the end of the fifth century. The Buddhist chronicles continued throughout the Middle Ages. Other works were written in Indochina, Thailand, Cambodia, China, and Japan, wherever Buddhism had spread. They provide retrospective information on history starting from the birth of the Buddha.

THE SHISHUNAGA-NANDA PERIOD (642–320 B.C.E.)

During the pre-Buddhist and Buddhist period, there was no imperial power in India. At that time, India was composed of a crowd of tiny states that were perpetually at war. The conflicts between the states—like those that plagued Europe during the Middle Ages—saw the employment of professional armies and hardly affected the general population, except in the republics formed by the Munda tribes who ferociously defended their independence. The boundaries of these states varied from time to time. Wars were paid for by annexing part of the territory belonging to the neighboring state and establishing a suzerainty that was rarely lasting. Matrimonial alliances sometimes managed to establish a temporary peace, although, on the other hand, they facilitated alliances against other states. Occasionally, two kingdoms would be united under the same sovereign, while maintaining their administrative autonomy.

There were sixteen important states, varying considerably in size and political structure. According to the grammarian Panini (fourth century B.C.E.), some of them were organized as republics, called *Samghas* or *Ganas*, while others were kingdoms, called *Janapadas*. The three major kingdoms in the north were Magadha (modern Bihar), Kosala to the north of the Ganges (in modern Uttar Pradesh), and Vatsa, south of the Ganges, whose capital was Kausambi on the River Jumna, not far from Allahabad. Among the other kingdoms, the most noteworthy were Kuru (close to Delhi), Panchala (in the Lucknow region), Surasena (Mathura, to the south of Kuru), Kashi (Benares), Mithila (north of Magadha), Anga (northwest of Bengal), Kalinga (southern Orissa), Asmaka (in modern Andhra), Gandhara (Taxila, Peshawar), and Kamboja (east of Afghanistan to the north of Kashmir).

At certain times, Gandhara annexed Kashmir. Hecataeus of Miletus (549–468 B.C.E.) mentions Kaspapyros (Kashyapapura = Kashmir) as one of the cities of Gandhara. Kamboja was usually associated with Gandhara. It included the Northwest Frontier Province in modern Pakistan and Afghani Kafiristan. Its capital was Rajapura (Rajaori), to the north of Kashmir. Two other kingdoms, Haihaya (probably Avanti, to the south of Rajasthan) and Vitihotra (probably Chedi in central India), are mentioned in the *Puranas*.

We find on all sides—in epic poems, religious and historical works, and plays—the concept of the ideal sovereign, the Kshatriya, who—in order to realize his full moral status—must conquer all the neighboring states and become "Sovereign of the World." He can make justice and virtue triumph. According to the literary image and later cliché, the dust at the emperor's feet should be swept away by the crowns of vanquished kings, prostrate before him. Only then does the conqueror gain the right to perform the horse sacrifice. A characteristic example of this conception of "World Sovereign" is found in *Ratnavali*, an elegant play for the theater, attributed to King Harsha (seventh century C.E.).

With the development of Magadha (modern Bihar) under Bimbisara and Ajatashatru in the sixth and fifth centuries B.C.E., the supremacy of Magadha was assured, laying the foundations of the Maurya Empire and the reign of the Emperor Ashoka. Prior to the development of the Magadha Empire, the Kingdom of Kashi (Benares) long played the predominant role in the north of India. Its origins are lost in prehistory. The ancient city of Benares (Varanasi), sacred to the cult of Shiva, was a kind of Babylon, the spiritual and cultural capital of India, a holy city, a city of letters and pleasures. It was the center of Indian civilization, whose kings were the suzerains of a large part of northern India and even of the south. Buddhist legends, known as *Jatakas*, constantly allude to the hostilities between the kingdom of Kashi and that of Kosala, which lay between Kashi and Nepal. Shortly before the birth of Gautama Buddha—who preached his first sermon at Sarnath, a district of Benares—the Kingdom of Kashi had succumbed to an alliance of neighboring kingdoms and had been annexed by and entirely integrated into the Kingdom of Kosala.

The annexation of Kashi made Kosala a powerful state. At the time of the Buddha, its sovereign was Prasenajit, one of the major kings of his time, about whom the Buddhist chronicles give a great deal of information. Very pious, he was greatly interested in Buddhism and neglected his kingly duties. During one of Prasenajit's visits to Gautama Buddha, the minister to whom he had entrusted state business proclaimed the crown prince Vidudabha as king. Prasenajit went to Ajatashatru of Magadha to ask his aid, but died on arriving in Rajagriha.

Vidudabha invaded the Shakya country (a minor state under the suzerainty of Kosala), where the family of Gautama Buddha reigned. The Shakyas say they descend from the solar race of Ikshvaku, an ancestry that may have been embellished by Buddhist historians. Vidudabha himself was the son of an illegitimate daughter of a Shakya king, and thus a kinsman of the Buddha. Despite his kinship ties, Vidudabha massacred the whole Shakya family, including women and children.

Meanwhile, the power of Magadha was growing. A war between Magadha, whose capital Pataliputra is modern Patna in the province of Bihar, and Anga, a kingdom lying to the east, ended in a complete victory for Magadha. The King of Magadha, Bimbisara (520–500 B.C.E.)—placed on the throne at the age of fifteen by his father Mahapadma—was a contemporary of the Buddha. He belonged to the Shishunaga family, an ancient non-Aryan clan, and desired to conquer the world. He implemented a skillful policy of alliances, in which marriages played a key role. According to the *Mahavagga*, he had 500 wives. In any case, the first of his wives was the sister of Prasenajit, King of Kosala (Lucknow region).

India in 600 B.C.E.

His second wife was Chellana, also known as Vasavi, daughter of Chebaka, one of the chiefs of the Lichchavis, a group of tribes forming a major republic in the north of Bihar, whose capital was Vaishali. Bimbisara's third wife was Khema, daughter of a king of the Punjab. His Kosala wife brought him the Kingdom of Kashi as a dowry, and a rapid war of conquest allowed him to annex Anga (northwest of Bengal). This concentration of power was the beginning of the Empire of Magadha, which was soon to spread its dominion over almost all of India.

Bimbisara's success was mostly due to the efficiency of his administration. He was a skillful politician, an excellent administrator, and a pious Buddhist, but also posed as a protector of Jainism. The fact of belonging to the new and moralistic religion that was Buddhism and having the support of the minority Jain religion freed Bimbisara from priestly control and Hindu orthodoxy. He could thus follow an independent policy, while maintaining the reputation of a strictly religious man, a reputation that was essential to gain the support of the Indian masses. This same policy was later adopted by the Muslim Emperor Ashoka and, in our own time, by Mahatma Gandhi.

According to Buddhist chronicles, Ajatashatru (500–475 B.C.E.), son of Bimbisara, killed his father and mounted the throne at the instigation of Devadatta, the Buddha's wicked cousin. He continued Bimbisara's work, however, and contributed to the development of the Magadha Empire. He stirred up two wars, one against his uncle Prasenajit of Kosala, and the other against the Lichchavis. The first of these wars, although not ending in absolute victory, turned to his advantage. Ajatashatru married the daughter of the King of Kosala and extended his political influence over the kingdom. His war against the Lichchavi republics lasted sixteen years and was very hard. In this war he used new weaponry: a catapult (*mahashilahantaka*) and a chariot (*rathamusala*) driven without horses that crushed the enemy soldiers. The powerful association of republics, of which the Lichchavis were the leaders, was keen to defend itself but Ajatashatru eventually managed to sow dissention among the Lichchavi chiefs and consequently subdue them.

Being thus solidly established, the Empire of Magadha gradually became the center of political activity in India. Ajatashatru's son and successor was Udayin, or Udayabhadra, who founded the city of Pataliputra Nagara, today known in its abbreviated form as Patna. This city, located on the right bank of the Ganges, was to become one of the most important in India. According to certain sources, Pataliputra had already been founded by Ajatashatru as a base for his operations against the Lichchavis. Buddhist sources make Udayin his father's murderer, whereas Jain works consider him, on the contrary, a good son who, at his father's death, was at Champa in west Bengal where he was viceroy.

During the reign of Udayin, the Kingdom of Avanti, whose capital was Ujjain near Rajputana, attempted to become a rival and annexed the Kingdom of Vatsa (Allahabad), between Ujjain and Varanasi, whose capital was Kausambi. Avanti and Magadha, however, avoided entering into any direct conflict, and Magadha maintained its predominance. According to the *Vayu Purana*, Udayin built a new city called Kusumapura (City of Flowers). A pious Jain, he was later assassinated by a novice in the pay of Palaka, King of Avanti, while he was listening to the teachings of a Jain monk. After Udayin, Anuruddha and Munda reigned, about whom very little is known. After them came Nagadasaka, called Darshaka in the *Puranas*. Next Shishunaga reigned, who made Girivraja his capital, annexed Varanasi (Kashi), and established his supremacy over Avanti, Vatsa, and Kosala.

The last king of this dynasty was Kalashoka, whom Curtius and Diodorus call Kakavarna (black as a raven). He was assassinated by a barber who was the queen's lover. The barber mounted the throne and founded the Nanda dynasty, putting to death all the descendents of the Shishunaga dynasty.

THE NANDA DYNASTY (425–325 B.C.E.)

There are very few documents giving precise information about the Nanda dynasty of Magadha and its actual duration. Jain, Buddhist, and other chronicles provide discordant information. According to the Jain texts, the dynasty lasted one hundred and fifty-five years; according to the

*Purana*s it lasted one hundred years; Buddhist documents give it twenty-two years. The dynasty's founder, Mahapadma, is described in Jain texts as the son of a barber and a prostitute. The Greek historian Curtius tells us that "his father was actually a barber who earned just enough to eat each day. But he had a fine presence and thus gained the queen's affection. Thanks to her influence, he obtained a position of trust, too close to the sovereign. He treacherously assassinated the king and, under the pretext of assuring the protection of the royal children, he usurped the supreme authority, put the young princes to death and begot the present king." The *Purana*s call Mahapadma "the greatest of villains" (*nichamukhya*). The commentary on the *Mahavamsha* modestly declares that the person's origins are unknown. The *Mahabodhivamsha* calls him "the terrible" (*ugrasena*, equivalent to the Greek *agrammes*). The *Arya Manjusri Mulyakalpa* explains that he was prime minister before becoming king, which seems likely. All the texts agree in counting nine sovereigns of the Nanda dynasty. According to the *Purana*s however, Mahapadma had eight sons who reigned in turn. We do not know, therefore, whether the nine Nandas were Mahapadma and his sons, or whether they are the descendants of one of them.

There is little information about the Nandas after Mahapadma, except the last one, Dhana Nanda. Xenophon speaks of his immense riches. According to Buddhist texts, he was extremely avaricious and imposed very unpopular taxes. Curtius says that his army included 20,000 horsemen, 200,000 infantry, 2,000 chariots, and 4,000 elephants.

Mahapadma Nanda created the first historical empire in India. He was also the first low-caste sovereign, as he did not belong to the Kshatriya clan (warrior princes). Mahapadma's accession caused a violent reaction in the princely families of the neighboring kingdoms. Mahapadma fought the coalition with extreme ferocity, managing to subdue the families and, in many cases, to exterminate them. A man of lowly origin, he did not observe knightly rules, and his low treachery got the better of the princes, for whom war and state management were the game of well-brought-up persons. The *Purana*s speak of Mahapadma as the "destroyer of the princely order" (*sarva kshatrantaka*). Among the families he destroyed are mentioned the Kurus, the Maithilas, the Surasenas, and others.

The empire of Mahapadma stretched from the Punjab to Bengal and to the south of the Deccan plateau. The city of Nava-Nanda-Dhera (City of the Nine Nandas), located on the banks of the River Godavari, south of the Deccan, would appear to indicate that the Nanda Empire reached that point. An inscription in the grotto known as Hathigumpha, close to Bhubaneshwar in Orissa, dating from the third century B.C.E. alludes to the Nanda conquest of Kalinga (the modern province of Orissa on the Gulf of Bengal). According to inscriptions at Mysore, Kuntala (to the south of modern Mumbai) also belonged to the Nanda Empire. Little is known of the Nandas' relations with the Achaemenids, who then occupied the Punjab.

The revolutionary ideas spread by Buddhism on a religious level thus led to a revolution of a political nature. The last of the Shishunagas were Buddhists or Jains. Devout, seeking common virtues rather than princely virtues, they had forgotten the great Hindu principle that "virtues that are not the virtues of your caste are not virtues." Kings were to be just, brave, and manly, not compassionate and devout. Neglect of this great principle—as Krishna reminded Arjuna in the *Bhagavad Gita*—caused the downfall of the Shishunagas, resulting in the elevation to the throne of a low-born intriguer such as Mahapadma and the ruin of all the high cultural values that the nobles had been born to protect.

6

The Iranian and Greek Invasions

THE IRANIANS

The great Aryan invasion that changed the face of the world, about the third millennium before our era, divided into several branches. Each of these mixed with earlier civilizations and in so doing became rapidly different. While the Indian and Achaean branches fairly rapidly assimilated important parts of the culture of the peoples they had subjected and partially annihilated, a large part of the branch known as Iranian more or less preserved its original character as nomadic warriors. The very rich and fertile country that stretches around the Caspian and the Oxus basin (Amou Daria), as far as the Hindu Kush and the Iranian plateau, had been one of the cradles of civilization. Over-exposed to invaders from the north and east, this region had a particularly tragic and troubled history. The peoples that occupied the land were in turn ruined and enslaved by other invaders, which is why so little of their history is known to us.

The Hurrians, who occupied the north of Mesopotamia and the region of Lake Van in Turkish Armenia during the third millennium B.C.E., spoke a Caucasian language related to Sumerian and to the Dravidian languages of India. They spread to Syria and Palestine and then withdrew during the second millennium. They reappear in the

Urartu culture, in the south of the Caucasus, in the ninth century B.C.E., and are the ancestors of present-day Georgians. Urartu bronzes have been found in Etruscan tombs. The Etruscans (Tusci, Tursinoi, etc.), who came from Lydia after the Trojan War in about 900 B.C.E., apparently belonged to the same pre-Aryan group. They are mentioned by Egyptian sources about 1200 B.C.E. as allies of the Lydians and the Achaeans. They were thus originally related to the Iberians of Spain and the Caucasus, and to the early inhabitants of Sicily, the Sicans, who, according to Thucydides, were Iberians expelled from Spain by the Aryan Ligurians.

The great pre-Aryan culture served as a basis for the development of the culture of the invaders. Medes, Scythians, Parthians, and Iranians gradually adopted whatever they had allowed to survive of the sciences, arts, and customs of their predecessors, whether of Urartu, Elam, Assyria, or Babylon. It is for this reason that it is so difficult to unravel what they later contributed to the civilization of India, since they themselves had already assimilated many of the earlier cultural elements that were closely tied to the more ancient cultures of the Indian subcontinent.

Little is known of the great empires of the Medes, Scythians, and Parthians, established by the so-called Iranian branch of the Aryan invaders on the ruins of previous civilizations. It is with the Mede Cyrus—who created the Iranian Achaemenid Empire and entered into conflict with the Mediterranean peoples—that the Iranians enter history as such. Later on, the Scythians and Parthians manifested their might in India, without any clear indication as to their contribution from the point of view of thought, science, the arts, or military and social organization. This strange fate, that seems to try to efface the great peoples of southern Russia from the pages of history, has continued almost until our own times. We easily forget that much of the culture attributed to the Arabs came in reality not only from Iran, but from those great centers of civilization located in what is today the territory of the southeastern republics of the Soviet Union, and from the north of Afghanistan. Avicenna was born at Balkh in Bactria, and Al Farabi probably in Azerbaijan. Since prehistoric times, Bukhara, Samarkand, Tashkent, and Merv had been centers of trade and civilization, and played a major role in the development of Iranian and Arab culture.

"Prior to the seventh century B.C.E. . . . there is further proof of relations between Persia and India through the facts of trade in antiquity, especially through the early commerce between India and Babylon, which, it is believed, was largely via the Persian Gulf."[1] India and Iran had maintained regular relations since the time when the Iranian and Indo-Aryan tribes had separated, about 2500 B.C.E. The name given to India in the Avesta, the sacred book of the Persians, is *Hindu*, and the Punjab, "land of the five rivers," appears in the first chapter of the Avestan Vendidad, as one of the sixteen regions controlled by the Iranians. Both the Vedas and the Avesta have common sources.

Besides political domination, cultural relations between India and Iran were constant and profound. It would be entirely false to envisage the development of the sciences and arts as independent phenomena in the Near East and in India. Before the Aryan invasions, there was a single, identical culture, and the new cultures developed by the Aryans who invaded Iran and northern India were also characterized by reciprocal contacts.

Archaeology provides us with little data about periods in which stone did not play a major role. Wood, the essential material for building temples and palaces in India, leaves no trace in a damp tropical climate. The first Indian architectural and sculptural elements in stone, however, are very clearly inspired by Iranian models.

Cyrus (558–530 B.C.E.), the founder of the Persian Empire, also conquered northwest India. According to Herodotus, "he conquered the lands of upper Asia and subjected all nations, without overlooking any." In his *Life of Cyrus* (I, I, 4) Xenophon tells us that, "Cyrus established his dominion over the Bactrians [to the north of Afghanistan] and the Indians." The term Indians here doubtless means the populations of the Indus valley. He adds (VIII, VI, 20–21) that Cyrus, after reducing Babylon, "launched on an expedition during which, they say, he subdued all the nations of Syria and the Erythraean Sea [the Indian Ocean], which was the boundary of Cyrus's empire eastwards."

During the reign of Darius I (522–486 B.C.E.) Persian dominion was

---

1. *Ibid.*, 294.

firmly established in the north and northwest of the Indian subcontinent. The province of Gandhara included the regions of Peshawar and Rawalpindi, while the "Indian" province comprised the Punjab (as far as Delhi), Sind (to the east of Karachi) and the entire lower Indus valley. These regions formed the twentieth satrapy that, in fact, corresponds almost precisely to modern Pakistan. There were Indian cavalry and infantry regiments in the gigantic army assembled by Xerxes in 480 to invade Europe. The Indians formed part of the contingent that fought against Leonidas and the Three Hundred at Thermopylae and at Plataea. According to Herodotus (VII, 65), "the Indians were clothed in cotton, had bows and arrows of bamboo, the arrows having iron tips." After Xerxes's defeat at Plataea, Persian power declined, and after the defeat of Darius III by Alexander at Arbela (330 B.C.E.), the Indian provinces broke loose from Persian control.

INDIA AND THE MEDITERRANEAN

Contacts between India and the Mediterranean world had existed since prehistoric times, and had continued throughout the Aryan period. "Hebrew sources mention that, during the reign of Solomon (970–933 B.C.E.), a ship equipped by Hiram, King of Tyre, made a journey to the east every three years, bringing back gold, silver, ivory, monkeys and peacocks, great quantities of sandal-wood (*almug*) and precious stones. The port whence this merchandise came was called Ophir ...], also called Sophara in the Septuagint. Sophir is still today the name for southern India in the Coptic tongue.[2] One of the great trade routes with the West crossed the Khyber Pass, through the Hindu Kush toward Balkh, the great center where all the trading routes met, from China, India, the Black Sea, and the Mediterranean. Another route followed the Oxus as far as the Caspian and from there to the Black Sea ports, while yet another went from Herat to Antioch, through Ctesiphon and Hecatompylos. These routes are mentioned by Pliny and Strabo.

---

2. K. M. Munshi, *The Age of Imperial Unity* (Bombay, 1951), 612.

The extending power of the Parthians and their successors the Sassanids separated India from the Mediterranean by the overland route, which greatly stimulated sea trade. Ships sailing to the Persian Gulf followed the coasts of India, Baluchistan, and Persia. Those travelling to the Red Sea crossed the Indian Ocean to Arabia and sailed northward to Suez, where the merchandise was transported overland to Egypt and the famous ports of Tyre and Sidon. Other vessels sailed up the Euphrates and joined the overland route coming from Persia. Strabo, who lived during the reign of Augustus, visited the port of Myos Hormos (founded about 250 B.C.E. by Ptolemy Philadelphus), to the north of the ancient port of Berenice on the Egyptian coast of the Red Sea. He mentions that one hundred and twenty vessels journeyed from this port to India, some of them going even as far as the Ganges estuary.

THE GREEKS

"For a thousand years, from the sixth century BC to the fifth century AD, there were Greeks in India. They traveled as explorers in the pay of the Persians and marched as soldiers in Alexander's army, they came as wandering philosophers and seaborne traders, as artists and ambassadors, as administrators and princes. They founded kingdoms and cities, and the list of Greek kings and queens who reigned in India and on its borders is as long as the list of English kings and queens who have reigned in England since the Norman Conquest. There were few parts of India into which the Greeks did not eventually penetrate. They invaded the valleys of the Indus and the Ganges, the plateaus of the Deccan and the beaches of Gujarat. As merchants they traded to the Malabar Coast and the coast of Coromandel, and as mercenaries they served in the palaces of Tamil kings. Until the British came no European race so thoroughly traversed and explored the great subcontinent.[3] Greek influence continued to be felt in architecture, especially in Kashmir, up to the Middle Ages.

When Alexander led his armies to India, in 326 B.C.E., he discovered

---

3. George Woodcock, *The Greeks in India*, (London, 1966), 13.

that many of his compatriots had already established themselves in the fertile mountains that dominate the Indus. For over two centuries, Greeks in the service of the Persians had visited India, had traded there and taken part in its administration. After Cyrus had subjugated the Greek cities of Asia Minor, his empire extended from the Hellespont to the other side of Afghanistan and circulation within its borders was easy. Thousands of Greeks had enrolled in the Persian army and administration.

In 517 B.C.E. Skylax, a Greek, was commissioned by Darius to explore the sea route from the Indus to the Red Sea. He embarked close to the town of Caspatyros that—according to the information provided by his contemporary, Hecataeus of Miletus—must have been located not far from modern Peshawar. Skylax sailed down the Indus with a considerable fleet and gained the coast of Arabia. His journey lasted two-and-a-half years. He wrote an account of it, a short fragment of which has come down to us in the writings of an obscure historian, Athenaeus, who lived several centuries later. The sole almost contemporary mention of this expedition is made by Herodotus, who was born about twenty years after Skylax's return.

Sanskrit sources indicate that important Greek colonies already existed on India's northwest frontier in the fifth century B.C.E. Starting from the fourth century B.C.E., the term employed by Indian literature and inscriptions to identify the Greeks is *Yavana*, related to the Persian *Yauna*, meaning "Ionian." It is difficult, however, to believe that this term was used only after Alexander's expedition. It most certainly comes from much more ancient contacts with the Mediterranean world, and perhaps with Crete, and was employed as a general term for all the Western "barbarians." The *Vishnu Purana* states that "To the east of Bharata [India] live the Kirata and to the west the Yavana."[4] The word *yavana* is used by the grammarian Panini (fourth century B.C.E.), who also mentions Greek literature (*yavanallipyam*). Buddhist literature calls them *Yona*. According to the *Law of Manu*—a very ancient and often re-edited text, the final version of which dates back to the beginning of the Christian Era—the

4. H. H. Wilson, *The Vishnu Purana*, (Calcutta, 1961), 127–129.

Greeks, owing to their martial virtues, are accepted as knights, despite their unclean customs and ritual shortcomings.

ALEXANDER

In the spring of the year 334 B.C.E. Alexander crossed the Hellespont, in the hope of establishing the greatest empire in the world. His army of forty thousand men was relatively small beside the vast armies of Persia and India at that time.

Alexander did not seek to establish a merely military empire, but a cultural one. He took with him three philosophers who were famous at the time, Anaxarchus, his disciple Pyrrho, and Aristotle's nephew Callisthenes. The latter was to die in Bactria, either executed or poisoned as the result of a plot. Anaxarchus was shipwrecked at Cyprus on his return journey, and King Nicocreon had him crushed between the stones of a mortar as punishment for his evil tongue. Only Pyrrho returned safe and sound and founded the Skeptic school, its teachings inspired by the doctrines of the Jain sages, whose teachings Pyrrho had followed at Taxila.

Alexander—called Sikandar in all the languages of the Near East—took five years to reach the borders of India. Crossing Persia and Seistan, then a fertile region, he gained the Kandahar area in modern Afghanistan. It was in this region, later to become a frontier province of the Maurya Empire, that Alexander first met the "Indian tribes." There he founded Alexandria of Arachosia. The name "Kandahar" is merely a corrupt form of "Alexandria." He then advanced to Ghazni, where he founded another town, and thence to the Kabul valley, the Paropanisadae of the Greeks. Advancing further north, he encountered the high chain of the Hindu Kush, which his soldiers mistook for the Caucasus. He camped for the winter in front of the then Indian town of Kapisa, and transformed the camp itself into a city, Alexandria of the Caucasus, the site of which is known today under the name of Begram.

In the spring Alexander crossed the Hindu Kush using the Pansjir-Khawak pass, in order to attack the Satrap of Bactria—Bessus, the murderer of Darius—who had taken the title of Emperor. Alexander pursued him through Bactria, Sogdiana (Bukhara), and Samarkand, as far as the region of Tashkent, then returned to winter in Bactria where he camped on the banks of the Oxus. He founded new cities, where he installed numerous Greeks who were already established in Bactria, former mercenaries in Persian service. These Greek cities were long to play an important role in the history of India.

Alexander recrossed the Hindu Kush and turned his attention to the last two provinces of the Achaemenid Empire, the satrapies of Gandhara (south of modern Afghanistan) and the Indus Valley. The last Achaemenids had lost control over these provinces, which is why, for more than half a century, the Greeks had had no source of information about their geography and populations. The error made by Herodotus in mistaking the Indus for the Ganges led to a very distorted view of Indian geography. With the aid of Indian refugees, Alexander gradually got a better idea of the subcontinent's geographical situation and political conditions. One of his informers was a prince of Gandhara called Shashigupta, whom the Greeks called Sasikottos, who had entered Persian service and then gone over to the Greeks. He also received a visit from Sandrakottos, a young refugee from Magadha, the great kingdom of northwest India. The young refugee told him of the disorder that reigned in the kingdom and at the court of Pataliputra, under the sway of the tyrannical low-caste usurpers, the Nandas. The young Sandrakottos was none other than the future founder of the Maurya Empire, Chandragupta.

Alexander made his plans taking due account of the rivalries between the various kingdoms that had sprung up again after the withdrawal of Persian power. He received an embassy from Ambhi, the king of Gandhara, who reigned at Taxila, offering an alliance. In actual fact, Ambhi wanted Alexander's assistance against his rival Porus, whose territory lay between the River Jhelum (Hydaspes) and the Chenab, halfway between Lahore and Rawalpindi. After leaving Bactria, Alexander had found Alexandria in the Caucasus in a chaotic state. He dismissed the governor, replacing him with a person of trust, Nicanor. There he installed his sick or wounded soldiers, as well as the descendants of the Greek families of the region. He followed the Kabul valley as far as Jalalabad, where he founded the city of Nicaea. There, Ambhi, accompanied by other princes of the region, came to meet him, bringing him a gift of twenty-five elephants.

In November Alexander gave Ambhi the task of accompanying the regiments commanded by his young favorite Hephaestion, who went through the Khyber Pass, but halted in the region of Peshawar in order to besiege the fortress of Pushkalavati. The siege lasted one month. The town was destroyed and then rebuilt, later becoming one of the major centers of Greek culture in India. In the meantime, Alexander had cleared the hills leading to Bajaur, protecting Hephaestion's left flank. He beat the Aspasians of the mountains and reduced the Assacenians in the Swat valley. He took numerous fortresses that were deemed impregnable, including Aornos on the higher reaches of the Indus, the fortress that, according to legend, had even repulsed the divine hero Krishna (Heracles). Alexander and his troops then rested in the Jalalabad region among the kindly Shaivite (Dionysian) peoples of Nysa who practiced the bacchanal and drank wine.

The inhabitants of the city of Nysa welcomed the conqueror as a Greek compatriot. The Nysans seem to be related to the modern Kafirs, who have now taken refuge in the high valleys of the River Kunar, in Afghanistan. They were Shaivites, and the Greeks recognized the country of Nysa as Dionysus' native land. Shiva's sacred mountain, Kailasa in Tibet, had, in popular religion, been mistaken on the one hand for Mount Meru—the Aryans' polar mountain, corresponding to the Greek Mount Meros—and, on the other hand, with the hill of Nysa, center of the cult of Dionysus-Shiva. It was all familiar ground. Several hundred Nysans joined their Greek brothers' army.

As a character, Alexander was to remain a demi-god or legendary hero throughout the Near East and in India. He is not unrelated to the concept of Maitreya, the Boddhisatva, who represents the future reincarnation of the Buddha born in the countries to the West. The legends of Iskander with the two horns, spread by the Muslims and Jews during the

Middle Ages, derive from the myth of Alexander. Many clan chieftains in the areas from the north of Pakistan to the upper valleys of Gilgit and the Karakorum chain, to the north of Kashmir, claim to be descendants of Alexander. As Woodcock remarks, the scant attraction Alexander felt toward women does not appear to justify such an abundant progeny. However, the presence of the Greeks in these areas—from the fifth century B.C.E. to the second century C.E.—does much to explain the light skin and classical faces of the population who took refuge among the mountains during later invasions. The Afridi of the north of Pakistan and the Kafirs of Afghanistan claim to be of pure Greek descent.

In the spring of the year 326 Alexander, having subjected all the tribes, crossed the Indus near Attock on a pontoon bridge built by Hephaestion and, after a few days, reached Taxila. Ambhi came to meet him and presented him with fifty-six elephants, many sheep, and three thousand bulls. He also offered to each of the chiefs of the army a golden crown and eighty pieces of silver.

Taxila was a major commercial and cultural center, where the three principal religions were practiced: Brahmanism, Buddhism, and Jainism. Alexander was fascinated by the Yogis' feats of endurance and the strange life of Jain ascetics, who wore no garment and attached no value to the things of this world. He tried to persuade one of the Jain philosophers, Dandamos, to go back with him to Greece. According to Arrian, "Dandamos replied that he was the son of Zeus as much as Alexander himself, and that he expected nothing from Alexander, since what he had sufficed him. He failed to see why the conqueror's soldiers had followed him so far, when their tribulations appeared to be endless. He desired nothing that Alexander could give him and wished that they would not try to restrain him. As long as he lived, India offered him everything he needed and the fruits in their season. When he died, he would be delivered from a companion of little interest, his own body.[5]

One of the Jain philosophers finally agreed to accompany Alexander.

---

5. Arrian, Anabasis of Alexander, in R.C. Majumdar, *The Classical Accounts of India* (Calcutta, 1960).

He was called Calanus and expected the Greeks to attend his classes naked. When he later fell sick at Susa, he refused the remedies and advice of the Greek physicians, saying that "he was happy to die as he was, which was preferable to a life that would make him abandon his rules of behavior." He made them prepare a pyre, said goodbye to the Greek generals, and to Alexander alone said, "We shall meet again in Babylon." He mounted the pyre. The flames surrounded the motionless ascetic. Astounded by his courage, Alexander had the trumpets sounded and granted him military honors.

Alexander appointed Nicanor as satrap of Gandhara and installed Philip at Taxila to share power with Ambhi. In the month of June he began his expedition against Porus. A great battle took place on the left bank of the River Jhelum (the Hydaspes), close to Jalalpur (between Rawalpindi and Sialkot). Porus's army included twenty thousand infantry, four thousand horse, three hundred chariots, and two hundred elephants. The fighting was fierce and a large number of Greeks were killed. However, on the day before the battle, heavy rains had made the ground muddy and slippery. The elephants, weary and enraged, turned on Porus's army and disorganized it. They were mostly killed or captured, and the battle turned to Alexander's advantage. Porus fought up to the last moment and only surrendered when he was wounded. Alexander went to meet him and was struck with admiration for the Indian king, "a man of magnificent stature, more than seven feet tall, and very handsome." Arrian recounts their conversation. "Then indeed Alexander was the first to speak, bidding him say what treatment he would like to receive. . . . Porus replied: 'Treat me, O Alexander, in a kingly way!' Alexander . . . said: 'For my own sake, O Porus, thou shalt be thus treated; but for thy own sake do thou demand what is pleasing to thee!' But Porus said that everything was included in that."[6] Alexander gave him his freedom, and replaced him on his throne. Later he made him his viceroy over all the territory between the Jhelum (Hydaspes) and the Beas (Hyphasis). He reconciled him with Ambhi and skillfully balanced the power of his two vassals.

---

6. *Ibid.*

To celebrate his victory, Alexander founded two new cities on the banks of the Jhelum. One was on the site of his camp, named Alexandria-Nicaea, the exact position of which is unknown. The other, on the site of the battle, he called Alexandria-Bucephalus in memory of his famous horse that died there, not of wounds, but of old age and fatigue, since he was over thirty. These two towns were to survive for many long centuries.

Alexander then decided to prepare a great offensive to subdue the powerful Empire of Magadha. He certainly did not take into account the distance his army would have to travel to reach Pataliputra (Patna) and the Ganges delta. The description given him by the young Chandragupta of the decadence of the Nanda Empire was somewhat exaggerated and the Greek conqueror consequently felt he could easily achieve the conquest of India, whereas he had merely invaded a frontier province of the vast subcontinent. Such errors of perspective often lead to the fall of the greatest conquerors.

He left Craterus to finish building his cities and prepare the fleet with which he planned to reach the sea—along the route followed by Skylax two centuries earlier—and headed east. It was the rainy season and the march was difficult. Despite this, the Greeks managed to reduce a people called the Glanchukayana, although they lost a certain number of men in crossing the River Chenab in flood. Having crossed the Ravi, Alexander took the capital of the Kathas by assault. When he reached the Mountains of Salt (Oromenos) in north Punjab not far from Lahore, the rich and powerful King Sophytes came to pay homage, dressed in gold-embroidered clothes and covered with precious jewels. Sophytes arranged a lion hunt for Alexander, for which a pack of hunting dogs of a special breed was used.

The name of Sophytes does not appear in the list of satraps and vassal kings who later carved up the territory. His kingdom seems to have been a trading center rather than a military power, though he controlled the trade routes from the Punjab to Kashmir. Sophytes had adopted Greek customs and attracted foreign craftsmen. Numerous silver coins have been found, finely engraved with his effigy, showing an Aryan profile and wearing a Greek helmet. The new mining methods employed in India starting from this period were probably due to the reorganization of Sophytes's metallurgical industries undertaken by Gorgias, Alexander's engineer.

Alexander continued his march as far as the Hyphasis, ready to descend toward the Ganges valley. He was never to go further than the west bank of the Hyphasis, however, where he experienced his first defeat—at the hands of his own soldiers. The total strength of the army had been greatly reduced, as he had lost more than half his troops. The survivors, exhausted by the damp heat of the monsoon and dismayed at the prospect of facing the enormous army awaiting them beyond the Thar desert, including a large contingent of war elephants, refused to venture further. They had gone beyond the limits of the ancient Persian Empire. Their last operation against the fortified city of Sangala had cost the lives of many men. Indeed, the tiny Macedonian army would have stood no chance against the armies of Magadha, one hundred times more powerful. The democratic organization of the Greek army spared Alexander a disaster comparable to the one experienced by both Napoleon and Hitler's armies in Russia.

Alexander assembled his men and asked them to follow him as far as the eastern ocean. After a long silence, Coenus spoke for the others, "Self-control in the midst of success is the noblest of virtues, O king! For thou hast nothing to fear from enemies, while thou art commanding and leading such an army as this, but the visitations of the deity are unexpected, and consequently men can take no precautions against them."[7] Alexander shut himself up in his tent for two days. Then he had the omens taken, which were unfavorable. He had twelve altars built and ordered sacrifices and games. Philostratos tells us that, four centuries later, Apollonius of Tyana saw these altars with his own eyes. Chandragupta Maurya who, a few years after Alexander, realized the Greek conqueror's dream of uniting all northern India under a single scepter, was also to offer sacrifices at these altars.

Alexander returned to Bucephalus and Nicaea and embarked on eighty boats, each of which had fifteen banks of oars on each side. The army also requisitioned local vessels. An army commanded by Craterus followed the

---

7. *Ibid.*, chap. XXVII, 56.

right bank, while Hephaestion with the elephants followed the left. Philip, who was to stay at Gandhara with a garrison, covered their rear.

On arriving at the junction of the Chenab and the Jhelum, Alexander set up camp and began to subdue the southern Punjab. His campaign against the Mahlavi (Malloi), in the region of modern Multan, and against the Kshudraka (Oxydrakoi)—the warrior republics, probably Bhils, occupying the lower course of the Indus—was very severe. The Macedonian himself was wounded, and his troops gave themselves over to massacres, the particular victims of which were the Sibi, "a savage tribe clothed in beasts' skins." He then started building two new Alexandrias that were never finished. Finally, he reached Patala (modern Hyderabad in Sind), on the Indus delta, and began to explore the region, trying out his boats on the ocean. Behind him, revolts broke out. At Kandahar, the Indians rebelled against Damaraxus. In the Swat, Nicanor was killed. Philip, who was guarding Taxila with Ambhi, replaced Nicanor as satrap of Gandhara, but was himself assassinated in 325 B.C.E. Alexander recognized Abhisara, King of Kashmir, who had prudently paid him tribute. Peithon was made satrap of Sind. Oxyartes, father of Roxana, Alexander's Iranian wife, reigned at Alexandria-in-the-Caucasus.

The armies were divided. Craterus, with the wounded and the elephants, took the easy route through Arachosia, over the Mulla pass. Nearchus departed with the fleet for the Persian Gulf. Alexander followed the desert coast of Baluchistan. In 323 he died in Babylon, as a result of his wounds and dysentery, thus making Calanus's prophecy come true.

THE SUCCESSORS OF ALEXANDER

Immediately after the death of Alexander, Chandragupta began attacking the Greek principalities. The Brahmans fomented revolts against the unclean foreigners. Peithon withdrew to Arachosia (Kandahar) in 316. After treacherously killing an Indian prince—probably Ambhi— Eudemus left India with one hundred and twenty elephants to join Eumenes' army. He was beaten and put to death with Eumenes by Antigonus, king of Babylon.

It took no great effort for Chandragupta to annex the Greek kingdoms, which had prepared the terrain for him. Due to their "barbarian"
customs and impiety, the Greeks had aroused profound hostility among
the Indian masses and the priests. Only the Greek kingdoms beyond the
Khyber Pass survived. For more than five centuries, they were to play an
important role in the cultural, scientific, philosophic, and artistic
exchanges between the Greek and Indian worlds. The disappearance of
the Greek Empire in India did not signify an end to contacts. The great
trading route running from the Mediterranean to Pataliputra remained
open, except for short periods, up to our own times. Later on, the Greeks
of Bactria, bearing the emblems of Alexander and invoking his name,
would once more descend on the Punjab and the Ganges plain.

A dozen years after the departure of Alexander's army, another Greek
appeared on the frontiers of India. Alexander's former companion,
Seleucus, now king of Syria, after taking Babylon from Antigonus the
one-eyed, annexed the entire region stretching as far as the Oxus (the
Amou Daria), to the north of modern Afghanistan. In 305 B.C.E. he
crossed the Indus with the aim of reestablishing the Greek satrapy of
India. There he found waiting for him the enormous army of
Chandragupta, including over nine thousand war elephants, which no
cavalry was capable of attacking.

Greek sources tell us that Seleucus found the enterprise too haz-
ardous and preferred to form an alliance with Chandragupta. He ceded
to Chandragupta the territories of Arachosia (Kandahar), and
Paropanisadae (Kabul), as well as certain parts of Aria (Herat), and
Gedrosia (Baluchistan). Seleucus also established an embassy at
Pataliputra and signed a treaty of friendship that was to remain in force
for many generations. In exchange for abandoning his claims to
Alexander's satrapies, Seleucus received five hundred elephants, a meager
recompense, implying, however, acknowledgement of his suzerainty over
the northern provinces. Furthermore, the elephants were to prove very
useful to him in pursuing his war against Antigonus. One of Seleucus's
daughters was given in marriage either to Chandragupta himself or to his
son. It is thus not impossible that the great Emperor Ashoka, grandson

of Chandragupta, had a Greek mother or grandmother. This alliance, which was to last for more than a century, also had a considerable impact on the increase in commercial and cultural exchanges between Syria and India, through Persia, Bactria, Alexandria in the Caucasus, and Taxila.

During the Hellenistic period, the great Western center for trade between India and Europe was Delos. In Syria special coins were minted for the India trade. Megasthenes, the ambassador of the Seleucids at the court of Pataliputra, wrote an important work on India that has unfortunately been lost, but was so often quoted by later historians that quite a lot of it is known. Megasthenes left Arachosia (the province between Kandahar and Ghazni) in 302 B.C.E., and spent nearly ten years at Pataliputra, visiting the neighboring countries down to the Ganges delta and the area of modern Calcutta. His observations are remarkably precise, except in reproducing legendary history.

There are otherwise very few indications as to the relationships between the Hellenistic kingdoms and India during the reign of the Maurya emperors. In 206 B.C.E., however, the Seleucid king, Antiochus III, descended the Kabul valley after a campaign in Bactria. According to the historian Polybius, "He crossed the Caucasus and descended into India; renewed his friendship with Sophagasenus [Subhagasena], the king of the Indians; received more elephants, until he had 150 altogether; and having once more provisioned his troops set out again personally with his army, leaving Androsthenes of Cyzicus the duty of taking home the treasure which this king had agreed to hand over to him."[8] According to D. R. Bhandarkar,[9] Subhagasena was an appellation of Salisuka, the Maurya emperor reigning at that time.

The Indo-Greek kingdoms lasted for more than two centuries, and we know of the existence of thirty-nine kings and two queens of Greek origin who reigned over Bactria and the Punjab. The history of the Greeks in Asia is, according to A. K. Narain, "the history of the ascent of an adventurous people, that filled the void created by the lack of any

8. Polybius, *History,* XI, 34, in R. C. Majumdar, *The Classical Accounts of India,* 449.
9. D. R. Bhandarkar, *Carmichael Lectures* (Oxford, 1921).

great power. When, in time, new peoples appeared on the scene, they had to give way before them. The Yavana (Greeks) could not maintain themselves indefinitely, and their power was bound to founder. Their kingdoms were conquered and their proud royal families melted into the racial mixture of northwest India, until even the last trace of them disappeared."[10] The destructions wrought by later invaders let nothing survive, and what we know of the history of the Greeks in India and Bactria has, as often as not, been reconstructed on the basis of numismatic evidence, as also on the impact of their knowledge on Indian scientific theories.

Among the successors of Seleucus who ruled in Bactria and the Hindu Kush between 220 and 150 B.C.E., the most important were Euthymedos I, Demetrius, Eucratides, and Menander. The coins, on the other hand, mention many other names, such as Agathokles, Pantaleon, and Diodotus.

Eucratides, king of Bactria, and his son Heliokles had conquered the Punjab down to the River Jhelum, while Demetrius had occupied Sind and the region of Karachi. Strabo tells us that Demetrius even advanced beyond the Hyphasis as far as the Ganges and even to Pataliputra. Patanjali (second century B.C.E.), in his commentary on Panini's grammar, gives us an example: "The Greek besieged Saketa [to the north of Varanasi], the Greek besieged Madhyamika [Nagari, close to Chitor in Rajasthan]." The *Gargi Samhita* says that "the cruel Yavana massacred thousands of men and invaded central India." This probably refers to the conquests of Eucratides, Demetrius, and Menander.

Opinions vary as to whether it was Demetrius or Menander who conquered Madhyadesha (the region stretching from the Indus to Benares). It appears that two of Demetrius's lieutenants, Menander and Apollodotus, advanced to the interior of India. Literary and archaeological evidence indicates that Demetrius reigned over Bactria and at the same time over his Indian possessions. Demetrius had to return to Bactria to face a revolt by Eucratides. He seems to have been killed in combat.

Menander, who reigned in the midst of the second century B.C.E., is one of the three Greek kings who played an important role in India. He

---

10. A. K. Narain, *The Indo-Greeks* (Oxford, 1957).

is frequently mentioned by Strabo, Plutarch, Trogus, Justin, and in Buddhist tradition. According to a Buddhist work in Pali, the *Questions of Melinda* (Menander), he was converted to Buddhism by a saintly man called Nagasena. Like all the other conquerors of India, the Greeks were in the end culturally absorbed by the Hindus.

The author of the *Questions of Melinda* describes Menander as follows: "He was unrivalled in discussion and was difficult to convince, he was superior to all the founders of the various schools of philosophy. With his physical strength, liveliness, and courage, Melinda was without equal in India."

After the death of Menander, Greek domination of the northwest provinces lasted for over half a century, but it was a period of rivalry, jealousy, intrigue, and decline. Such a situation was to the advantage of the Parthians (Pallava), Scythians (Shaka), Yueh Chi (Kushana) and other peoples of the north, who invaded the territory of the Indo-Greeks. The last Greek kingdom vanished about 50 B.C.E.

GREEK INFLUENCE ON INDIAN CULTURE

The brief campaign of the Macedonian conqueror—which could have been just a military adventure without consequences—strengthened the age-old ties between the civilized world of India and the other civilized world beyond the Persian Empire. These relationships were to develop later on. The Greeks were not barbarian invaders, like those that periodically descended from the northwest frontiers. The two cultures did, in actual fact, have a deep influence on each other.

At the same time, by weakening the warrior tribes to the northwest, Alexander's adventure facilitated the later triumph of the Mauryas and the extension of their empire. Furthermore, his expedition left permanent bases in the form of the Hellenistic kingdoms, some of which were to last several centuries. The Greek kingdoms in the north of India were a source of direct artistic and scientific contact, whose traces can be found in the sciences and arts of India down to the Middle Ages and, indeed, to our very own times. A hybrid form of art known as Greek-Buddhist (although

Indo-Scythian in reality) developed in Afghanistan (Gandhara) and in the Punjab. Its value has certainly been exaggerated, but this kind of art did exist, always present and available to Indian artists. The Greek, and later on, Roman, concepts of science, mathematics, and astronomy had a decisive influence on the Indian sciences. The *Romaka Siddhanta* and the *Pulisa Siddhanta*, which replaced the ancient treatises on astronomy, came from Alexandria. In his works on astronomy, Varahamihira mentions the Greek authors and Sanskritizes many Greek words. The Sanskrit theater adopted some of the characters of Greek comedy, such as the fool *(vidushaka)* and the parasitical *bon-viveur (vita)*. The term *yavanika* (Greek) is even today used to designate the theater curtain. In music the impact of Greek theories is clear, at the same time creating considerable confusion, since the theories themselves do not really apply to Indian musical art. Greek coins were imitated. Many sovereigns employed Greek mercenaries as bodyguards. Greek traders, ambassadors, and scholars visited the major Indian courts.

Yet, the consequences of Alexander's expedition must not be exaggerated. Contacts with the Greek world existed in any case, and the political, economic, and social system of India was not at all changed by it. Greek influence on the arts and literature remained an external and secondary aspect, affecting no principles. Indian artists were much too personal, too refined, and too developed to retain any lasting influence. Greek-Buddhist art is interesting above all as a historic curiosity. This hybrid art had no impact, however, on the masterpieces of Greco-Roman or Hindu art, which turned in different directions, in compliance with the spirit of their very independent cultures. We must await the Middle Ages and Gothic art to find Western art forms that, in concept, are like those of the Hindus, a phenomenon that so far has never been explained. It is certain, however, that Greek influence is not foreign to certain aspects of Buddhism, and that Greek and Persian techniques have had an impact on Hindu art. Up to that time, the Indians had only used wood and terracotta in architecture and the plastic arts. There is no trace of stone monuments or sculptures before the reign of Ashoka. The famous pillars he raised, although Persian in style, show in their details—especially in the treatment of the animal friezes—a delicacy and realism unknown to the Persians; they are doubtless the work of Greek artisans. The manufacture of the horse of Sarnath and the bull of Ramapurva in Bihar is, in its realism, typically Greek. There is nothing similar in the Indian or Persian art of the period.

At the same time, Indian influences were felt in the Mediterranean world. Ashoka sent missionaries to Egypt (to Alexandria), Cyrene, Macedonia, and Epirus. In his edicts he proclaimed that even in those far-off countries, Buddhist law had its followers. Alexandria was one of the major centers for exchanges between India and the Western world, not only of a commercial kind, but also artistic, philosophical, and scientific. Clement of Alexandria does not hesitate to say that "the Greeks had stolen their philosophy from the barbarians." The analogies between the Samkhyan and Pythagorean philosophies are evident, as William Jones remarked at the end of the eighteenth century. In the sixth century B.C.E., at the time of Pythagoras, the Achaemenid Empire stretched from India to Greece, making Persia the great meeting point between India and the Mediterranean world. Schröder noted that almost all the philosophical or mathematical doctrines attributed to Pythagoras were current in India at the time, in a much more developed form.[11]

Eusebius, quoting Aristoxenes, recounts that an Indian had met Socrates and had asked him what was the goal of his philosophy. "The study of the human phenomenon," Socrates replied. The Indian laughed and said, "How can a man understand the human phenomenon, when he is ignorant of divine phenomena?" This means, in any case, that Indian philosophers were travelling to Greece and spoke Greek in the fifth century B.C.E. The basic concepts of the Samkhyan philosophy are found in Anaximander, Heraclitus, Empedocles, Anaxagorus, Democritus, and Epicurus.

There is a considerable Hindu, Jain, and Buddhist contribution in the thought of the Skeptics, as in that of the Neo-Platonians. Many of the sects that developed in Palestine in the first century B.C.E. were inspired by Indian concepts. The Essenes and Christianity at its outset were certainly deeply influenced by ideas from India. A great number of

---

11. Schröder, *Pythagoras und die Inder* (Leipzig, 1884).

the events surrounding the birth of Christ, as related by the Evangelists, strangely recall legendary tales of Krishna and Buddhism. That the Gnostics and the Neo-Platonians, as well as the Gospel of St. John, drew on Indian sources, is now a widely accepted fact. The notion of the *logos* appears to be derived from the concept of *vak*.

There is no doubt that around the time of the birth of Christianity, the culture and religions of India played an important role in the Near East. The similarities between Christianity and Buddhism are not mere coincidences. The structure of the Christian church resembles that of the Buddhist *chaitya* (temple). The rigorous asceticism of certain early Christian sects recalls that of the Jains and Buddhists. The veneration of relics and the use of the rosary are Indian practices. Buddhism is mentioned for the first time by Clement of Alexandria (150–218 of our era). According to Archelaos (around 278 C.E.), Terebinthus declared that he was the new Buddha.[12] Buddhist influence on Manichaeism is quite clear. One Manichaean treatise, written in the form of a Buddhist *sutra*, speaks of Mani, employing the Jain term *tathagata*, and mentions Buddhism and the Bodhisattva.

According to the Syrian writer Zenob, there was a Hindu colony on the upper Euphrates as early as the second century B.C.E. It was only in 304 of our era that St. Gregory destroyed their two temples and broke their images.

---

12. J. W. McCrindle, *Ancient India as Described by Ptolemy* (Calcutta, 1927), 185.

PART THREE

The Great Empires

7

The Maurya Empire

With the Maurya Empire, India enters 'history,' in terms of the meaning we give to the word. Starting from this time, we possess important original documents, written by Indians and foreigners, as well as numerous archaeological and epigraphic documents in languages that we can read and understand with certitude.

The Maurya Empire (317–180 B.C.E.) was the first great effort at unifying India during historical times. The *Artha Shastra*—a highly important work on the administration, justice, and politics of the Maurya Empire, written by a certain Kautilya (or Chanakya), a minister of Chandragupta—gives us a detailed glimpse of living conditions and state organization. This picture is completed by a politically-based play in Sanskrit, the *Mudrarakshasa* by Vishakadatta, in which the action occurs during the Maurya period. *Indika*—the book on India written by the Greek ambassador to Maurya, Megasthenes—survives in part as quotations and abstracts in the works of later writers. Buddhist and Jain chronicles also contain important information. The edicts of the Emperor Ashoka, engraved on stone and erected in the various provinces of the empire, mark the various events of his reign. Many of these edicts have survived.

This period sees a leap forward in Greek information. In addition to Skylax—the first Greek traveler to give a first-hand written description of India—other sources, some better or less informed, were utilized by Diodorus, Strabo, Arrian, Pliny, and Plutarch. Greek commentators often contested Megasthenes's important work, comparing it with the more or less fantastical accounts of other authors. The *Indika,* however, seems to have been the best informed foreign document existing on India at the time of the Mauryas.

The monuments of this period are numerous and indicate a high level of technology and artistic refinement. The use of metals was very widespread, and the iron pillars of India, found without a trace of rust, are evidence that metallurgical techniques unknown elsewhere in the world were used.

The city of Pataliputra, at the confluence of the Ganges and the Sone, was 80 stadia long (15 kilometers) and 15 wide (3 kilometers). It was surrounded by a moat that was 20 meters deep and 75 meters wide, filled with water from the Sone, into which the sewers emptied. A massive wooden palisade, built along the moat, protected the town. Loopholes allowed the archers to shoot their arrows. The city's walls had 64 gates and 570 towers.

CHANDRAGUPTA

Chandragupta, the founder of the Maurya dynasty, appears to have been the son of a low-caste concubine of the last Nanda king. Later on, efforts were made to provide him with a noble, though obscure, origin, but he was certainly of low extraction. Justin and Plutarch, who call him Sandrakottos, mention his humble origins. According to the Jain chronicles, he came from a village of peacock farmers (*mayura*), whence the name Maurya.

Chandragupta began his career by conquering the Punjab, where the people were weary of foreign domination. Taking as a pretext the murder of King Porus by Eudemus, in about 317 B.C.E., he assembled from among the republican tribes of the Punjab an army that Justin calls "a band of robbers and mercenaries." He took the leadership of a vast liberation movement and, with the aid of his counselor Kautilya, managed to throw the foreigners out of the Punjab. He then organized a powerful army and undertook to conquer the Ganges valley.

Chandragupta made an alliance with the "King of the Mountains" (Parvataka), who brought him the aid of an army of Greeks, Iranians, and other northern peoples. At their head, Chandragupta first attacked the Greek kingdoms. According to Justin, "After the death of Alexander, India shook off the yoke of servitude and put the (Greek) governors to death. Their liberator was Sandrakottos." The Greek satrap Eudemus judged it prudent to quit Indian territory in 317 B.C.E. Chandragupta then turned eastward and attacked the Nanda Empire. He besieged Pataliputra, the capital, and easily reduced it. He put to death the king, Dhana Nanda, and all the members of his family. According to the *Milinda-panha*, he indulged in great massacres. His counselor, the Brahman Kautilya, crowned him emperor, and Chandragupta undertook to subject the whole of the Indian subcontinent, which he gradually managed to do, except for the extreme south. Chandragupta's empire then stretched from Pamir to Bengal and, southward, included the state of Mysore (modern Karnataka). Saurashtra (Kathiawar) was also part of the empire.

Once he had consolidated his power, Chandragupta devoted himself to the political unification and organization of his vast territories, adopting an administrative system that was so efficient and so complete that the various later conquerors of India, including the Muslims and the British, only made very superficial changes.

Chandragupta had adopted the Jain religion. In India Jainism and, later on, Buddhism have always been the refuge of the powerful whose birth gave them no status in the severe Hindu hierarchy. We shall see, that Mahatma Gandhi turned to Buddhism many centuries later for the same reasons, even though by that time it was no more than a phantom religion in India.

According to Jain tradition, Chandragupta renounced the world in the last years of his life and lived as a Jain ascetic with the holy Bhadrabahu at Shravana Belgola in Karnataka State, still a place of pilgrimage, famous for its giant statue of a naked Jain ascetic. There, Chandragupta let himself die by abstaining from food, in the manner recommended by Jainism.

We are fairly familiar with the political organization of Chandragupta's empire, thanks in part to the information provided by Megasthenes, but more especially to the great treatise on the art of government written by Kautilya, Chandragupta's famous minister. Kautilya's treatise has been preserved in its entirety and constitutes a unique document on the political and social organization of ancient India. It represents one of the best courses of political Machiavellianism ever conceived. The Maurya Empire was a centralized despotism, founded on military power, but disguised as a constitutional monarchy and decentralized by being split up into autonomous provinces, administered by governors or viceroys. This system—the only one possible for such a vast empire— took its pattern from the Achaemenid system.

The king was the head of the administration. He had all powers: military, juridical, legislative, and executive. Kautilya despises the republics and democracies just as he does tyrannies. He considers constitutional monarchy as the best form of government. According to him, "royalty is the incentive to national expansion and the common weal. It represents the unity of interest of the various sections of the community; it is the power that directs and governs personal and political relations and facilitates the life of each individual and his possibilities of progress."

According to Kautilya, sovereignty rests on three forces (*shakti*): political ability (*mantra shakti*), money (*prabhu shakti*), and enthusiasm (*utsaha shakti*). Only by means of these combined forces does he who wishes to win (*vijigishu*) attain his goal. The king has to maintain and consolidate his authority in his own kingdom, then impose that authority on neighboring states. His policy thus rests on the different relations that are possible with neighboring states, divided into various categories forming the different degrees of his "zone of influence" (*mandala*). According to the nature of the states, he must put into effect one of the six forms of political action: entente, war, neutrality, hostility or cold war, alliance, and deception.

Establishing the king's zone of influence first required a permanent entente with the closest states, so long as such states possessed all the elements of sovereignty: a government, a territory, fortresses, financial resources, and allies. Otherwise it was better to annex them. The circle was extended to include the allies of the members of the entente, like the spokes of a wheel whose center is the emperor. The states lying beyond the zone of influence were considered as potential enemies, undecided, or neutral.

According to Megasthenes, Chandragupta employed an enormous number of spies, who provided secret reports on every important question concerning the city and the army. Trustworthy men were chosen for this task, and they used prostitutes as informers.

Government organization and the making of laws was entrusted to a Council of Ministers (*mantriparishada*) and to two assemblies, the "City Council" (*paura*) or "Council of Citizens" and the "Council of the Kingdom" or "Council of the People" (*jana pada*). These assemblies were consulted by the sovereign on all important questions of policy and administration, before he placed his seal of acceptance or rejection on decrees. Kautilya established the rule that the king must take the good of the people into account in governing: "The tranquillity of the king depends on the contentment of his subjects, his prosperity on theirs; he must not consider good what pleases him, but what pleases his subjects."

The king had to consult his ministers. The council's role was "to propose projects, to bring works undertaken to a successful conclusion, to examine new possibilities, to maintain discipline in the administration." When, later on, Ashoka's excessive liberality to the Buddhist monasteries seemed to endanger the state's finances, the council remonstrated and the king had to renounce certain projects.

The number of ministers seems to have varied. The *Shukranitisara*, a great treatise on the political art drawn up somewhat later on, speaks of eight ministers as an established number. Mention is sometimes made, however, of twelve, sixteen, or even twenty ministers. According to Kautilya, the number should not be fixed, since it varies according to need. The crown prince, the commander-in-chief, the chamberlain, the treasurer, and the intendant of the elephants attended the council.

The ministers represented the various departments, called *tirtha*. The eighteen principal members of the council were, under Chandragupta:

1. The King's Counselor (*mantri*)
2. The High Priest (*purohita*)
3. The Commander-in-Chief (*senapati*)
4. The Crown Prince (*yuvaraja*)
5. The Palace Governor (*dauvarika*)
6. The Chamberlain (*antarvanshika*)
7. The Minister of Prisons (*prashastri*)
8. The Minister of Revenue (*samahatri*)
9. The Minister of the Treasury (*sannidhatri*)
10. The President of the Court (*pradeshtri*)
11. The Minister of the Armies (*nayaka*)
12. The Governor of the Capital (*paura*)
13. The Minister of Morals and Customs (*vyavaharika*)
14. The Minister of Mines and Factories (*karmantika*)
15. The President of the Council (*mantriparishad adhyaksha*)
16. The Quartermaster for the Armies (*dandapala*)
17. The Minister of Fortifications (*durgapala*)
18. The Minister for Frontiers (*antapala*)

In order to have legal force, the ministers' proposals had to bear the seals of the president of the council and of the king's counselor, with the final approval and seal of the emperor himself. Kautilya describes the functions of the City Council (*paura*) and Council of the Kingdom (*jana pada*) in Book VIII, Chapter XVIII of the *Artha Shastra*. When the king imposed unjust punishment or over-heavy taxes, they protested. Kautilya advised the king to win the favor of the assemblies. The assembly sent petitions to the king, in the event of distress, famine, or theft. In his Girnar edict Ashoka declared that he discussed religious questions with the members of the assemblies. The assembly of the kingdom represented the rural population as well as those of the towns.

The empire was divided into provinces. The five major provinces each had its capital: Girnar (in Kathiawar), Taxila (northwest frontier), Ujjain (central India), Tosali (Gulf of Bengal), and Suvarnagiri (south). They were governed by princes of the royal family. The governors appointed certain officials, who were, however, controlled by envoys from the central power. Among these, the *rajuka* was responsible for justice and death sentences, the *pradeshikas* (provincials) acted as controllers of the revenue and magistrates, and the *antamahamatras* (ministers of the frontiers) monitored the populations who escaped the empire's control.

According to the *Artha Shastra*, the army was composed of four elements:

1. Members of the warrior caste, professional soldiers, called *maula*, who formed the base of the contingent
2. Mercenaries (*bala*), recruited from subject countries and abroad
3. Conscripts, soldiers supplied for short periods by the corporations
4. Warriors from the forest tribes, used to lead astray and harass the enemy (considered to be the bravest members of the army)

Kautilya considers three arms highly important: the infantry, the cavalry, and the elephants. It appears that chariots were advised against after the defeat they had met with from the more mobile armies of Alexander. The *Artha Shastra* gives much detail about strategy and maneuvers, vanguard, reserves, camps, and so on. Equipment was considerable and included both fixed and movable machinery. The forts had moats, submerged gates, and secret entrances. For taking forts, Kautilya advises the use of sappers, flooding, fire, and betrayal. According to Megasthenes, the War Council numbered thirty members, divided into six committees, whose functions were the navy, transport, infantry, cavalry, chariots, and elephants.

The army included more than six hundred thousand men. The soldiers received regular pay and the state also provided them with arms and kit. Outside of their military duties, soldiers led "a life of absolute freedom and pleasure." Their pay was sufficient for them to live comfortably and for others to live off them. Even in camp, they had servants "who looked after their horses, cleaned their weapons, led their elephants, repaired their chariots, and served as drivers."

According to Arrian, "The footsoldiers carry a bow made of equal length with the man who bears it. This they rest upon the ground, and pressing against it with their left foot thus discharge the arrow, having drawn the string far backwards: for the shaft they use is little short of being three yards long, and there is nothing which can resist an Indian archer's shot, neither shield nor breastplate, nor any stronger defence if such there be. In their left hand they carry bucklers made of undressed ox-hide, which are not so broad as those who carry them, but are about as long. Some are equipped with javelins instead of bows, but all wear a sword, which is broad in the blade, but not longer than three cubits; and this, when they engage in close fight (which they do with reluctance), they wield with both hands, to fetch down a lustier blow. The horsemen are equipped with two lances . . . and with a shorter buckler than that carried by the footsoldiers. But they do not put saddles on their horses, nor do they curb them with bits like the bits in use among the Greeks or the Celts, but they fit on round the extremity of the horse's mouth a circular piece of stitched raw ox-hide studded with pricks of iron or brass pointing inwards, but not very sharp: if a man is rich he uses pricks of ivory Within the horse's mouth is put an iron prong like a skewer, to which the reins are attached. When the rider, then, pulls the reins, the prong controls the horse and the pricks which are attached to this prong goad the mouth, so that it cannot but obey the reins."[1]

Megasthenes provides a detailed description of the administration of the capital, Pataliputra. It seems probable that other large cities were organized in the same manner. There were six municipal committees, each of five members, supervising industry, foreigners, the registry office, the markets, product quality, and the payment of a sales tax of ten percent.

The city commissioners are divided into six groups of five each. One group looks after the arts of the handicraftsmen. Another group entertains strangers, for they assign them lodgings, follow closely their behavior, giving them attendants, and either escort them forth

---

1. Arrian, *India*, XVI, in R.C. Majumdar, *The Classical Accounts of India*, 230–231.

or forward the property of those who die; and they take care of them when they are sick and bury them when they die. The third group is that of those who scrutinize births and deaths, whether better or worse, may not be unknown. The fourth group is that which has to do with sales and barter. But the same man cannot barter more than one thing without paying double taxes. The fifth group is that of those who have charge of the works made by artisans and sell these by stamp, the new apart from the old; and the man who mixes them is fined. The sixth and last group is that of those who collect a tenth part of the price of the things sold; and death is the penalty for the man who steals. The six committees are together responsible for public works, the temples, harbor infrastructure, and so on.[2]

According to the *Artha Shastra*, the city was governed by a mayor (*nagaraka*), who managed the uniformed police (*sthanika*) and the secret police *(gopa)*. The police kept a register of persons and goods, and inspected the hotels, gaming houses, and pleasure spots. A supervisor of manufactures placed his seal on products sold at market. A similar organization is indicated for the towns of southern India in the *Shilappadikaram*. There were firemen, and the police patrolled the streets at night. There was a curfew and any strangers wandering about at night were arrested, except during festivals.

The administration was under the control of various supervisors. The most important were the supervisors for agriculture, who oversaw the distribution of seed, agricultural machinery, silos, canals, reservoirs, irrigation, and working conditions. They received the produce from the crown lands and were paid a sixth of the produce from other land.

The supervisor of mines and metals oversaw the working of the mines and gathered the percentages owed to the state. The mint struck silver and gold coins. There were special supervisors for salt mines, jewelers, butchers' shops, forests, and so on. There was a passport office and

2. *Indika*, quoted by Strabo, XV, I, 50–52, fragment 34, in J.W. McCrindle, *Ancient India as Described by Megasthenes and Arrian*, 268, and in R. C. Majumdar, *The Classical Accounts of India*.

one for the surveillance of foreigners. Kautilya mentions the land register and the various measurements used for land. Property boundaries were checked. In the event of famine in one region, populations were transferred. Masters, scholars, and faithful officials received lands.

The state ensured the living conditions of the old, the poor, the sick, the weak, widows, orphans, and young children. Roads were carefully kept in repair. On the great royal road that ran between Taxila and Pataliputra (nearly 2000 kilometers), milestones indicated the distances. According to Pliny, road menders kept this road in perfect condition. This same road, only slightly modernized, but rather narrower, was called the "Grand Trunk Road" by the British. Only the bridges have been rebuilt since the reign of Chandragupta.

The king was responsible for justice but, according to Manu and Kautilya, kings were subject to the law and could, on principle, even be punished. The judiciary was independent. Courts with scribes and lawyers were set up, where judges could sit for hearings. Cases were judged according to the evidence, by inference, and by analogy with customary law. Appeal was possible and the last court of appeal was the King's Council. Even when the king was absent, he was responsible for any judicial errors. An excellent example appears in the *Shilappadikaram*, where the king dies of shame because he had failed in his duty to give justice, by having an innocent man put to death on police evidence.

There were two kinds of court: the civil court, dealing with matters of contract, inheritance, disputes, marriage, dowry, loans, and interest rates, and the criminal court for all matters concerning the police. The penal code was very severe. Megasthenes mentions that a person accused of false witness was punished by the mutilation of one of his limbs. Whoever mutilated another himself lost the same member, as well as his hand. If he were the cause of an artisan's losing his hand or eye, he was put to death. The code allowed torture, ordeal, and mutilation, but it was possible to redeem oneself by paying a fine. Sentences were given very quickly.

In the villages a council of five elders arbitrated any of the usual disputes. Small villages had a council of three judges, aided by three jurists. The "Council of Five" still exists even today in the villages. For offences that do not involve the community, people are always judged by their peers.

The king's court was noted for its luxury. The king only appeared in public with great ceremony. According to Curtius, he was carried on a gilded palanquin adorned with pearls, and wore fine muslin, embroidered with gold and purple. Behind him marched his soldiers and guards, some carrying branches with birds perched on them. The king's personal guard was made up of women, who surrounded him even when he was hunting, driving chariots, riding horses or elephants. As a rule, these women were foreigners, as often as not Greek.

The king's amusements included hunting (he had a special breed of dogs for lion hunts), ox races (oxen were as fast as horses), and animal combats (fights between bulls, rams, rhinoceros, or elephants). On religious feast days, the king paraded with his elephants caparisoned in silver and gold, four-horse chariots, servants bearing gold and silver pots decorated with precious stones, tamed animals, such as lions, leopards, and buffaloes, and numerous birds.

When the king went out on an official occasion, his guard included twenty-four elephants. Specially trained parrots flew around the royal palanquin. The royal palace, according to Greek authors, was "decorated with gilded pillars and winding golden vines on which silver birds perched." Around the palace were vast gardens, with evergreen trees, and artificial lakes stocked with enormous fish, on which boats sailed.

Society was divided into castes or corporations, corresponding to the various professional groups. Each caste had its own special privileges. Kautilya is against the predominance of certain castes and demands equality before the law for both Brahman and artisan. The system of "equivalencies," instead of equality, which gives each corporation its own rights and privileges, was a very useful tool for avoiding class struggles in Hindu society.

Women had considerable rights in matters of marriage, contracts, and divorce. A woman could remarry if her husband had been absent for a long time, if he were sick and incurable, if he were impotent, excluded from his caste, a delinquent, a traitor, or cruel. A man could repudiate his wife if she were barren, or gave him only daughters. The *Artha Shastra* deals with the proper treatment of women, regarding board pensions, adultery, abduction, rape, and so on.

Prostitutes had a special supervisor who looked after their well being and their education in the various arts. They were also employed as spies.

Homosexuality was very widespread and male prostitutes had established privileges that they still have today in orthodox Hindu society, though modern puritan society affects to confuse them with eunuchs.

Prosperity and well-being were great. According to Megasthenes, "The inhabitants [of India], having abundant means of subsistence, are of unusual height and bulk of body. They are also found to be well skilled in the arts, as might be expected of men who inhale a pure air and drink the very finest water. And while the soil bears on its surface all kinds of fruits which are known to cultivation, it has also under ground numerous veins of all sorts of metals, for it contains much gold and silver, and copper and iron in no small quantity, and even tin and other metals, which are employed in making articles of use or ornament, as well as the implements and accoutrements of war."[3]

Megasthenes mentions the great number of rivers and the quantity of cereals. "It is accordingly affirmed that famine has never visited India and that there has never been a general scarcity in the supply of nourishing food . . . since there is a double rainfall in the course of each year." He also notes another reason for this prosperity. "Whereas among other nations it is usual, in the contests of war, to ravage the soil and thus to reduce it to an uncultivated waste, among the Indians, on the contrary, by whom husbandmen are regarded as a class that is sacred and inviolable, the tillers of the soil, even when battle is raging in their neighborhood, are undisturbed by any sense of danger, for the combatants on either side in waging the conflict make carnage of each other, but allow those engaged in husbandry to remain quite unmolested. Besides, they never ravage an enemy's land with fire, nor cut down its trees."[4]

---

3. Fragment I, quoted by Diodorus Siculus, II, 35, 42, in R.C. Majumdar, *The Classical Accounts of India*, 232–233.

4. *Ibid.*, 233.

Towns built on riverbanks or beside the sea were of wood, while on the hillsides they were of brick or beaten earth. India's naval dockyards, which belonged to the state, were famous throughout history. The sailors were paid by the state, and the admiral of the fleet hired the ships and crews to tradesmen for transporting goods and passengers. When the British annexed the country much later on, they utilized the Indian dockyards—which were much better organized than those in the West—to build most of the ships for the British navy, for as long as ships were made of wood.

ARTS, CULTURE, RELIGION

Sanskrit was the official language of the Maurya Empire. While most of the written works were in Sanskrit, some Buddhist authors employed the language used in everyday life—a simplified Sanskrit mixed with the popular tongue. A large number of persons were literate and a great number of literary works are mentioned, but none has survived. Only technical, philosophical, and religious works have survived, together with some works on musical theory. Nothing remains of the poetry, nor of the highly important theatrical literature, although the great treatise on dramaturgy and the dance-theater, the *Natya Shastra*, was based on the theater of the time.

Kautilya, the author of the *Artha Shasta*—written in refined and elegant language—is also credited with a work on chemistry, another on poetry, and a third on medicine. The *Yoga Sutras* of Patanjali and his grammar are also of the Maurya period. The *Kama Sutra*, Vatsyayana's great work on eroticism, is also contemporary, and provides many details about life and customs.

As a rule, the Buddhists and Jains preferred to use the common tongues, or Prakrits. The most important writer in Prakrit at that time was the Jain pontiff Bhadrabahu, author of the *Kalpa Sutras*. A work on astronomy is also attributed to him. The work in Pali called *Kathayattu* was completed during the third Buddhist council, which met at Pataliputra in the reign of Ashoka. The Buddhist *Tripitakas*, *Jatakas*, and *Dharmasutras* are also attributed to this period.

In its various forms, Brahmanism remained the general religion, with its social system of castes and its different rules for the "four ages of life" (*ashrama*). Megasthenes mentions Shaivism and Vaishnavism. He also names the Buddha and speaks of the naked ascetics, the Jains. Buddhism continued to be the religion of a minority, despite the efforts made to spread its beliefs. It was not until the Mahayana period, early in our era, that Buddhism, having integrated many Hindu beliefs, became a relatively popular religion.

After the Aryan conquest and the end of the Indus civilization, stone and baked brick ceased to be widely used in architecture, reappearing only near the end of the sixth century B.C.E. Frames were made of wood, as were the defense works of fortresses, none of which endured. Excavations have brought to light the foundations of major towns, but all the decorative elements, columns, and so on, were made of wood and did not survive. However, we have detailed descriptions of the architecture and layout of towns in the *Artha Shastra*, Megasthenes' *Indika*, the *Shilappadikaram*, and architectural treatises such as the *Manasara*. Indeed, although the monuments themselves have not survived, their architectural tradition has; many temple buildings and houses still existing today in the Himalayas, in Nepal, and especially in southern India, correspond exactly to the descriptions of the structures of the Maurya era. At the same time, Buddhist monks dug cells and sometimes even entire monasteries in the rock, and many of these highly ornate caverns still exist at sites like the famous Ajanta and Ellora caves. Their style always copies the wooden structures of the period, providing important documentation on architecture, sculpture, and decoration. The caves of Ajanta have also preserved some excellent frescoes.

The funerary monuments known as *stupas*—hemispherical hills built on cremation grounds, or later on to protect relics—were originally earthworks, subsequently built of brick and stone covered with decorative motifs and sculptures. The famous stupa built by Ashoka at Sanchi was of brick. It was covered with stone three centuries later. A wooden balustrade, delicately sculpted with figures and decorative elements, surrounded it. This balustrade was later replaced by an exact copy in stone that still exists today. Historians recount that sculptors of ivory and wood were employed to sculpt stone. This proves that the beginning of stone sculpture in India dates from the Maurya era, and was probably due to the influence of Greek and Persian artisans. The monolithic pillars erected by Ashoka and the columns used in his palace at Pataliputra are of highly polished stone, using a technique whose perfection has never been rivaled. The capitals are in the Persian style, and the decorative motifs are of Greek manufacture. If the sites were unknown, they would without hesitation have been given an Achaemenid origin.

This is not the case with the stupa or cave sculpture, which is entirely Indian in style, and highly realistic, showing an art that is very developed and often almost decadent. Here, there is a visible meeting of two quite distinct artistic traditions, an autochthonous tradition found throughout the country as a whole, and an Achaemenid influence, doubtless because Persian and Greek craftsmen were welcomed at the Pataliputra court. At Sarnath and at Gaya, the balustrades are cut out of large blocks of stone and have little decoration. Further examples of this period include sculptures in the caves belonging to the monks of the Ajivika sect, while the Lomasha Rishi cave provides a precise replica of wooden models. At Sarnath, however sculptures of remarkable delicacy have survived.

BINDUSARA

According to the Buddhist and Jain chronicles, Chandragupta had several sons. Of them, Bindusara was chosen as his heir and given the title of *Deva-nampriya* (Well-Beloved of the Gods). Strabo calls him Allitrochades, as well as Athenaeus and Amitrochates. This name was probably a transcription of Amitraghata (slayer of his enemies). According to the *Rajavalikatha*, a Jain work, the original name of this prince was Simhasena.

Bindusara extended the empire to the far south, subjecting the kingdoms of Chera (Kerala), Chola (Tamil country), and Satyaputra (Kongu country, nowadays called Coimbatore, close to the Nilgiri), but he never managed to overcome the armies of the south, and his domination was nominal. The ancient Tamil literature of the Sangam alludes to the Maurya conquest, which is called "Vamba Moriyar," but provides no details. Except for this expedition of little consequence, Bindusara was not a conqueror. Rather, he was the organizer of the empire. He bequeathed to Ashoka what Chandragupta had created, without any territorial additions, but strong internal consolidation. According to the Tibetan author Taranatha, Kautilya (Chanakya) helped Bindusara "to destroy the nobles and kings of the sixteen kingdoms and thus to become absolute master of the territory between the eastern and the western oceans."

Kautilya continued to serve Bindusara. According to Buddhist traditions, Bindusara sent his son Ashoka to crush a revolt at Taxila. Ashoka was received by a delegation of citizens, who assured him that they did not oppose the emperor or himself, but only their bad viceroys. From Taxila, Ashoka annexed the kingdom of Khasha. He continued the destruction of the ancient Kshatriya order, who were the representatives of the ancient pre-Aryan nobility.

Two Greeks resided at Bindusara's court. These were Deimachos, the ambassador of Antiochus Isoter of Syria, and Dionysus, ambassador of Ptolemy II Philadelphus of Egypt. Their writings have not survived. Bindusara maintained a friendly correspondence with Antiochus. Hegesander recounts that he asked Antiochus to buy and send him some dried figs, sweet wine, and a Sophist. Antiochus replied, "We shall send the wine and figs, but Greek law does not allow us to sell our Sophists." Bindusara died probably in 274 B.C.E. His reign, according to the *Puranas*, lasted twenty-five years.

ASHOKA

Ashoka, whom all the inscriptions call *Devanampriya* (Well-Beloved by the Gods) like his predecessor, or *Piyadasi* (Pleasant to Look Upon), mounted the throne in 274 B.C.E. According to Buddhist sources, his coronation ceremonies took place four years later. The milestones of Ashoka's reign can be easily established from his famous stone-engraved edicts. There is, however, some confusion as to the precise date of his accession, since the Tibetan chronicles and the Buddhist, Chinese, Indian, and Sri Lankan texts all give slight variations. The Sri Lankan chronicles present Ashoka as a cruel and ferocious tyrant. On the death of Bindusara, he is supposed to have massacred his brothers and sisters and, in particular, his elder brother Susima, in order to seize power. He was then about twenty years old. His coronation was probably delayed owing to the bloody conflicts following Bindusara's death.

While still an adolescent, Ashoka had been appointed viceroy of Ujjain, then of Taxila. He already possessed experience in government and did not delay in renewing his grandfather's policy of conquest. The main event of his reign was the annexation of Kalinga, the powerful kingdom on the east coast of India, south of Bengal. Previously invaded by the Nandas, Kalinga had rapidly regained its independence. But Ashoka's war was without quarter and the population was almost entirely annihilated. Losses in the Kalinga armies numbered one hundred thousand dead, one hundred and fifty thousand prisoners, and an enormous number of wounded. Ashoka set up a viceroy at Tosali, one of the capitals. After his complete victory, Ashoka had Edict XIII recorded: "In truth, the Well-Beloved of the Gods desires to do ill to no man. He practices moderation and impartiality even toward those that behave badly. For him, the best of conquests is conquest by virtue ... A conquest made by these means causes us great joy."[5]

The horrors of this war made a deep impression on the young emperor. According to the Buddhist chronicles, it was only a short while afterward that he was converted to Buddhism by a venerable monk called Upagupta. Buddhism, a younger and hence less rigid religion than Jainism, was probably the religion preferred by his father. Ashoka went to live for one year in a monastic community, and then began a pious life of pilgrimages. He set up religious discussion centers, promulgated edicts on ethics, and made considerable gifts to Buddhist communities, as well as—being a prudent sovereign—to the Brahmans and Jains. He excavated the underground temples of Barabar and gave them to the ascetic

---

5. Hultzsch, ed., *Corpus Inscriptionem Indicarum* (Oxford, 1925).

Shaivite sect, the Ajivikas. He provided wells in the villages and founded hospitals and centers for growing medicinal herbs. He condemned ritual ceremonies as useless and sought to emphasize human charity, and respect for the family, masters, priests, and monks.

The Buddhists built hemispherical tumuli, called *stupas*, to serve as tombs for holy men and to protect their relics. In the fifteenth year of his reign Ashoka enlarged the Buddha's stupa, near Kapilivastu. He then had many other stupas built, among which he distributed the Buddha's relics. The Chinese pilgrim Hiuen Tsang (seventh century) records that Ashoka had had eighty-four thousand stupas erected—probably an exaggeration. Ashoka published edicts exhorting the members of the Buddhist community to avoid dissension and internal disputes and set forth selected passages from the Buddhist scriptures that he deemed especially suitable for the monks' meditation.

In about the twenty-first year of his reign Ashoka summoned a great council to Pataliputra to define Buddhist orthodoxy and refute heresy. This council is mentioned in the *Mahavamsha*, the famous history of Buddhism in the Pali language dating from the fifth century. According to Sri Lankan traditions, eighteen sects present were deemed heretical. The council lasted nine months and proclaimed that the tradition known as *Sthaviravada* represented the sole orthodox form of Buddhism. It was then that Upagupta composed the *Kathavastu*, which refuted the eighteen forms of philosophy deemed heretical and defined the Buddhist canon, known by the name of the "Small Vehicle" (*Hinayana*). After the council, Ashoka sent missionaries into every country in the world, from Greece (Yavana-dvipa) to Java.

The Emperor Ashoka imposed on himself the task of inculcating Buddhist virtues on the peoples he governed. Like many empire-builders, he was quick to use virtue and religion to impose his power and police, under a cover of morals. At no time did Ashoka abandon the idea of uniting the whole of humanity under his scepter, but he pursued his design by missionary rather than warlike methods. He invented the fifth column of puritanism. "He intervened beyond the political borders of his empire, spreading the beliefs and practices of Buddhism. He recognized no natural confine to his missionary activity, if not the very limit of the inhabited parts of the earth's surface."[6] Buddhism offered him an ideal tool for emasculating warlike peoples. In his Kalinga edicts he appealed to the people on his borders, stating that he considered all his subjects as his children and that even unsubdued populations and criminals would be treated with justice, moderation, and charity. "All men are my children. I desire the well being and happiness of my children in this world and the next, and I have the same feeling toward all mankind."

The virtues taught by his edicts were "to practice charity to all living beings, to make gifts to the Brahmans, monks, one's dependants, one's parents and acquaintance; to tell the truth, observe purity of thought, honesty, lenience, gratitude, self-control, patience, respect for the life of animals, fear of sin, moderation in spending and in gain, respect for one's parents, for older people, masters, to treat well the Brahmans, monks, friends and parents, servants and slaves; to avoid cruelty, spite, anger, pride and envy; to endeavor to do good works, alleviate the suffering of the elderly, the poor and the sick; to practice tolerance and respect for other religions; to avoid sectarianism, etc."[7]

Such a plan involved almost total inquisition, and the establishment could—"to its great regret and simply out of duty"—punish whomever it wished. In the thirteenth year of his reign Ashoka appointed super-ministers of morals and religion (*dharma-mahamatras*), who had the right to inspect every administration department, including that of his own palace. The setting up of absolute power by means of puritanism is probably the greatest invention of Ashoka's reign. It explains how Buddhism became such an arm of cultural and political expansion, utilizing methods similar to those with which the Inquisition established the temporal power of the Church in the later Christian world.

The utilization of such methods of moral persuasion also explains why Buddhism was so totally swept away from India after the fall of the great empires. "The first rise of the Maurya dynasty may have marked an

---

6. Arnold J. Toynbee, *Between Oxus and Jumna* (London, 1961).

7. Amulyachandra Sen, *Ashoka's Edicts* (Calcutta, 1956).

attempt to restore the Brahman power and so check the rising influence of the heterodox communities. . . . This policy was certainly abandoned by Ashoka, whose zeal for Buddhism may have been one of the main causes for the downfall of his great empire immediately after his death."[8]

Ashoka's inquisitors were his special ministers for religion and virtue, ranking above all the administrative officials, and sent out to each province of the empire for a period of five years. Ashoka forbade the killing of, or causing suffering to, animals. He was thus forced to set an example. In 259 B.C.E. he limited the number of animals killed in the royal kitchens to one peacock and three roe deer. Two years later, he proclaimed that he was a vegetarian. He forbade all animal sacrifices. He replaced safaris by royal pilgrimages (*vijaya yatra*). He authorized the gelding and branding of animals only on specified days. He created hospitals for animals as well as for men throughout India and in many western countries. He continued the ancient practice of freeing prisoners once a year, and granted those condemned to death three days' reprieve. Thus, Ashoka established his power as an "angel of peace," the first sovereign to try to build an empire on the basis of universal ethics and religion, with the support—it goes without saying—of the inquisition and the police.

In the administrative sector Ashoka applied the Hindu doctrine of the "birth debt" to relations between the king and his subjects, and between the king and his officials. In this doctrine, each man at birth contracts a moral debt toward the state, toward his parents, and toward his teachers. He must pay this debt by his services, before acquiring any personal merits. Nowadays, this notion is implicit everywhere in compulsory military or civil service.

Ashoka reigned over the greatest empire known to the history of India prior to the Moguls. Pataliputra, the present Patna, center of the ancient kingdom of Magadha, continued to be the capital. The location of his inscriptions and the pillars he erected following the Achaemenid practice clearly indicate the bounds of his empire, including the whole of the north of India and Pakistan, but not the extreme south. Important centers were

8. J. B. Bory, S. A. Cook, and F. E. Adcock, *The Cambridge History of India*, vol. I, 148.

Kausambi (close to Allahabad) and Lumbinivana, the Buddha's birthplace, to the northeast; Atavi, the forest region along the east coast, and Kalinga (Orissa) with its capital Tosali; Suvarnagiri to the south; Ujjain in central India (in modern Madhya Pradesh) and Vidisha (modern Bhilsa); Taxila to the north (near Peshawar). According to the historical work known as the *Rajatarangini*, Kashmir was also part of the empire, and it was Ashoka who built the town of Shrinagar. On the northwest frontier lay the kingdom of the Greek Amtiyaka (Antiochus II). Antiochus is called Yavanaraja (king of the Greeks). In the *Mahavamsha* the Yavana capital is called Alasandra (Alexandria). This may have been Alexandria of Egypt, or one of the other cities founded by Alexander. Antiochus did not reign over the lands to the east of Herat; thus, Gandhara, Arachosia, and other areas ceded by Seleucus must have belonged to Ashoka's empire. To the far south, the border lay along the River Pennar, to the north of Karnataka, and the Tirupathi mountains. The Dravidian states of Chola (Karnataka and Tamilnadu), Pandya (Trichinopoly), Chera (Kerala) and Satyaputra (south of Karnataka) remained independent. The ancient Pandya capital was Urayur and their kingdom included Madura. Assam did not belong to the empire.

The vassal states included the land of the Andhra, whose capital Andhrapura lay on the River Telvaha, and that of the Pulinda, in the Vindhya mountains of central India. On the western coast lay Aparantaka or Paschaddesha (Gujarat), Saurashtra (Kathiawar), under Tushaspa—the Persian or Greek governor—who resided at Giringara. Vidarbha or Berar was located in the center of India. To the south of the Vindhya mountains lived the Rashtrikas, Bhojakas, and Pitinakas, who were semi-independent republican tribes. The Rashtrikas seem to have been the ancestors of the Rashtrakutas and the Reddy of Andhra. The Bhojakas, whose kings bore the hereditary title of *Bhoja*, lay to the north of Maharashtra. The Pitinakas probably represent the peoples of the region of Paithan or Pratisthana, on the Godavari. Among the northeastern kingdoms were the Gandharas (from Peshawar to Taxila), and the Kambhojas (from the northeast of Afghanistan).

The empire directly or indirectly ruled by Ashoka was thus immense, running from the Hindu Kush to Bengal, and from the Himalayas to the

River Pennar in the south. It included Kalinga in the east and Saurashtra (Kathiawar) in the west.

Ashoka died at Taxila in 232 B.C.E. after—according to Tibetan documents—reigning thirty-seven or thirty-eight years. His empire was at once divided up. He had many sons, of whom the three most important were Mahendra, Kunala, and Jalauka. His principal successor was Kunala, who reigned for eight years over the center and west of the empire. The Buddhist chronicles tell us that Kunala's eyes had been put out by order of Ashoka, at the instigation of a jealous wife of the emperor.

Kalhana's *Rajatarangini* mentions that Jalauka reigned over Kashmir. He also conquered the Greeks of Bactria and annexed a part of the plains around Delhi. Kunala's successor was Dasharatha, also called "The Well-Beloved of the Gods," who dug cells for the monks of the Ajivika sect in the rocky hills of Nagarjuni. Jain tradition and the *Matsya Purana* mention another descendant of Ashoka, Samprati, who reigned at Pataliputra and Ujjain. Samprati was a protector of Jainism and sent missionaries to Persia and to the Greek kingdoms. The last of the Mauryas was Brihadratha, assassinated by order of one of his generals, Pushyamitra, around 180 B.C.E.

The splitting up of Ashoka's empire has been attributed to his policy of peace. This merely echoes the legend of the pious and benevolent emperor, a legend that he himself created. In actual fact, while teaching his subjects the virtues of non-violence and submission, Ashoka maintained his power by force, adding thereto the subtle arms of informants, inquisition, and puritanism. Moralism has always caused the downfall of empires, loyal citizens being unable to help fight political treason for fear of being themselves denounced on moral grounds, where no one is entirely innocent. Treason and crime flourish wherever moral transgressions and political dissension are prosecuted; gangsters have always and everywhere financed prohibitionist movements. Ashoka never reduced his powerful army and he did not hesitate to threaten the forest peoples with severe punishment if they did not change their way of living. His Kalinga campaign remains as one of the most ferocious wars of extermination that have ever taken place in the history of India.

According to Haraprasad Shastri, a further important reason for the empire's decline was Ashoka's anti-Brahmanic policy. Although he claimed to treat all religions with respect, he in fact forbade the great sacrifices that were the core of Hindu worship. His "super-ministers of virtue" (*dharma-mahamatras*) were hated, and disorganized the entire social structure of Hinduism for which individual freedom in matters of worship and personal ethics is a basic principle. The splitting up of the Maurya Empire marked the beginning of the decline of Buddhism, which disappeared from India a few centuries later without leaving a trace. Jainism—also a puritan religion, but never a state religion—survived and still numbers many followers today. Puritan despotism, founded on informers and obligatory virtue, produced the same baneful results—murder and discord—both in the emperor's own family and among the peoples of the empire. As a result, foreign invaders were often welcomed as liberators.

8

The Shungas and the Kanvas

THE SHUNGAS (187 TO 75 B.C.E.)

The murder of Brihadratha, the last of the Maurya emperors, by Pushyamitra (187 to 151 B.C.E.) sealed the division of the Maurya Empire. To the east, according to the *Puranas*, the Shungas and the Kanvas succeeded the Mauryas, while in the west, according to Greek and Jain sources, independent republics were established. The political geography of India about 180 B.C.E. shows: in the northwest, the Indo-Bactrian and Indo-Parthian kingdoms; in central and eastern India, the Shunga and Kanva empires, whose capital was Vidisha (Bhilsa); in Kalinga, the kingdom of Kharavela; and in southern India, the Satavahana Empire. For the history of this period, the most important source is the *Puranas*, which provide fairly precise information, as well as other documents such as the *Mahabhashya* by Patanjali and the *Gargi Samhita*, together with later literary works such as the *Malavikagnimitra* by Kalidasa, the *Divyavadana*, and the *Harsha-Charita* by Bana.

From Greek sources, we know that the last of the Mauryas were incapable of maintaining Ashoka's subtle methods of tyranny. Popular discontent was able to find expression and disorder infiltrated all political and military organizations. The Maurya armies suffered defeats at the hands of the Greeks of Bactria. Patanjali mentions Greek attacks against Saketa (Ayodhya) and Madhyamika (near Chitor in Rajputana). Greek detachments had even reached the walls of Pataliputra. Pushyamitra was the commander-in-chief of the Emperor Brihadratha's armies. His victories over the Greeks were one of the factors that led him to take power to defend the country against foreign invasion, and to reestablish an authority that would enjoy popular support. During a parade—for which Pushyamitra had assembled all the troops to be presented to the emperor—he had Brihadratha killed.

Pushyamitra's origin is disputed. When he took power after the murder of his master, he was forced to provide a somewhat idealized genealogy. According to the grammarian Patanjali, Pushyamitra descended from the ancient Shunga family, a clan of Brahmans to which the Vedic sage Bharadhvaja belonged. The Shungas are mentioned in Vedic texts such as the *Ashvalayana Shrauta Sutra*. His name ending, *"mitra,"* leads to the assumption that he was of Persian origin. On the other hand, in Kalidasa's *Malavikagnimitra*, Agnimitra—Pushyamitra's son and the second of the kings of this dynasty—is presented as belonging to the Baimbika family, descendants of the sage Kashyapa. Both the *Puranas* and the *Harsha-Charita*, however, consider that Pushyamitra actually descended from the ancient Shunga family.

According to Kalidasa, Agnimitra, while viceroy of Vidisha, invaded Vidarbha (Berar) and defeated King Yajnasena, brother-in-law of a minister of the last Maurya emperor. Vidarbha was divided between Yajnasena and his cousin Madhavasena, under Pushyamitra's suzerainty. After this victory, Pushyamitra, in a gesture of extreme magnificence, offered the horse sacrifice—a great sacrifice that only triumphant kings may offer. The horse destined for sacrifice had to be left free, without anyone daring to touch him. The Greeks halted the horse on the banks of the Indus. They were attacked and defeated by the armies of Pushyamitra, and the horse was led to the place of sacrifice.

Later, Agnimitra's son had to fight the Greeks again on the banks of the River Sindhu, which may be the Indus, but is more probably the river of the same name between Mathura and Allahabad. The Greeks in question were certainly princes of Bactria, and Demetrius, Menander, and Eucratides probably directed the invasions. The Indian victories were facilitated by dissension among the Greeks. In the meantime—in an inscription at Hathigumpha (the elephant grotto near Bhubaneshwar)— King Kharavela, in the twelfth year of his reign, proclaimed his victory over a king of Magadha, who can only be Pushyamitra, but who is called by the curious name of Bahasatimita. This name has been explained in various ways, Mita being equivalent to Mitra and Bahasati to Brihaspati (Jupiter), who is the regent of the *Pushya* constellation (the sixth lunar house).

Under Pushyamitra, the Shunga Empire had three capitals: Pataliputra, Ayodhya, and Vidisha. The empire, which covered only the central part of the former Maurya Empire, stretched as far as Narmada and Vidarbha (Berar) in the south. According to the Buddhist historian Taranatha, Jalandhara (Jullundur) and Sakala (Sialkot) in the Punjab remained under Greek influence. Pataliputra remained as the most important capital. The Andhras and Kalingas had regained their independence.

Maurya Buddhist propaganda and the methods employed to disorganize Brahmanic society had been one of the causes of the dynasty's unpopularity. Pushyamitra reestablished the Brahmanic order and deprived the Buddhists of the honors and assets that had been showered upon them. According to Buddhist tradition, he gave himself over to terrible persecutions, destroying the monasteries and burning the monks. He is said to have put a price of one hundred gold pieces on the head of each monk during his triumphal march on Sakala in the Punjab. He reestablished the Brahmanic sacrifices—in particular the horse sacrifice—that had been outlawed by Ashoka.

In actual fact, Pushyamitra appears to have practiced the habitual tolerance of the Hindus in matters of religious freedom, but he did violently oppose the Buddhist concept of an organized church and the utilization of religious and moral pressure for political ends. It is certain that the Buddhists resisted and were not happy at losing their power and privileges. Pushyamitra had to reduce them to reason in order to establish religious freedom, one of the basic principles of Brahmanism, but not of Buddhism. Hinduism has always refused to organize itself as a church and impose its religious and moral code. Indeed, many Buddhist monuments were erected during his reign, including the stupas of Barhut and Sanchi.

When Pushyamitra died in about 151 B.C.E. after reigning for thirty-six years, his son Agnimitra mounted the imperial throne and reigned for eight years. His successor was Sujyeshta, who was succeeded by his son Vasumitra. Vasumitra had to repulse a renewed attack by the Greeks of Bactria. According to Bana, it seems that he was assassinated by a certain Mitradeva, during a theater performance. After him, the throne passed to Udaka, whom the *Puranas* call by various names: Andhraka, Antaka, Ardraka, Odrula, Bhadraka. After him came Bhaga, whom the *Puranas* call Bhagavata, who reigned for thirty-two years. In the fourteenth year of his reign Heliodorus, ambassador of the Greek king of Taxila, Antialcidas, erected a column at Besnagar in honor of the divine bird Garuda.

The last king, Devabhuti, was a dissolute man, who lost his life as the result of the scarcely honorable intrigues of his Brahman minister Vasudeva Kanva. He was killed in 75 B.C.E. by a young slave who managed to get close to him by disguising himself in the queen's clothes.

The Shunga period, lasting one hundred and twelve years (from 187 to 75 B.C.E.), was—as is so often the case in times of political disorganization—marked by a great flourishing of the arts. The kings encouraged literature and the sciences. The famous grammarian and philosopher Patanjali lived at the court of Pushyamitra. The theater, music, and the plastic arts flourished. The stupas of Barhut and Sanchi have preserved for us sculptures of extremely refined artistry from that time. Despite the wars to repel the Greek expeditions, the Shungas maintained friendly relations with the Greek kingdoms of the north, and the cultural and scientific exchanges between the two worlds are attested to in many fields.

THE KANVAS (77 TO 30 B.C.E..)

After murdering his king, the minister Vasudeva usurped the throne and founded the new dynasty of the Kanvas or Kanvayanas. This dynasty counted only four kings—Vasudeva, Bhumimitra, Narayana, and Susharman—who reigned over Magadha nine, fourteen, twelve, and ten years respectively. Certain parts of the empire remained in the hands of Shunga princes, the Andhras or Andhrabhrityas, who were to put an end to the Kanva dynasty and, at the same time, to the rest of the Shunga Empire.

The Andhras, who conquered Magadha and all the neighboring kingdoms, do not appear to have managed to establish themselves. After their expedition, the north of India was divided into numerous small kingdoms. The history of Magadha remains obscure until the arrival of the Guptas, in the third century of our era.

9

The Romans, Scythians, and Parthians

THE ROMANS

The Romans became interested in trade with India very early. Imperial Rome, continuing the tradition of the ancient empires of the eastern Mediterranean, imported luxury products—gold, precious stones, cloth, spices, monkeys, and peacocks—in increasing quantities. To avoid the land route, made difficult by the Parthians, the Romans sought to develop the maritime routes. An expedition was sent by Augustus in 25 B.C.E. to reopen the sea route to India. Aden was occupied shortly after by Egyptian and Greek traders.

In 45 C.E. Hippalus claimed to have discovered the monsoons. However, as Kennedy remarks, the monsoons had been known since the most ancient times by all those that sailed along the coasts of Africa and Arabia, and the usual trade route with the Red Sea never went along the inhospitable coasts of Gedrosia (Baluchistan).[1] The direct voyage is described by Pliny in his *Natural History*. The ships departed from the port of Okelis, at the neck of the Red Sea, reaching Muziris (Cranganore on the Malabar coast) in less than forty days. It took less than three

---

1. *Journal of the Royal Asiatic Society* (London, 1898), 272–273.

months to transport merchandise from India to Alexandria, the major entrepot of the Western world. At the beginning of our era, at least one ship departed every day from Egypt bound for the East. The sailors knew every detail of the western coast of India.

The great demand for Indian luxury products at Rome must have led to a considerable increase in trade, once this route was protected from thieves and pirates. During the first century before and the first century after the beginning of the Christian Era, the island of Dioscorida (Socotra) at the mouth of the Red Sea was peopled by foreigners, "a mixture of Arabs, Indians, and Greeks," who lived there for their trade. The *Periplus of the Erythraean Sea* mentions that large vessels were regularly sent from Barygaza (Bharuch, near Bombay) to the entrepot of Ommana, in Persia. The Indians also traded with Madagascar and had an important colony there. The Indonesian language, mixed with Sanskrit, was current on the island, whose ancient name was Malay. According to a tradition still alive in Madagascar, its inhabitants came from Mangalore, on the Malabar coast. Later on, trade between India and the West focused at the major ports on the coast of Azania (Kenya and Tanganyika), especially Rhapta in Tanganyika, and Kilwa, Songo, Mnara, Sanjeya, Kati, Kua, and so on. These towns remained prosperous up to the fifteenth century, when the Portuguese and other Western adventurers destroyed them completely.

The consolidation of the Roman Empire assured peace, facilitated communications, and made trade routes safer. Pliny estimates that over fifty million sesterces (fifteen million gold francs) were spent in India each year, explaining the quantities of coins found there. By studying these coins, it is possible to discover when trade with the Roman Empire was at its most active. Almost non-existant under the Consulate, Indian-Roman trade attained its maximum under Nero, stopped after Caracalla, and then recovered slightly under the Byzantine Emperors. Roman merchants installed themselves in India, especially in the region of Madura (Madurai). The ruins of a fairly important Roman town have been discovered close to Pondicherry, on the southeast coast of India (Coromandel). Tamil literature between the first and third centuries C.E.

mentions the numerous foreigners living in the ports of southern India—rich merchants and sailors who loaded and unloaded the vessels. It also confuses Greeks and Romans, describing them as "Yavanas of an uncouth and graceless tongue."

Trade with Rome via the land route also continued, despite the difficulties created by the Parthians and Sassanids. According to O. B. Priaulx, silk, worth its weight in gold at the time of Aurelian, was sold in the reign of Julian at a price accessible to all.[2] Palmyra and Petra also became great centers of trade with India at this time. Merchandise arriving by sea up to Vologesia on the Euphrates was transported via the land route as far as Palmyra. Goods coming through the Red Sea were transported from the ports of Alana and Leuke Kome as far as Petra. When Petra was destroyed in 105, Palmyra increased in importance, until its destruction by Aurelian in 273, after which trade passed into the hands of the Arabs. When trade with India became active again under Constantine, Roman vessels carried the merchandise up to the port of Adule on the African coast of the Red Sea. This route remained as the main trading route up to the sixth century.

Many Indian states sent embassies to Rome under Augustus. Indian embassies were sent to Trajan (98–117), Hadrian (117–138), Antoninus Pius (138–161), Heliogabalus (218–222), Aurelian (270–275), Constantine (323–353), and Julian (361–363). Two embassies to Justinian, in 530 and 552, are also mentioned.

The Romans who visited India and the Indians who visited the Mediterranean world were thus numerous. Dio Chrysostom (about 117 C.E.) mentions an important Indian colony living permanently at Alexandria. He also mentions translations of Homer in Indian languages. The Brahmans who visited Alexandria in 470 were guests of the Consul Severus.

A Greek comedy, a parody of *Iphigenia in Tauris*—written in the second century C.E. and found in a papyrus text at Oxyrhynchus in Egypt—

---

2. Osmond de Beauvoir Priaulx, *The Indian Travels of Apollonius of Tyana and the Indian Embassies to Rome* (London, 1873).

tells the story of a Greek lady called Chariton. She is shipwrecked on the west coast of India, between Bombay and the Malabar coast, where she meets a king who speaks to his officials in a tongue found to be Kanada. An Indian statuette has also been found at Pompeii, and Clement of Alexandria, who died around 220, left a fairly precise account of the Hindu doctrine of transmigration and the worship of relics by Buddhists. Christian missionaries, after St. Thomas, visited India, while Christian communities have existed in the south of India since the third century. All of these evidences speak to the facilitated communications of the consolidated Roman Empire.

THE SCYTHIANS (SHAKAS) AND PARTHIANS (PALLAVAS)

The disappearance of the Bactrian Greeks, toward the middle of the first century B.C.E., was due to the pressure of the Scythians and the Parthians. The Scythians, called Shakas by the Hindus, were a group of outlying Iranian tribes. The cuneiform inscriptions of Darius I mention three branches of Scythians. According to Herodotus, Scythian contingents formed part of Xerxes's army during his invasion of Greece. Coming down from the north, they had penetrated Arachosia (Kandahar in Afghanistan), but had long been kept in check, thanks to the power of the Parthians, the Macedonians, the Syrians, and the Indo-Bactrians. They took advantage of the weakening of the Bactrian kingdom to seize part of the ancient Hellenic empire. They then advanced through Afghanistan into Sind, over the Bolan pass. They settled in Sind, and gradually advanced toward the Punjab.

The Parthians, whom the Hindus called Pallavas, had established a vast empire around their original homeland, to the southeast of the Caspian. They were Iranian tribes, originally from the north, who had mixed with the local populations. The Parthians were thus related to the Scythians. The insurgence and development of Parthian power created a barrier between Syria and its eastern provinces that had revolted during the reign of Antiochus II (286–247 B.C.E.). So effective was this barrier that it is only thanks to modern scholarship that we know anything about the Greek-Bactrian kingdoms that, at times, had extended their influence as far as the mouth of the Narmada, to the north of Bombay (Mumbai). India's political isolation was made complete by the Scythian conquest of Bactria in about 135 B.C.E. After the Maurya Empire, contacts gradually diminished and sea trade replaced trade via the land route. For the West, India became an increasingly mysterious land of fabulous riches.

In about 70 B.C.E. Greek domination east of the Indus reached its end, except for the Hazara region. The Greek kingdoms of Gandhara, the Kabul valley, and Badakshan managed to maintain their position for another quarter of a century. But when Hipastratus, the last king of Gandhara, died in about 50 B.C.E., the Parthians ravaged the kingdom of Gandhara. The only Greek kingdom that lasted a little longer was Parapamisadae, near Peshawar, where Hermaeus was king; it managed to defend itself and even to reconquer Ghazni and Arachosia. His kingdom was, however, gradually reduced by the Parthians and the Kushanas (Yueh Chi), who had already repelled the Shakas (Scythians). In 30 B.C.E. Hermaeus and his wife Calliope died, and the last of the Greek kingdoms passed into Parthian hands.

The northern Punjab was settled by dynasties of Scythian viceroys, called satraps, who reigned over Gujarat and Ujjain. The first of the Scythian kings of India was Manes, who settled at Pushkalavati (close to Peshawar) and at Taxila, in about 78 B.C.E. His successor, Azes I, mounted the throne toward 58 B.C.E. After him came Azes II and Gondophores, both of whom were viceroys of Arachosia before becoming king. Gondophores's name is associated with the legend of St. Thomas, Apostle of the Parthians, who—according to the legend—died at Madras (Chennai) in southern India. Gondophores was to found a vast empire, including Sind and Arachosia, free from Parthian control. After him came Pakores, who appears to have reigned only over the Punjab. It was at about this time that the powerful Kujula clan settled in the Punjab. Kadphises I (Kujula) drove out the Parthians from the northwest and occupied Taxila and Kashmir.

The Shakas, whose influence had begun to be felt much earlier, ruled western India from approximately 120 to 380 of our era. Their coins, sculptures, and names show that they became quickly and completely Indianized. Very rapidly, they mixed with the local populations, leaving few racial traces. The Shakas were simple folk and their palace at Sircap was a building of little architectural pretension. They adopted one or another of the religions of India, worshipping Shiva, Buddha, or Mahavira, and protecting the various religions. According to an inscription at Nasik, a Shaka prince, Usavadatta, made generous donations for the upkeep of the Brahmans and the Hindu temples. The Marathas now living in the region of Mumbai and Pune descend from the Shakas, mixed with the ancient Rashtrikas. They remained a warrior people and later played an important role in the struggle against the Muslim and then British invaders.

Although an initial Shaka era must have existed around 140 B.C.E., the Shaka era that is still in force today began in 78 C.E. It is known by the name of *Salivahana Shaka*. This era is utilized in inscriptions and in the *Puranas*.

YUEH CHI KUSHANAS

In 174 B.C.E. a nomad tribe called the Yueh Chi—driven out of its traditional homeland in the Kansu (Lanzhou area of China) by the Huns—occupied Shaka territory between the Jaxartes and the Oxus. Toward 126 B.C.E. new pressures pushed these nomads further south. They then occupied Bactriana, where they settled. In 48 C.E. one of the Yueh Chi tribes, the Kushanas, under their king Kadphises, left Bactria and occupied Gandhara, driving out the last Greek king, Hermaeus. Later on, they extended their control over the small Greek, Shaka, and Parthian kingdoms, and founded an empire comprising the Punjab, Sind, North Gujarat, and a part of central India.

One of the theories held by Kalgren and Sten Konow is that the Kushanas were a new wave of Iranian tribes related to the Shakas. Greek, Latin, and Chinese works mention that the peoples of Bactriana were conquered by the Siawang, meaning by the Shakas and that one of the Shaka tribes was the Kueishung, or Kushanas. However, according to

Tarn, the Kushanas were the Asii, the dominant element of the Yueh Chi. This appears more likely, since the Chinese annals of the Han dynasties, the *Tsien Hanshun* and the *Hon Hanshu*, speak of the sway of the Ta Yueh Chi in the region of Ta-his. It was this power that was extended later on. The Yueh Chi, a warrior people from the east, had occupied Bactria in about the second century B.C.E. and then had come up against the Parthians and Scythians. They maintained their contacts with central Asia and were a link between China and India.

During their westward migrations in 165 B.C.E., the Yueh Chi were driven back by the Huns (the Hiung-nu). Later, the Yueh Chi hordes attacked another tribe, the Wusun, killed their chief, and occupied Kipin (the north of Kashmir). They had established a center to the north of the Oxus and had divided into five groups. A Yueh Chi king fought by the side of Chinese generals.

The accession of Kadphises I to the throne marks an important date in Yueh Chi Kushana history. He created and consolidated their empire, establishing his supremacy over Bactria around 30 B.C.E. and becoming the sole sovereign of the Yueh Chi. He drove out the Parthians and occupied Taxila and the Kashmir valley. During his reign, the Kushana Empire stretched from the Persian border to the Indus and even to the Jhelum. It included both Sogdiana (Samarkand) and Afghanistan.

Kadphises I died at the age of eighty. His son, Kadphises II, ambitious and enterprising, fought the Chinese on one side and conquered Sind on the other. In his reign the empire's frontiers extended as far as Mathura. He apparently adopted Shaivism, as indicated by the images of Shiva and his bull on the obverse of the coins bearing his effigy.

KANISHKA

Historians have disputed the dates of Kanishka's reign, some placing him before Kadphises I, and others after Kadphises II. This latter version appears to be more probable, since Kanishka's coins are frequently found with those of Kadphises II. Kanishka must therefore have succeeded to the throne in the second century B.C.E., about 120 according to Sten

Konow, or between 120 and 160 according to V.A. Smith. Majumdar's theory that his reign began in 248 contradicts the Tibetan documents that make him a contemporary of King Vijayakirti of Khotan, whose reign started in 120.

According to the Chinese chronicles, Kanishka came originally from Khotan and belonged to one of the smaller Yueh Chi tribes. An able general, he was the most capable of the Kushana monarchs. He began his career as King of Wema in the Ganges valley, subdued the other viceroys, and established his authority over the Punjab and Sind. He conquered the northwest of India and established his capital at Purushapura (Peshawar). He then invaded central India and fought the kings of Saketa and Pataliputra, after which he turned westward and defeated the Parthian king.

An early expedition against the Chinese Empire came to nothing, but during a second expedition, he defeated the Chinese king Pan Yung, the son of Pan Chao, and annexed the provinces of Kashgar, Yarkand, and Khotan. His empire then stretched from central Asia to central India, including Gandhara (Afghanistan), Kashmir, and the Pamir region. He had contacts with Rome, and his coins imitated Roman models.

Kanishka converted to Buddhism, and his name has remained famous in the annals of that religion. He was not a religious man, but he found political support in Buddhism, whose propagation served as a pretext for his conquests, presented as crusades. Internally, on the other hand, he sought to maintain a balance between various religious factions.

Ashoka in his time had standardized the doctrine of *Theravada* or "Little Vehicle" (Hinayana) Buddhism. After his death, conflicts reopened among the various schools, and Kanishka had once again undertaken to codify doctrine. A great council was summoned at Kunnavala Vihara, in Kashmir, under the presidency of Vasumitra. The Tibetan annals recount that this council took place at Jullundur. Kanishka gathered five hundred monks to put an end to controversies. According to the Chinese pilgrim Hiuen Tsang, the newly redefined Buddhist canon was inscribed on copper plates and buried in a stupa built for the purpose. The new canon defined a very different religion than the one defined by the council called by Ashoka. This new Buddhism is known as the "Great Vehicle" (Mahayana).

Although his coins bear the images of Greek, Zoroastrian, Mithraic, and Hindu (Shiva and Durga) deities, and although he was the first king to put the image of Buddha on his coins, Kanishka's personal character was cruel and temperamental. The famous Buddhist sage Ashvaghosha refused to come to his court. He was generally detested and the people were weary of his wars, ambitions, and depredations. It seems that he died in his bed, suffocated by those around him, as he lay sick in 162.

The development of Mahayana had begun before Kanishka, starting from the third century B.C.E., but its doctrine was only settled in the second century of our era. It was to serve India's cultural and political expansion. The first Buddhist doctrine was a simple one, with no great philosophical claims. When Buddhism expanded, it rapidly mixed with popular Hinduism and assimilated the magical practices of Shaivite Tantrism and Yoga techniques, including *mantras* (the reciting of formulas) and *dhyana* (meditation). The resultant religion—whose principles were defined by the council summoned by Kanishka—was a profoundly different religion from original Buddhism. The admirable philosophical contents of the canons of this later Buddhism were mainly the work of Ashvaghosha. This Hindu convert wished to make a synthesis of Buddhism and Hinduism, with the addition of elements coming from the various religions found in northwest India, such as the Greek religion, Christianity, Zoroastrianism, and the religions of central Asia.

Little is known about Kanishka's administrative system, but the prosperity of the Kushana Empire implies a very efficient organization. Kanishka was a great builder. He built numerous stupas and monasteries, such as Purushaputra and Pushkalavati. He founded a new city, Kanishkapura, in the center of which he erected a wooden tower above the Buddha's relics that was considered one of the wonders of the world for a long time. This tower was more than 200 meters high. Its iron roof was surmounted by a copper-plated parasol. The sides were decorated with statues of the Buddha, probably his first anthropomorphic images, since up to then he had been represented only by symbols. The statues represented the Buddha in the form of the Greek god Apollo. The tower was still in existence in the sixth century and was a marvel to travelers. Its columns were finished with Corinthian capitals.

During Kanishka's reign a new school of sculpture known as Greco-Buddhist appeared in Gandhara; it applied Greek aesthetic principles to Indian subjects. This school saw a development from the first to the fourth centuries, a period of very close contacts with the West, giving rise to a bastardized, conventional art, of little value as compared to the refined art of other contemporary Indian schools. Greco-Buddhist art is particularly interesting from a historical point of view, as a sort of exotic extension of the Hellenistic schools of Alexandria or Pergamon, or the Romano-Asiatic or Romano-Syrian schools. During the same period, a purely Indian school flourished at Sanchi, Barhut, and Mathura. The image of Buddha created at Mathura was to serve as a prototype for later sculptures.

Coins mention three Kanishkas. His immediate successor seems to have been Vanishka, probably his son. After him came Atuvishka, who founded the city of Atuvishkapura in Kashmir. He reigned for a long time, and his wealth is borne witness to by the number of gold and copper coins minted during his reign. His successor was Vasudeva I, the last important monarch of the Kushana dynasty. His name indicates that he was a convert to Hinduism. He seems to have lost control over the northern and northwestern provinces. On his death, in 178, the empire began to decline under the rule of Kanishka II. The latter's successors, Vasudeva II and Kanishka III, were weak and incapable of resisting the pressure of Sassanid power in the west. In the vacuum left by the decline of Kushana power the tribes reappeared, organized as republics, such as the Yaudhayas, the Malavas, and the Kunindas.

The Kushana domination of India was always a foreign occupation. They considered central Asia as their true home, and never got used to the Indian climate. Their rule was particularly marked by the development of considerable trade with the Roman Empire on the one side and with China on the other. For a time, the Kushana Empire was the center point of the major civilizations.

THE WESTERN SATRAPS

The system of satrapies, or vice-royalties, established by the Persians had continued, even though the satraps had, more often than not, become hereditary and independent sovereigns. There are two main groups of western satrapies, the Kshaharatas and the Kardamakas.

The Kshaharatas appear to have been Pallavas and the Kardamakas Shakas. Two Kshaharata kings—Bhumaka and Nahapana—have left a name. Nahapana built an empire stretching from Pune to Ajmer, which included Malwa and Kathiawar. His reign ended in 124, probably as a result of his defeat by Gautamiputra Satakarni, of the Andhra dynasty of the Satavahanas.

After the death of Nahapana, the other dynasty of western satrap—founded by Chastana, belonging to the Kardamaka line—took power. He reigned at first jointly with his son Jayadaman and, after the latter's death, with his grandson Rudradaman. The next king, Rudravarman I, was the most illustrious of the western satraps. Rudravarman's successors continued to rule over western India until the fourth century. They disappeared in 395 when Chandragupta II killed the last of the satraps, Rudrasimha III.

10
The Andhra Empire

THE SATAVAHANAS
(FIRST CENTURY B.C.E. TO THIRD CENTURY C.E.)

After the fall of the Maurya Empire, the peoples of the south remained independent of the Shunga Empire and united under the suzerainty of the most powerful among them, the Andhras, whose country of origin lies between the rivers Godavari and Krishna. The Andhras were probably not originally from the country to the north of Madras that bears their name today, but came from the center of the Deccan. It was only toward the second century of our era that they annexed the southern country today known as Andhra, close to the mouth of the River Krishna.

Originally, the Andhras were one of the powerful non-Aryan tribes mentioned by the *Aitareya Brahmana* (VII, XIII, 18), prior to the fifth century B.C.E., occupying the Vindhya mountains, toward the sources of the Narmada. One of Ashoka's edicts mentions the Andhras of this region. Pliny, probably utilizing information taken from Megasthenes, speaks of the powerful king of the Andhra country, mentioning his thirty fortified cities and army of one hundred thousand footsoldiers, two thousand horse, and one thousand elephants.

The Satavahanas—whom the *Puranas* call Andhras—belong to a very ancient dynasty that had ruled a part of central India for centuries.

Originally, they probably came from the Mysore region, but they annexed the eastern lands, the Andhra country in particular, where they set up their capital.

The first of the Satavahanas was Simuka, who, according to the *Puranas*, destroyed the last vestiges of Shunga power. Simuka formed alliances with the Maratha kings of the western Deccan. He played the role of suzerain for the whole of the south of India. According to *Purana* chronology, it appears that Simuka—who was of non-Aryan origin and considered low-caste by the Aryans—founded his dynasty around 30 B.C.E. and reigned for twenty-three years. He dethroned the last Kanva and exterminated the last Shungas toward the end of his reign. His dynasty was to last nearly three centuries.

Krishna, Simuka's brother, succeeded him and reigned for eighteen years. The two brothers had extended their empire as far as the Nasik region, to the northeast of Bombay (Mumbai). They took the title of *Dakshinapatheshvara* (Lords of the Territories of the South). Dakshinapatha is the name generally given to the Maratha country south of Bombay, and indicates that the empire included the west coast of India. The next sovereign was Simuka's son or nephew, Satakarni, a name borne by many of his successors. Satakarni reigned eighteen years and was a contemporary of Pushyamitra of Magadha and of Kharavela, king of Kalinga. He married a Rashtrika (Maratha) princess, and established an alliance with the Maratha country.

After a war in which Satakarni fought Kharavela, the Satavahanas appear to have maintained friendly relations with the Kalingas, to the northeast of their empire, who were also survivors of the ancient pre-Aryan civilization. Satakarni's empire went right across India, from one side to the other, with the Shunga Empire to the north and, to the south, the Dravidian kingdoms that had remained independent. Satakarni proclaimed his imperial power by means of the "horse sacrifice," probably after his victory over Pushyamitra. His successor, Satakarni II, reigned fifty-six years and consolidated Satavahana power.

The Satavahana administration continued to use the system established by the Mauryas. The sovereigns conformed to the rules of conduct laid down by Kautilya in his *Artha Shastra*. The king centralized all powers and symbolized the ideals of courage, justice, and magnanimity. He was assisted by a Council of Ministers. The country was divided up into provinces, each under a governor.

Satakarni's capital was Pratisthana, modern Paithan, on the northern bank of the River Godavari, near Aurangabad in the state of Maharashtra. This point is confirmed by Ptolemy in his *Geography*. The Rivers Tapti and Narmada separated the Andhra Empire from the kingdoms of Ujjain and Vidisha. Ujjain was one of the most famous cities of India, and one of the Hindus' sacred towns. The famous temple of Shiva that lay in the forest of Mahakala, to the north of the town, was to be destroyed by the Muslims in the thirteenth century.

Three parties thus shared power around Ujjain: the Greeks of Taxila to the north, the Shungas to the east and the Andhras to the south. Vidisha remained under Shunga domination, but Avanti and Ujjain were annexed by the Andhras. This was, moreover, the source of a conflict between the Shungas and the Satavahanas that was to last up to the second century, with fluctuating fortunes. In the meantime, the Scythians (Shakas) had solidly established themselves in the Indus delta. They were called upon to help free the town of an Andhra tyrant, Gardabhilla, and for some time they occupied Ujjain, during the reign of Satakarni II.

The Scythian occupation is mentioned in the *Periplus of the Erythraean Sea* (written about 70–80 C.E.). It tells of the rich markets of Dachinavades (*Dakshinapatha*), such as Suppara (modern Sopara, near Mumbai) and Calliena (modern Kalyan), "which in the time of the former Saraganus [Satakarni I] was an open market, but which since it fell into the hands of Sandares [a Scythian king] has become difficult of access. The Greek ships risk being seized, led out of their way and conducted under guard to Barygaza [modern Bharuch, at the mouth of the Narmada]."

The Scythians were repulsed once more by Vikramaditya, son of Gardabhilla, who reestablished Andhra suzerainty over Ujjain. This Vikramaditya has sometimes been mistaken for his famous homonym who lived four centuries later and was the patron of the great poet

Kalidasa. The seventh king of the Satavahana dynasty was Hala, who conquered Sri Lanka in about 78 of the Christian Era. He probably founded the Salivahana, or Shaka, era, which is still in force today. He was a protector of the arts and letters, and was himself a poet in Prakrit-Maharashtri, the official language of his kingdom. After him, Satavahana power declined, and the west of their empire fell in the hands of the Scythians, the western satraps. The Scythians' retreat was only temporary. The Scythian king Nahapana, who reigned from 119 to 125 C.E., attacked the Satavahana Empire and annexed the south of Rajputana.

Numerous monarchs are mentioned between Satakarni II and Gautamiputra in the *Puranas* (10, 12, 13, 14, or 19 kings, according to the lists). We know nothing of their history, although many may have belonged to collateral branches, reigning over different parts of the Deccan. The twenty-third king, Gautamiputra Satakarni (who reigned from about 106 to 130 C.E.) mounted the throne at a time when the Satavahana fortune was at its lowest ebb. He managed to reestablish the might of the dynasty of which he was one of the greatest kings. The Scythian and Parthian Empire was at that time divided into numerous independent principalities. Gautamiputra attacked the satraps, conquered and killed the Scythian king Nahapana as well as the satrap Usavadatta, and totally destroyed the Scythian dynasty of the Kshaharatas. He also conquered the Greeks. Once more, the Satavahana Empire stretched from the eastern to the western ocean. Gautamiputra's conquests extended from Kathiawar and north of the Vindhya mountains to the far south. He took the title of "Sovereign Whose Subjects Drink the Water of the Three Oceans," meaning the Gulf of Bengal, the Arabian Sea, and the Indian Ocean. Even under this powerful sovereign, however, the Satavahana Empire never went beyond the Malwa and the Kathiawar peninsula in the northwest. The Scythians remained masters of what is now Pakistan.

Gautamiputra, a convinced Hindu, also gave his protection to other religions, and particularly to Buddhism. This handsome man, with a pleasant and radiant face, of noble demeanor, with long muscled arms, was respectful to his mother, benevolent, and fearful even of wounding his enemies. He inspired everyone with courage and trust. It was said of him that he was the refuge of good men, the seat of fortune, and the fount of courtesy. As sovereign, he was respected and obeyed by other kings, he was compassionate toward the sufferings of his subjects, and was just in levying taxes. He was just as interested in the well-being of the low as of the high castes, but was opposed to their mixing and strictly upheld the corporate structure and racial division that is the feature of Hindu society.

Gautamiputra died young, and his son Vasishtiputra Pulumayi, who succeeded him, found himself at the head of a vast and mighty empire. The Kshaharatas, however, reorganized under Rudradaman I, managed to reconquer most of the territories annexed by Gautamiputra in two campaigns between 130 and 150 C.E. Pulumayi compensated for his failure in the west by his conquests in the east. He conquered the Telugu country and set up his capital at Navanagara or Pratisthana on the River Godavari.

According to Ptolemy, Siriptolemaios (Shri-Pulumayi), son of Gautamiputra Satakarni, continued to reign at Baithana (Pratisthana), while Ozene (Ujjain) fell into the hands of Tiasthenes (Chastana). This indicates that the northern provinces had been occupied by the Kardamaka Shakas. The Scythians thus retook possession of the northern territories, and Gautamiputra's successors reigned over a considerably reduced empire. According to the *Puranas*, Pulumayi's successor was Shivashri Satakarni (toward 159–166), who fought the Scythians with some success. He was followed by Shivaskanda Satakarni (167–174), after whom came Yajnashri Satakarni (174–203), the dynasty's last great king, who extended his empire in central India and toward the north. He is mentioned by the Chinese pilgrim Hiuen Tsang under the name of So-to-po-ha (Satavahana). Yajnashri reigned twenty-nine years. He rekindled the war against the Kshaharatas and managed to win back several provinces. After him, under the reigns of Vijaya (203–209), Chandashri (209–219), and Pulona (219–227), who were weak and incapable kings, the empire disintegrated and split up gradually into independent principalities. The Abhiras took possession of the territories around Nasik and made them an independent state.

The chiefs of the Kura family forged a kingdom for themselves in the south of Maharashtra. One of the Satavahana princes, Rudra Satakarni, made an independent state of the Andhra country. Another branch reigned over Berar, until it was exterminated by the Vakatakas. The Chutusatakarnis of Vanavasi conquered the west of the Deccan, while Santamula I of the Ikshvaku family of Nagarjunakonda seized the eastern Deccan. The very name of the Andhra dynasty finally disappeared, and was replaced by the Pallavas. Not until modern times did an Andhra province reappear, comprising the territories on the eastern coast where the Telugu language is spoken.

The Satavahana era is highly important because it marks the renaissance of Hindu philosophical, cosmological, and social concepts and the final defeat of Buddhism. The Brahmans regained their predominant role, and the castes once more formed the essential social structure. The principle of religious tolerance, which is fundamental to Hinduism, allowed the various sects to keep going and even, in the case of Jainism, to gain new vigor. It was also at this time that the cultural center of Hinduism moved definitively further south.

Maharashtri-Prakrit was the official language, replacing the Pali or Ardhamagadi of the Maurya period. Literature flourished. The Jain philosopher Kundakundacharya wrote numerous works in Prakrit. Gunadhya compiled a collection of histories in Paisaci dialect, known as the *Brihatkatha*. A new Sanskrit grammar, less difficult than Panini's, was composed by Sarvavarma for the use of the Satavahana princes.

In the field of arts, the excavations of Amaravati and Nagarjunakonda reveal a very refined art, showing the influence of the Gandhara and Mathura schools, but with greater freedom and ease and an exuberant style. This was one of the great periods of Indian art. Figures are harmonious, graceful, and sensual. Plants and animals are very true to life, treated with spirit and vigor. The frescos of Ajanta that began with the Satavahanas (starting from the second century B.C.E.) are unrivalled in the history of Indian painting.

KALINGA

Kalinga country, now known as Orissa, stretches along the northwest coast of the Gulf of Bengal. It includes the towns of Cuttack and Puri and the ancient city of Bhubaneshwar, whose temples are famous for their beauty and number. Kalinga was, and remains, one of the most interesting regions in India, because its culture and population belong to the pre-Aryan civilization and have largely escaped Aryanization. It is one of the regions where a great number of ethnic, linguistic, artistic, and religious features of pre-Vedic India continue to exist. In many sectors, the originality of its culture has continued down to our own times, whereas the Angas of Bengal, with whom the Kalingas are always associated in the *Puranas*, were more systematically Aryanized.

The Kalingas suffered cruelly from Ashoka's conquest. For political reasons, the Mauryas had divided the country in two with two capitals, one Tosali (modern Dhauli, near Bhubaneshwar) and the other Samapa (modern Jangada). Shortly after the death of Ashoka, however, Kalinga regained its independence and was reunited. From the second century B.C.E., the country became one of the most powerful states in India, under the Chedi dynasty, founded by Mahameghavahana and his successor Vakradeva.

The third sovereign of this dynasty was Kharavela, a contemporary of Satakarni and Pushyamitra. He was a very great king. The monasteries he excavated in the rock for the Jain ascetics at Udayagiri, close to Bhubaneshwar, the present capital of Orissa, include some of the most refined and beautiful monuments that India has ever produced. A wall inscription at Udayagiri, only a part of which has survived the weather, recounts the childhood and adolescence of Kharavela, and up to the twentieth year of his reign. The rest of the inscription is very damaged and difficult to interpret. The precise dates of Kharavela's reign are unknown, but are most probably between 180 and 130 B.C.E.

Kharavela spent the first fifteen years of his life playing the games suited to a young prince. He studied writing, the art of coining, book-keeping, administration, and legal procedure. At sixteen, he was installed as crown prince (*yuvaraja*) and at twenty-four was crowned as king (*maharaja*) of Kalinga. Although a pious Jain—he is sometimes called *bhikshu-raja*, the mendicant king—he protected all the religions in his states with impartiality.

In the second year of his reign Kharavela launched a military expedition, for the simple pleasure of adventure. He crossed the states of his friend and neighbor, Satakarni, with whom he had no bone to pick, without any serious consequences from the resultant clashes. He conquered the Rashtrikas of the Maratha country and the Bhojakas of Berar, two of Satavahana's vassals. These expeditions were, however, primarily acts of bravado, in a knightly society in which kings were first and foremost soldiers. They did not lead to annexations, but were a kind of tournament, according to the pre-Aryan tradition, and in no way affected the lives of the people.

On the other hand, Kharavela harassed the kings of the north, in particular the sovereigns of Magadha, against whom the Kalingas harbored a quite justifiable resentment. In the eighth year of his reign he destroyed the fortress of Gorathagiri, in the hills of Barabar, and took the town of Rajagriha (modern Rajgir), near Gaya. The Greek king Dimata (Demetrius)—who had sent an expedition against Pataliputra—was so afraid that he fled to Mathura.

In the eleventh year of his reign Kharavela turned southward and destroyed the town of Pithuda (Sanskrit Prithuda, the Pitundra of Ptolemy), the capital of the Maisoloi (*masulipatam*), close to Madras. The following year, he beat Brihaspatimitra of Magadha on the bank of the Ganges. He brought back considerable booty from Magadha and from Anga (Bengal), as well as numerous Jain statues. In the same year he defeated the Pandya king in the far south of India.

Kharavela was a great lover of music and organized spectacles and festivals. He took an interest in the well being of his people, developed irrigation, and was a major builder. He had to rebuild his capital after it had been devastated by a cyclone, and had a wonderful palace built for himself. The monuments built up to the medieval period (tenth to twelfth centuries) in the regions of Bhubaneshwar, Puri, and Konark are among the most beautiful in India.

We possess few documents about the Mahameghavahana dynasty after Kharavela. His successor appears to have been called Vadukha. Pliny (first century C.E.) says, "The tribes called Calingae are closest to the sea. The royal town of the Calingae is called Parthalis (Tosali). Sixty thousand foot soldiers, a thousand horsemen, and seven hundred elephants guard the king and protect him in case of war." The Kalingas are not mentioned in the *Periplus* (70 C.E.) or in Ptolemy's *Geography* (140 C.E.). The latter does, however, mention one of the Kalinga ports, where vessels departed for the "Land of Gold" (Burma), sailing straight across the sea. Kalinga continued to play a highly important role in the expansion of Indian culture overseas. Indeed, the Indians were, and still are, called *Kling* (Kalingas) throughout the countries of southeast Asia, from Burma to Java.

THE BARASHIVAS
(THIRD AND FOURTH CENTURIES)

The third and fourth centuries C.E. are sometimes spoken of as a dark age for northern India. This idea comes from the lack of Buddhist documents and the low value specialists set on the *Puranas* until recently. The progress of archaeology is, however, throwing light on a very important period, during which Hinduism reacted against foreigners—Greeks, Pallavas, Shakas—and the modern religions they patronized, such as Buddhism, and even Vedism. The people had never abandoned pre-Aryan Shaivism, and only tolerated other religions to the extent that they did not interfere in Shaivite rites, beliefs, and customs. The Nagas, who were established at Mathura, Padmavati, and Ahichatra, set up a confederation of republican tribes. Their chiefs were called the Barashivas. They were given this name because they wore an emblem of Shiva around their arm. They celebrated ten horse sacrifices—vast ceremonies commemorated by the *Dasavamedha Ghat* (The Stair of the Ten Horse Sacrifices)—at Varanasi, the major center of Shaivite religion. The Vakatakas of Berar cooperated with the Barashivas. The Sanskrit language returned to its prime position, in place of the Buddhists' Prakrit. Although this period is relatively little known, since it saw the creation of no great empires, it was the time of the development of the culture on which the Gupta Empire and the glorious age of Vikramaditya was to thrive.

Although ancient Brahmanism had survived in India during the Buddhist era, it had lost the support of royal power in most of the country and had consequently abandoned much of its intransigence. The Brahmans had gone back to their studies and the ascetic life of earlier times. They had been influenced by Buddhist and Jain doctrines, resulting in their adoption of non-violence, vegetarianism, and the theory of transmigration. Thus, the grounds for the Buddhist reform had ceased to exist, and Hinduism had assimilated almost all the important precepts of Buddhism.

The restoration of Brahmanism was to culminate slightly later, in the astonishing personality of Shankaracharya (born in Kerala toward the seventh century). During the preceding two centuries, Hinduism developed as we know it today: It was a very strict religion from a social point of view (caste system), but very liberal and open from a religious, philosophical, and ethical point of view. It left the human being great freedom for personal development, welcoming all forms of religion, which were seen as valid attempts in the search for the divine. Persecuted religions have always found refuge and the right to be themselves in India. This is why we find Indian Christian and Jewish communities dating back to the first centuries, and the Parsis, refugees from Iran, as well as numerous other sects finding refuge in India. It was only with Islam—and later on with the arrival of the Portuguese and St. Francis Xavier—that India rediscovered intolerance and the choice between circumcision and death, between the cross and the pyre.

It is without any doubt the institution of the caste system and its highly complex organization—in the form of corporations, with dedicated professions assuring an independent role to each racial, cultural, or religious group, thus obliging them to cooperate while prohibiting them to mix—that has made India the refuge of all persecuted peoples.

11

The Golden Age of the Guptas (300–600 C.E.)

CHANDRAGUPTA (319–330)

After the end of the Kushana Empire in the second century, we know little of the history of northern India up to the appearance of the Gupta dynasty at the beginning of the fourth century C.E. It is at this point that north India enters its "golden age." It becomes conscious of its nationhood, and extends and consolidates its empire, supported by an efficient administration. Religious movements assert themselves; literature and the arts flourish. This great period of cultural expansion, especially eastward, led to the establishment of what may be called "Outer India." Indochina and Indonesia were entirely Hinduized, and India's spiritual influence spread as far as China and Japan, where it was to have a profound impact on thought, religion, and the arts. For an examination of the Gupta era, we possess numerous archaeological and literary documents, as well as Chinese documents, such as the journal of Fa Hsien, who stayed for three years at Pataliputra.

The founder of the Gupta dynasty seems to have belonged to the Jat caste of Rajputana, indicating that he was probably a Scythian. According to the *Kaumudimahotsava*, Chandragupta I (319–330) had been raised by a king of Pataliputra called Sundara-varman.

Chandragupta is said to have assassinated the old king and exiled his son. He married a Lichchavi princess, Kumaradevi, and refounded the empire. The Gupta era, which is still the current one, begins with the date of his accession. Chandragupta chose his most capable son as his successor, and it was this son, Samudragupta, who built up the powerful structure and established the glory of the Gupta Empire.

SAMUDRAGUPTA (330–380)

Samudragupta was the most noble and most capable of the kings of this dynasty. Although less extensive than that of the Mauryas, his empire had greater luster. There was no region of India that did not feel the influence of the Gupta era, an age of refined and delicate culture that may bear comparison with eighteenth century France.

Samudragupta sought to establish the political union of India under his scepter. His early campaigns were directed toward the plains of northern India, subsequently toward the southern kingdoms, then to the border areas, and lastly to the forest tribes. His northern campaigns led to the annexation of the semi-independent kingdoms. In the south his campaigns were simply expeditions aimed at demonstrating the emperor's might. He won battles, humiliated kings, and gained enormous booty, after which he withdrew with his armies, maintaining a rather theoretical suzerainty. In the west he established his dominion over Rajputana, the Punjab, and Kashmir. Among the border kingdoms that voluntarily accepted his suzerainty, the most important were Bengal, Assam, and Nepal.

After a series of campaigns to establish his might, Samudragupta offered a grand horse sacrifice. He was a faithful Hindu, unlike his Maurya and Kushana predecessors, who had sought the support of Buddhism. He rejected the reforms of foreign origin introduced by Kanishka and the Shakas. He reformed the coinage, striking gold and copper coins and medals, but no silver ones. He was a good and just sovereign. He took an interest in the social and economic problems of the less privileged classes and often pardoned his enemies.

Samudragupta was a well-read king, and played the harp. A recently rediscovered theater play, *Krishna Charita*, is attributed to him. Striving to follow the rules concerning kingly duties as defined by the Hindu scriptures, Samudragupta identified his success with the happiness and prosperity of the peoples of his empire. He avoided war whenever his clever diplomacy made it possible. His policy was very flexible: wars of annexation and extermination in the north, wars of capture followed by restitution and the reestablishment of kings in the south. Observing the law of Manu that fixed the borders of India at the mountains of the Hindu Kush and Pamir, he never attacked Persia, which, weakened by the Romans, could easily have been conquered. This voluntary limitation of his territorial ambitions was one of the causes of the solidity of his empire.

The empire itself was conceived as a federation of kingdoms around a central royal power. Each state retained its independent administration, but the various countries were gathered together in a political union. Such a union—that left the individual states feeling free but united them against a common threat—was one of the major political successes of the Gupta Empire.

VIKRAMADITYA (380–415)

Like his predecessor, Chandragupta II—who succeeded to the throne in 380—had been chosen by his father to succeed him. Like Louis XIV, he considered the empire as a noble inheritance. Through his conquests, he managed to maintain and even enlarge it. His surname, Vikramaditya, is still one of the most glorious names in Indian history.

Samudragupta had not attacked the Scythians or Shakas, who continued to occupy Gujarat and the Kathiavar peninsula. Taking advantage of a conflict between the satraps, Vikramaditya invaded their kingdoms with a mighty army and exterminated them. He then transferred his capital from Pataliputra to Ujjain. The annexation of these western provinces added regions of exceptional fertility to the empire but, above all, gave free access to the coastal ports and control over the highly important sea trade with Europe and Egypt. The empire thus stretched from Bengal to Baluchistan and northward as far as Bactria.

It was during the reign of Vikramaditya that the Chinese traveler Fa Hsien visited India. In the account he left, he speaks of the empire's prosperity and describes its capital as a center of culture. Buddhism, already on the decline, co-existed harmoniously with Brahmanism there. The court of Ujjain was a center of the arts and sciences, ornamented by the "Nine Jewels" of knowledge, who included the great poet Kalidasa, the famous astronomer Varahamihira, and Vasubandhu, the celebrated Buddhist philosopher.

THE GUPTA ADMINISTRATION

Like the Maurya monarchy, the Gupta monarchy was constitutional. The sovereign respected the laws and, in so doing, respected the peoples he governed. Although his titles suggested that he was almost divine, the emperor was not deified, or considered a god. Royalty was hereditary, but the crown did not pass, by right, to the eldest son. The king chose his successor. The members of the royal family were employed as viceroys in the provinces.

The Council of Ministers (*mantriparishada*) had no executive power, and merely gave its advice to the sovereign. The prime minister (*mantrimukhya*) presided over the council's resolutions and transmitted the results to the king. Ministerial posts were hereditary. Among the main executive offices were the Chief of the Armies, the Controller of Morals, the Director of the Police and Justice, and the Controller of Military Expenditure.

The empire was divided into provinces (*desha*) and regions (*bhukti*), and subdivided into departments (*vishaya*). The provinces were placed under governors (*goptri*), the regions under princes, and the departments under prefects (*vishaya-pali*). The villages had a village headman. As a rule, the governors belonged to the royal family. The princes were appointed by the emperor, and the prefects either by the princes or directly by the emperor. In general terms, the administrative system continued the structures established by the Mauryas.

The main sources of revenue were taxes on private property and the leasing of crown lands. There was little corporal punishment, with offences being punished by fines. The corporations played an important role, owning collective assets and fixing their own rules of conduct and their own organization, so long as they did not infringe upon the laws. The corporations elected a president, established rules for bonuses, insurance, and pensions. They fixed prices and wages and took charge of families in case of sickness. Trade with Egypt, Rome, and Persia flourished.

Completely reformed, Buddhism incorporated the ritual practices of Shaivism and of the cult of the goddess (Shakti), as well as the magical and erotico-mystical rites of Tantrism. Buddhism was thus gradually reintegrated into Hinduism, and the Buddha was accepted in the Hindu pantheon as an incarnation (avatar) of Vishnu.

The schools of philosophy under the Guptas developed the doctrine of the Word (*Shabda*), envisaging the Word as the primary cause of the world and as cosmic law. This "universal law," revealed in the Vedas, was deemed to be the sole transcendent reality, the gods being merely superior forms of created beings.

The orginal atomic theory of the world was also developed in the Gupta schools of Nyaya (logic) and Vaisheshika (science). At this time several major Hindu theories also appear regarding: the unreality of matter—being only energy; the identity of matter and thought; and the relative nature of space—being different in the atom and in the perceptible world (an atom is therefore, in itself, as vast as a solar system). The schools of Samkhya (cosmology) and Yoga (extrasensory perception) completed the scholarship of the other Gupta institutes. Their conclusions as to the limits of space and the relativity of time currently appear to be on the way to being corroborated.

The ancient Jain religion, moralistic and atheistic, was encouraged by the Guptas. It regained its prominence in its two aspects: *shvetambara*, whose followers wear white, and *digambara* (clothed in space), in which nudity is obligatory. Shaivism also regained a strong influence, the Pashupata sect in particular. At the same time, devout Vaishnavism, in the form known as Bhagavata, founded the sentimental cult of Krishna that became extremely popular. Many Gupta kings were fervent followers of the Krishna cult. This religion split into two sects—the Pancharatra and the Vaikhanasa—on which many texts were written at the time. The cult of the goddess, or female principle (Shakti) also played an important role, ranging from the popular cult of the Mother Goddess to the much higher symbolic conceptions of Tantrism. In the *Tantras* and the *Agamas* we find a particular philosophy called Shakti-Vishishtadvaita (qualified non-dualism of the "energy" principle).

The Gupta age is considered a great period for Sanskrit literature, or at least it is a period from which the greatest number of literary texts have reached us. It was probably at this time that the celebrated poet and playwright Kalidasa lived. Although the great poet's dates have been contested, he must have been a contemporary of Chandragupta II (380-415). Many of his plays have become classics, not only in India, but throughout the world. Two other famous playwrights of this period are Vishakadatta, who wrote the *Mudrarakshasa*, and Dinnaga, who wrote the *Kundamala*.

Kalidasa's art—though considered to be the acme of India's literary art—is extremely bombastic. As with many other aspects of Gupta art, it is also rather affected and decadent. It considerably weakened Sanskrit literature by making pedantry and preciosity the literary models to be followed. Unfortunately, Kalidasa's prestige was so great that all attempts to return to less affected norms were rejected by men of letters and the related works have not survived.

Owing to its very refinement, Gupta art is decadent. It is a product that has assimilated the outside influences of the great Iranian, Scythian, and Greek international complex that had impacted Indian life. It does not truly represent Indian culture, although it is strongly marked by it. It is a palace art, an art of riches, which does not rest on the popular foundation of a vigorous tradition. This is equally true in the domain of Gupta literature, philosophy, and religion.

This period is often reminiscent—in spirit, if not in form—of the Hellenistic culture, or the eighteenth century in France. Indeed, we shall presently see a reaction take place—similar to that of the European Middle Ages—with art plunging its roots once again into the people's true culture, religion, and philosophy. This reaction was to give rise to a new art, profoundly symbolic and vigorously stylistic, during the great period of Hindu culture known to us as the medieval period, which flourished from the ninth to the twelfth centuries.

Huns and Muslims destroyed most of the Gupta monuments. Among those that survived, one of the most striking is the famous small temple of Deogarh, in central India. Ajanta's rock-hewn monasteries also still contain major frescoes of the Gupta period, a unique and wonderful specimen of the pictorial art of that time; a few frescoes still exist in the rock-hewn temples at Ellora and Bagh.

THE HUNS (FIFTH CENTURY)

The Huns were a race of ferocious barbarians from the steppes of central Asia who, in the fifth century, launched their devastating hordes against the finest provinces of the Roman Empire in the West and the Gupta Empire in India. Toward the end of the reign of Kumaragupta (415–455), successor of Chandragupta II, the Huns started their attacks. Previously, the empire's stability had been threatened by revolts of the Pushyamitras—a powerful tribe of central India, living in the Amarkantak region at the source of the Narmada—but Skandagupta, then crown prince, managed to reduce them. When he himself came to the throne in 455, he successfully faced down formidable attacks by the Huns, who were under the generalship of Toramana and his son.

Skandagupta's victory over the Huns had enormous consequences. Since they could no longer penetrate India, they launched themselves on the West. Their continual pressure on eastern Europe was the result of having been checked in their efforts to penetrate India. After the death of Skandagupta in 467, however, they renewed their attacks and managed finally to invade the border provinces in the fourth century, establishing their dominion there in the sixth century. The empire was subsequently split up, and the Huns dominated Rajputana, the Punjab, and Kashmir. Their cruelty and tyrannical character have been mentioned by several authors, and in particular by the Chinese pilgrims.

When the Huns entered the Punjab, however, their aggressiveness had already been tempered and their occupation brought no serious consequences. In 465 the chief of the White Huns, Toramana, ruled the Punjab, and as far south as Malwa. His son Mihiragula established his capital at Sialkot. Their advance was frustrated however, thanks to the princes who rallied around the Gupta power. At Eran, in eastern Malwa, a king named Baladitya (perhaps Bhanugupta) managed to halt the Huns in a celebrated battle. It was not until 533–534 that Yashovarman of Mandasor, an ambitious and energetic king of western Malwa, finally broke the Huns' power.

The arrival of the Turks isolated the Huns in India from the rest of the Hun Empire in central Asia. They continued to reign over small principalities in the northwest of India and Malwa until they were absorbed by their repeated marriages with Rajput families.

THE DECLINE OF THE GUPTA EMPIRE

At the death of Skandagupta (467) a period of anarchy broke out. Narasimhagupta and Buddhagupta made an effort to reassemble the forces of the crumbling empire, but failed as a result of family strife, invasions, and revolts by kings who had been submissive till then. Several sovereigns took the title of *Maharaja* (Emperor) to affirm their independence.

Under the direction of Bhataraka, the Maitrakas—an ancient dynasty of Rajput origin—seized power at Vallabhi. Druvasena, the third king of that dynasty, still acknowledged Gupta suzerainty, but after him the kings became independent. Bengal also detached itself from the empire. There, Isanavarman, of the Maukhari family from Kanauj, fomented an armed rebellion. He then made an alliance with the Vardhamanas of Thanesar for mutual defense against the Hun Mihiragula. The Vakataka kings, with whom Chandragupta II had made alliances through a skilful matrimonial policy, also separated from the empire and, in the reign of Narendrasena (445–465), entered Malwa in triumph.

THE LAST GUPTAS (SIXTH TO SEVENTH CENTURY)

After the splitting up of the Gupta Empire the state of Magadha—the center of their empire—fell into the hands of a dynasty known as the last Guptas, who reigned for one hundred and fifty years, from the middle of the sixth century to the end of the seventh century. The names of these kings all end in *-gupta*. They do not, however, appear to be connected with the ancient Guptas, and probably had to adopt the name for reasons of prestige. Little is known about the first three: Krishnagupta, Harshagupta, and Jivitagupta. The fourth, Kumaragupta, conquered the chief of the Maukharis—Isanavarman—and died at Prayag (Allahabad). His successor, Damodaragupta, continued the war against the Maukharis. After him, Mahasenagupta appears to have reestablished to a certain extent the status of the kingdom, and was victorious in a war against Susthitavarman. He died tragically, and his two sons, Kumaragupta and Madhavagupta, took refuge at Thanesar, where they entered the service of Harsha and Rajyavardhana.

The last of the Guptas was Adityasena, who reestablished his sovereignty over Magadha, made an alliance with the Maukharis, and effected a rapprochement with the kings of Bengal. During his reign, the dynasty's influence and prestige were ruined by an invasion of the Chalukyas of Badami. Adityasena's successors were colorless minor princes. Yashodharman of Kanauj invaded Magadha and killed the king there, but was himself defeated by Muktapida Lalitaditya of Kashmir. After this, the north of India plunged once more into the confusion of a multitude of tiny states.

After the Gupta Empire came to an end, many local dynasties regained importance. The best known are the Maitrakas of Vallabhi (Kathiawar), the Maukharis of Kanauj (on the bank of the Ganges, to the north of Kanpur), the Vardhamanas of Thanesar (close to Lahore), Yashovarman in Malwa (near Indore), the Karkotakas of Kashmir, the Varmans of Kamarupa (Cooch Bihar), Sashanka of Bengal, the Kesharis of Orissa, the Gangas of Kalinga, the Vishnukindins of Vengi (north of Madras), and, in the south, the Pallavas of Kanchi, the Cholas

(Trichinopoly), the Pandyas (east coast) and the Cheras (west coast), the Kadambas of Bavanasi (Kuntala in Karnataka) and, further to the north, the Chalukyas of Badami. The Maitrakas were called Shiladitya at the time of Harsha and were spoken of by Hiuen Tsang and I Tsing as the great patrons of the University of Vallabhi. The Maukharis of Kanauj, whose empire extended as far as Bengal, made an alliance with Prabhakara-Vardhana of Thanesar in an attempt to slow down the Huns' advance.

For a certain time, Kanauj took over from Magadha as the cultural and political center of northern India. It was, however, a powerful empire no longer, and whenever the kings of the south made incursions north-ward, they did so as conquerors. Indeed, the centers of imperial power in India had passed to the south of the subcontinent, where the Chalukyas of Badami and the Rashtrakutas now played the role that had once belonged to the Guptas. This period of the history of India could be called the Karnataka (southern) era, just as the eighteenth century (C.E.) could be known as the Maratha era.

12

The Deccan Kingdoms
(Third to Sixth Centuries)

THE VAKATAKAS

The disappearance of the Satavahanas in the third century left the Deccan without any paramount power. The Vakatakas—a Brahman dynasty who reigned over Berar—modestly took their place. The Vakatakas were protectors of the arts, and some of the best frescoes of Ajanta were painted at their order. The dynasty's founder, Vindhyashakti, conquered part of the Vindhya Mountain territory and a part of eastern Malwa. His capital was Purika. After him, his son, Pravarasena I, mounted the throne and solidly established his power during his very long reign (280–340). His conquests seem to have led him southward as far as Karnal, in the modern day province of Andhra. He also took advantage of the crisis which beset the Kshatrapas, or satraps of the west, and reduced them to vassal status. His empire comprised all the central provinces (Madhya Pradesh), Berar, Malwa, the Kshatrapa domains, and a large portion of the Deccan. He took the title of *Samrat* (Emperor) and offered innumerable Vedic sacrifices, including four horse sacrifices. At that time, he was the most powerful of India's monarchs.

According to the *Puranas*, the four sons of Pravarasena I reigned after his death over different parts of his empire. His real successor was his grandson Rudrasena I, who reigned from 340 to 360. In about 348 Samudragupta attacked Rudrasena, who was defeated. The next king was Prithivisena I, who reigned from 360 to 390, and tried to reestablish the family fortunes. He conquered Kuntala and strengthened his influence over central India. His power preoccupied Chandragupta II Vikramaditya, who made an alliance with him and gave his daughter Prabhavatigupta in marriage to Prithivisena's son, Rudrasena.

Rudrasena reigned only five years, and then his wife became regent. She was the mother of two young children. This was the opportunity for Chandragupta to increase his influence. The queen assisted him in his campaigns against the Shakas. When her elder son died, her second son, Pravarasena, mounted the throne in 410. He took the name of Prithivisena II and reigned up to 445. He remained under the influence of the Guptas, however, and Chandragupta is said to have sent the poet Kalidasa as ambassador to his court.

Narendrasena succeeded his father and reigned from 445 to 465. His reign was troubled: The Pushyamitras and the Huns threatened India, and the Nalas invaded the Vakataka kingdom, but Narendrasena managed to organize his forces and expel the invaders from his lands. He killed their king, Arthapati, and became the sovereign of Mekala. Taking advantage of the Guptas' difficulties, he occupied Malwa for some time.

Prithivisena III, the son of Narendrasena, was the last king of the main branch. After him, the monarchy passed to a secondary branch of the family, of whom the last king was Harisena (480–515), an ambitious and powerful sovereign. At his death, the Vakataka Empire disintegrated and neighboring kingdoms annexed its provinces.

THE KADAMBAS AND THE GANGAS

The country known as Karnataka extends geographically from the Cauvery to the Godavari. Karnataka comes from *karu nadu,* "high plateau," in the language of the country, Kanada, one of the major Dravidian languages. The most ancient dynasties of the Karnataka country that are known historically are the Kadambas of Vanavasi, who governed the northwest of the modern state of Karnataka, and the Gangas of Talaka, whose kingdom was located further south.

The Kadambas, contemporaries of the Pallavas of Kanchi, inherited the southern part of the Satavahana Empire when it broke up. The dynasty's founder was a Brahman, Mayura Sharma, who had studied the Vedas at Kanchi. Having quarreled with a Pallava spy, he asked the king for justice. Not obtaining it, he threw away his prayer items and took up arms. He managed to organize a band of adventurous young men and—having subdued the neighboring kings and keeping the Pallava army in check—he founded his own kingdom. Inscriptions attribute to him quite improbable conquests, going as far as the Punjab. In actual fact, he established his dominion solidly over the Karnataka country as a whole. After him the most outstanding sovereign was Kakusthavarman, who reigned from 425 to 450 and established matrimonial alliances with the Gangas, the Guptas and the Vakatakas. The dynasty later divided into two branches. The same thing happened to the Gangas, and the Pallavas did their best to encourage these divisions. Among the early Gangas, Purvinita (605-650) was famous as a soldier and man of letters. He fought victoriously against the Pallavas and managed to put a Chalukya prince on the Pallava throne. A poet in the Kanada tongue, he translated a work from the Paisaci dialect into Sanskrit.

Toward the middle of the sixth century, the Kadambas and the Gangas were overshadowed by the Pallavas' rise to power on the one side, and that of the Chalukyas of Badami on the other.

THE CHALUKYAS OF BADAMI

The Chalukyas were natives of the Karnataka country. Minor princes in the service of the Satavahanas and the Kadambas, they took advantage of the weakening of the central power and created a kingdom of their own whose capital—Badami—became one of the major cultural centers of India. The monuments still existing at Badami, Aihole, and Pattadakal are among the most extraordinary ever conceived in India. The sculptures that decorate the Chalukya temples show a unique elegance, refinement of manufacture and expression, and are furthermore totally exempt from foreign influence. At the same time, the Chalukya Empire won great prestige and maintained relations with distant lands, relations that were founded on cultural values more than on military or economic might.

Pulakeshin I (547–567)—the grandson of Jayashimba, who fought the Pallavas, and son of Rajashimba—was the first Chalukya king, and ruled from Vatapi (Badami), on a hilltop close to the River Malaprabha, eight kilometers from Pattadakal and fourteen kilometers from Aihole. Once he had ensured his independence, he offered a horse sacrifice to affirm his sovereign power.

Kirtivarman I (567–598) succeeded his father Pulakeshin, and considerably extended his territory. He ensured the control of the richest ports on the west coast. On the death of Kirtivarman, his son being too young, his brother Mangalesha (598–608) succeeded him and continued his work of conquest. He annexed the ports of Goa and Revatidvipa. He attempted to put his own son on the throne, but Pulakeshin—the son of Kirtivarman who had been exiled—managed to overcome him with the aid of loyal friends and put him to death.

Pulakeshin II (608–642) was the greatest Chalukya monarch and the most powerful sovereign of southern India. He seized the throne, taking advantage of the disorders following the death of Mangalesha. He rapidly consolidated his power and undertook a series of conquests that considerably extended his lands, including Gujarat in his kingdom.

Pulakeshin's ambitions clashed with those of the Vardhamanas, and with those of Harsha in particular. War became inevitable. Harsha subsequently lost an important battle to the north of the Vindhya Mountains and had to flee. Harsha's discomfiture at this time is confirmed by the Chinese traveler Hiuen Tsang who visited the Karnataka country in 641. Pulakeshin then built fortresses to the north of the Vindhya Mountains and along the whole length of the River Narmada. He took the title of *Parameshvara* (Supreme Sovereign) and called his empire *Maharashtraka* (The Great Kingdom). He later conquered Kalinga, beat the Cholas close to the Cauvery, and received the submission of the Cheras and Pandyas. In the end, he clashed with the Pallavas, but came out victorious from this adventure after conquering King

Mahendravarman I, who had to take refuge at Kanchi. Having thus assured his uncontested sovereignty over the whole of the south of India, he reigned in peace in his capital, Badami.

It is believed that an embassy sent by Pulakeshin to Khusru II of Persia is represented on the famous Ajanta frescoes (Cave 1).

Hiuen Tsang writes of Pulakeshin's nobility and might, as well as describing the character of the people. "The inhabitants are proud and war-like, grateful for any good that is done to them, but seeking revenge if someone wrongs them. They are generous to anyone who makes a request, but cruel to those who insult them. These warriors get drunk before battle and also intoxicate their elephants. The king, trusting in the strength of his army and elephants, treats his neighbors with disdain. His vassals serve him loyally." Pulakeshin was not cruel, however. When a general lost a battle, Pulakeshin did not punish him, but forced him to wear women's clothes. As often as not, the humiliated general killed himself.

Pulakeshin's victory over the Pallavas was not to last long. After the death of Mahendravarman I, Pulakeshin again invaded the Pallava coun-try, but on this occasion was defeated by the young king Narasimha in three bloody battles. The Pallavas then pursued the Chalukyas as far as their capital Badami and sacked it. This bitter defeat completely disor-ganized the Chalukya Empire; it remained humiliated and submissive for thirteen years, leaving the Pallavas the uncontested sovereigns of the south.

When Pulakeshin died, he left the central government to his eldest son Vikramaditya (655–680), while his second son Chandraditya gov-erned the border provinces. The restoration of the country's unity and the family's prestige was the difficult task that Vikramaditya attempted to bring about. He was assisted in this by his maternal grandfather, the Ganga king Purvinita.

Taking advantage of the disorder that reigned in the south, Vikramaditya mortified the Cheras, Cholas, Pandyas, and Kalabhras by his constant attacks. He then attacked the Pallavas, decisively beating Parameshva-Ravarman I and taking the town of Kanchi, despite its forti-fications, ramparts, and the great moat that surrounded it. Thus he almost avenged his father. The Pallava king, however, took refuge in a fort and launched a surprise attack on the sleeping Chalukya camp. Vikramaditya escaped "clothed only in a towel." This misadventure was not, however, to have important consequences.

Vinayaditya (678–696), who succeeded his father, had a peaceful reign. The Pallavas and all the kings of the south paid him tribute. It is even claimed that he received tribute from the king of Persia, which would appear somewhat improbable. His son, Vijayaditya II, reigned from 696 to 733. He too fought the Pallavas and built one of the most beautiful temples at Pattadakal, the temple of Sangameshvara.

As soon as he reached the throne, Vikramaditya II (733–743) decided to revenge himself on the Pallavas, who had humiliated his ancestors. He organized an expedition and inflicted a terrible defeat on them; he occupied the town of Kanchi without destroying it, since for the southern lands "it was a jewel in the belt on a maiden's body." The Pallavas' defeat was total. Vikramaditya then easily subdued the Cheras, the Pandyas, the Cholas, and the Kalabhras and erected a victory column on the shores of the southern sea.

The last of the Chalukya kings was Kirtivarman II, who continued to wage war against the weakened Pallavas, without weighing the risk of the growing power of the Rashtrakutas on his northern border. The Rashtrakuta king, Dantidurga, attacked Kirtivarman and totally defeated him in 753. Dantidurga then continued his advance southward and subdued the kingdoms in the far south. He had no sons. His uncle, Krishna, succeeded him and completed his work by destroying definitively the empire of the Chalukyas of Badami.

Although the Chalukya kings were devout Hindus, worshipping both Shiva and Vishnu, Jainism—with its deep roots in the country—continued to prosper, and Buddhism was tolerated there. The Hindu and Jain monuments built under the Chalukyas are among the most beautiful in India. Aihole is described as "the cradle of Hindu architecture." The style of the sculptures, very distinct from the realistic Gupta style, gives the first example of the balance between stylization, grace, and expression that is so characteristic of that great Hindu art known as medieval, which probably remains unrivalled.

Aihole had more than seventy temples, the most beautiful of which belong to the period between 450 and 650. The temples at Pattadakal, a few kilometers from Aihole, date from the seventh century and betray a certain influence of the art of Kanchi. The Virupaksha temple, forty meters tall, is one of the most magnificent monuments of Chalukya art. Its sculptures and decorations are of exquisite quality, both in the perfection of their style and in their sensitiveness. The famous fresco of the Buddha's temptation at Ajanta is the only masterpiece of Chalukya painting that has survived.

13
The Vardhamanas
(Sixth to Seventh Century)

HARSHA

Quite a lot is known about the history of the Vardhamanas, since two important historians have left us relatively faithful accounts. One is the poet Bana, who lived at the court of Harsha and wrote his biography, the *Harsha-Charita*. The other is the Chinese traveler Hiuen Tsang, whose account, the *Si-yu-ki*, is a detailed description of the court and great deeds of King Harsha.

The Vardhamana dynasty was founded in the sixth century by Pushyabhuti, a king of great bravery who acquired supernatural powers by practicing Shaivite Tantrism under the direction of the famous ascetic Bhairavacharya. Pushyabhuti forged a kingdom for himself not far from Thanesar (near Lahore) and helped the last Guptas in their wars against the Huns. His son, Rajyavardhana, was a sun-worshipper. The latter's son, Adityasena, married a Gupta princess with whom he had a son called Prabhakara-Vardhana.

Prabhakara-Vardhana was distinguished for his victories in Sind, Gujarat, and Malwa (the region of Kota, Bundi), and more especially over the Huns, then established in the northern Punjab. According to Bana, "the Huns seemed like gazelles before this lion. He was a burning fever for the King of the Indus, he troubled the sleep of Gujarat. He appeared like the pest for the sovereign of Gandhara, like a thief to Lata (south of Gujarat) and like an axe for Malwa's vine of glory."

Prabhakara-Vardhana had two sons, Rajyavardhana II and Harshavardhana, plus a daughter, Rajyashri. When old age began to undermine his strength, the Huns once more threatened the country's security. He formed a coalition to halt their advance. The young Rajyavardhana, accompanied by Harsha, went off to fight them at the head of an immense army. When he returned victorious, he learned that his father had died and his mother had sacrificed herself on his funeral pyre. Rajyavardhana decided to renounce the world and to become an ascetic, leaving the kingdom to his younger brother Harsha. The latter refused indignantly, "Does he take me for the most despicable of men, ready for a foul deed of any kind? Am I not, I too, the descendent of Pushyabhuti, son of my father, and his own brother? Does he believe me bereft of any feeling?"

While the two brothers were thus chopping niceties, King Devagupta of Malwa—who had made an alliance with Sashanka of Gauda (Bengal)—attacked Grahavarman of Kanauj, who had married Rajyashri, the sister of Rajyavardhana and Harsha. Grahavarman was killed and Rajyashri imprisoned. The two brothers left their quarrels and, at the head of an army of ten thousand horse, Rajyavardhana attacked Malwa, which he took without difficulty. King Sashanka of Bengal, pretending to submit, invited Rajyavardhana to a banquet, where he had him murdered.

Harsha thus found himself alone, without his parents, without his elder brother, without knowing what had happened to his sister. He was then eighteen years old. Bana describes the young prince's fury as he took a solemn oath: "On the dust of the feet of my god, I swear that if within a few days I have not delivered the land from the Gaudas, and have not caused to echo the noise of the chains attached to the feet of all those kings incited to insolence by the suppleness of their bows, I will throw myself on a pyre, just as an insect throws itself into the lamp flame."

At the head of a mighty army, Harsha subdued all the neighboring kingdoms, and found his sister who, having taken refuge in a hermitage of the Vindhya forest, was about to commit suicide.

Bana's account stops at this point. For the rest, the main source of information is the work of the Chinese pilgrim, Hiuen Tsang. According to him, Harsha's conquests extended as far as Bengal, but he suffered a serious defeat when he attacked the Chalukya Pulakeshin II, king of the Deccan. In a great battle, which took place around 620, Harsha's army was severely decimated and he had to withdraw in haste.

Harsha's empire comprised the area of Uttar Pradesh, a great part of Bihar (Patna), Bengal, and Orissa. He was the revered suzerain of Sind, the Punjab, and Kashmir, as well as Nepal. The limit of his empire southward was the River Narmada (from Bharuch to Jubbulpor). He exchanged embassies with numerous sovereigns, including the Emperor of China.

Harsha was a great emperor in his virtues, his political ability, his conquests, his solicitude for the people, and the justice of his laws, as well as in his patronage of the arts and sciences. His conquests were limited, being checked by the southern powers (Pulakeshin II in particular) and by his conflicts with Sashanka of Bengal. His dominion only extended to the north of India, but even those states that did not accept his suzerainty sought his friendship and acknowledged his ascendency.

Harsha's administration was similar to that of the Guptas. The Council of Ministers *(mantriparishada)* was very powerful, and officially proposed the king's election. Harsha himself was elected king by the council on the death of his brother. The king's power was absolute, but each sphere of administration enjoyed considerable autonomy. This has always been a principle of Hindu administration. The country was divided into provinces, districts, and communes. Each village functioned like a small republic as far as local affairs were concerned; the solidity and independence of the village administrations were the strong point of the administrative system. According to Hiuen Tsang, "Harsha was just in his administration and punctilious in exercising his responsibilities. He forgot to sleep and eat, in his concern for doing good. He visited and inspected his whole empire. Temporary constructions were erected for his visits." A military career was a hereditary profession at this time, and according to Hiuen Tsang, the army during Harsha's reign was also extraordinarily disciplined and efficient.

With regard to criminal justice, there was no forced labor, and everyone was free to busy himself with his own affairs. Criminals were few. The use of the ordeal, however, made justice somewhat problematical.

Hiuen Tsang tells us that, to establish guilt, the ordeal was practiced in four ways: by water, fire, weights, or poison. "In the water ordeal, the accused party was put into a sack and a stone in another. The sacks were both thrown into the water. If the sack containing the stone floated, and the man sank, it meant he was guilty. In the ordeal by fire, the accused party had to kneel on red coals, walk over them, take fire in his hand, or lick it. If he was not burnt, he was innocent. In the ordeal of the weights, the accused party was placed in the dish on one side of the scales and a large stone was placed in the other. If the stone was lighter, it meant he was innocent. In the poison ordeal, a violent poison was inserted at a certain point of a leg of lamb, of which the accused party was made to eat a piece. If he survived, he was innocent." Punishment for being an unworthy son, or for disloyal behavior, or for an offence against social morals, was the cutting off of the nose, ear, hand, or foot of the guilty party, or else banishment.

Harsha ruled for over thirty years. He had been raised in the religion of Shiva, but later converted to Mahayana Buddhism. From that time on, each year he summoned a Buddhist assembly that lasted twenty-one days. He surrounded himself with scholars from all parts of India, especially from the University of Nalanda.

Hiuen Tsang tells us that he instituted the religious festival called "Assemblies of Great Liberation" (*mahamoksha-parishada*), which fell every five years and lasted one month. Images of the Buddha, Shiva, and the Sun were carried in procession, and Harsha distributed all the riches he had accumulated, of which nothing remained save "the horses, elephants, and military equipment, which were necessary for maintaining order and protecting the royal power. He gave away his jewels and personal objects, his clothes and his necklaces, his earrings, bracelets, rosaries, the jewels of his neck and forehead. Having given everything away, he begged from his sister (Rajyashri) an old garment and, having put it on, he worshipped the Buddhas of the ten regions of space and expressed his joy that his goods had been distributed for the purpose of earning religious merit."

Even more severely than Ashoka, Harsha forbade the killing of animals and the eating of their meat. He built a bronze temple at Nalanda, one hundred feet high, as well as hospitals and rest houses to shelter travelers along the roads. He called Buddhist synods, at which the monks debated questions of theology or ethics in his presence. He exiled monks whose behavior was not exemplary. At the palace, food was prepared every day for one thousand Buddhist monks and five hundred Brahmans. Despite Harsha's efforts, however, Buddhism everywhere declined. Its holy places fell into ruin and were abandoned.

Harsha was also a very generous patron of literature and the arts. Three remarkable plays in Sanskrit—*Ratnavali, Priyadarshika,* and *Nagananda*[1]—are attributed to him. He also composed Buddhist hymns. Major writers lived at his court. The main ones were Mayura and the poet Bana, who wrote Harsha's biography and a famous verse novel, *Kadambari.* A play, *Parvali-parinaya,* and a volume of verse, *Chandishataka,* are also attributed to Bana. Harsha made considerable donations to the Buddhist University at Nalanda in Bihar, which attracted students from all over the world. This university was at the apex of its glory when Hiuen Tsang visited it. It had three great buildings, a library, and an observatory. The entrance examinations were very difficult, and studying the Mahayana texts was obligatory.

Harsha died in 646 or 647. He had no son. His daughter's son, who took the name of Druvasena IV, succeeded him. The dynasty was not long-lived however, and Harsha's extremely centralized empire split into numerous small kingdoms.

It was at this point—in 640—that the Arabs reached the frontiers of India. They occupied the Makran desert, took Herat and Kabul between 650 and 663, and, in 712, invaded Sind.

---

1. Translated by Alain Daniélou (Paris, 1977).

HIUEN TSANG

Born in 600 CE of a family that practiced Confucianism, Hiuen Tsang converted to Buddhism and became a monk at the age of twenty. Not very satisfied with the Chinese translations of fundamental Buddhist texts, he wished to visit the land where Sakyamuni had preached his doctrine. He left Siam (modern Thailand) for India in 629 and didn't return to China until 645.

Hiuen Tsang's great work, the *Si-yu-ki*, provides a detailed description of living conditions in India in the seventh century. At his time, the Huns had destroyed Peshawar and Taxila. The great centers of Hindu and Buddhist culture were Shrinagar in Kashmir, Kanauj, Prayag (Allahabad), and Varanasi (Kashi). The two latter cities were, as they are today, major pilgrimage centers for Hindus. Hiuen Tsang gives a precise description of living conditions in India, and speaks of the caste institution. He admired the Brahmans for their love of study and the frugality of their life, and mentions the Kshatriyas—or warrior caste—to which the kings belonged, and the wealthy Vaishyas, who dealt with trade. He speaks of the Shudras, who formed the farming caste. He also mentions the "untouchables," who practiced unclean occupations, and says that the dwellings of butchers, acrobats, executioners, and scavengers were marked with a special sign. They had to live outside the town and walk on the left side in villages.

Like that of orthodox Hindus today, clothing of the time consisted of two pieces of seamless draped cloth. Both men and women wore earrings and many jewels. Except for monks and Brahmans, most people ate meat and fish and drank various kinds of strong drink. The remarriage of widows was viewed with horror, and sati—the widow's suicide on her husband's funeral pyre—was considered to be an act of holiness. Old men also renounced living. "The friends of those who feel too old, or have an incurable disease, or wish to renounce life, offer them a farewell reception on a boat in the middle of the Ganges. After this, they drown themselves, deeming that they will thus be reborn in paradise."

Hiuen Tsang boasts of the honesty of the Indians, and their rich agriculture. He describes the architecture of towns and villages and the furnishings of palaces. The army was divided into four parts: infantry, cavalry, elephants, and chariots. The soldiers, brave and well paid, were armed with spears, bows, swords, sabers, war-axes, pikes, halberds, javelins, and various kinds of slings for stones. The administration was just, and taxes not very heavy. Some states had a legal code, and others none.

Hiuen Tsang stayed five years at Nalanda University, where more than seven thousand monks lived. He mentions a very considerable literature in Sanskrit and other works on history, statistics, and geography, none of which have survived. He also writes of officials whose job it was to write records of all important events. At Nalanda, studies included the Vedas, the Upanishads, cosmology (Samkhya), realist or scientific philosophy (Vaisheshika), logic (Nyaya), to which great importance was attached, and Jain and Buddhist philosophy.

Studies also included grammar, mechanics, medicine, and physics. Medicine was highly effective, and surgery was quite developed. The treatises of this period are still in use in Hindu schools of medicine. Their pharmacopoeia was enormous, and astronomy was very advanced. The earth's diameter had been calculated very precisely. In physics, Brahmagupta (about 628) had discovered the law of gravity.

YASHOVARMAN OF KANAUJ

No document survives about Kanauj between the death of Harsha and the accession of Yashovarman in about 730. This king sent an embassy to China in around 731. According to one of the Jain chronicles, he was descended from the ancient Maurya dynasty. His ambition was to conquer the whole of India, and his armies went as far as Bengal. However, he ran up against the King of Kashmir, Muktapida Lalitaditya, and was himself reduced to vassal status. All the same, Yashovarman occupies a place in history for his patronage of arts and letters. He wrote plays, and the famous playwright Bhavabhuti resided at his court. One after the other, Yashovarman's successors were defeated by the kings of Kashmir and Bengal, and finally, by Bhagabhatta II, King of Bhinal in Rajputana, who set up his capital at Kanauj.

PART FOUR

The Medieval Period

(Eighth to Twelfth Centuries)

14

The Eastern and Southern Kingdoms

THE RASHTRAKUTAS OF MALKHED (700–1000)

The greatest dynasty in the south was that of the Rashtrakutas. Manyakheta (Malkhed, between the Krishna and the Godavari, not far from Sholapur) was the center of a stable empire, extending from Kanyakumari to the Ganges plain. No other southern power played such a role in all the history of India, up to the arrival of the Marathas. Under the Rashtrakutas India developed its major contribution to the world of theory—the non-dualist philosophy (Advaita) of Shankara. They protected Hindus, Jains, and Buddhists. The Rashtrakutas were also patrons of the arts and literature. Numerous poets in the Kanada tongue and in Sanskrit lived at their court. Major works on musical theory and on other arts are a hallmark of the scientific curiosity of the period. Architecture also reached a peak under the Rashtrakutas, with the temples of Ellora and Elephanta bearing glorious testimony to the refinement of the arts.

The Rashtrakutas claimed to descend from the ancient Yadavas, but this fact has been seriously questioned. They first appear as petty local sovereigns, vassals to the Chalukyas. The dynasty's founder was Dantidurga, a remarkably able prince, who is said to have fought victoriously against all the kings of the far south, as well as those of Kalinga,

Malwa, Lata, and Koshala. He died without issue in 756, at the age of thirty-seven.

His uncle Krishna (756–775) succeeded him. He invaded the country of Ganga (Karnataka) and received the submission of its king, Shri Purusha. He obliged the Chalukya king in the east, Vishnudharman IV, to acknowledge his suzerainty. He also conquered Konkan (of the Goa region). He was a great builder and had the famous temple of Kailasa— one of the marvels of Indian architecture and sculpture—hewn from the rock at Ellora. His successor, Govinda (775–780), was indolent and left the government to his younger brother, Dhruva, a capable and brave prince. Dhruva sought to seize power and a conflict ensued in which Dhruva was victorious.

Dhruva (780–794) wanted to revenge himself on the Ganga king Shivarama, who had supported his brother. He invaded the Ganga country and captured and imprisoned Shivarama. He then attacked the Pallavas, and forced Dantivarman to pay him tribute. He invaded the Chalukya country to the east, and obliged Vishnuvardhana to give him his daughter in marriage. He rapidly became the most powerful sovereign in the Deccan. He then attacked the northern kingdoms and invaded the Pratihara kingdom to the northeast of Agra, forcing king Vatsaraja to flee to the Rajputana desert. Dhruva then marched on Malwa (east of Rajputana), whose Pala sovereign, Dharmapala, he then defeated. On Dhruva's death, no state in India could rival the Rashtrakuta kingdom's power.

Following his father's dispositions, Dhruva's third son, Govinda III, succeeded him. His elder brother then sought to claim power, with the aid of twelve confederate kings. Govinda overcame the revolt and did not take vengeance on his brother, whom he appointed as vice-regent of the Ganga country. He entrusted the government of the Lata country to his other brother. In the meantime, the Pratihara sovereign, Nagabhata II, had conquered Kanauj and had set up his capital there. Desirous of keeping the growing Rashtrakuta power in check, he formed a confederation and attempted to hold sway over Malwa. Govinda launched his army against them and won a signal victory. He continued his advance and received the submission of Chakrayudha of Kanauj and his protector, Dharmapala, King of Bengal.

A coalition of southern kings (Pallava, Pandya, and Chera), joined by the Gangas of Orissa, sought to take advantage of the monarch's absence to attack Rashtrakuta territory. Govinda returned by forced marches and inflicted a terrible defeat on the southern confederates, not far from Badami, close to the River Tungabhadra. He also received the submission of the king of Sri Lanka. One of his daughters married the Pallava king Nandivarman III. Toward the end of his reign, he had to tackle another revolt, this one fomented by his son Krishna who had fled to Talakad. Govinda sent his general Bankesha against him, and the latter brought Krishna back as a prisoner. Having attained a position unrivalled in India at that time, he reigned from 793 to 813.

Amoghavarsha I Nripatunga (813-878) was very young when he succeeded his father. Although faced with initial difficulties, he was helped to overcome them by his uncle Karka, King of Gujarat, and his prime minister, Patalamalla. He crushed the revolts of the Pandyas and the Chalukyas in the east and made an alliance with the Gangas and Pallavas. The Arab traveler Suleiman, who visited the Rashtrakuta Empire—where Arab merchants circulated freely—described Amoghavarsha as one of the four great kings of the earth. The other three were the Emperor of Constantinople, the Caliph of Baghdad, and the Emperor of China.

At the end of his reign, in order to avert a calamity that threatened his people, the king cut off the fingers of his left hand and offered them to the Goddess Mahalaksmi of Kolhapur. He then abdicated and became a Jain monk. He was a patron of the arts and literature, and an important work in the Kanada tongue and another in Sanskrit are attributed to him.

Krishna II (880–914) succeeded his father Amoghavarsha. His reign was marked by wars with the Chalukyas, with varying outcomes. Vijayaditya III took Malkhed, the Chalukyas' capital, and Krishna had to acknowledge the conqueror's suzerainty. Later on, he successfully attacked Vijayaditya's successor Bhima, but Bhima prepared his revenge and took the kingdom of Vengi in the Andhra country from the

Rashtrakutas. Indra III (914–928), the grandson of Krishna II, waged war against the Pratiharas and marched as far as Delhi. After him, several sovereigns reigned for short periods up to the coming of Krishna III.

The Rashtrakutas' power regained its luster under this prince (939–966), who conquered numerous fortresses in the north of India, and then turned to attack the Cholas, who had themselves subjugated the other southern kingdoms. Krishna's brother-in-law, Buguta II of Talakad, aided him in this venture. Their success knew no bounds. Kanchi was occupied, then Tanjore. The Chola king Parantaka fled to Sri Lanka. Krishna then attacked the Cheras and Pandyas and occupied Rameshvaram, in the far south of India, where he erected a "victory column" facing the sea.

After Krishna, his brother Khottiga, already an old man, mounted the throne in 966. The Paramara king, Siyaka of Malwa, invaded the Rashtrakuta Empire and sacked Malkhed the capital in the spring of 972. Khottiga died in September of the same year. His nephew Karkka succeeded him, but was only to reign for eighteen months. A minor Chalukya prince, Tailapa, who had been a vassal of the Rashtrakutas, revolted. After a bloody battle, he put Karkka to flight and established the dynasty of the Chalukyas of Kalyani. The last Rashtrakuta, Indra IV, took refuge with the Ganga king, Narasimha II, living near the Jain sanctuary of Shravanabelgola until his death in 982.

THE PALAS OF BENGAL

Bengal, which had belonged to the Gupta Empire, affirmed its independence in the second half of the fourth century and became the rabid enemy of the Maukharis of Kanauj. The country acquired a certain power under Sashanka, but then fell back into anarchy, thus becoming an easy prey for its western neighbors. The anarchy ended only with the Pala dynasty.

Gopala, the founder of this dynasty, was elected by the people. He rapidly extended his authority over the whole country, and then over Magadha. Toward the end of his life, however, he was defeated by

Vatsaraja, the Pratihara sovereign of Kanauj. Gopala was a devout Buddhist, and founded the University of Odantapuri, near Nalanda.

Dharmapala (769–815), Gopala's son and successor, reestablished the might of the Pala dynasty. He dethroned Indrayudha of Kanauj, replacing him with a man of his choice, Chakrayudha. Nagabhata II Pratihara managed to defeat Dharmapala and occupy Kanauj. This event, however, hardly affected Dharmapala's empire, which stretched from the Gulf of Bengal to Delhi and from Jalandhara to the Vindhya Mountains.

Dharmapala was succeeded by his nephew, Devapala (815–854). After brilliant successes that allowed him to extend the empire still further, he was defeated by the young Pratihara king, Mihira Bhoja. Devapala, a Buddhist, was violent in his attacks on other religions, a policy that was always rather dangerous in India, since the people as a whole had never accepted Buddhism and were hostile to this falsely egalitarian and sentimental religion adopted by the leisured classes.

After Devapala, the dynasty declined. His successor, Vigrahapala (854–857) abdicated in favor of his son Narayanapala (857–911). Under the latter's long reign, the empire disintegrated little by little.

In the middle of the tenth century an invasion by a mountain tribe, the Kambhojas, interrupted the course of the dynasty, which was reestablished, however, by Mahipala, who reigned from 992 to 1040. After him there came kings of little character and the Pala Empire gradually fell apart.

THE PALLAVAS OF KANCHI

The Pallavas were one of the most remarkable dynasties of the medieval period. Their capitals lay to the west, not far from Sholapur and Vengi, in the Andhra country to the east, between the rivers Krishna and Godavari.

The Pallavas' origin is a matter of controversy. Totally ignored by the ancient history of the Tamil country, they suddenly appear on the scene. They were most probably Parthians, driven out of northwestern India. For a long time, their official language was Maharashtri Prakrit. They must therefore have resided in the west of India. Their defeat by Gautamiputra in the second century forced them to take refuge to the south of the Satavahanas' domain. Indian historians have made every effort to provide them with an autochthonous origin, but their efforts lack conviction. The first Pallavas appeared at Kanchi toward the third century. Officials of the Satavahana Empire, they declared their independence when the empire declined. They reigned for two centuries as petty sovereigns, up to the arrival of King Simhavishnu (570–600), with whom Pallava greatness begins. He subdued the traditional southern kingdoms (the Cheras, Cholas, and Pandyas), conquered Sri Lanka, and vanquished the Kalabhras.

His son, Mahendra-varman (600–630), took an interest in the arts of peace as well as those of war. He attempted to attack the Chalukyas in the west, but Pulakeshin II, who had just defeated Harsha, repulsed the attack and Mahendra-varman had to withdraw. He built the rock-hewn monolithic temples of Mahabalipuram (Mamallapuram) and Pallavaram. Also attributed to this period are the sculpted caves of Varaha and Gopalakrishna of Mahabalipuram, as well as the Jain paintings at Sittannavasal, close to Pudukottai. Mahendra-varman composed literary works and was a renowned musician. The long inscription on musical theory that he had engraved on the rock at Kudumiyamalai is a unique document on the art music of the time. Although born into the Jain religion, he converted to Shaivism, and his reign marked a major renewal of Shaivite and Vaishnavite Hinduism and a decline in Buddhism and Jainism.

Narasimha-varman (630–655) succeeded his father. Shortly after his accession, Pulakeshin II attacked the Pallava Empire and threatened Kanchi, its capital. Narasimha-varman gathered his army, marched against the Chalukya, and defeated him three times, at Pariyala, Manimangala, and Suramara. He continued his advance and took Badami, the Chalukya capital, which he occupied for fifteen years. He also subdued the kings of the south and invaded Sri Lanka, where he placed on the throne his friend, Prince Manavarma.

Hiuen Tsang visited Kanchi in 640 and has left important information about the size of the Pallava capital. Like his father, Narasimha-varman was a great builder and it is to his reign that the celebrated stone chariots—the monolithic *rathas*—of Mahabalipuram are attributed.

Mahendra-varman II, who succeeded his father, reigned only two years. After him came Parameshvara-varman, who was attacked and beaten by the Chalukya Vikramaditya I. His son, Narasimha-varman II, had a peaceful reign and played a great role in the arts. Giving up monolithic architecture, he had stone buildings constructed for the first time in southern India. Up to that time, architecture had always used timber. It was he who had the temple built on the waterside at Mahabalipuram and the Kailasanatha at Kanchipuram.

His successor Parameshvaram II was severely beaten by Vikramaditya II, a defeat that left the Pallava country long in chaos. During the long reign of Nandivarman II (over fifty years), the Pallava Empire began to crumble. The king had to defend his lands against the Gangas, the Pandyas, and the Chalukyas of the east. In about 740 Vikramaditya II sent a new expedition against the Pallava Empire. Nandivarman was unable to resist and fled, abandoning his capital to the mercy of the invaders. This time, the Chalukyas triumphed and occupied Kanchi.

Dantivarman (826–844) succeeded Nandivarman. He was beaten by the Rashtrakuta, Govinda III. The Pandyas also began to threaten Pallava power. However, Dantivarman's son, Nandivarman III (844–866), managed to beat the Pandyas and subjugate them once more.

The last of the Pallava kings was Aparajita (879-892), who managed to beat the Pandyas, but was himself totally overcome by Aditya I Chola. This defeat marked the total extinction of Pallava power.

By and large, the Pallavas respected the various religions. Under their administration a devotional movement known as *bhakti* developed in south India, giving Hinduism a new orientation. The Shaivite poet-saints, the Nayannars, and the Vaishnavite poet-saints, the Alvars, henceforth played a considerable role in Hindu religious life. Their simple faith, and their attitude of devotion and fraternity, tended to replace the theology and philosophy of the men of letters as the focal point of Hindu religious life.

The Pallavas supported educational and cultural establishments, and

Kanchi became a great cultural center. An important Sanskrit literature was developed in the south at this time. Some of the sovereigns themselves were poets of renown. The importance they attributed to Sanskrit would seem to confirm their northern origin.

In the domain of the arts the Pallavas created an architectural style that was to become typical throughout southern India and is known as "Dravidian." One aspect of this style is represented by the *mandapans*— vast roofed halls supported by rows of sculpted pillars. Great bas-reliefs, sculpted in rock or incorporated in the temples, still show the beauty of Pallava art, of which the *Austerities of Arjuna* and the *Descent of the Ganges* at Mahabalipuram are magnificent specimens.

THE PANDYAS

The Pandyas are one of the legendary dynasties of the Tamil country, whose origins are lost in prehistory. Although these kings are mentioned incidentally at all periods, the only precise documents about them start from the conflicts with the Pallavas and the Chalukyas of Badami in the sixth century. The most outstanding king of this period was Kadungon (590–620), of whom we know only that he freed the Pandya country from Kalabhra domination. Hiuen Tsang leaves a few not very obliging comments on the Pandya country, which he calls Malakuta. Since Buddhism was on the decline there, and Jainism was flourishing, the views of the Chinese pilgrim were quite naturally hostile.

The reign of King Arikesari Maravarman (670–710) saw the beginning of the Pandyas' quarrel with the Pallavas, and the expansion of Pandya power at the expense of the Cheras. This king was followed by Kochchadaiyan Ranadhira (710–740), who conquered Kongu and overcame the Marathas. Then came Maravarman Rajasimha I (740–765), who fought the Pallavas and had some successes against the Chalukyas of Badami. Varaguna I (765–815) continued to wage war against the Pallavas, who had made an alliance with the kings of Kongu and Kerala, but Varaguna came out victorious. He ruled over Tanjore, Tiruchirapalli, Salem, Coimbatore, and Travancore in the south.

Shimara Shrivallabha (815–862) succeeded his father and continued his expansion policy. He invaded Sri Lanka. The other powers—the Gangas, Cholas, Pallavas, Kalingas, Magadhas, and so on—formed a coalition in an attempt to stall the growing power of Shrimara, who managed to defeat their combined forces at Kudamukku (Kumbakonam). A few years later, however, the Pallava king, Nandivarman III, succeeded in crushing the Pandya king's army at Tellaru, and in driving it back into its own country. Shrimara's successor was Varaguna-varman II (862–880), who attempted to regain the prestige lost by his father. He attacked the Chola country, but was beaten by the combined forces of the Cholas and the Pallavas. He was succeeded by his younger brother, Parantaka Viranarayana (880–900), and then the latter's son, Maravarman Rajasimha II (900–920). The Cholas had by then won considerable importance, after beating the Pallavas. Parantaka I Chola invaded the Pandya country after the battle of Vellur in 915. The Pandya king, Rajasimha, fled to Sri Lanka and ended his days in exile in Kerala. The Pandyas had to accept Chola domination, despite periods of relative independence, up to the thirteenth century, when Maravarman Sundara Pandya (1226–1238) reestablished Pandya might.

THE CHOLAS OF TANJORE

In the ninth century the Chola kingdom was crushed between the Pallavas and the Pandyas. Then, while he was a Pandya vassal, Vijayalaya Chola (850–871) revolted, took Tanjore, and made it his capital. Vijayalaya's son, Aditya I, made an alliance with the Pallavas and helped them to crush the Pandyas. After this, he turned against his protector Aparajita Pallava, put an end to the Pallava dynasty, and solidly established the foundations of the Chola Empire.

The next Chola emperor, Parantaka (907–953), managed to overcome the combined forces of the Pandyas and the Sri Lankans. Attacked by Krishna II Rashtrakuta, he beat the Rashtrakutan army at Vallala. In 949 he penetrated Rashtrakutan territory, but this time was not successful. His army was routed, after a battle in which his son Rajaditya was killed. The Rashtrakutas then occupied the Tamil country, and the Cholas were once more reduced to vassal status.

Nevertheless, Parantaka was a great king. A votary of the god Shiva, he covered the roof of the temple of Chidambaram with gold. He was a patron of the arts and letters. After him, his second son Gandaraditya (953–957) reigned in modest state, followed by Parantaka II (957–973) and Uttama Chola (973–985). This last-named king was so unpopular that he had to cede the throne to his nephew Rajaraja.

The latter (985–1014) inherited a diminished kingdom that had suffered considerably from the Rashtrakuta occupation. He managed to reestablish Chola power, which he organized and increased greatly. In the end his empire stretched from the far south to the east as far as Orissa and to the west as far as Quilon and Coorg. After conquering the Chera country, and then the Pandya, the king invaded Sri Lanka and sacked its capital Anuradhapura. He invaded and annexed the Karnataka country, made an alliance with the Chalukya king of the east, Vimaladitya, and helped him to conquer the Andhra country. He also annexed the Maldive Islands, after which he reorganized his states, chose his administrators wisely, and ensured the goodwill of the various peoples. His reign was marked by a vast production of Tamil literature. A devotee of the god Shiva, he built the Brihadeshvara temple at Tanjore. Southern India was now divided between two great empires, the Cholas of Tanjore and the Chalukyas of Kalyani.

Rajaraja's son, Rajendra (1014-1044), continued his father's work. He consolidated his conquests and annexed the empire's northern territories more closely. His ambitions then turned northward, where he successfully attacked Orissa and Bengal. His victorious army devoutly brought water back from the Ganges. An enormous temple to Shiva—one of the most beautiful in southern India—was built and consecrated with this holy water at Ganga-Konda-Chola-puram. Rajendra undertook two naval expeditions, the first against Sri Lanka and the second against the countries of southeast Asia. He received the submission of the kings of Java, Palembang, and Malaysia. The Tamil traders established major entrepots in Java, Sumatra, and Malaysia.

The son of Rajendra I, Virajendra, and after him his brothers Rajendra II and Viramahendra, continued attacks on the Chalukya Empire. Rajendra II was killed, but the Chola army advanced as far as Kolhapur. In about 1068 the Cholas invaded the Karnataka country and put to flight the sons of Someshvara I. The latter, who was suffering from an incurable fever, drowned himself in the River Tungabhadra.

After a series of family quarrels, a Chola prince called Kulottunga—son of one of Rajendra I's daughters—succeeded in taking the throne and reigned for fifty years over the Tamil and Andhra countries. He continued to extend his lands, and beat the Kalingas and the Sri Lankans. His main work was the establishment of a very accurate cadastral plan. A worshipper of Shiva, and highly intolerant, he persecuted the Vaishnavites. Ramanuja—the famous philosopher and inventor of the branch of metaphysics known as qualified non-dualism (Vishishtadvaita)—had to flee to Melkote in the state of Mysore (modern Karnataka) to escape Kulottunga's religious persecutions. After Kulottunga, his son Vikramachala reigned, and made major gifts to the temple of Chidambaram. He was the patron of the famous poet Kamban, who wrote a Tamil version of the *Ramayana*. In the Tamil country the reigns of Kulottunga II and Kulottunga III—lasting up to the end of the twelfth century—saw the development of some major religious movements such as the Shaivite renewal.

The Cholas were at last attacked by the Pandyas in the south and the Kakatiyas and Chola-Telugus in the north. The north of Karnataka was occupied by the Yadavas of Devagiri, and the south by the Hoysalas.

Under the Cholas, the voting system for the election of village councils was developed, with voting papers placed in an urn. All citizens voted, except those who, owing to ill conduct, had been deprived of the right to vote, and the untouchables, who were prohibited by caste.

In the Chola Empire and neighboring kingdoms, the center of social life was the temple, an enormous organization centralizing religious, moral, economic, and charitable activities. According to K. A. Nilakantha Sastri, "The mediaeval temple in India has few parallels in the annals of mankind. It acted as chief proprietor, employer, consumer of materials and work, as bank, school, museum, hospital, in short as the kernel around which there collected all that is best in civilized life, controlling it with a humanity deriving from a profound sense of duty (*Dharma*)."[1]

The Cholas were great patrons of literature and the arts. Thus the Chola era saw a considerable development in Tamil literature. In architecture and painting, the Cholas continued the tradition of the Pallavas and Pandyas. It is to this period that the most magnificent bronzes of southern India belong.

THE CHALUKYAS

At the time when the Chola king, Kulottunga II, was uniting the whole of the Tamil country (around Madras) and the Andhra country (on the east coast) under his scepter, the Chalukya prince Vikramaditya rebelled against his brother Someshvara II and seized power. Rejecting the influence of Kulottunga II, he established his dominion over the center of the Indian subcontinent and proclaimed himself Emperor of Karnataka. Vikramaditya (the sixth of that name) abolished the Scythian (*Shaka*) era then in force and established the Chalukya-Vikrama era, beginning in the year 1072 C.E. His capital, Kalyani, became one of the most brilliant in India. At this court Vijnaneshvara wrote *Mitakshara*, his famous commentary on the *Yajnavalkya Smriti*, which became and remains even now the Hindus' legal code (except in Bengal, where the code is the *Dayabhaga*). There, too, the poet Bilhana composed his *Vikramankadeva-charita*.

During his reign, Vikramaditya VI saw three powerful dynasties appear in the Karnataka country—the Yadavas of Devagiri to the north, the Kakatiyas of Warangal in the Andhra country, and the Hoysalas of Mysore—all of whom, however, continued to acknowledge the suzerainty of the Chalukyas.

The successor of Vikramaditya VI, Someshvara III, was a great man of letters. He wrote an encyclopedic work, the *Abhilashitartha Chintamani* or *Rajamanasollasa*. He also took an interest in southern

---

1. K. A. Nilakantha Sastri, *Early History of the Deccan* (Calcutta, 1960).

musical theory. His successors, however, were weak. The Yadavas and the Hoysalas consequently gained in importance. At the center of the Karnataka country, Kalachurya Bijjala, a dependent of the Chalukyas, occupied Kalyani and set up the Kalachuri dynasty. His reign is important since it was the time of the Shaivite renewal, in the form of the major sect known as the Virashaivas, of which Basava was one of the promoters. According to the Virashaivas, Bijjala was a Jain who persecuted the Virashaivas and was assassinated by Basava. It appears, however, that Bijjala merely abdicated in favor of his son Someshvara, who continued the dynasty until 1180.

The appearance of the Virashaivas is a phenomenon peculiar to India. As if history had not existed, we see reappearing in this sect the rites, beliefs, customs, and philosophy of prehistoric Shaivism that had remained the people's religion, despite being ignored by Brahmanic scholars for almost four millennia. Shaivism abruptly came to the surface again, having been given its stamp of approval thanks to the character of Basava, making it clear that a large part of the Indian population had never been affected by the rites, customs, and beliefs of the invaders who had succeeded each other since the first Aryan conquest. This is the case in all the regions of India. The principle of non-interference in the customs and institutions of the various castes has allowed even the most ancient religions to keep going indefinitely, so long as they are practiced with discretion and without proselytizing.

15

The Rajputs
(Ninth to Twelfth Centuries)

THE RAJPUTS

The role of the Rajputs in the history of northern and eastern India is considerable, as they dominated the scene between the death of Harsha and the establishment of the Muslim Empire.

Contradictory opinions have been put forward as to the origin of the Rajputs. Owing to the number and duration of foreign occupations in northern and northwestern India, the reigning families are inevitably of very mixed race. From a racial point of view, the Rajputs present no characteristic recalling those of the Munda tribes or Dravido-Gangetic peoples. They belong to a group of populations that spreads from the south of what was the Soviet Union to the mouth of the Indus—principally Indo-Aryans mixed with Scythians, Parthians, Indo-Iranians, Greeks, and Huns.

The Rajputs' chivalrous spirit lent them such prestige, as representing the model of the Hindu ideal of knightly kings, that the southern and central dynasties of India felt the need to forge their own genealogies in order to be called Rajputs—a name that is synonymous with "princely"—although very often the noble titles of these dynasties were far more ancient than those of the Rajputs.

At the same time, the Rajputs themselves sought to link their families with the ancient pre-Aryan dynasties. They claimed to be descendants of Lakshmana, the brother of the hero Rama of the *Ramayana*, who is represented as having a pale skin, whereas Rama himself was dark skinned. What is certain is that numerous Greek, Scythian, Parthian, and Hun conquerors mixed with the ancient families whose origins are lost in pre-history. But here history, legend, and fairy tales merge to such an extent that it is impossible to unravel the facts.

As conceived by the Rajputs, the monarchy was hereditary and absolute, and kings observed the Hindu rules as to the duties of princes. Respect for the written law and the principles of chivalry tempered the exercise of power. The division of society into corporations or castes was the basis of social organization. The dangers presented by the brutality of the various northern invaders had led to the fairly strict confinement of women. The practice of sati—in which the wife burns herself alive on the pyre of her dead husband—was considered a deed of great virtue. Although on principle, Hindus only recommended this practice for women belonging to the royal and warrior caste, it does appear to have been practiced by other castes, as witnessed by a great number of commemorative monuments. Great emphasis was laid on the birth of male progeny and female infanticide at birth was widespread.

The new philosophical and religious movements created by Shankara and Ramanuja had spread throughout northern India. Ramanuja's Vaishnavite philosophy was universally accepted in the east and center of the subcontinent. Shaivism was dominant in the west and north. Some kings also supported Jainism. Buddhism had practically disappeared. During the Rajput period, Hindi and other popular tongues replaced Sanskrit for literary purposes, and a new mystical poetry developed—simpler, more human, and more alive than conventional Sanskrit poetry.

The Rajput period was the most extraordinary era of Hindu architecture and sculpture. Temples were built at Khajuraho, and many others of the same style were built throughout central India and Rajputana. This period—one of the flourishing of a religious art that is both symbolical and human—is strikingly similar to the flowering of Gothic art in

Europe three centuries later. Sculpture attained a perfect balance between stylization, based on proportional and symbolic diagrams, and a sense of the real and human. The gods and goddesses covering the temples thus are highly individual beings, with a beauty unrivalled in the history of art. The diagrams and proportions utilized in architecture and sculpture of the time belong to a cosmological theory claiming to correspond to the very principles underlying all the world's structures, as well as to both the perceptive mechanisms through which we are aware of the outside world, and the psychological and emotive reactions that direct our deeds.

THE GURJARA-PRATIHARAS

The Gurjara-Pratiharas of Kanauj (to the northwest of modern Kanpur) are an important Rajput dynasty that attained imperial dimensions, similar to that of Samudragupta or Harsha. It has been conjectured that originally the Gurjarats were nomads who accompanied the Huns. Although this is not improbable, they mixed with Indian families so rapidly and so thoroughly that this fact is important only with regard to the origin of their sovereignty. The Gurjarats were and still are a nomadic tribe of what is now Rajasthan. At the beginning of the Middle Ages, certain members of this tribe managed to seize power and establish a strong dynasty known by the name of Pratihara (porter), since one of their ancestors had served as a door-keeper during the sacrificial ceremonies performed by one of the Rashtrakutan kings.

The Pratiharas of the Avanti dynasty—founded by Nagabhata I (about 740)—distinguished themselves in the struggle against the Muslim invaders. Their capital was at Ujjain. The third sovereign, Devaraja or Devashakti, was defeated by Dantidurga, the founder of the Rashtrakutan dynasty, who temporarily occupied Avanti. The two dynasties remained in a state of war for nearly two centuries. Vatsaraja (775–800) succeeded his father Devaraja and sought to consolidate his southern border against the Rashtrakutas. His efforts were in vain, however; the Rashtrakuta Dhruva invaded the north of India and vanquished both Vatsaraja and the Pala king Dharmapala. The struggle of these three dynasties to dominate the valleys of the Ganges and the Jumna—and in particular the town of Kanauj—was to be a major factor in the history of India during the course of the following century.

When Nagabhata (800–840) succeeded Vatsaraja, he decided firmly to reestablish the fortunes of the Pratiharas. He concluded alliances with the kings of Andhra, Sind, Vidarbha (modern Berar, whose capital is Amaravati), and Kalinga in an attempt to contain the Rashtrakutas to the south and the Arabs of Sind to the west. He attacked Kanauj and defeated King Chakrayudha, the protégé of the powerful king of Bengal, Dharmapala. Later on, he succeeded in beating Dharmapala himself. He had reestablished the greatness of the Pratiharas.

However, his success was of short duration. Govinda III Rashtrakuta, having settled his problems in the south, turned against Nagabhata, whose armies he totally destroyed. Govinda advanced victorious as far as the foothills of the Himalayas and received the submission of Dharmapala and Chakrayudha. Nagabhata, however, managed to stay put in Kanauj, to which he transferred his capital after Govinda's retreat. He again fought the Palas, who had to acknowledge Pratihara supremacy.

Bhoja (840–890) was the greatest emperor of the Pratihara dynasty. He regained the prestige lost by his predecessors and established a vast empire. He also built the famous temples at Osiyan, in Rajasthan. He raised the spirits of his allies among the Gurjara clans and established a hierarchy that was to survive for nearly a thousand years. Many Rajput princes who had to abandon their privileges in 1947–48 were descendants of Bhoja's generals.

The Rashtrakutas were engaged in a difficult struggle with the king of the Chalukyas of the east (the Andhra country), Vijayaditya III. They were thus not in a position to oppose the development of Bhoja's empire as it became even greater than Harsha's, including east Punjab, Uttar Pradesh, Rajasthan, Gwalior, Malwa (Ujjain), Gujarat, and Kathiawar. Bhoja halted the Arab advance on the northwest frontier and took part of Sind back from them. The Arab merchant Suleiman has left some impressions of Bhoja: "The king of Jurz possesses a considerable army, and no Indian prince has such excellent cavalry . . . He is extremely rich, his camels and horses are numerous. In no other region of India does one encounter so few thieves."

Mahendrapala (890–908) continued the work of his father. He added Magadha (Patna) and a part of Bengal to the empire. The famous poet and playwright Rajashekhara lived at his court. With the next emperor, Mahipala, the power of the Pratiharas declined. Mahipala was beaten by the Rashtrakuta king Indra III in 916, but managed to recover from this defeat. According to the Arab traveler Al Masudi, the King of Kanauj had four armies, each with between seven and nine hundred thousand men.

Mahipala's successors lacked character and diplomacy. The Chandellas of Kalinjar (Bundelkhand) attacked Kanauj, and the Muslims too renewed their attacks. Finally, Trilochanapala was defeated by Mahmud of Ghazni in 1019. "The imperial city was delivered to pillage and massacre. . . . The great Pratihara Empire was dead, but its carcass remained, which was given over to the vultures."

Toward the end of the eleventh century, Chandradeva, of the Gahadavala dynasty, took Kanauj and established his rule over Ayodhya and Delhi. The greatest king of this dynasty was Govinda (1114–1155). He favored Buddhism and his wife Kumaradevi restored the monastery of Sarnath. His grandson Jayachandra reigned at Benares (Varanasi). He was defeated by Shihab-ud-din on the plain of Chandwar, near Etawah, on the bank of the Jumna. Benares was pillaged and Jayachandra killed. One of his sons escaped the massacre and became the forefather of the Rathors of Jodhpur.

THE PARAMARAS OF MALWA (UJJAIN)

The Paramaras, formerly known as the kings of Avanti, played an important role, largely owing to their association with some very well known writers in Sanskrit literature. When Govinda III Rashtrakuta annexed Malwa, he set up the family of one of his subordinates there, who took the name of Paramara. In the tenth century Harsha Siyaka, a descendant of the Paramaras, defeated the Chalukyas of Gujarat and the Chandellas (of Bundelkhand). He attacked Khottiga, the last Rashtrakuta sovereign, and burned his capital of Manyakheta (Malkhed). After many victories over his neighbors, Harsha Siyaka was himself defeated by the Chalukya king Tailapa II, who had already beaten the Rashtrakutas. He was imprisoned and beheaded when he attempted to escape. On the death of Harsha Siyaka's son, Munja, Bhoja, the son of Sindhuraja, succeeded him. Bhoja reigned for fifty-five years and rebuilt his capital, Dharanagara. He fought his neighbors with various results, but was able to keep the Muslims out of Malwa. Bhoja himself was a writer of renown and a major patron of letters. He wrote over twenty works on the arts and sciences.

At the end of the eleventh century, the Rajput dynasties controlled the whole of the north of India. The centers of their power were Ranthambar, Gwalior, Kalinjar, Jaipur, and Ajmer.

When Mohammed of Ghour succeeded to the throne of Ghazni, the Rajput dynasties opposed him. He was beaten at the battle of Tarain in 1191, but returned the following year, and this time it was Prithviraj of Ajmer who was defeated, made prisoner, and assassinated in cold blood. Ajmer was given to one of his sons, but was later annexed by Qutb-ud-din-Ibaq. Mohammed of Ghour annexed the whole country as far as Benares, and the Rajput families were dispersed. Although often traversed by the Muslims, several of the Rajput states still managed to survive.

16

Colonial Expansion

Ptolemy's *Geography* (140) mentions the sea routes between India and Malaysia and numerous trading centers in southeast Asia. In Sanskrit literature, Burma is known as *Suvarna Bhumi*, the land of gold. This name is also given occasionally to the Malay Peninsula and to the Sunda Isles. Ashoka sent Buddhist missionaries to Burma. Otherwise nothing is known of the country's history at that time. The first Indian king about whom archaeological documents have been discovered dates from 162 C.E. The temples at Pagan show strong Indian influence and the architects of the Ananda temple at Pagan were certainly Hindus. The kings of Burma adopted Hindu laws and the Pali language appears everywhere beside the Mom tongue. Although Buddhaghosha came from Sri Lanka to preach Buddhism in 639, orthodox Hinduism played the predominant role. The Schwezigon pagoda was built at Rangoon at the beginning of the eleventh century. In Siam (modern Thailand), the Hindu kingdom of Sukhodaya was established in the ninth century.

CHAMPA AND KAMBOJA

Indochina was divided between the two powerful kingdoms of Champa and Kamboja. From a territorial point of view, Champa corresponded to Annam, part of modern Vietnam. The first Hindu kingdom of Champa was founded by King Shrimara in 102 C.E. There too Shaivism was the main religion. The kingdom of Champa was to last for thirteen centuries, from 150 to 1471. In the sixteenth century the Annamites and Mongols from the north ravaged and occupied the country.

Kamboja corresponds to modern Cambodia (Kampuchea). In the Chinese annals, Kamboja is called Fou-nan. The country was colonized by Hindus starting from the first century C.E. According to legend, a sage called Kambu Svayambhuva married Mera, a celestial nymph, and created a solar dynasty. According to another legend, it was a certain Kaundinya who came to Kamboja from India, married a Naga princess called Soma, and established a lunar dynasty. This latter version is confirmed by the Chinese writer K'ang T'ai, who visited Fou-nan at the beginning of the third century.

> At the beginning, the sovereign of Fou-nan was a woman called Lieou-ye (willow leaf). In the country of Mo Fou in India, there was a man named Houen-chen who worshipped a spirit with love and passion. The spirit was touched by his piety, and one night Houen-chen saw in a dream a man who gave him a divine bow and commanded him to board a ship and depart over the sea. The next day, Houen-chen entered the temple and found a bow at the foot of the tree in which the spirit dwelt. He procured a great boat and sailed away. The spirit directed the winds so that Houen-chen reached Fou-nan. Lieou-ye wished to capture the boat. Houen-chen raised his bow and shot. The arrow drove through the boat of Lieou-ye from one side to the other. Dismayed, she surrendered, and Houen-chen became the master of Fou-nan.[1]

According to K'ang T'ai, "the inhabitants were ugly, curly-haired, and the men went around naked. Their manners were unpolished, but they were not thieves. Agriculture was rudimentary. . . . The vessels they used for food were of silver. They paid taxes in gold and silver, in pearls and per-

---

1. K'ang T'ai, Rapport d'une ambassade du Fou-nan de 245 à 250, in K. M. Munshi, *The Age of Imperial Unity* (Bombay, 1951), 656–657.

fumes. They had books and libraries of archives. Their writing was like that of the *Hons* in central Asia."[2] Kaundinya forced the inhabitants to wear clothes, reformed the institutions, and organized agriculture on the Indian model.

The most ancient Sanskrit inscriptions that have been found in Cambodia date from the sixth century. Bhavavarman, founder of the Khmer dynasty, was a great conqueror. He founded a new capital, Bhavapura, and built many temples inspired by the Chalukya-Pallava style. Bhavavarman's successors developed Khmer power, which finally covered Siam, Laos, the south of Burma, almost all Indochina, and Malaysia. This family reigned until the eighth century.

In the ninth century Yashovarman annexed the south of Annam (Champa) and all the other southern kingdoms. He was a great builder of reservoirs and monasteries, as well as the town of Yashodharmapuram, the leading city of Angkor. Angkor Thom was created by Jayavarman VII at the end of the twelfth century. At its center was the renowned Bayon, a temple of Shiva. Jayavarman VII (1182–1201) was Kamboja's last great king. He vanquished the King of Champa. His kingdom covered almost all of Indochina, from the China Sea to Bengal. His capital, Angkor Thom, was one of the world's great cities. Up to the fifteenth century, Kamboja had Hindu kings and Shaivism was the main religion. Mahayana Buddhism, introduced in the ninth century, made a curious mixture with Shaivism, while the cult of Shiva-Buddha spread as far as Java and Sumatra. The Khmer language adopted many Sanskrit words, and a great number of Tantric works were translated or composed.

THE ISLANDS

Java, or *Yava-dvipa* (the isle of Java), is mentioned in the *Ramayana* and in Ptolemy's *Geography*. Called *Lankasuka* in Tamil inscriptions and in the Javanese and Malay chronicles, it could even be the Lanka of the *Ramayana*, making it a legend of Indochinese origin.

---

2. *Ibid.*, 656–657.

Hindu culture began to influence the Sunda Isles around the first century C.E. According to Javanese tradition, about twenty thousand people emigrated from Kalinga to Java during this period. They founded a kingdom called Ho Hing, which is the Chinese transcription for Kalinga. The capital was Kedah, mentioned in the Tamil literature belonging to the first centuries of the Common Era, and in particular in *Manimekhalai*. The most ancient Sanskrit inscription found in Java dates from the fourth century.

Hinduism was very widespread in Java, where a very considerable number of images of all the Hindu gods are to be found. Buddhism was also present, in a form that had been highly assimilated by Hinduism, and the Buddha belonged to the Hindu pantheon. Javanese literature is deeply influenced by Sanskrit. Except for the Vedas, Javanese translations can be found of most of the major classical works on philosophy, religion, rites, laws, and so on. Although quite different from those of India, dancing and music observed the same ideal as regards the role of the theatrical arts as a means of teaching the people.

Very few temples remain on Java from the Hindu period. The most important ones are the temples of Prambanan, in the center of the island. The enormous building of Borobudur—originally a temple of Shiva later transformed into a Buddhist *stupa*—is still one of the most extraordinary monuments in the world. It has no less than four hundred and thirty-two images of the Buddha in meditation.

Sumatra, the largest of the Sunda Isles, is located halfway between India and China, and belonged to the Indian sphere of influence long before the Common Era. Indian influence was to continue for more than one thousand years. Little is known, however, about the island's history prior to the establishment of Shri Vijaya's kingdom in the fourth century.

I Tsing, who visited the island in 671, speaks of the importance of the kingdom of Shri Vijaya, which had annexed many isles in the archipelago and part of the Malay peninsula. Buddhism was the main religion. In the eighth century the ancient dynasty was replaced by one founded by Sailendra, a Buddhist who also established his sway over Java, and whose influence stretched as far as Annam and Kamboja. Arab travelers have left several descriptions of the splendor of the court of Sumatra and the power of its kings. Sumatra was invaded by a Chola king in the eleventh century and, until the thirteenth century, the island remained an almost integral part of India.

Bali, or *P'o-li*, lying to the east of Java, is the sole island where Hindu culture has survived to our own time. The caste institution is still very strict, the dead are burned, and even today some women perform sati. Bovines are never slaughtered, and pork is the only meat eaten. The dance is governed by the principles of the great Hindu treatise on dancing and the theater, the *Natyashastra*.

The isle of Sri Lanka is called by different names in Pali, Greek, and Arabic: Tambapanni, Simhala, Tamrobane, and Serendib. Sri Lanka's identification as the Lanka of the *Ramayana* appears to be very late. The origin of the name *Simhala* is attributed to a king Vijayasimha, who is said to have come from Kalinga. King Ashoka sent emissaries (including his own son) to preach Buddhism in the island. The famous Buddhist monasteries at Polonnaruva and Anuradhapura were built in the second century B.C.E. The relations and conflicts between Sri Lanka and India were a constant aspect of the island's history. In the thirteenth century the Cholas occupied Sri Lanka, and the Shaivite religion once more dominated the island for a certain time.

PART FIVE

Muslim Domination

17

The Arabs, Turks, and Afghans

THE ARABS

The Arabian Peninsula—which was not always the arid desert it became through the fault of men—was known by the ancient Hindus. The city of Makheswara, today known as Mecca, was one of the sacred places of the cult of Shiva-Dionysus, mentioned in the *Puranas* and famous for its black stone, considered as a symbol of the *lingam* (phallus) of Shiva.

Since prehistory, the south of Arabia had been a great center of trade between India, on the one hand, and the cities of east Africa, the Mediterranean, Crete, Phoenicia, and Egypt, on the other. The Semitic peoples we know as Arabs—a simple and warlike people—had gradually subjected or assimilated the other elements of the population well before the appearance of Islam. Like the Hebrews, they had probably already invented a philosophy with monotheistic trends.

The Prophet Mohammed was born in 570 C.E. He opposed the return of the ancient pantheistic and universalistic cosmological concepts, which had gradually been reintroduced into the Judeo-Christian world. He proposed a new reform, founding a new religion, Islam, which preached an intransigent and popular monotheistic faith, freed from the nuances of more ancient philosophies. It is easy to persuade a people that its customs, habits, and laws are better than anyone else's, and that it is in some way a chosen people. The less this is justified, the more the conviction of superiority is affirmed with violence. The monotheistic conception lends this feeling of superiority a kind of divine sanction, since "the only God" naturally belongs to the tribe. The tribe then puts its hands to "God's work," since God is apparently incapable of organizing his own propaganda. This is what leads monotheistic peoples to be aggressive, intolerant, and destructive. The more intransigent the monotheism, the more imperialistic it inevitably becomes. Mohammed's monotheism was not a philosophy but a dogma, demanding a simple and uncompromising faith.

Armed with their faith and their spears, sure of having the only God on their side, the Arabs launched on their world conquest with enthusiasm and passion. A little more and they would have succeeded fully. As it was, the banner of Islam soon waved over the ruins of temples, libraries, and cities of a vast territory stretching from Spain to central Asia. The Islamic ideal was imposed on an immense number of peoples, the only survivors being those that adopted the religion of the new conquerors.

From the moment when the Muslims reached India, its history has no further interest. It is a long and monotonous recital of murders, massacres, plunder, and destruction. As always, it is in the name of a "holy war," of their faith, of the only God, whose agents they believe themselves to be, that barbarians have destroyed civilizations, annihilated peoples, and considered doing so a meritorious deed. Under the command of temporal and spiritual chiefs, called caliphs, who took command of the Islamic world starting from 632, the Muslim conquest was to continue for long centuries in Europe, India, southeast Asia, central Asia, and China. There were of course interludes, under "good" caliphs or emperors who sought to practice tolerance and to take an interest in the sciences, arts, and philosophies of non-Islamized countries. These are the ones who created the major periods of Islamic civilization. But they were only interludes, always succeeded by destructive fanaticism.

From the start, the Arabs had coveted the rich lands and great trading ports of India. As early as 637, an Arab army was sent to seize Thane, near

Bombay (Mumbai). This expedition was followed by others, directed at Broach (Bharuch) in the Gulf of Khambhat, the gulf of Debal in Sind, and Al-Kikan (the Kalat area, in Baluchistan). About the middle of the seventh century, the satrapy of Zaranj in the south of Afghanistan fell into Arab hands, followed by Makran in Baluchistan. The Arabs several times attacked the King of Kabul, who was probably a descendant of the great Kanishka. Kabul managed, however, to maintain a precarious independence, up to the closing years of the ninth century. At the same time, the lord of Zabul, in the upper valley of the River Helmund near Kandahar, fell, despite a courageous resistance.

Having conquered Baluchistan, the Arabs launched their forces against Sind. At that time, Sind was ruled by Brahmans. King Dahar managed to repel the first expeditions sent by al-Hajjaj, the governor of Iraq. The latter then sent his son-in-law Muhammad ibn-Kasim at the head of a considerable army. Dahar was betrayed by Buddhist monks and by some of his vassals, who helped the Arab troops to cross the Indus. During a heroic battle, close to Raor, in 712, Dahar was beaten and killed. His widow directed a magnificent but vain resistance from the fortress of Raor. The invaders then made for Bahmanabad and Alor, and took Multan, thus assuring their domination over the whole of the lower Indus valley. After Muhammad ibn-Kasim, a new governor, Junaid, continued the series of conquests and sent expeditions against Marwar, Mandor, Dahnaj, Bharuch, Ujjain, Malwa, and Gujarat. The Arabs subsequently occupied Sind, Cutch, Kathiawar, Bharuch, Malwa, and the west of Rajputana.

When the power of the Baghdad caliphs began to decline, the Muslim governor of Sind became practically independent. In 871 the province became the fief of the Safavid chief Yaqub ibn-Lais. At his death, Sind was divided into two principalities, Mansurah, close to Bahmanabad, and Multan. No longer having the united might of the Islamic world behind them, the Muslims of Sind had to defend themselves against the Hindu princes and negotiate with them. The Chalukyas to the south, the Pratiharas to the east, and the Karkotas to the north managed to arrest the Arab advance eastward. It was at this point that a new danger arose, with the founding of the kingdom of Ghazni by Alptigin in about 962.

MAHMUD OF GHAZNI

A courageous and enterprising man of Turkish origin, Alptigin was a former Samanid slave from central Asia. He managed to forge an independent kingdom for himself at Ghazni and to annex part of the Kingdom of Kabul. A little after his death in 963, his son-in-law Sabuktigin succeeded him. King Jayapala of the Shahiya dynasty, who reigned over a vast territory stretching from the south of Afghanistan to the Kangra valley (to the south of Kashmir), vainly attempted to stop the depredations caused by the Muslims' expeditions, called—"holy wars"—against his states. After the death of Sabuktigin, his son Mahmud succeeded him and inflicted a crushing defeat on Jayapala, close to Peshawar, in 1001. Humiliated, Jayapala committed suicide by being burned alive on a pyre in 1002. His son Anandapala withdrew to the steep slopes of the "Mountains of Salt" region (Nandana), where he did his best to organize resistance. His efforts were continued by his successor Trilochanapala, with the aid of the King of Kashmir and the princes of central India, particularly the Chandellas of Kalinjar.

Mahmud, moreover, having taken Multan, inflicted a number of defeats on the Hindu troops. He launched a series of sudden and unpredictable expeditions to terrorize them. Trilochanapala was assassinated. Mahmud took Thanesar in 1014 and attempted—without success—to conquer Kashmir. He burned the temple of Mathura. In 1018 he sacked Kanauj and put an end to the Pratihara Empire. He received the submission of Gwalior and Kalinjar in 1022-23. Finally, in 1026, he destroyed the famous temple of Somanatha in Kathiawar, one of the principal Hindu holy places.

Mahmud died in 1030, but his successors, the Ghaznavid sultans, continued his policy of raids, destruction, and pillage, rather than annexations as such. During one of these expeditions, the holy city of Varanasi was sacked, and its wonderful temples and palaces systematically destroyed. Arab historians like al-Biruni have expressed their admiration for the heroism and magnanimity of the Shahiya kings and other Rajput princes. On both sides, these conflicts were carried out with great courage, but also with merciless ferocity.

Despite syncretism and spiritual exchanges between Muslims and Hindus in the higher spheres of thought, throughout the history of India the Muslims were insatiable invaders. The vast scope of their expeditions, over time, pillaged the fabulous riches of India and demoralized those who guarded them. The annexation of the Punjab had considerable consequences. It drained the country's military and economic strength. It opened wide the gates to the northwest and shook the whole social and economic structure. Neither the Arabs nor the Ghaznavid Turks managed to annex India, but they prepared the way for the final conflict, that— two centuries later—was to destroy the kingdoms of the Ganges plain.

The empires of the Pratiharas in the Ganges plain and the Palas in Bengal were starting to crumble. Responsibility for defending India against new invaders from the northwest was thus left to the minor kingdoms, established by former vassals who had proclaimed their independence. In the face of danger, internal revolutions were often needed to rid certain threatened countries of their incompetent kings. Thus it was that the Pratihara king Rajyapala was executed by a subordinate "in the country's interest." Dissension among the minor states and the lack of a common ideal made India an easy prey for the invaders, despite the admirable courage of most of the Indian princes.

Great efforts were made to repair some of the damage caused by the invaders, but the disaster was sometimes irreparable. Bhima I, King of Gujarat, had the temple of Somanatha rebuilt. One of his generals, Vimala, built the famous temple called Vimala Vasahi on Mount Abu. Magnificent temples were built at Shatrunjaya, Girnar, and Abu. Hostility on principle to the new religion was, however, contrary to the Hindu spirit. King Arjuna of Gujarat donated funds for a mosque built by a Muslim ship owner at Ormuz, at the mouth of the Persian Gulf, and he granted subsidies for Shiite festivals. In 1297, however, Gujarat was annexed by the sultan Ala-ud-din Khalji of Delhi.

The Chandellas of central India enlarged their country and were patrons of the arts. They had new temples built at Khajuraho and Mahoba. The most important role was played by the kings of the Kalachuri dynasty, Gangeyedeva and his son Lakshmikarna. Gangeyedeva took under his protection the holy cities of Varanasi and Prayag (Allahabad). Lakshmikarna concluded strong alliances, with Bengal, central India, and Kalinga in particular. Had he not died young, he probably would have reestablished an empire capable of defending itself against the invaders. A combination of princes from Gujarat, Malwa, Bundelkhand, and the Deccan, however, put an end to the ambitions of his successors.

Madhyadesha, the upper valley of the Ganges, passed into the hands of the Gahadavala dynasty, founded by Chandradeva at the end of the eleventh century. His grandson Govindachandra consolidated an empire that covered Uttar Pradesh and Bihar and managed to defend the Hindu and Buddhist holy places against the Turks. A rival empire was, however, set up by Chauhan Vigraharaja at Ajmer and Delhi. This latter town had been founded toward the end of the eleventh century by a Tomara king, from whom Chauhan took his new capital. Sadly, the conflict of the Gahadavalas and Chauhans weakened them to such an extent that they were easily swept away by the new invasion that was being prepared in the deserts of Afghanistan.

MUHAMMAD OF GHOUR AND THE SLAVE DYNASTY

Under the successors of Sultan Mahmud, the Ghazni Empire disintegrated. The princes of Ghour—a small principality in the mountains southeast of Herat—who were of Persian origin, took advantage of the weakness of the Ghazni sultans in an attempt to become the dominant power.

Qutb-ud-din Muhammad of Ghour and his brother Saif-ud-din were ferociously executed by Bahram Shah of Ghazni. In order to revenge them, their brother Ala-ud-din Husain pillaged Ghazni and burned the town, the fire lasting seven days and seven nights. Bahram's son, Khusrav

Shah, then had to quit Ghazni when it was invaded by a Turkmen tribe, the Ghouzz; he fled to the Punjab. The princes of Ghour succeeded in repelling the Ghouzz in 1173. The son of Ala-ud-din was killed in combat. His cousin and successor Ghiyas-ud-din Muhammad retook Ghazni and appointed as his vice-regent there his younger brother Shihab-ud-din, more widely known as Muhammad of Ghour.

In 1175 the latter commenced his expeditions against the kingdoms of India. He first attacked the Ismaili sect of Multan, considered to be heretics by other Muslims. After meeting with failure in Gujarat in 1178, he occupied Peshawar and established a fort at Sialkot in 1181. Forming an alliance with Vijaya Dev of Jammu against the last Ghaznavid representative, Khusrav Malik, who was still reigning over Lahore, he made him prisoner and brought him to Ghazni. He then continued his advance into India and came into conflict with the Rajputs, particularly Prithviraj, the mighty king of Ajmer and Delhi. The most important of the north Indian kingdoms was that of Jayachandra of Kanauj, who lived at Varanasi. He was jealous of Prithviraj and when—according to the epic songs of the time—the latter carried off his daughter who was a famous beauty, his hate knew no bounds and he refused to aid his rival when he was attacked by Muhammad of Ghour. Legend tells us that he even invited and encouraged the Muslim invader.

During the winter of 1190–91, Muhammad attacked the Punjab and a great battle took place at Thanesar. Muhammad was wounded and withdrew to Ghazni. He invaded India again in 1192 with a powerful army, and this time managed to beat the Rajputs. Prithviraj and his brother were taken prisoner and put to death. The Muslim Empire's foundations in India had been laid and, from then on, the Rajputs' efforts to seize the initiative were in vain. Various parts of northern India were annexed in a few years by one of Muhammad's most faithful officers, the Turk Qutb-ud-din Aibak, who was a slave from Turkestan. Bought by a trader from Nishapur, who had him raised with his own children, he was then sold to a merchant, who resold him to Muhammad of Ghour. The dynasty he was to found in India is for this reason known as the "Slave Dynasty."

In recognition of his services, Muhammad left Qutb-ud-din in full charge of the new territories and wholly free to undertake fresh enterprises. In 1192 Qutb-ud-din took Hansi, Meerut, Delhi, and Ranthambhor. In 1194 he defeated and killed Jaichand, the king of Varanasi and Kanauj. In 1197 he attacked Gujarat and sacked its capital. In 1202 he besieged the famous fortress of Kalinjar, in central India, and succeeded in reducing it to ruins, taking an enormous booty and fifty thousand men and women prisoners. Kalinjar never fully recovered. Its ruins can still be seen today, invaded by the jungle. Qutb-ud-din then took Mahoba, which had replaced Khajuraho as the capital of Bundelkhand, and Badaun, one of the richest cities in India. In the meantime, another of Muhammad's lieutenants, Ikhtiyar-ud-din, attacked Bengal, whose rulers took refuge close to Dacca.

On the death of his elder brother, Ghiyas-ud-din, Muhammad of Ghour became the titular sovereign of Ghazni, Ghour, and Delhi, of which he had long been the de facto ruler. His power was soon threatened, however. In 1205 the shah of Khwarazm in central Asia inflicted a defeat on him that had repercussions throughout the empire. Despite this, Muhammad managed to repress rebellions at Ghazni, Multan, and in the Punjab, and crushed his old enemies, the Khokars. When he returned to Lahore, however, he was assassinated in rather obscure circumstances. His body was brought back to Ghazni for burial.

Muhammad of Ghour had no sons. At his death, his viceroys assumed full power in their respective territories. Taj-ud-din Yildiz, the governor of Kirman, ascended the Ghazni throne. In India the various Muslim governors recognized the suzerainty of Qutb-ud-din, who took the title of *Sultan*. He immediately came into conflict with Taj-ud-din and for some time occupied Ghazni. His repression, however, exasperated the population, who secretly recalled Taj-ud-din. The latter prepared his revenge and Qutb-ud-din had to flee. India and Afghanistan thus became two separate empires.

Qutb-ud-din died shortly afterward, in 1210, of a fall from his horse while playing polo at Lahore. As a sovereign, he had been respected for his justice and generosity, but also for his severity. An ardent Muslim, he made great efforts to spread the Islamic faith in India. He built a mosque in Delhi and another at Ajmer.

When Qutb-ud-din died, the chiefs of Lahore "so as to avoid disorder" immediately chose his successor. This was Aram Baksh, who appears to have been his favorite. Aram did not possess the necessary qualities for governing, and the nobles of Delhi soon conspired against him and invited the governor of Badaun, Shams-ud-din Iltutmish, to replace him. Iltutmish advanced against Delhi with his whole army, defeated Aram close to Delhi and seized power.

Iltutmish belonged to a tribe from Turkestan. In his early youth, he had been extremely handsome and his intelligence was brilliant. His brothers were jealous of him. He was sold as a slave and ended up by being bought for a very high price by Qutb-ud-din, then viceroy of Delhi. Qutb-ud-din thought highly of him and made him governor of Badaun, giving him one of his daughters in marriage. He was emancipated and ennobled in recognition for his bravery and ability during the campaign against the Khokars.

The new sultan immediately had to tackle the threatened dissolution of the empire, whose various provinces were proclaiming their independence. First of all, he had to repress a revolt by the emirs and consolidated his power over the kingdom of Delhi and its dependencies, Badaun, Oudh, Varanasi, and Siwalik. In 1214 Taj-ud-din Yildiz was driven out of Ghazni by the shah of Khwarazm, whose lands extended around the east of the Caspian. He took refuge in Lahore, undertook the conquest of the Punjab and sought to assert his power against Iltutmish. The latter marched against him, took him prisoner, and then went on to take Lahore and annex Sind.

In about 1228 Iltutmish received from the Caliph of Baghdad a robe of honor and the title of *Sultan-i-azam* (Great Sultan), thus confirming his power as legitimate "over all lands and seas that he had conquered." This strengthened his authority considerably. Between 1230 and 1231, Iltutmish subdued Bengal. Gwalior, which had regained its independence, was again taken toward the end of 1232. The Kingdom of Malwa was annexed in 1234 and the fortress of Bhilsa fell soon afterward. Ujjain was then sacked. During his last expedition in the Mountains of Salt, in the Punjab, Iltutmish fell sick. He was taken back to Delhi on a litter and died in April 1236, having reigned for twenty-six years.

Iltutmish had established Muslim domination firmly over India. A skilful politician and strategist, he was also a patron of Persian letters and Islamic arts. He built the famous Qutb minaret, to which he gave the name of one of his protégés, Khwaja Qutb-ud-din, a native of Baghdad. He also built a magnificent mosque. He was a devout Muslim and never failed to say his prayers. In inscriptions, he is called the "protector of God's territories."

During the reign of Iltutmish, the Mongols appeared for the first time on the banks of the Indus in 1221. They were led by their famous chief, Genghis Khan, born in 1155, whose real name was Temuchin. He was a brave, enterprising, and patient man. He had the bright idea of organizing the barbarian tribes of central Asia, grouping them together, and giving them laws and institutions that were to last for generations, leading to the creation of an army of remarkable cohesion and effectiveness. With surprising rapidity, Genghis Khan invaded the immense lands of central and western Asia. When he attacked Khwarazm (Khiva), to the east of the Caspian, the sovereign of that country fled to the Punjab. After pillaging Sind and Gujarat, Genghis Khan fell back on Persia. However, the Mongols dared not face the might of Iltutmish. They withdrew from India, which was thus for a time saved from the ravages of their terrible hordes.

The eldest son of Iltutmish, governor of Bengal, had died in 1229. Since the sovereign's other sons were unfit, Iltutmish appointed his daughter Raziyya as his successor. The idea of having a female sovereign greatly displeased the court, so the throne was given to Rukn-ud-din Firuz, the second son of Iltutmish. Rukn-ud-din was a dissolute man who thought only of his pleasures and spent without counting the cost. The actual ruler was his mother, Shah Turkhan, a former Turkish servant. The kingdom was plunged into disorder and the authority of the central power was completely disrupted. In the end, the nobles imprisoned the queen mother and then Rukn-ud-din, who died in prison in 1236.

Although Raziyya had difficulty in asserting herself at first, she managed to do so with skill and courage. Even the farthest provinces of Bengal and Sind accepted her authority. Wise and just, gifted in the arts of peace and war, she presided over the assemblies and loved playing "king," dressed as a man. However, her weakness for an Abyssinian slave, Jalad-ud-din Yaqut, whom she had appointed chief of the stables, displeased the court nobles, who were Turks. They fomented a revolt, led by Ikhtiyar-ud-din Altuniya, governor of Sarhind. The queen marched against him at the head of a great army, but in the fighting Yaqut was killed and the queen made prisoner. She attempted to get out of her difficulty by marrying Altuniya and marching with him against Delhi. Their troops abandoned them, however, on 13 October 1240, and Raziyya and her husband were put to death the next day.

Her successors were incapable of ruling, and the resultant confusion was increased by the incursions of the Mongols, who penetrated the Punjab and seized the beautiful city of Lahore, ravaging it ferociously. The Mongols then advanced on Uch and were repelled, with great losses. In 1246 the nobles decided to put on the throne Nasir-ud-din Mahmud, the youngest of Iltutmish's sons. Nasir-ud-din, an amiable and pious man, was more interested in calligraphy than in anything else. Real power was in the hands of his minister Ghiyaz-ud-din Balban, who did his best to repress the rebellions and managed to repel the Mongols.

Balban had been born in Turkestan, in the Ilbari tribe. Taken by the Mongols, he had been sold as a slave at Baghdad. He was later bought, together with forty other slaves, by Iltutmish who, appreciating his intelligence and ability, made him his personal page. Balban quickly came to play an important role at court and, after the death of Iltutmish, became the personal representative of Nasir-ud-din, to whom he had given his daughter in marriage. When Nasir-ud-din died in 1266, he designated Balban as his successor.

The new king found himself faced by a difficult situation. The treasury was empty, the country disorganized, and the nobles arrogant. The Mongols' repeated incursions hung over everything as a constant threat. He started by reorganizing the army, then asserted his authority over the

territories around Delhi. He pursued the Rajputs of Mewar (Alwar)—
who had formed bands of pillagers, holding travelers and merchants for
ransom—through the jungles and put them to the sword. He reestablished the central power, in district after district, rebuilding fortresses,
and putting them in the charge of Afghan officers on whom he could
count. Having consolidated his power basis, Balban was able to take on
the Mongols, who threatened the northwest and had settled at Ghazni
and in Transoxiana. They had taken Baghdad, killed the caliph, and were
launching increasingly murderous incursions in the Punjab and Sind.

In 1271 Balban marched on Lahore, governed by his cousin Sher
Khan Sunqar, who fought the Mongols courageously. Balban did not like
him and had him poisoned, a grave error that encouraged the Mongols.
Balban then appointed his two sons as governors of Multan and Samana
respectively. During a further incursion in 1279, the Mongols were
beaten by the combined armies of Multan, Samana, and Delhi.

Taking advantage of Balban's difficulties in the northwest, Tughril
Khan, the Turkish governor of Bengal, proclaimed his independence. The
sultan sent an army, commanded by Amir Khan "of the long hair." The
latter was beaten, and a furious Balban had him hanged in front of the
gate at Delhi. Another army suffered the same fate. Balban himself then
took all his troops and managed to find Tughril, who had fled into the
jungle. The Turk was beheaded and his companions imprisoned. Balban
had all of the rebel's kin and henchmen massacred and installed his own
son Bughra Khan as governor of Bengal. When the Mongols attacked
again in 1285, Muhammad—Balban's eldest son and governor of
Multan—advanced against them and was killed in an ambush. This was
a very hard blow for the old sultan, who died two years later at the age of
eighty.

Balban's court was the last word in magnificence and he welcomed
numerous princely exiles from central Asia. He had an acute feeling for
the sultan's majesty and never appeared, even before his intimates, without dressing in state. He would not allow men of humble origin to
occupy important posts. His court adopted the etiquette and ceremonies
of the ancient kings of Persia. The famous Persian poet and philosopher

of Turkish origin, Amir Khusrav, frequented his court. Balban, a devout Muslim and moralist, made it a point of honor that justice should be administered with impartiality. He maintained many spies throughout the various provinces. He did not actually reorganize the administrative structure. His concept of the state was that of a dictatorship, whose stability depended on the personal strength of the sovereign. Balban saved the sultanate from falling apart for some time and halted the advance of the Mongols, but he did not establish a lasting empire.

Kaiqubad, Balban's grandson, was eighteen when he ascended the throne. His grandfather had raised him according to the most absurd moralistic code, and his preceptors' mission had been to ensure "that he should never let his eyes fall on a pretty girl, or taste a cup of wine."

As soon as he came to power, Kaiqubad's only preoccupation was to regain the time he had lost, and he was little worried by the empire's problems. The ambitious Nizam-ud-din, the son-in-law of the Mayor of Delhi, took over effective power and threw out the kingdom's former officials. Disputes set the court's Turkish faction against what was known as the Khalji faction. Firuz, the leader of the Khalji party, managed to have the leaders of the Turkish party killed. Kaiqubad was in the end assassinated in his palace of mirrors by a nobleman whose father he had put to death. Firuz had Kaiqubad's son—still in his cradle—killed at once and took power.

The Slave Dynasty thus ended ignominiously. They could have established a stable monarchy, but their egocentricity, puritanism, and cruelty lost them the trust and friendship of their subordinates, who were continually involved in escaping their tyranny.

THE KHALJI DYNASTY

Jalad-ud-din-Firuz, the new sovereign, did not please the court at Delhi, because he was not a Turk, but Afghan or Pathan. With his arrival, the Turks had lost the Delhi Empire. As a cover-up, an attempt was made to find a vague Turkish origin for him, more or less forgotten during his ancestors' long stay in Afghanistan. At the same time, the generosity and nobility of his character, together with his sense of equity and justice, gradually won him some sympathy.

The new sultan was seventy years old. He was too understanding and sensitive to reign at such a troubled time. He pardoned rebels but, on the other hand, imprudently allowed the execution of a dervish suspected of treason. He refused to attack the rebellious fort of Ranthambhor for fear of "sacrificing the lives of numerous Muslims." He was vigorous, however, in attacking the Mongols, of whom a horde of an estimated one hundred and fifty thousand men had once more descended toward the north of India in 1292. The Mongols were severely beaten, but Firuz generously allowed them to return home. Ulghu, a descendent of Genghis Khan, together with a large group of Mongols, decided to embrace Islam. They demanded and received permission to settle near Delhi. These converted Mongols are known as the "new Muslims." The sovereigns of Delhi were later to repent of allowing this Mongol infiltration. The sentimental notion that members of a conquered people who adopt the religion of their conquerors are more easily assimilated and dominated has been fatal to all empires down to our own times.

Ala-ud-din Khalji, Firuz's nephew, was an orphan who had been raised by his uncle with great care and tenderness. The sultan gave him his daughter in marriage and entrusted him with a principality in the region of Allahabad. Ala-ud-din immediately launched on various adventures, without consulting Delhi. He commanded an expedition against Malwa in 1292 and took the city of Bhilsa. He heard talk of the fabulous riches of the kingdom of Devagiri, to the west of the Deccan, ruled by a prince of the Yadava dynasty, Ramachandradeva. Ala-ud-din departed secretly, at the head of some thousands of horsemen.

Ramachandradeva was not expecting an attack, and his army was mostly engaged on an expedition to the south. After vain efforts, he had to accept the extremely harsh conditions of the conquerors, who departed with an enormous booty of gold, silver, silk, pearls, and precious stones, and the promise of annual tribute. This expedition opened the way to Muslim domination over the Deccan and the south of India. Ala-ud-din had no intention of sharing his treasures. He persuaded the elderly sultan to come and see him, and the latter, blinded by his affection, was caught in a trap and assassinated. Ala-ud-din had himself proclaimed sultan at his camp on 19 July 1296.

As soon as she learned the news, the queen mother placed her younger son Ibrahim on the throne at Delhi, since the eldest son, Arkali—who governed Multan—had refused to succeed his father. Ala-ud-din immediately marched on Delhi. After a feeble attempt at resistance, Ibrahim fled to Multan with his mother and his minister Ahmad Chap. Pursued by Ala-ud-din's brother, they were captured, together with Arkali. Their eyes were put out and they were taken back to Delhi and imprisoned in the Hansi fort. All Arkali's children were put to death, and Ala-ud-din remained the uncontested master of the empire.

During his reign, the Mongols remained a constant source of anxiety. They made a first incursion in 1298, but were beaten back at Jullundur. Two thousand of them were taken prisoner and sent to Delhi in 1299. Furious at their defeat, the Mongols then prepared another invasion of India, with the aim not of pillage, but of annexing the country. They entered on the northern frontier and without much difficulty reached Delhi, where the citizens were taken by panic.

Zafar Khan, the commander of Ala-ud-din's troops, was killed during a heroic battle, but the Mongols were alarmed, and withdrew. They attempted a new incursion in 1304, and then another in 1307–08. This time, it was their own chief who was killed, and many of their captains were captured and put to death. Terrified by Ala-ud-din's cruelty, the Mongols suspended their incursions for the rest of his reign. Ala-ud-din took advantage of this by consolidating his defenses and strengthening the fortresses on the northwest.

In the meantime, the "new Muslims"—the converted Mongols—were becoming agitated. Ala-ud-din had excluded them from any public office. Using the pretext that they had conspired to assassinate the emperor, he had over thirty thousand of them ferociously massacred in a single day.

During the reign of Ala-ud-din, Muslim domination extended over most of India. In 1297 he sent his brother at the head of a powerful army to conquer Gujarat, whose rich ports were pillaged. The Hindu King

Karnadeva II fled, but the Queen, Kamala Devi, whose beauty was renowned, was captured and brought back to Delhi, along with a young eunuch called Kafur. Kamala Devi was to become the favorite wife of Ala-ud-din and Kafur his most influential minister—almost head of state—before and after Ala-ud-din's death. Ala-ud-din then attacked the Rajput princes. He took Ranthambhor, then the celebrated fortress of Chitor. On each occasion, the besieged, having lost all hope, performed the terrible rite called *jauhar*. A great fire was lighted inside an enormous cave, and all the women were given to the flames, to save them from dishonor. The Rajputs then left the fort and—launching themselves against their assailants—were all massacred.

After Chitor, Ala-ud-din conquered Malwa and killed the king, Mahlak Deva. Then it was the turn of Ujjain, Mandu, Dhar, Chenderi, and so on. Having affirmed his dominion over all northern India, the sultan turned his attention to the rich kingdoms of the south. In 1307 Kafur, now commander-in-chief of the army, took Devagiri, after putting the Yadava kingdom to fire and sword. In March 1310 he took Warangal, whose king had to give up all his treasure. Kafur brought back to Delhi one thousand camels loaded with booty. In November 1310 he returned with a mighty army and took Halebid (Dorasamudra). He then proceeded southward and, taking advantage of local dissension, invaded the Chola and Pandya kingdoms on the Coromandel coast (Tamilnadu), and the Chera kingdom on the Malabar coast (Kerala). In 1311 Madura, the capital of the Pandyas, was pillaged. Kafur continued his expedition as far as Kanyakumari and returned to Delhi in October 1311 with an incredible booty: six hundred elephants, twenty thousand horses, ninety-six thousand quintals of gold, and cases of pearls and precious stones.

The whole of southern India henceforth acknowledged the suzerainty of Delhi and paid tribute. The methods employed by the Muslims—the sacking of towns, the massacre of their inhabitants, and the pillaging of temples—left a profound bitterness among the populations, who only awaited the right moment to revolt. Worried by such rebellions, the sultan concluded that something was wrong in the empire's administration. After consulting his counselors, he attributed his difficulties to four causes: 1) the sultan's lack of personal attention to state business; 2) wine; 3) friendly relations among the nobles; and 4) the abundance of money.

Having decided to prevent any possibility of revolt, he set up a system of repressive regulation. He began by attacking private property. All pensions or usufructs were suppressed. All villages belonging to a landowner, or from which someone enjoyed an income, were confiscated. Under any pretext, people were overburdened with taxes, to the extent that, according to the contemporary historian Barni, no one any longer had even a piece of silver, except the state's agents and bankers.

The sultan then set up a vast spy network. His spies had to report on everything, even the talk and transactions at the bazaar. This created such a climate of insecurity that noblemen feared to talk together, even in an isolated place. The use of alcohol and drugs was strictly forbidden, as was betting. To set an example, the sultan had all the palace wine cups broken. He also forbade receptions and meetings, except with an authorization that only he could give. This rule was applied so strictly that meetings and dinners ceased completely, and the nobles no longer had any communication with each other. The farmers had to give the state half their produce. The sultan wished to reduce the common people to such a state of misery that no superfluous object could be found among them. They could possess neither arms, nor ride on horseback, nor wear beautiful attire, nor amuse themselves in any way and had to walk with lowered head. Forced by hunger, Hindu women had to work as servants for the Muslims. These laws were enforced so rigorously that the tax collectors were feared more than the pest. Ala-ud-din needed a strong army, but, unwilling to increase his soldiers' pay, he fixed the price of all essential commodities at a very low price, including slaves, horses, arms, etc. Stocks of wheat or rice were forbidden, and had to be surrendered to the royal reserves. Merchants were strictly controlled, and if the weights they employed were incorrect, a piece of flesh weighing the same as the difference was cut from their body. Probably never, in any country, had tyranny been so total. The sultan was hated by all. As he got older, he became embittered and weak spirited, soon becoming little more than a puppet in the hands of his favorite, Kafur, who was probably not without a hand in his death on 2 January 1316.

According to Barni, Ala-ud-din shed more innocent blood than any other prince had ever done. Out of jealousy, he betrayed, assassinated, or blinded all those who had helped him. He was a brave and skilful soldier and a great builder of fortresses and mosques, but the empire he had built crumbled, because all those he had humiliated had no other thought than vengeance.

Kafur was even worse than his master. After the death of Ala-ud-din, he published what he claimed was the emperor's will, disinheriting Khizr Khan, the sultan's eldest son, in favor of his youngest son, who was five years old. The latter was thus acknowledged as king, with Kafur as regent and de facto dictator over the empire. He at once put out the eyes of Khizr Khan and of the sultan's second son, Shadi Khan. He imprisoned the queen and confiscated all her possessions. Ala-ud-din's third son, Mubarak, managed to escape. Kafur then tried to exile all the nobles and slaves who had supported the Khaljis. Such an enterprise was impossible, however, and Kafur was assassinated inside the palace itself. The nobles then called Mubarak and made him regent. After sixty-four days of regency, however, in April 1316, Mubarak put out the eyes of the official sultan, his young brother, and seized the throne, taking the name of Qutb-ud-din Mubarak Shah.

Mubarak's reign was initially a success. He suppressed his father's severest edicts, freed prisoners, and returned lands to their owners, which quite naturally made him popular. He totally neglected state business, however, abandoning himself to a life of pleasure and giving himself over to love, music, alcohol, and making handsome gifts of money. He fell completely under the influence of a low-caste man from Gujarat, a convert to Islam, whom he named Khusrav Khan.

Gujarat revolted, but the sultan's authority was easily reestablished by his father-in-law Zafar Khan. When Devagiri tried to shake off Delhi's yoke, Mubarak himself led the army. The Yadava king, Harapala Deva, fled, but was caught and made prisoner. Mubarak had him flayed alive, and the Yadava kingdom was annexed by the empire. Mubarak remained at Devagiri for one year, building a great mosque there and leaving a Muslim governor before returning to Delhi. These triumphs swelled

Mubarak's vanity. He rejected the spiritual authority of the caliphs and proclaimed himself supreme head of Islam. Despite his friends' warnings, he maintained his trust in Khusrav, who organized his pleasures. When he thought the right moment had come, Khusrav had the sultan stabbed to death by one of his low-caste associates in April 1320, thus putting an end to the Khalji dynasty.

Khusrav took power and ascended the throne as Nasir-ud-din Khusrav. He showered gifts and honors on his kinsmen and those of his tribe who had helped him. He distributed the state's wealth to the nobles, who had been forced to acquiesce in his usurpation. He also spread terror, however, by massacring all the former sultan's friends and servants. He favored the Hindus, thus rousing the wrath of the Muslim nobles who, led by Ghazi Malik, governor of the frontier provinces, marched on Delhi. Khusrav was defeated and beheaded on 5 September 1320. All his henchmen were massacred. Ghazi Malik at first refused the throne, but since no descendent of Ala-ud-din remained, the nobles persuaded him to accept and he took the name of Ghiyas-ud-din Tughluq.

THE TUGHLUQ DYNASTY

The father of Ghiyas-ud-din had come to India at the time of Balban. He had married a Hindu of the warrior caste of the Jats of the Punjab. Born poor, Ghiyas-ud-din had gradually acquired an important position due to his bravery and virtue. He had been India's defense against the Mongol invasions. He was also a devout Muslim. Under his reign, the court of Delhi became very austere. He did his best to put the state finances and administration in order. He encouraged agricultural development and dug canals, but his laws were tainted with the spirit of oppression that characterized the attitude of the Muslim administrations toward the people, who had remained Hindu. Barni explains that he established taxes so that too much prosperity would not lead his subjects to rebel, often reducing them to such a degree of misery and poverty that they were no longer capable of exercising their professions properly. He reorganized the post, justice, and the army, and then undertook the consolidation of the empire. He sent an army against Warangal, a kingdom that had refused to pay tribute. Warangal was besieged, the Hindu sovereign sent as a prisoner to Delhi, and the town was renamed Sultanpur. Ghiyas-ud-din then subdued Bengal, but on his return in 1325, he died when a wooden triumphal arch built by his son Jauna collapsed as he passed by. The historians of the time considered that this "accident" had been carefully prepared.

Jauna was proclaimed sultan three days after his father's death, and took the name of Muhammad bin Tughluq. Numerous documents exist about his reign, particularly the memoirs of the historian Barni—who lived during the reign of his successor—as well as those of the famous poet and man of letters who lived at his court, Amir Khusrav, and, lastly, the account of the Arab traveler Ibn Batutah. These texts provide us with much information. Muhammad bin Tughluq was a man of letters and vast culture, interested in philosophy, mathematics, astronomy, and physics. A skilful dialectician and great strategist, as well as a charming and often generous man, he lacked any sense of reality. He would not allow facts to give the lie to his vision and was obstinate to the point of folly. This lack of balance was the reason for the surprising failure of a sultan who possessed every talent for success.

His plans frustrated, he accused all of treachery and rebellion, and found himself totally isolated. He condemned people to death on the slightest suspicion, cruelly punishing whole populations when he imagined they did not love him. This gentle man was one of the cruelest sultans of India. He decided to increase the taxes paid by the peasants who farmed the fertile plains of the Ganges at a time when famine was raging, and he exacted the greatest rigor in collecting these taxes. The peasants were reduced to such misery that they had no other choice than to abandon their farms. The sultan had them brought back forcefully, with terrible punishments. The results were catastrophic at both human and economic levels. The sultan attempted agricultural reform, but his measures came too late to remedy this disaster.

In 1327, in order to protect himself from Mongol incursions, the sultan decided to transfer his capital from Delhi to Devagiri, which he renamed Daulatabad. This town was located close to Ellora (in modern Maharashtra), and suffered a burning and unhealthy climate. Since the citizens of Delhi hesitated to leave their homes, the sultan had them taken by force and, according to Barni, "there remained neither a cat nor a dog in the deserted streets of the former capital." Many of the exiles died on this forced journey of more than 1000 kilometers. Some time later, the sultan acknowledged his mistake, and transferred the capital back to Delhi, but very few of its former inhabitants survived this new exodus, and Delhi remained a semi-deserted city.

The sultan changed the coinage, introducing copper coins for the first time; as they were only too easy to imitate, millions of false coins were struck, ruining the treasury. Fortunately, the sultan's ambitious plans to conquer Khorasan and Iraq could not be undertaken for lack of money. An entire army was lost in an expedition to Garhwal in the Himalayas in 1338. Revolts broke out in various regions of the empire. The sultan's own cousin, who governed Sagar in central India, refused to pay tribute. He was captured, brought back to Delhi, and flayed alive. A more serious revolt occurred at Multan. Muhammad marched on Multan and—after defeating the troops of the governor Bahram Aiba—he had him seized and beheaded, and his head was hung at the city gate. The governor of Mabar in southern India, Jalal-ud-din Ashan Shah, proclaimed his independence in 1335. The sultan marched in person against Madura, but a cholera epidemic forced him to withdraw, and Madura became an independent Muslim kingdom until it was annexed by Vijayanagar in 1378. Bengal, then Oudh, also proclaimed their independence. When the emperor sought to repress one revolt, another broke out. During an expedition against Sind, he was taken by a fever and died. The army—with wives and children—found itself without its head and in the greatest state of confusion, harassed by the rebels from Sind and by the Mongol mercenaries whose services the sultan had hired.

To avoid a disaster, the army commanders begged Firuz, the cousin of Muhammad-bin Tughluq, to take over the command and to accept the crown, which he did with some reluctance. At the same time, however, Khwaja-i-Jahan, the sultan's representative at Delhi, proclaimed as king a child whom he said was Muhammad's son, and who probably was. After consulting with the nobles and jurists at Multan, Firuz insisted on his claims and Khwaja-i-Jahan submitted. Firuz exiled him, but he was beheaded on the way by his escort.

Firuz was a weak and vacillating man. He possessed none of the qualities needed to reestablish the unity of the empire. He gave away victories that were almost certain, from the fear of "shedding Muslim blood," as in the case of his two campaigns against Bengal. He also accepted a vague submission by Orissa. A difficult and costly campaign in Sind allowed him to reduce that province, but he refused to attack the Deccan.

He was devout and wept when he had to attack Muslims. At the same time, he persecuted the Hindus and did his best to convert the followers of other religions. He strengthened the application of the additional taxes recommended by Koranic law for non-Muslims or other "heretics," although he also suppressed certain city tolls and thus facilitated trade. By and large, the price of essential commodities remained low, while the construction of several major canals improved agricultural potential. The sultan created new towns and gave new names to ancient cities. He built many mosques, bridges, and gardens. He created a kind of labor exchange, to facilitate the recruitment of workers. He also attempted to make the administration of justice more humane. According to his own words, "Under the reign of other kings . . . many forms of torture were employed, such as the amputation of hands, feet, ears, or nose, the putting out of eyes, the pouring of molten lead down the throat, the using of hammers to break bones in hands and feet, the burning of the body with red-hot irons, the hammering of nails into hands, feet, or breasts, the cutting of tendons, the sawing of bodies in two, and so on. The Lord, great and magnanimous, has inspired me to seek his grace in making me prevent the illegal putting to death of Muslims and the infliction of cruel tortures on them or on other men."

The number of slaves increased enormously during Firuz's reign, because he allowed a part of the provincial dues to be paid in the form of slaves. A historian of the time speaks of one hundred and eighty thousand slaves in the capital.

During his last years, Firuz partly lost his reason. He wished to share power with the eldest of his surviving sons, Muhammad Khan. The latter was only interested in his amusements, however, and Firuz appointed as his successor his grandson, Tughluq Khan. Firuz died on 20 September 1388. The reign of Tughluq Khan did not last long. He was an early victim of conspiracy. The nobles of Delhi proclaimed his cousin Abu Baqr as sultan, while at the same time the partisans of his uncle Muhammad proclaimed *him* king in 1389. Abu Baqr was forced to abdicate in 1390. Muhammad died in 1394. His son Humayun succeeded him, but died a few months later. The youngest of Muhammad's sons, Nasir-ud-din Mahmud, succeeded him. None of these princes had anything by way of character, but were puppets in the hands of the nobles.

The rule of the Muslim sultans of Delhi and their conquests had led to the establishment of numerous Muslim-governed provinces that— with the weakening of the central government—became independent kingdoms. The most important in the north were Bengal, Jaunpur, Malwa, Gujarat, and Kashmir and, toward the south, Khandesh and the Bahmani kingdom, which was divided into five sultanates: Berar, Ahmadnagar, Bijapur, Golconda, and Bidar. The surviving Hindu kingdoms were: Nepal; Kamarupa, to the north of Bengal; Assam; Mewar in Rajputana; Orissa to the east; and the Vijayanagar Empire to the south.

TIMUR

Timur (whom we call Tamerlane) was a Turk who ascended the throne of Samarkand in 1369. He immediately undertook a series of conquests in Persia, Afghanistan, and Mesopotamia. The riches of India tempted him, and the weakness of the Delhi government provided him with a favorable opportunity. By invoking the propagation of the Islamic faith, he obtained the consent of his nobles. His invasion of India was the most ferocious that the country had ever known up to then.

In1398, Timur sent his grandson to annex Multan. The town was besieged and taken. Timur then left Samarkand, in April 1398, with a mighty army. After crossing the rivers Ravi and Jhelum, he appeared in

October before the town of Talamba, northwest of Multan. The town was sacked and all its inhabitants either massacred or reduced to slavery. Timur continued his advance, razing the towns and massacring their inhabitants. He reached Delhi in December. Mahmud attempted to resist at the head of an army of ten thousand horse, forty thousand foot, and one hundred and twenty elephants covered with armor, but the army was routed and Mahmud fled to Gujarat.

The next day, Timur entered Delhi, took one hundred thousand male prisoners and put them all to death the day after. The city was given over to the Turkish soldiers, who pillaged, raped, and massacred its inhabitants for many days. A great number were taken away as slaves: those that were good craftsmen were sent to Samarkand to build the famous Friday Mosque, whose plans Timur had had drawn up.

Timur had no intention of staying in India. After a fortnight he went home, destroying everything in his path. He took Firuzbad on 1 January 1399, and Meerut on 9 January. He beat two Hindu armies that attempted to stop him at Haridwar. He took Kangra on 16 January and sacked Jammu. Wherever he went, the inhabitants were massacred. Timur crossed the Indus on his return on 19 March, leaving one of his officers as governor of Lahore and Multan. Following the massacres, famine and pest took hold of Delhi, killing most of its surviving inhabitants. The city remained almost abandoned. In 1401 Mallu Iqbal, Mahmud's minister who had taken refuge at Baran, returned to Delhi and recalled Sultan Mahmud, who had suffered bitter humiliation in Gujarat. Mahmud was to remain a puppet in the hands of Mallu Iqbal, up to the latter's death in a fight against the governor of Multan in 1405. Mahmud continued his vague and colorless reign until his death in 1413.

THE SAYYIDS AND THE LODIS

After the death of Sultan Mahmud, the nobles of Delhi chose one of themselves—Daulat Khan Lodi—to succeed him. In 1414, however, Khizr Khan—who governed Multan on behalf of Timur—once more seized Delhi and imprisoned Daulat Khan. His domination lasted seven years, and was uneventful. Delhi was now only a small town, with no power over its former empire. Khizr Khan claimed descent from the Prophet, although he had very little Arab blood in his veins. His dynasty is known as the Sayyid dynasty.

Mubarak Shah, the son of Khizr Khan—whom the latter had chosen as his successor—then ascended the throne. He was assassinated in 1434, the victim of a conspiracy. One of Khizr Khan's grandsons, Muhammad Shah, succeeded him. His son Alam Shah did not wish to reign and power passed to Buhlul Khan Lodi, governor of Lahore.

Buhlul Khan belonged to the Afghan tribe of the Lodis. Although the Kingdom of Delhi was at this time only a minor state, this hardy warrior made his neighbors respect him. He reestablished Muslim prestige in India. He died in 1489, while returning from an expedition against Gwalior. At his death, his second son, Nizam Khan, took power under the name of Sultan Sikander Shah. An energetic man, he reestablished Delhi's dominion right to the border with Bengal and signed a non-aggression pact with Hussain Shah of Bengal. He was reputed to be moderate and just, but his justice only stretched to Muslims. He founded the town that was later to be called Agra, and died there in 1517.

His eldest son, Ibrahim, succeeded him at Agra. A faction of nobles, however, wanted the kingdom to be divided between him and his younger brother Jalal. Ibrahim managed to seize Jalal and have him assassinated. Ibrahim was a skilful soldier, but a bad diplomat, and attempted to control the Afghan nobles who held the kingdom's provinces and key posts by using severe measures. He managed merely to alienate their loyalty. When he tried to deal severely with Dilwar Khan, governor of Lahore, the latter appealed to Babur, the Timurid king of Kabul, with the result of renewed Turkish domination in India.

THE MUSLIM STATE AND ITS INFLUENCES

The Muslim state was a theocracy, of which the sultan was the temporal and spiritual head. The sultan was an absolute autocrat, using religious pretexts to justify his conquests, massacres, and violence. The Hindu nobles were hostile and were largely massacred. There was never any real Muslim aristocracy, and no kind of parliament or assembly.

The sultan had a council of friends and officers, known as *Majlis i Khalwat*, that he consulted on certain problems. Koranic law was the only law recognized. The penal code was particularly severe, and torture was employed to obtain evidence. Judgement was summary and sentences were usually death or mutilation. The sultan's sources of revenue included: the *kharaj*, taxes collected from major Hindu landowners; the *khalsa*, revenues from crown lands; the *khams*, a fifth of any war booty as the sovereign's share; various taxes (*abwab*) on houses, pasturage rights, water, and so on, as well as taxes on trade; and the *jitya*, the special tax on all non-Muslims. As a rule, taxes on agriculture amounted to half the produce. A large part of the wealth of the Delhi court came from booty obtained by ravaging towns and whole regions of India, and reducing part of the population to slavery. These processes led to the general impoverishment of a prodigiously rich country, and much later—when European exploitation had replaced Muslim exaction—were to lead to the profound poverty of contemporary India.

Since ancient times, India had been one of the greatest producers of textiles in the world: cotton, wool, and silk cloth, brocades, and prints. Other major industries included metal (gold, copper, bronze), paper, ceramic, arms (the quality of Indian steel and iron were famous), scents, jewels, ivory, indigo, opium, and spices. Hindu craftsmen were among the best in the world. Up to the nineteenth century, Kashmir shawls were an art of unrivalled refinement. A single shawl could represent two years of work for six persons. Thanks to excellent reservoirs and a very widespread irrigation system, agriculture provided two harvests each year.

The sultans and Muslim nobles practiced wide scale slavery. Ala-ud-din owned fifty thousand slaves, Firuz Shah over two hundred thousand. The Muslims' common tongue was Persian and great efforts were made to impose Persian culture and language in India. Amir Khusrav could say that Delhi was the rival of Bukhara, the great university city of the Persian world.

All previous invaders of India had contributed to its culture, religion, arts, and skills, and such elements had been rapidly assimilated. This was not to be the case with the Muslims, whose contribution was essentially negative. There were, of course, certain influences, resulting from efforts made by both Hindus and Muslims to know each other better.

Under Arab and Turkish domination, exchanges of ideas with Hindus were inevitable in religion, the sciences, and arts. This fact was to have a profound impact, on the Hindu world, on the one hand, and on the Arab world—and consequently the Christian world—on the other. A large number of Sanskrit texts on philosophy and mathematics were translated into Persian and Arabic. Through these Arabic versions, Europe got to know Hindu fables, the first texts of the Upanishads, and many of India's scientific concepts. The Arab astronomer, Abu Mas'har, lived for ten years at Varanasi in order to study Hindu astronomy. The Shiite philosophy of Iran is impregnated with Indian metaphysics and its concepts are almost identical to those of the Vedanta. Iranian *Zekhr* chants and dances are very similar to those of the Indian *Kirtana*.

At the same time, India assimilated certain elements that Islam contributed, often indirectly. The movement known as *bhakti* (devotion), which was to play a major role in the religious life of India, is partly due to Islamic influence. Religious feeling for the Hindus—distressed by the loss of their hieratic, ritual, and aristocratic social order under Muslim domination—took refuge in this kind of simple faith and sentimental and irrational piety. For this doctrine of charity and love, social, ethnic, and ritual differences appeared to be of little importance. The great saints and poets that promoted this new cult include Chaitanya (1485–1533), Kabir (1450–1518), and Nanak (1469–1538), who founded the new Sikh religion, a kind of Hinduized version of Islam, to which numerous Muslims were converted. For Kabir, the doctrine of love embraces all human beings:

> The Hindu and the Turk are made of the same glory. Allah and Rama differ only in their names. The barber seeks God, like the washerman or the carpenter. The poet Raidas himself is a man of God. The prophet Svapacha was only a tanner by caste. Hindus like Muslims have attained the final goal, where there are no more differences. The

path to Heaven does not pass through fasts, prayers, or the reciting of holy texts. The veil of the temple of Mecca is in actual fact in the heart of men. Make your spirit the Qa'aba, your body the temple that surrounds it, your mind your master. Sacrifice anger, doubt, malice, let your patience be your five prayers. The god of the Hindus and the Muslims is the same. Religion is not a matter of fine words. He who sees men as equals is religious. Religion does not mean visiting temples, or sitting in a posture of contemplation. Religion is not made of a missionary spirit and pilgrimages. If you remain pure among the impurities of the world, you will find the path of true religion.

But we shall see that this religion of love was later to give rise to a sect of warriors and, sometimes, fanatics.

The principles of Islamic architecture, originally of Mediterranean origin, have nothing in common with Hindu architecture. The only contribution of India's traditional art in buildings of the Muslim period was through the employment of skilled Hindu craftsmen in their decoration. The Muslims destroyed most of the wonderful Hindu monuments. Only a few temples in towns abandoned in the forest, like Khajuraho, or too distant, such as Konark, have survived.

They were replaced by the banal buildings of Islamic art, the same wherever they are, whether in Spain or Egypt, in Bactria or Delhi. For political reasons, the European conquerors gave Muslim architecture an extraordinary advertising campaign, and it was only at the approach of independence that the foreign traveler was encouraged to visit India's great temples and not merely the Taj Mahal. It is only in recent history that medieval Hindu sculpture, purposely neglected, has begun to regain the place it deserves among the highest forms of art.

18
The Vijayanagar Empire

At the beginning of the fourteenth century, five brothers—sons of a certain Sangama, and refugees from the Telugu country—laid the foundations of a city on the left bank of the River Tungabhadra, to the south of the Deccan plateau, facing the fortress of Anegundi. They were the disciples of a learned and wise Brahman, Madhava Vidyaranya, and his brother Sayana, the famous commentator of the Vedas. These five brothers established an empire—the Empire of Vijayanagar—whose aim was to defend the ancient religion, social structure, and culture of the Hindus against Islamic and modernist inroads.

The Empire of Vijayanagar grew with great rapidity. Under its first sovereigns, Harihara I and Bukka I, it extended its suzerainty over a great number of principalities, including most of the Hoysala territory. Vijayanagar was able to hold in check the Muslim Bahmani kingdom (Hyderabad) to the south, as well as the power of the sultans of Delhi. In 1374 Bukka I sent an embassy to China. When he died in 1378 or 1379 his son, Harihara II, took the title of Emperor. Harihara was a devotee of Shiva, and—in accordance with Hindu principles—he respected the other religions.

The history of Vijayanagar is a long history of difficult wars. During the reign of Harihara II, his son Bukka II attacked Firuz Shah Bahmani in 1398, but was beaten in 1399, and Vijayanagar had to pay a considerable tribute. In the meantime, the authority of Vijayanagar had stretched over the whole of the south of India, including Mysore, the Kanada country, Chingleput, Trichinopoly, and Kanchipuram. Harihara II died in 1406 and—after disputes among his sons—Deva Raya I ascended the throne. He suffered several defeats in his wars with the Bahmani sultans and died in 1422. His successor, Devi Raya II, also suffered several defeats, but was responsible for a considerable reorganization of the administration. He accepted Muslims in his army and established the office of "Controller of the Southern Seas."

An Italian, Nicolo Conti, visited the city of Vijayanagar in 1420. The Persian Abdur Razzaq stayed there in 1443. Other travelers—Italians, Persians, and Portuguese—have left wonder-struck descriptions of the city and the empire. According to Edoardo Barbosa, in 1516 the town was a center of international trade in "diamonds, Pega rubies, silks from China and Alexandria, cinnamon, camphor, musk, pepper and sandalwood." Men from all nations could be met there. The city's circumference was nearly 100 kilometers. According to Abdur Razzaq, the empire possessed three hundred seaports and maintained trade relations with Malaysia, Burma, China, Arabia, Persia, East Africa, Abyssinia, and Portugal.

Music was greatly appreciated. Even the king's wives played some instrument, and most of the palace officials were women. The Brahmans exercised a predominant influence in state business. The languages of the empire included Sanskrit, Telugu, Tamil, and Kanada, in each of which a considerable literature grew. Numerous poets, philosophers, historians, and musicians lived at court. Architecture underwent a great revival and some of the surviving temples are among the most remarkable monuments in India.

Deva Raya II died in 1446 and his son Mallikarjuna succeeded in maintaining the kingdom's integrity, despite the combined attacks of the Bahmani sultan and the Hindu king of Orissa. After his death in 1465, his successor, Virupaksha II, was unable to resist the attacks of the Bahmani sultan, who was then occupying part of the Vijayanagar territories between the Rivers Krishna and Tungabhadra. The empire's most faithful vassal, Narasimha Saluva of Chandragiri, then deposed

Virupaksha and seized the throne in 1486. His heart's desire was to accomplish the sacred mission for which the empire had been built up. He charged his best general, Narasa Nayaka, to govern after him. Narasa Nayaka left the throne to the son of Narasimha, but took over the government. However, at his death in 1505, it was his son, Vira Narasimha, who assumed royal power, deposing the last of the Saluva sovereigns.

At the death of Narasimha, his younger brother Krishnadeva Raya succeeded him. He was to become the greatest sovereign of Vijayanagar and one of the most famous in the history of India. Krishnadeva decided to consolidate the organization of his states before attacking his northern neighbors. It was not until 1510 that he marched against the prince of Mysore, who had shown insubordination, and took the fortress of Shivasamudram. He then forced the other chiefs of the region into obedience. In 1512 he advanced toward the frontier of Bijapur and took possession of Raichur. Wisely counseled, he did not attack the Muslim states, but turned against Orissa. He took the fortress of Udayagiri near Bhubaneshwar in 1514, and took prisoner the uncle and aunt of the king of Orissa. He treated his prisoners with respect and consideration. In the following year he took the fortress of Kondavidu and other less important forts. The assistance received by the king of Orissa from the sultans of Golconda and Bidar did not manage to halt the advance of Krishnadeva. He captured Prince Virabhadra and other nobles, but instead of imprisoning the prince, he appointed him governor of a province. In the end the king of Orissa was forced to sign a peace treaty.

Krishnadeva's last great victory was against Ismail Adilshah, close to Raichur, in 1520. The territory of Bijapur was conquered and the fort of Gulbarga razed. The Empire of Vijayanagar now stretched from one sea to the other and included the whole south of the subcontinent. Krishnadeva established friendly relations with the Portuguese, who managed to take Goa from the Muslims. In 1510 he authorized the Portuguese governor Albuquerque to build a fort at Bhaktal.

Krishnadeva died in 1529 or 1530 and was succeeded by his brother Achyuta Raya. Neither he nor his successors, however, were able to keep the empire intact. Maladroit alliances antagonized all the neighboring

India in 1525

kingdoms. The sultans of the Deccan formed a confederation and, on 23 January 1565, the vast army of Vijayanagar was beaten. The minister, Rama Raya, who governed the empire, was killed by the hand of Husain Nizam Shah. The magnificent city of Vijayanagar was delivered up to pillage. For more than five months, the Muslims did their best to destroy everything—temples, palaces, and magnificent residences. Contemporaries say that the scenes of massacre and horror were beyond anything the mind can imagine. The conquerors took away such riches in gold, jewels, furniture, camels, tents, gear, drums, banners, girls, boys, slaves, arms, and armor that every soldier left a rich man. The kings allowed everyone to keep what he had seized, except for the elephants. Of the most beautiful and most prosperous city in India, only smoking ruins were left.

This tragedy did not, however, mark the end of the Empire of Vijayanagar. The sultans quarreled among themselves and Tirumal, the brother of Rama Raya, reorganized the empire and set up another capital at Penugonda. Toward the end of his career, he dethroned the titular emperor, Sadashiva, and usurped the throne. His son, Ranga II, succeeded him and continued his work, followed by his brother Venkata II, who reigned from 1586 to 1614 and moved the capital to Chandragiri. In 1612 he allowed Raja Wodeyar to found the kingdom of Mysore, the sole one to survive the disintegration of the empire when it fell because of the egoism and dissension of its vassals and the ambition of the Muslim states.

The Vijayanagar Empire produced in India—dilapidated and debased by the ferocious Muslim occupation—a prodigious cultural renewal at all levels, including philosophy, the sciences, arts, architecture, and social organization. India returned to life. A very large part of what we know of the history of Indian thought comes from texts restored and commented on at this time.

The chivalry, humane justice, and respect for life and property that we find even in the wars fought by the emperors of Vijayanagar make a surprising contrast with the cruelty, barbarity, massacres, rape, and whole populations reduced to slavery, characteristic of the Muslim empires. Neither Muslims nor Christians were discriminated against in the Hindu empire. Barbosa remarks with astonishment that "the king allows such freedom that anyone can go, come and live according to his religion, without anyone to worry or ask him whether he is Christian, Jew, Muslim or Hindu." In the Muslim states the murder of an "unbeliever" was extolled as a virtue. Later on, we shall see sad examples of this in the modern Islamic State of Pakistan.

19

The Mogul Empire

Apart from the group of "new Muslims," the Mongols had never formed a permanent part of the Indian population, but they continued to harass the peoples close to the frontiers. Timur's invasion and permanent occupation of the Punjab installed Mongol power in India for the first time. One of his descendants, Babur, undertook the systematic conquest of northern India with the intention of dwelling there definitively. The emperors known as the "Great Mongols," or Moguls, were the descendants of the second son of Genghis Khan, who had reigned over central Asia and Turkestan. At the time when they settled in India, however, their army was a mixture of Turks and Mongols. The Turko-Mongols that converted to Islam were one of the latter's principal world triumphs. They established Muslim domination over India, as well as over the Near East. The Turks took Constantinople in 1453, and Suleiman the Magnificent (1520–1566) added southeastern Europe to the Turkish Empire. In Persia Ismail Safavi (1500–1524) founded the Safavid Empire.

The Turko-Mongol occupation of India can be divided into three phases. From 1526 to 1530, they subdued the Afghans and the Rajputs. From 1530 to 1540, Humayun attempted to conquer Malwa, Gujarat, and Bengal, but was thrown out of India by the Afghan Sher Shah. During the third phase, from 1545 to 1556, Humayun established the Mogul Empire, which was later consolidated and extended by Akbar.

BABUR

Babur was a Chaghatai Turk who descended from Timur through his father and from Genghis Khan through his mother. At the age of eleven, he had inherited the minor principality of Farghana, which today lies in Chinese Turkestan. His early years were difficult and his attempts to enlarge his modest realm were opposed by his cousins and by the Uzbek chief Sharbani Khan. In 1497 and in 1503 he tried unsuccessfully to annex the city of Samarkand. He ended up by being dispossessed of his own inheritance and had to wander for nearly a year. However, he never abandoned his dreams of conquest. Taking advantage of the Afghans' revolt against the Uzbeks, he managed to make himself master of the city of Kabul in 1504, whence—with the aid of Shah Ismail Safavi of Persia— he again marched in 1511 against Samarkand, and was once more checked in his enterprise.

Then he decided to turn his efforts toward the southeast and launch a series of expeditions against Indian territory. He skillfully took advantage of the hostility of certain nobles toward the court of Delhi. Called upon for aid by Daulat Khan of the Punjab, and by Alam Khan—the uncle of Ibrahim Lodi, one of the pretenders to the throne—he descended toward the Punjab and occupied Lahore in 1524. However, his allies rapidly understood the danger of his ambitions and turned against him. Babur withdrew to Kabul and there prepared his army with a view to conquest. In 1525 he attacked and occupied the Punjab, forcing Daulat Khan to submit. He marched against Delhi and—with his small well trained army of twelve thousand men—met the immense army, one hundred thousand strong, of Ibrahim Lodi in the famous Battle of Panipat. According to Babur's own remarks, his enemy "was an inexperienced soldier, whose movements were badly calculated, who marched in a disorderly manner, halted or withdrew without method, and attacked without any tactics." Thanks to his skill in maneuvers and to his artillery, Babur won the battle. Ibrahim Lodi was killed, together with his best officers. Without delay, Babur occupied the cities of Delhi and Agra.

Although the Battle of Panipat is deemed to be the Mogul Empire's starting point, Babur immediately faced redoubtable adversaries—the Afghan chiefs on one side and the Rajput nobles led by Rana Sanga on the other. The principalities of the Afghan and Rajput chiefs were practically independent, under the purely nominal suzerainty of Ibrahim Lodi. Babur first took care of getting rid of a good number of Afghan chiefs, of whom only a few partisans of the Lodi dynasty agreed to join forces with Rana Sanga.

The latter was a brave and capable man who had reorganized the Hindu Rajput clans against the weakened Muslim Empire. Without the arrival of Babur and the Mongols, he would probably have succeeded, and the history of India would have been very different. Accompanied by the princes of Marwar, Amber, Gwalior, Ajmer, and Chanderi, as well as the Sultan Mahmud Lodi, whom he had acknowledged as the legitimate sovereign of Delhi, Rana Sanga marched against Babur with an army that numbered eighty thousand horse and five hundred elephants. Babur—whose army was much smaller—estimated the danger. In front of his soldiers he broke his wine cups and vowed to take no other inebriating drink until victory was his. His speech mesmerized his troops.

The battle took place at Khanua, to the west of Agra. The Rajputs fought with heroic bravery, but Babur, using the same tactics as at Panipat, was triumphant. The Rajputs' defeat was total, despite their desperate resistance. Rana managed to escape, but died soon afterward. Babur left the Rajputs no time to recover. He crossed the Jumna and took the Chanderi fortress by assault. Following their defeat, the Rajput clans ceased to be an important factor in the political life of India for more than thirty years. Babur's Indian expedition—which could have been no more than an episode in his life—led him to take on responsibilities that were to fix his destiny there. His fortune was now established, and his future battles aimed solely at enlarging his empire. His center of activities was no longer Kabul, but Delhi. After defeating the Rajputs, Babur attacked the confederation of Afghan chiefs and inflicted a cruel defeat on them near Patna, on 6 May 1529. His empire now stretched from the Oxus to Bengal, and from the Himalayas to Gwalior.

He was not long to enjoy his success, however. He died at Agra on 26 December 1530. His body was taken to Kabul, where he was buried in his favorite garden. Legend has it that Babur's son, Humayun, had been grievously sick, and that Babur had prayed hard for the sickness to be transferred to himself. As Humayun gradually got better, Babur's health declined, and he expired shortly after his son's recovery.

He had had time only to impose himself on India by force of arms, not to organize his new states. He thus left his son an empire without any economic, legal, or political structure. The organization of the Mogul Empire was to be the work of his successors.

A soldier of fortune and a ferocious conqueror, Babur had delighted in massacres and useless destruction. Together with the Mongol's energy, he employed the sagacity of the Turk and the faith of the devout Muslim to subject and destroy the Hindu world. As often the case with cruel and bloody men, he was also an affectionate father, a good master, and a devoted friend in the close circle of his family and group. A poet, he loved music and the arts. His memoirs—written in Turki, his maternal tongue, and translated later on into Persian by Abdur Rahim Khan-i-Khanan— provide us with a historical and literary document of great worth.

HUMAYUN

Three days after the death of Babur, Humayun ascended the throne. He was twenty-three years old. The responsibilities that fell to him were staggering. He was surrounded on all sides by hostile forces. His cousins, as well as his three brothers, were all pretenders to the throne and were only waiting for the right chance to seize it. The Rajputs and the Afghans, defeated on the battlefield, had not really been subdued. The empire had no coherent administration. It needed a military genius and a skilful politician to maintain what Babur had conquered by force of arms. Humayun did not possess these virtues. A gentle and cultivated man, incapable of perseverance, he liked to shut himself up in the pleasant cloisters of the harem and inebriate himself with opium, when he should have been preparing to face his enemies. He pardoned those whom he should have punished. He was a charming companion in private life, but had none of the qualities that make a great king. Humayun's first mistake was his clemency to his brothers, whom he should have removed from power. Unable to believe their true sentiments, he made Askari governor of Sambhal, Hindal governor of Alwar, and gave Kabul and Kandahar to Kamran. The latter, after obtaining some military successes, also received the Punjab and the district of Hissar. Humayun thus prepared the disintegration of Babur's empire, and with the Punjab lost the main source of recruitment for his army.

On a military level, Humayun won some relative successes. He besieged the fortress of Kalinjar and agreed to lift the siege once he had received from the raja a considerable amount of silver. He conquered the Afghans at Durah and put the Sultan Mahmud Lodi of Jaunpur to flight. He then besieged Chunar, the fief of Sher Khan, but abandoned the siege after receiving the purely nominal submission of the Afghan chief. Turning westward, he wanted to attack Bahadur Shah of Gujarat, whose growing power worried him. Bahadur Shah—taking advantage of declining Rajput power—had annexed Malwa and besieged the famous fortress of Chitor. Queen Karnavati of Mewar had asked Humayun's aid to defend Rajputana, but Humayun refused. Bahadur Shah then took Chitor, with the help of Portuguese gunners and a Turkish engineer of Constantinople named Rumi Khan. Humayun thus lost a precious chance to regain the Rajputs' sympathies. He did attack the army of Bahadur Shah, whom he defeated close to Mandasor, and pursued him to Mandu, Champaner, and Ahmedabad, then to Cambay. Bahadur Shah finally took refuge on the isle of Diu.

Humayun's victory was not to last long. With his brother Askari and most of his officers, Humayun dreamt only of celebrating his victory with parties and sundry pleasures, to the extent that, even in his camp, no discipline was observed at all. The sultan of Gujarat took advantage of the fact and easily succeeded in retaking his lost territories. Humayun, who had to face new dangers in the east, no longer had time to deal with it. In one year he had reconquered two great provinces, only to lose them again the following year.

SHER SHAH

The Afghan chiefs, deeply hostile to the newcomers who had seized power, found in Sher Khan Sur a strong character capable of coordinating their efforts and of organizing resistance. Sher Khan's grandfather was an Afghan of the Sur tribe, who lived close to Peshawar. He had emigrated to India in quest of military adventure and had settled in the Punjab with his son Hasan. Hasan's son Farid was born in the Punjab in 1472. Hasan had found employment at Sasaram in Bihar, and took Farid with him. His father's favorite wife, however, did not like Farid, who soon quit his paternal home and launched alone on a life of risk and intrigue. At Jaunpur, he was brilliant in his studies of Persian language and literature. On the death of his father, he inherited his duties and found great favor with Bahar Khan Lohari, who gave him the title of *Sher Khan* (the Tiger Lord), after he had, alone, succeeded in killing a dangerous tiger.

Bahar Khan's entourage, however, jealous of the favor Sher Khan enjoyed, undermined his prestige with the sovereign and he was dispossessed. He then went into service with Babur, who was highly appreciative of his talents, appointing him vice-governor of Bihar and tutor to the younger son of his former patron, Bahar Khan. Sher Khan became virtually the governor of Bihar and—having won the army to his cause—proclaimed the country's independence. Taj Khan, prince of Chunar, had been assassinated by his own son. Sher Khan married the prince's widow and became master of that powerful fortress. Humayun besieged Chunar in 1531, but Sher Khan was successful in making an apparent submission in time.

When he began to have difficulties with the other Afghan chiefs, who were jealous of his success, he made an alliance with the king of Bengal, Mahmud Shah. Sher Khan conquered the confederate army at Sujargarh, close to the city of Bihar. Taking advantage of Humayun's expedition against Gujarat, he attacked Gaur, the capital of Bengal, using a by-path. Mahmud Shah preferred to make peace by ceding considerable territory and paying him a tribute of three hundred thousand gold pieces. Many of the Afghan chiefs, impressed by these successes, then joined him. Sher Khan returned to the charge and attacked Bengal, this time intent on annexing it. In October 1537 he once more besieged Gaur. Troubled, Humayun advanced against Bihar, but instead of relieving Gaur, for six months he besieged Chunar, whose garrison resisted bravely. In the meantime, Sher Khan reduced Gaur, which fell in April 1538.

Held in check at Chunar, Humayun advanced toward Bengal and entered Gaur in July 1538. Sher Khan carefully avoided any direct conflict and—while the imperial army was occupied in Bengal—himself pillaged Mogul territory in Bihar, at Jaunpur, and as far as Kanauj. Humayun (who had spent his time celebrating at Gaur) decided to return to Agra. Sher Khan and his Afghan allies took up position to bar his return. The Moguls suffered a major defeat at Chaunsa on the banks of the Ganges, close to Buxar, in June 1539. Most of the emperor's soldiers were drowned or made prisoner. Humayun himself was only saved by a water-carrier, and crossed the Ganges on inflated waterskins. Sher Khan now found himself the lord of vast lands, stretching from Kanauj to Assam and from the Himalayas to the Gulf of Bengal. He took the title of *Sher Shah* and had coins struck in his name. In the following year Humayun once again marched against him, but his army, lacking enthusiasm and badly directed, was put wholly to rout near Kanauj on 17 May 1540. Once more, Humayun managed to escape but—dispossessed of all he owned—was forced to lead the life of a vagabond for fifteen years. The empire of northern India had passed again into Afghan hands.

Babur's sons could not be persuaded to put their quarrels aside, despite the efforts of Humayun, who had taken refuge at Lahore. Sher Shah attacked the Punjab in an attempt to subdue the warrior tribes of the Gakkar country. He ravaged the land, but did not manage to subdue the Gakkars, since he was forced to hasten his return to Bengal, where the governor he had appointed had rebelled. He drove out the rebel and skillfully divided the country into districts, each governed by an officer reporting directly to himself.

Sher Shah then departed again for the west in order to attack the Rajputs. He took Malwa in 1542 and next attacked the fortress of Raisin.

The Rajputs agreed to surrender if they were given a safe-conduct to evacuate the fort. Sher Shah accepted, but the Afghans threw themselves on the besieged as they left the enceinte. Then—in accordance with their laws of chivalry—the Rajputs killed their women and children so that they would not fall into Muslim hands, and let themselves be killed to the last man. Sher Shah then succeeded in reducing Marwar, after several terrible engagements in which he lost many thousands of men. He managed to extend his sway over the whole of Rajputana, from Ajmer to Abu. He next turned against central India and succeeded in taking the fortress of Kalinjar. At the moment when his power seemed to be definitively established, he died accidentally from an explosion of cannon powder, on 22 May 1545.

During his short five-year reign, he had not only won a number of military successes, but had also undertaken major reforms in all branches of the administration. The judicious nature of his reforms has astonished historians. Many of the forms of organization he had set up or borrowed from the former Hindu empires were to last even under British domination. He systematically associated Hindu officials with the administration and did his best to create an empire that would be acceptable to the population as a whole. His agrarian reforms are the foundation of the Indian system even today. He abolished vexatious taxes and suppressed internal customs. He built roads and restored the famous "Grand Trunk Road" that runs from the east of Bengal to the Indus, connecting Calcutta, Varanasi, Delhi, and Lahore. The roads are wide, bordered with trees, and were dotted with *sarails*, or guesthouses, where travelers could stay for the night.

Sher Shah was buried in a magnificent mausoleum at Sasaram, between Varanasi and Calcutta. Without him India would never have known the reign of the "Grand Moguls." The Afghan Empire that Sher Shah had built did not, however, last long. His second son, Jalal Khan, was proclaimed king and took the title of *Sultan Islam Shah*, popularly known as "Salim Shah." Salim took ferocious measures against his elder brother, and succeeded in maintaining his power, the might of the army, and the effectiveness of the administrative reforms started by his father.

He died young, however, in 1554, and disorder was let loose. His son, still a child, was assassinated by his maternal uncle, Mubariz Khan, who seized the throne and took the name of Muhammad Adil Shah. This spineless man, despite the efforts of his capable low-caste minister, Himu, lost one province after the other and was unable to check the intrigues of Sher Shah's two nephews who laid claim to the throne.

Humayun took advantage of the situation. He had wandered miserably from place to place, ill-treated by his brothers, whose ill-will pursued him in his misfortune. He tried to obtain aid from the Rajputs, but without success. He had married a Persian and his son, Akbar, was born on 23 November 1542 at Amarkot. In the end, he petitioned the shah of Persia, Shah Tahmasp, who gave him an army of fourteen thousand men, on condition that he embrace the Shiite faith and cede Kandahar if he were successful. Humayun occupied Kandahar and Kabul in 1545. He imprisoned his brother Kamran, had his eyes put out, and sent him to Mecca, together with his second brother Askari. His last brother, Hindal, was killed one night in an ambush. In February 1555 Humayun took Lahore. He occupied Delhi and Agra in July of the same year. He had thus recovered part of his empire when he died, on 24 January 1556, from an accidental fall on the staircase of his library. Akbar, aged thirteen, was at that time in the Punjab with his tutor Bairam. He was proclaimed as Humayun's successor on 14 February 1556.

At this time, Mogul supremacy in India was far from being assured. The country rapidly lost the benefits of Sher Shah's reforms. The provinces had, in practice, become independent states once more. Furthermore, a terrible famine complicated matters. The Portuguese had settled at Goa and Diu. The Afghans continued to occupy a large part of the country. Akbar's inheritance was consequently precarious and his task difficult.

Himu, the skilful minister of Adil Shah Sur, took over command of the troops and advanced against the Moguls, with a mighty army that included fifteen hundred elephants. He occupied Delhi and Agra and met Akbar's troops on the famous battlefield of Panipat. The battle turned in his favor, but an arrow blinded him in one eye. He swooned and his soldiers dispersed in disorder. According to legend, he was killed by Akbar himself, on the advice of Bairam. Other sources say that Akbar refused and that it was Bairam who killed Himu. The conquerors soon occupied Delhi and Agra.

AKBAR

The second Battle of Panipat marked the permanent establishment of the Moguls in India. The Rajput clans were demoralized, then rallied by a skilful policy. Gwalior, Ajmer, and Jaunpur were annexed between 1558 and 1560. Akbar was still a ward of his tutor Bairam. The young and spirited emperor felt he was being bullied. His mother, Hamida Banu Begum—together with his nurse Maham Anaga and the latter's son Adam Khan—persuaded him to rid himself of his cumbersome protector. Akbar summoned Bairam, announced his dismissal, and sent him to Mecca. Bairam protested, but dared not revolt. He was killed during the journey by an Afghan whose father he had killed.

Akbar assumed full power. For two years more, however, he remained under the thumb of his nurse and Adam Khan. The latter occupied Malwa in 1561, giving himself over to such pillage and acts of cruelty that the historian Badauni condemns him in no uncertain terms. In the end, Akbar had Adam Khan killed. His mother, Maham Anaga, died of sorrow forty days later. In May 1562, at the age of twenty, Akbar freed himself from the influence of the harem and remained sole master of the empire.

Akbar's policy was one of conquest and annexation. A monarch, he said, must always make new conquests, otherwise his enemies take up arms against him. For more than forty years, he continued to annex one state after another. The key of his policy was to win an alliance with the Rajputs, the most noble and bravest warriors in India. He managed to do so, and associated them widely in government, giving them the command of major sections of the army. Akbar's empire was thus the result of coordinating skilful diplomacy with the Mongol spirit of adventure, allied with the Rajputs' courage and spirit of chivalry.

Greatly influenced by his Persian mother, Akbar had none of his predecessors' fanaticism. In his philosophy, conception of values, and religion, he was much closer to the Persian Shiites than to the strictly Sunni Arabs, Turks, and Mongols, for whom murdering the "unfaithful" was a meritorious deed. Akbar found the Rajputs a proud and difficult ally, however. Offended because Baz Bahadur, the dethroned sovereign of Malwa, had found refuge and protection at Mewar, Akbar besieged Chitor and succeeded in overcoming its resistance. The occupants let themselves be killed to the last man. The women and children submitted to the rite of *jauhar*, and threw themselves into a blazing room. According to Abul Fazl, thirty thousand persons died there.

Discouraged by the fall of Chitor, the Rajput princes submitted. The last to acknowledge the emperor's sovereignty was Raja Ramchand of Kalinjar. Possession of this renowned fortress in central India greatly strengthened Akbar's military might. The sovereigns of Bikaner and Jaisalmer even gave their daughters in marriage to the Muslim emperor, which for Hindus was quite unprecedented. The only one who would not submit was Pratap, King of Mewar. Pursued by his enemies from rock to rock, feeding his family on wild fruit, he is still a legendary hero in India—a symbol of the Rajputs' indomitable courage and spirit of chivalry. He even managed to retake some of his fortresses before dying at the age of fifty-seven on 19 January 1597.

Akbar then undertook the conquest of the rich province of Gujarat and, after several expeditions, annexed it to the empire. This province was one of the empire's most important sources of revenue and provided contact with the sea and with the Portuguese. Up to then, the Moguls had never had any relations with seafaring peoples, and their lack of interest in sea trade had greatly facilitated the intrusions of Europeans. After Gujarat, it was the turn of Bengal, against which Akbar launched several expeditions in 1575 and 1576 before managing to reduce it. Orissa was also annexed by the empire in 1592.

Afghanistan—under the turbulent government of Akbar's half-brother, Mirza Muhammad Hakim—was a perpetual danger. Akbar marched on Kabul in 1581, with fifty thousand horse, five hundred elephants, and numerous infantry divisions. Mirza Muhammad submitted and took an oath of loyalty. The emperor pardoned him and Kabul was formally annexed in 1585. Like all the governments of India, Akbar's government had to tackle the problem of the northwest frontier, the route of every invasion. Master of Kabul, he had to secure his possession of Kandahar, where the high mountains of the Hindu Kush were lower, offering an easy passage to invaders. This region was occupied by tribes that were very attached to their independence, and were on principle hostile to any dominant power. The Uzbeks and Yusufzai were a perpetual menace, as well as the Roshniyas, disciples of Bayazid, whom they considered to be the new Messiah. Their religion was based on communism and the destruction of Islam's enemies. Akbar managed to conciliate the Uzbeks and establish ties of friendship with their chief, Abdullah Khan. He defeated the Roshniyas and crushed the Yusufzai, of whom, according to Abul Fazl, many were killed and a great number sold as slaves in Turan and Persia.

Kashmir was annexed in 1586, Sind in 1591, and Baluchistan in 1595. Kandahar was a major trading center for merchandise from central Asia. Harassed by the Uzbeks, the Persian governor capitulated to Akbar's envoy in 1595. The empire's frontiers seemed henceforth to be safe.

Akbar then directed his forces toward the Deccan, in the center of the Indian peninsula. He had two aims: to subdue the sultanates of Ahmadnagar, Bijapur, Golconda, and Khandesh, and to contain the growing influence of the Portuguese. Although relations with the latter were amicable on the surface, he feared their interference in politics and also the skill with which they had drained part of India's resources. No religious fanaticism was in play, as would be the case with his successors. Akbar first attempted to establish his suzerainty through diplomacy, then sent an army against Ahmadnagar, which was defended with extraordinary bravery and will by a woman, Chand Bibi, the Queen of Bijapur. After various episodes, Chand Bibi was assassinated, and the Mogul army occupied the city in 1600. Its official annexation, however, did not take place until later, under the reign of Shah Jahan.

Akbar next attacked Khandesh. He took the capital, Burhanpur, and for six months besieged the formidable fortress of Asirgarh. He succeeded finally by ruse and treachery, and bought the defenders' submission with large sums of money. According to one of his historians, the gates of the fortress were "opened with golden keys." This was the last of Akbar's conquests. The extent of his empire was now immense, but was far from having any kind of administrative unity, and many territories had only made nominal submission. Akbar returned to Agra in May 1601. His latter years were saddened by the revolt of his only surviving son, Salim, who had proclaimed himself king at Allahabad, and had made an alliance with the Portuguese to fight against his father. Salim put to death Akbar's historian and friend, Abul Fazl. In the end, a reconciliation was arranged, but Akbar died of dysentery on 17 October 1605. He was sixty-two.

Born of a Persian mother, the daughter of a learned Sufi, Akbar had none of the fanaticism of the other emperors. His intelligence and love of the arts, his interest in the people, and his religious liberalism have made him a legendary figure, to the extent that many stories and fables—often much older—are now attributed to him. In the popular mind, he has remained the perfect sovereign, the very symbol of greatness and imperial magnanimity, as was Ashoka before him.

At Kabul, he had the chance to meet many Sufi holy men and men of letters, refugees from Persia, and had been deeply impressed by the Sufis' liberal and mystical thought, Sufi doctrine being almost identical to that of Hindu Vedanta. Through his Rajput wives, Akbar had been in close contact with Hindu mysticism. He was profoundly shocked by religious conflict. He willingly spent hours in meditation and dreamed of a new religion—a synthesis of all creeds and all human spiritual aspirations—that would help him to harmonize the discordant elements of his empire. Officially, he observed Sufi rites up to 1575. Under the influence of Sheikh Mubarak and his two sons, he had a "Temple of Religions" built at Fatehpur Sikri, where questions of philosophy and theology could be discussed. He first summoned the Islamic theologians, and was deeply shocked by the narrowness and mediocrity of their concepts, their morbid orthodoxy, and their hostility to all. He then appealed to the Hindu philosophers such as Purushottama and Devi, to the Jains—including Hari Vijaya Suri, Vijaya Sen Suri, and Bhanuchandra

Upadhyaya—to Parsi priests, and even to Christian missionaries from Goa. He was so deeply interested in their discussions that each thought he had been converted to their faith.

His new religion—expounded in the *Din-i-Ilahi*—represented an effort to attain that essence of reality that each religion approaches in a different way. This effort, at times profound, at times puerile, to seek to understand the nature of the world and the goal of religion without prejudice, required a universal tolerance. The generosity, honesty, and impartiality of his thought—that make Akbar one of the greatest spirits the world has known—have been held up to ridicule alike by Muslims and Jesuits, such as Bartoli, both furious at not having been able to convert the emperor. It appears strange that the Jesuits, as well as the Muslims, accused him of betraying Islam. In actual fact, he remained faithful to the principles of the Koran, but opposed the tradition of murder, tyranny, and conquest practiced by both Christians and Muslims under the banner of faith.

Fundamentally, Akbar was a humble man, although everything about his person breathed greatness. His son Jahangir remarks in his memoirs that "in his actions and his movements, Akbar was not as ordinary men. The glory of God was manifest in him. He knew no fear and was always ready to risk his life in battle. With exquisite courtesy, he charmed all those that approached him." He knew neither how to read nor write, but collected a vast library, and many scholars, poets, and philosophers were ordered to read to him. His culture was so wide, his memory so astonishing, and his spirit so lively that whoever spoke with him could never have imagined he was illiterate.

Unlike his predecessors, Akbar respected the institutions and feelings of the peoples he conquered. The structures of the Mogul Empire established by him were based on cooperation and the goodwill of the man of the street. He freed the Hindus—the great majority of his subjects—from the inequality and humiliation from which they had suffered since the Muslims' arrival. He suppressed discriminatory taxes on "infidels" and forbade any distinction between Muslims and non-Muslims in appointments to the more important posts throughout the empire. He was a patron of the arts and literature, and his reign was one of the most brilliant periods in Indian history.

JAHANGIR (1605–1627)

Some weeks after the death of Akbar, Salim was crowned at Agra and took the title of *Nur-ud-din Muhammad Jahangir Padshah Ghazi*. He was thirty-six. He sought to win the people's favor by means of a general amnesty for all prisoners and by highly liberal measures. He appointed as his top officials those who had supported him in his conflicts with his father. At the very beginning of his reign, Jahangir was strongly shaken by the revolt of his eldest son Khusrav, dearly loved by Akbar, who despised his father. The young prince—who was very handsome and of noble bearing—was adored by the people. Khusrav fled to the Punjab and fomented a rebellion. Jahangir marched against his son at the head of a mighty army. He was so upset that, on the very first day, he forgot to take his usual dose of opium. The rebels were easily defeated close to Jullundur. The prince and his main supporters were made prisoner. Khusrav was led before his father, during a public audience, in chains, with his feet bound. Imprisoned, he was to die sadly in 1622. His two main henchmen, Husain Beg and Abdul Aziz, were sewn into the hides of a cow and an ass and promenaded on asses, facing the tail, through the town.

The religious head of the Sikhs, Guru Arjan, was accused of having given money to the young prince. He defended himself by saying that the gift was not politically motivated, but was in accordance with his religious duties and with his gratitude toward the Emperor Akbar. Jahangir had him condemned to death and confiscated all his goods. This brutal deed was a grave political error, since it turned the Sikhs—who until then had always been a peaceful community—into dangerous enemies of the empire.

Jahangir had a complex character. An affable man who loved nature and flowers, he wished to be a just king. According to the ancient Hindu custom, he had attached to a stone pillar in front of the palace gate a chain made of tiny bells, which any citizen could ring to demand justice.

He was upset because the elephants shivered when they were washed with cold water in winter. He was a lover of women and had many love affairs, but was weak in dealing with harem intrigues. At the same time, he plotted assassinations and spoke of them without the slightest remorse; he also liked to have those that had displeased him whipped to death in his presence. Indeed, with his dreamy imagination, indecision, and insensibility, his character was typical of the opium addict. A painter, a fine connoisseur of literature and the arts, in religion his attitude was vaguely deistic and, like his father, he liked to converse with representatives of various religions. From the point of view of ritual observance, however, he remained faithful to Islam.

In 1611 Jahangir married Nur Jahan. This young woman of amazing beauty and great intelligence was—according to Mutamid Khan's *Iqbal-Nama-i-Jahangiri*—the daughter of a Persian emigrant. At seventeen, she had married a Persian adventurer, Sher-Afghan, who obtained an administrative post at Burdwan in Bengal at the outset of Jahangir's reign. The emperor's interest in Sher-Afghan's young wife was probably the cause of her husband's death. Jahangir accused Sher-Afghan of "having a tendency to rebellion," and he was cut into pieces by the emperor's soldiers. His wife, Mir-un-nisa, was brought to court with the baby daughter to whom she had just given birth. Four years later, the emperor married her and made her his principal queen. He gave her the name of *Nur Jahan* (Light of the World). The young woman's ambition knew no limits. She acquired considerable influence over the emperor, had her father and brother appointed to important posts at court, and married her daughter to Jahangir's youngest son, Prince Shahryar.

During his reign, new contacts were made between India and Europe. Jahangir won several military successes. A revolt of the Afghans of Bengal was crushed in 1612, and Jahangir's conciliating policies rallied them definitively to the empire's cause. His attitude toward the Rajputs was similar. Military successes, followed by a generous peace, turned them into allies who remained unswervingly loyal to the empire until Aurangzeb's fanaticism once more made them implacable enemies.

Jahangir conducted a vague war against the Deccan. His army lacked enthusiasm, and its leaders quarreled amongst themselves. They were opposed by a remarkable character—Malik Ambar, son of an Abyssinian slave—who, through his exceptional sagacity and capacities of organization, had become the prime minister of the Kingdom of Ahmadnagar. However, one of Jahangir's sons, Khurram, managed to occupy the city of Ahmadnagar during a military operation that had no sequel. Enchanted, Jahangir gave Khurram the title of *Shah Jahan* (King of the World) and increased his civil list. These costly and interminable operations did not, however, affect the frontiers of the Mogul Empire; they remained as they were in 1605. Jahangir's reign also saw the taking of the fortress of Kangra in the Himalayas in 1620.

The first disaster for the empire was the loss of Kandahar, annexed in 1622 by Abbas, the clever shah of Persia (1587–1629). Jahangir ordered his son Shah Jahan to retake Kandahar, but the young prince, fearing the intrigues of Nur Jahan, refused to depart. Exasperated by the queen's hostility, Shah Jahan finally fomented a rebellion against his father, which made Jahangir desist from retaking Kandahar. Shah Jahan's little army was easily beaten close to Delhi in 1623 by the imperial forces, commanded formally by his brother Parwez but in reality by the skilled general Mahabat Khan. Shah Jahan wandered in exile until he was reconciled with his father in 1625.

Mahabat Khan's success aroused the jealousy of Nur Jahan and her brother, and their intrigues led to the rebellion of this capable statesman. By means of a surprise attack, he managed to seize the emperor's person, close to the River Jhelum, as Jahangir was making his way to Kabul. Nur Jahan escaped and vainly attempted to rally the troops to free the emperor. She ended by joining him in prison, from which they escaped to join a strong army that the emperor's supporters had gathered. But her triumph was not to last long, since Jahangir died on 28 October 1627. Mahabat Khan soon rallied to Shah Jahan.

SHAH JAHAN (1628–1658)

Shah Jahan was in the Deccan when his father died. Two of his brothers, Khusrav and Parwez, were already dead, but the youngest, Shahryar, was in the north. Encouraged by Nur Jahan, Shahryar proclaimed himself emperor at Lahore. Asaf Khan, the father of Mumtaz Mahal, Shah Jahan's wife, dispatched a messenger to him, with the order to return to the north. Asaf Khan provisionally placed on the throne one of Khusrav's young sons, and marched on Lahore. He routed Shahryar's troops, made him prisoner and had him blinded. In the meantime, Shah Jahan had returned to Agra and was proclaimed emperor in February 1628. The young prince who had served as interim emperor was imprisoned and later sent to Persia. Shah Jahan "dispatched to the other world" all his potential rivals. He was later to see two of his own sons put to death, another exiled, and he himself would end his days in prison.

The reign of Shah Jahan began calmly and with optimism. He managed to crush two revolts. The more serious was by the Afghan prince Khan Jahan Lodi, who was supported by the King of Ahmadnagar and by many Maratha and Rajput chiefs. Shah Jahan finally defeated him at Tal Sehonda, to the north of Kalinjar, and had him cut into pieces, together with his two sons.

The Portuguese—who had been the beneficiaries of an imperial charter allowing them to settle in Bengal, near Satgaon, in 1579—had gradually strengthened their positions and built major settlements at Hugli, to the north of present-day Calcutta. They began practices that displeased the emperor, such as levying taxes on Indian merchants, particularly on tobacco, which had become an important item of trade. They also captured Hindu or Muslim children, converted them to Christianity and sold them as slaves. In this way they seized two young slave-girls belonging to Mumtaz Mahal, the emperor's wife. The more-or-less forced conversions practiced by Portuguese Jesuits added to Shah Jahan's fury. He ordered the Governor of Bengal to punish the Portuguese. Hugli was besieged and taken, many Portuguese were killed, and the rest led away prisoner to Agra.

Shah Jahan also wished to recover the province of Kandahar. By skilful negotiations and promises, he managed to seduce the Persian governor from his duty and open the city. The shah of Persia, Abbas II, waited for winter, when it would be difficult for the Moguls to send reinforcements, and retook the city in 1649. Shah Jahan then sent several expeditions—

first commanded by his son Aurangzeb, and then by his favorite son Dara Shukoh—but without success. These campaigns cost an enormous sum and their lack of success damaged the empire's prestige considerably. Shah Jahan dreamed of reconquering Balkh and Badakshan as well as Samarkand, the capital of his ancestor Timur, even though such an enterprise was of no interest to India. The difficulties and cost of transporting a great army through the steep passes of the Hindu Kush were almost insurmountable obstacles. Shah Jahan took no account of all that. Taking a civil war as a pretext, he sent an expedition with his son, Prince Murad, who succeeded in occupying Balkh, but fell sick and had to return to India. Aurangzeb was then sent at the head of a great army, but in the meantime the Uzbeks had organized their resistance. Aurangzeb had to withdraw to India after suffering considerable losses, owing partly to the cold and snow. This bootless expedition cost the treasury enormous sums.

Shah Jahan had greater success in the Deccan. By making use of treachery, such as buying the commanders of enemy forts, and attacking violently when necessary, in 1636 he managed to annex Khandesh, Berar, Telingana, and Daulatabad. Aurangzeb was appointed governor, but he resigned in 1644, embarrassed by the intrigues of his brother Dara Shukoh, Shah Jahan's favorite. After the Balkh campaign, he was again put in charge of the Deccan, where he reorganized both the administration and finances, aided by a very capable Persian minister, Murshid Quli Khan. Under various pretexts, Aurangzeb annexed the rich independent kingdoms of Golconda and Bijapur. In both cases, just as he was about to succeed, Shah Jahan, under the influence of Dara Shukoh, sent him orders to abandon the campaign, causing Aurangzeb great bitterness.

The last days of Shah Jahan were saddened by a terrible clash between his sons, a struggle that broke out as soon as he fell ill in September 1657. Shah Jahan had four sons: Dara Shukoh, aged forty-three; Shuja, aged forty-one; Aurangzeb, aged thirty-nine; and Murad, aged thirty-three. He also had two daughters: Jahanara, who was on Dara Shukoh's side; and Raushnara, who preferred Aurangzeb. Dara Shukoh was the emperor's favorite and chosen successor. Dara Shukoh was a liberal, a man of culture, interested in Sufism and Vedanta doctrines. Very like Akbar in his attitude and wish to respect the various religions of India, he was a suspicious character to orthodox Muslims. Aurangzeb, on the contrary, was a wily diplomat and able general, but a rigidly orthodox Sunni and a fanatical and convinced Muslim. The other brothers were far from being in the same class. Good soldiers, *bon viveurs*, and honest administrators, they could not measure themselves against Dara Shukoh and Aurangzeb.

Dara Shukoh was the only one of the four who was at Delhi when Shah Jahan fell sick. Without waiting for him to die, Shuja proclaimed himself emperor in Bengal and Murad did the same in Gujarat. The latter joined up with Aurangzeb and the two brothers made a pact to share the empire between them. They then marched on Delhi with a great army. Dara Shukoh came to meet them with fifty thousand soldiers. It happened that his elephant was wounded in the battle, which took place to the east of Agra on 29 May 1658, and his troops, believing him dead, fled in disorder. He himself fled to Agra. Aurangzeb took Agra, refusing to come to friendly terms with Shah Jahan. The dethroned emperor was imprisoned in the cruelest conditions, just like an ordinary prisoner, and deprived of any comfort. He spent his last years in prayer and meditation, in the company of his daughter Jahanara, until his death, which did not take place until eight years later, in 1666. He was seventy-four years old.

Aurangzeb had himself crowned emperor in Delhi on 21 June 1658. He then sought to eliminate his brother and ally Murad. He drew him into a trap and imprisoned him, first in the fort of Salimgarh, then in the fortress of Gwalior, where he was executed on 4 December 1661. Shuja was defeated in a battle near Allahabad in January 1659. Pursued through Bengal, he took refuge at Dacca, then in Arakan, where he disappeared, probably assassinated. Aurangzeb's eldest son, Prince Muhammad, who had joined Shuja's party, was imprisoned for life and died in 1676. The son of Dara Shukoh, Suleiman, abandoned by his soldiers, took refuge with the Hindu raja of Garhwal, in the Himalayas. The raja treated him with kindness and respect, but in the end gave him up to his enemies. This extraordinarily handsome young prince was led in chains before Aurangzeb and demanded to be put to death immediately, rather than being gradually poisoned. Aurangzeb promised that no harm would be done to him, but did not keep his word. The prince was imprisoned, and every morning his guards forced him to drink an infusion of poppy heads, called *pousta*, which causes a state of complete degradation and rapid physical decline. Suleiman died in May 1662.

When Aurangzeb took Agra, Dara Shukoh fled to Lahore, where he sought to organize resistance in the Punjab. A month later, Aurangzeb took Lahore. Dara Shukoh took refuge at Multan, then at Gujarat, then Rajputana, and lastly in Afghanistan. His wife, Nadira Begum, died on the journey. The Afghan chief whose life Dara Shukoh had saved betrayed him and delivered him to his enemies, with his two daughters and his second son, Siphir Shukoh. Dara was promenaded as a prisoner through the streets of Delhi, riding a small mud-stained elephant. The French physician François Bernier, who witnessed the scene, recounts that the whole people lamented and wept, as though a calamity had fallen on the land. Aurangzeb had Dara Shukoh judged by the Muslim priests, who condemned him as a heretic. Dara was beheaded and buried in a corner of Humayun's tomb.

AURANGZEB ALAMGIR (1658–1707)

Aurangzeb's long reign falls into two parts. During the first, from 1658 to 1681, he was busy organizing northern India. In the second, he moved to the Deccan with his court and government. Moving the imperial power southward was to have disastrous results. The emperor's remoteness, together with his fanaticism, plunged India into chaos. In the Deccan itself, the rising nationalism of the Marathas did not allow him to establish calm and security. Aurangzeb had himself crowned twice. The first hasty coronation took place in July 1658, after his occupation of Agra, while the second, with much pomp and solemnity, was held in June 1659. He took the titles of *Alamgir* (World Conqueror), *Padshah* (Emperor), and *Ghazi* (Leader of the Holy War).

The Ahoms, a people of Mongol origin from the north of Burma, had, since the thirteenth century, gradually extended their influence over the Brahmaputra valley, Assam, and part of Bengal. Their capital was Garhgaon. The Ahoms had become Hinduized and had adopted Hindu customs and habits. In 1658 they had occupied Gauhati and seized a considerable store of arms, horses, and sundry goods belonging to the Mogul government. Worried by their expansion, Aurangzeb dispatched the governor of Bengal, Mir Jumla, against them with a considerable army. The Ahoms offered little resistance and allowed their capital to be occupied, allowing the Muslims to seize much booty. They did, however, organize guerrilla warfare and ceaselessly harassed the imperial army. The region has the heaviest rainfall in the world and an unhealthy climate, and the Muslim soldiers were slowly decimated by disease. Mir Jumla himself died in 1663. Thus, in men and materials, the cost of this apparently easy victory was enormous. A few years later, the Ahoms retook the area.

Mir Jumla's successor undertook to eliminate the Portuguese pirates operating in the Gulf of Bengal, annexing the island of Sondip that served them as a base. He also took Chittagong from the King of Arakan, who had made an alliance with the Portuguese.

The turbulent tribes of Afghanistan and the northwestern frontier—being incapable of organizing a stable agriculture and a productive economy—lived mainly on expeditions against the rich cities of the northwest Punjab. Aurangzeb sent several armies against them, with varying success. The Afridis, led by their chief Akmal Khan, had risen in 1672. Gradually the Khattaks and all the other Pathans joined them in a general revolt. In the end, Aurangzeb himself had to take command of a major expedition to eliminate this perpetual danger. By means of gifts, posts, and skillfully distributed privileges, he managed to buy the principal Afghan chiefs, employing arms only against recalcitrants. When he returned to Delhi in 1675, he appointed as governor of Afghanistan Amin Khan, a shrewd man who managed to ensure the neutrality of certain clans by means of subsidies, and by setting the tribes against each other. The Khattak hero Khush-hal continued fighting for several years, but was finally given up to the Moguls by his own son. The pacification of Afghanistan was extremely costly, and its indirect impact was negative for the empire. It deprived the army of its main source of recruitment, and of its best soldiers—the Afghans—of whom the emperor had urgent need to fight the Rajputs. The Maratha chief, Shivaji—taking advantage of the fact that most of the Mogul army was occupied in the northwest—made triumphal raids through Golconda, the Karnataka country, Bijapur, and Raigarh in 1675 and 1676.

Aurangzeb was first and foremost a Sunni Muslim, and as such belonged to the formalistic, puritan, and intransigent section of Islam. Having won the throne as the champion of strict orthodoxy against the liberal Dara Shukoh, he always preferred to sacrifice the empire's material interests in order to maintain the rigor of his religious policy. He did his best to ensure the strict application of Koranic law, which recommends holy war against infidels and their forced conversion to Islam. He imposed on his entire entourage the gloomy gravity of puritan living and the strictest observation of religious rules. He appointed censors of public morals, threw astronomers and artists out of his court, forbade most festivals and ceremonies and the practice of the arts, particularly music. The former court musicians, whom no one dared employ, sought to draw the emperor's attention to their miserable plight by organizing a funeral procession that passed, lamenting, in front of the palace balcony. When Aurangzeb demanded to know who they were grieving for, the musicians replied, "Music, killed by your orders, for which we, its children, are grieving." The emperor's reply was: "I admire your piety. Dig it a tomb so deep that it will never rise again." He forbade the production, sale, and use of wine and *bhang* (a beverage made with Indian hemp or hashish). Dancers and public women were expelled from the kingdom. "Indecent" songs, processions, and merry-making ceased to be tolerated. From 1663, the practice of sati was forbidden. In 1679 the sultan reordered the heavy tax, the *jitya*, to be paid by non-believers.

By identifying the interests of the Muslim faith with those of his lands—in a country as diversified as India, where the Muslims were a minority—Aurangzeb made a serious mistake. He made the Mogul monarchy highly unpopular and was the main cause of the decline and fall of the empire. The first revolt against religious oppression was by the

Jats of the Mathura region in 1669. Their chief Gokla was put to death and the members of his family forcefully converted to Islam, but this did not change matters. In 1688 another revolt occurred and its leader, Rajaram, was also killed. In 1691, after the death of Aurangzeb, a powerful resistance, led by Churaram, was organized against the Moguls. There was another revolt in Bundelkhand (the region of Khajuraho), led by the Bundela Prince Chhatrasal. Chhatrasal's father had already revolted against Aurangzeb and had committed suicide to avoid being imprisoned. From 1671 onward, Chhatrasal was the champion of Bundelkhand freedom. He managed to establish an independent kingdom in eastern Malwa with Panna as its capital, where he died in 1731. The revolt by the Satnamis, in the region of Patiala and Alwar, had a less happy outcome. They were peasant monks, unskilled in the art of war. They were easily overcome by the Mogul army and systematically massacred almost to the last man, leaving the region depopulated.

THE SIKHS

Guru Nanak, the founder of the Sikh religion, died in 1538. He preached the fundamental unity of all religions and wished to harmonize the material and spiritual aspects of life. His disciple, Angad, succeeded him from 1538 to 1552, and after him came Armadas, from 1552 to 1574. The next religious head of the Sikhs was Ramdas, from 1574 to 1581. Akbar, who greatly admired the latter, donated some land with a spacious lake at Amritsar, where the Sikhs' famous temple was built. The fifth Guru, Arjan Mal (1581–1606), composed the Sikhs' holy book, the *Adi Grantha*, collecting the teachings of his predecessors together with poems composed by Hindu and Muslim saints. Arjan put the finances of the Sikh church on a sound footing by tithing the faithful. His wealth and influence were the main reasons that led Jahangir to put him to death. Arjan's son, Har Govinda, was his successor from 1606 to 1645. Imprisoned for twelve years at Gwalior for refusing to pay the fines that his father had been condemned to pay, he organized the Sikh community on a military basis. He managed to defeat the army of Shah Jahan in

1628, but then had to take refuge in Kashmir, where he died in 1645, after naming as his successor the youngest of his grandsons, Har Rai (1645–1661), who in turn was succeeded by his son Har Kishan (1661–1664).

Tel Bahadur, who succeeded him, opposed the religious measures promulgated by Aurangzeb. Brought to Delhi, he was offered the choice between conversion to Islam and death. He chose death and, according to the inscription of his statue, "he gave his head but did not give the essential" (*sira diya, sara na diya*). His son and successor, Guru Govinda, was a remarkable organizer and established the Sikh laws and rites as they exist today, including baptism with water stirred by a dagger and the duty of wearing five articles beginning with the letter *K:* long hair (*kesha*), a comb (*kangha*), a sword (*kripana*), shorts (*kachcha*), and an iron bracelet (*kara*). After their baptism, the Sikhs receive the title of *Singh* (lion). In battle they must never turn their back on the enemy. Guru Govinda composed a supplement to the Sikhs' holy book, called *Dasvain Padshah ka Grantha* (The Book of the Tenth Sovereign). He played an important role in politics and in the revolts against Aurangzeb. He supported the claims of Aurangzeb's third son, Bahadur Shah, to the throne, and followed him to the Deccan, where a fanatical Afghan assassinated him on the bank of the River Godavari.

THE RAJPUTS

Since the time of Akbar, the Rajputs had been faithful allies of the Mogul Empire. But Aurangzeb's Muslim fanaticism and particularly the "tax on the infidel" that he levied made them indignant. In 1678—taking advantage of the death of Jaswant Singh, the raja of Marwar (Jodhpur)—Aurangzeb annexed Marwar and appointed to it his own administrators. He recognized a nephew of Jaswant Singh as a purely nominal sovereign. In February 1679, Ajit Singh, the posthumous son of Jaswant Singh, was born at Lahore. Aurangzeb proposed to recognize his rights if he became a Muslim. This proposal roused the indignation of the Rajput princes so much that they vowed to sacrifice their lives rather than accept the domination of the Mogul emperor. A long series of struggles ensued, in which the imperial army occupied the towns and sacked them, while the populations—who had withdrawn into the mountains and the desert—attacked them ceaselessly and carried off their supply convoys. Prince Akbar, Aurangzeb's son, was profoundly opposed to his father's policy and, dreaming of recreating a Hindu and Muslim unity, he joined the Rajputs. He went to the court of the Maratha king, Shambhuji.

In the end, the exhausted imperial armies had to give up the struggle and the emperor signed a peace treaty with Mewar (Udaipur). The war with Marwar continued, however, for more than thirty years until, after the death of Aurangzeb, his son Bahadur Shah recognized Ajit Singh as raja of Marwar in 1709. Through his ambitious and clumsy policy, Aurangzeb had lost his best allies, the only ones that could help him to contain the Afghans on the border.

THE DECCAN

During the first part of his reign, Aurangzeb took little notice of the Deccan, leaving it to his governors. Neither had he measured the importance of the growing nationalism and Maratha power. After the death of Shivaji in 1680 and the flight of Prince Akbar to his successor, Shambhuji, whom Aurangzeb called "the infernal son of an infernal father," the emperor decided to put the affairs of the Deccan in order. He left Ajmer and reached Burhanpur in 1682. He was full of enthusiasm, not understanding that he was about to dig his empire's grave. For the first four years, he attacked the Marathas, trying unsuccessfully to seize Prince Akbar. Turning to the sultanates, Aurangzeb managed to obtain the capitulation of Bijapur, exhausted by famine after one-and-a-half years of siege, from April 1685 to September 1686. The first thing Aurangzeb did was to destroy the wonderful frescoes and paintings in the palace. The city was devastated and never recovered.

In February 1687 Aurangzeb attacked Golconda. The siege of the citadel lasted eight months, and the imperial troops suffered greatly from disease and incessant guerrilla attacks. The emperor finally had recourse to treachery. For a considerable sum, he managed to buy an Afghan officer in the service of the sultan of Golconda, and the officer opened the main gate. The sultan of Golconda was sent to the fortress of Daulatabad, with a pension, and the empire annexed Golconda. However, the annihilation of the Deccan sultanates was entirely to the Marathas' advantage, since it eliminated their local rivals. Turning against the Marathas, Aurangzeb initially had some success. Raigarh was occupied and Shambhuji executed on 11 March 1689. His children and family were imprisoned.

In the following few years Aurangzeb extended his conquests southward, forcing the Hindu kingdoms of Tanjore and Trichinopoly to pay tribute. In 1690 Aurangzeb seemed to be at the peak of his power, with an empire stretching from Kabul to Chittagong, and from Kashmir to southern India. Indeed, the empire had become too vast for a hated sovereign, with neither allies nor friends. His enemies were rising everywhere, and he could punish them but not reduce them. From the distant Deccan, he could not control northern India, where the administration was corrupt. Everywhere the local chiefs were defying the authority of the central power, and all was disorder and tumult. Culture and the arts seemed to have been abolished. Of Aurangzeb's reign there remains neither a monument nor a work of art, nor a single manuscript of any interest. The treasury was emptied by his incessant and interminable wars. The soldiers were badly paid and mutinied on all sides. In the end, the emperor's only financial resource was the revenues from Bengal that were sent regularly by its governor who had remained faithful to Aurangzeb. The court awaited the arrival of the messenger from Bengal with understandable impatience.

The Marathas reorganized and began harassing the emperor's troops. In his last years Aurangzeb saw his empire founder. He proposed to share it with his rebel sons, but they refused. He wrote pathetic letters to his son Azani, "I came into this world alone, and I shall leave it alone. I have not done any good for the country, nor for the people, and I have nothing to hope from the future." Aurangzeb died on 3 March 1707 at Ahmadnagar. His body was carried to Daulatabad and buried close to the tomb of the famous Muslim saint, Burhan-ud-din.

If holiness consists of the rigorous and inhuman keeping of religious rules and of propagating them by any means, Aurangzeb was a saint. If, on the other hand, holiness consists of respecting the work of the Creator and of all the paths that lead to him, Aurangzeb was merely an odious and cruel fanatic.

THE MARATHAS

The Marathas had played an important role in medieval India, but had lost their independence under Ala-ud-din. It was not until the seventeenth century that they managed to organize themselves as an independent state. Shivaji was the hero of the Maratha union. The city of Pune is the center of the Maratha country, or Maharashtra, which, protected by its mountains and rivers, is very difficult to conquer. The bad rough ground, lack of rain, and the harshness of the climate there help to make the Marathas a hardy and vigorous people. Holy men—Ekanath, Tukaram, Ramdas Samarth, and Vaman Pandit—had for centuries preached a doctrine of piety, divine love, and the equality of mankind, a doctrine which helped the Marathas become a united people, without caste distinctions. Ramdas, the tutor of Shivaji, made a deep impression on his contemporaries, owing to his ideal of social reforms and of national renewal. Language too was a bond between the Marathas. A considerable amount of literature in the Marathi tongue, mostly of religious inspiration, developed in the fifteenth and sixteenth centuries.

Shahji, Shivaji's father, had served in the armies of the sultan of Ahmadnagar, and had reached an important position there. After the annexation of Ahmadnagar by Shah Jahan, Shahji entered the service of Bijapur in 1636, and had received an important land grant located in Karnataka country, in addition to what he already owned near Pune. Shivaji was born in 1627 or 1630, close to Junnat. His father had remarried and had left Shivaji's mother, so Shivaji was raised by a Brahman called Dadaji Khondev. His mother's heroic character, intelligence, and noble feelings had a profound influence on the career of Shivaji, who was raised to be a brave and adventurous soldier, anxious to free his country from foreign tyranny. Through his father, he descended from the Rajputs of Mewar, and through his mother, from the Yadavas of Devagiri. He lived among the rude mountaineers of the Malwa country, who became his faithful companions and best soldiers.

In 1646 Shivaji took the fortress of Torna, near which he built the fort of Raigarh. He then took over several other forts belonging to various principalities, either by force, ruse, or money. In the end he controlled a considerable territory. His first conflict with the Moguls took place in 1657. He was obliged to make his submission to them, at the same time as Adil Shah of Bijapur. Shivaji then turned to the north of Konkan. He took Kalyan (near present-day Mumbai), Bhiwandi, and Mahuli, thus stretching his domains southward as far as Mahad.

With the aim of putting an end to the growing might of Shivaji, the sultan of Bijapur sent a strong army in 1659, commanded by Afzal Khan, with the order to bring Shivaji back alive or dead. Unable to get him to leave his fortress, Afzal Khan proposed a peace treaty and invited him to a conference. Aware of Afzal's intentions, Shivaji put on armor under his robes. When Afzal attempted to strike him with a dagger while embracing him, Shivaji slashed him and killed him with the steel claws of his gauntlets, called "tiger's claws" (*bagh-nakh*). Shivaji's partisans then attacked the Muslim camp and its leader's private army dispersed. Shivaji next took Kholapur. This time, however, he had to face the imperial army. Aurangzeb occupied Pune and hunted down the Marathas of Kalyan. Guerrilla warfare ensued, lasting two years. Shivaji gave proof of his speed, audacity, and sense of adventure, which demoralized and routed the imperial army and made him a prototype of the people's hero, a "superman." In April 1663, with a few partisans, he secretly entered the harem of the Mogul governor, Shasta Khan, in the very middle of the Muslim camp at Pune. He cut off the governor's thumb, killed his son, the captain of his guards, and six of the harem women, then withdrew in the same way as he had come.

In 1664 Shivaji attacked and took the rich port of Surat. The Mogul governor fled. Shivaji pillaged the city and carried away an enormous booty. Only the Dutch and English settlements were able to resist him and avoid pillage. Aurangzeb sent two of his most skilful generals—the raja of Amber, Jai Singh, and Dilir Khan—who carried out a series of operations and managed to encircle Shivaji's territories with enemies. Besieged in his capital, Shivaji had to accept a treaty on 22 June 1665, by which he ceded more than half his fortresses to the Moguls and promised a contingent of five thousand horse for the Mogul army.

Jai Singh did his best to persuade Shivaji to come to the court at Agra, promising him great honors and guaranteeing his safety. Shivaji had a naïve desire to see the splendors of the court and the emperor in person. Encouraged by his courtiers and his astrologers, he reached Agra on 9 May 1666. Aurangzeb received him coldly and placed him among the ranks of minor nobles in command of five thousand men. Humiliated, Shivaji accused the emperor of breaking his word and swooned. He was put under surveillance and found himself a prisoner. He never lacked stratagems, however. Pretending that he had to send gifts of fruit and cakes to the Brahmans and nobles every evening by way of thanking the gods for having been healed of his pretended illness, he waited for his guards to relax their vigilance. He and his son then hid in the baskets of fruit and escaped from Agra. Disguised as a beggar and taking a roundabout route, he reached home on 30 November 1666, having left his son in the care of a Brahman at Mathura.

For three months, he stayed relatively quiet, busy organizing his estates. Aurangzeb sanctioned his use of the title of *Raja*. However, the war was to begin again in 1670. Shivaji retook almost all the forts he had ceded in 1665. In October 1670 he again sacked the port of Surat and beat the Mogul generals on all fronts. On 16 June 1674 he crowned himself king of Raigarh in the midst of splendid ceremonies, and took the title of *Chhatrapati* (Lord of the Parasol, meaning King of Kings). Shivaji availed himself of the cooperation of the sultan of Golconda and, in 1677, conquered Genji, close to Pondicherry, and Vellore. He died at the height of his success, on 14 April 1680, at the age of fifty-three. His lands then stretched from the region of Madras to Bombay, including a large part of the modern state of Karnataka. Many ports, however, were in the hands of new powers from the West, who were apparently only interested in trade. Among these were the Portuguese, the Dutch, the English, the Ethiopians, and, more recently, the French. This was the case, in particular, of Daman, Salsette, Bassein, Chaul, Goa, and Bombay. Janjira was in Ethiopian hands. Shivaji did not disturb them.

Shivaji was an astonishingly gifted conqueror, as well as an excellent organizer and administrator, and a liberal and enlightened sovereign. His council of eight ministers was remarkably effective. A viceroy, also assisted by eight ministers, governed each province. His agrarian reforms greatly improved agricultural productivity and the conditions of the peasants. Over the regions that were not under direct Maratha control, Shivaji levied a special tax called the *chauth*, on payment of which the territory was not vexed by Maratha soldiers.

The army was carefully organized and remained in a constant state of alert. It comprised ten thousand foot soldiers, forty thousand horse, twelve hundred and sixty elephants, three thousand camels, and considerable artillery, bought from the French at Surat. A great war fleet had also been built up. No woman, whether married, a prostitute, or a dancer, was allowed to accompany the army. Shivaji united the Marathas, who until then had been scattered, and made a powerful nation of them, despite the opposition of four great powers—the Mogul Empire, the sultan of Bijapur, the Portuguese, and the Ethiopians at Janjira. The Marathas were to become the dominant power in India in the eighteenth century, disputing the empire with the English, until they were crushed by Lord Hastings. With unpolished customs, and respectful of holy places, other religions, and women's honor, the Marathas dreamt of giving control over their own country back to the Hindus. They would have succeeded had it not been for the intervention of the British as allies of the Muslims.

Shambhuji, Shivaji's son and successor, was a pleasant man, more interested in his amusements than in state business. During his reign, the Marathas' spirit of adventure lost its dash. Shambhuji was a brave man, however, and valiantly fought the considerable army that Aurangzeb led into the Deccan. Lacking foresight, he was taken by surprise and made prisoner by one of the emperor's best officers. With him were captured, on 11 February 1689, his minister, the Brahman Kavi-Kulash, and twenty-five of his most important generals. Shambhuji and Kavi-Kulash were brought to the imperial camp at Bahadurgarh. The prisoners were promenaded through the town, disguised as clowns, and were subjected to all kinds of indignities. They were tortured, meticulously and ferociously, for over three weeks to make them reveal where the Marathas' treasure was hidden. After this, their limbs were cut off, piece by piece, and thus they died, on 11 March 1689. Mogul troops occupied most of the Maratha fortresses, and their capital Raigarh capitulated. The Muslims seized Shambhuji's whole family, including his baby son Shahu. However, the youngest of Shambhuji's brothers, Rajaram, managed to escape, disguised as a beggar. After many adventures, he reached Genji, close to Pondicherry, which had been annexed by Shivaji in 1677.

The Maratha Empire seemed to have been crushed, but the spirit that Shivaji had infused into the Marathas was not tamed. The whole people, under the various local chiefs, took part in incessant guerrilla warfare against the imperial army. Daring groups harassed the Muslim troops and their raids penetrated even inside the emperor's camp. Against these unforeseen initiatives, every strategy seemed vain. In order to be left in peace, many of the local governors ended up paying considerable tribute to the Marathas.

Aurangzeb's troops besieged Genji for eight years. The fortress was finally taken in January 1698, but Rajaram had escaped and, returning to Satara, he assembled a strong army. Satara was besieged in turn and surrendered only on 12 March 1700, after Rajaram's death. The emperor in person occupied one after another of the Maratha fortresses, but what he took one day was retaken the next, and the imperial army was worn out by this interminable game. Rajaram's widow, Tara Bai, took over the command as regent for her son, Shivaji III. With great competence, she succeeded in reorganizing the administration and in smoothing over disputes between the supporters of the various contenders. Her own party favored Shivaji III. The party of Rajaram's other wife, Rajas Bai, favored the latter's son, Shambhuji II. There was also a party that was faithful to Shahu, the son of Shambhuji I. Tara Bai sent out commandos to pillage the provinces held by the Moguls. In 1703 the rebels devastated Berar, in 1706, Gujarat.

Baroda was sacked. In May 1706 a small Maratha army attacked the imperial camp at Ahmadnagar and was only driven back with great difficulty. According to a historian of the time, Bhimsen, "the Marathas controlled the whole kingdom completely and blocked the roads. By theft and pillage, they escaped poverty and acquired great assets."

The Marathas had modernized their army. They now possessed artillery and rifles, bought from the Europeans, as well as bows, arrows, camels, and elephants. Their equipment was not at all inferior to that of the Mogul army. They were elusive and Aurangzeb's efforts to crush them proved useless. The Maratha people were about to become a power against which Aurangzeb's weak successors could do nothing.

In his will Aurangzeb advised his three sons to divide up the empire, but they preferred to fight it out. In the internecine struggles that ensued, Azam, who governed Gujarat, and Kam Bakhsh, who reigned over Bijapur, were defeated and killed. Mu'azzam, who had been Governor of Kabul, ascended the throne in 1708 and took the title of *Bahadur Shah*, though he is more widely known by the name of Shah Alam I. He died in 1712, and his four sons fought among themselves to win power. Three of them were killed and the survivor, Jahandar Shah, proclaimed himself emperor. Shortly afterward, he was deposed and strangled in the fort at Delhi by his nephew Farrukhsiyar, who was crowned emperor in 1713.

Farrukhsiyar was an undecided man, cowardly and characterless, and showed no gratitude toward his two ministers, Abdullah and Hussain Ali, who had helped him to power. Furious, they deposed him in turn, blinded him, imprisoned him in frightful conditions as a common criminal, and finally put him to death.

The two ministers then placed on the throne two brothers, Rafi-ud-Darajat and Rafi-ud-Daulat. Then—in the belief that they had found a more obedient puppet—they crowned an eighteen-year-old, Roshan Akhtar, the grandson of Bahadur Shah, who took the name of Muhammad Shah and reigned from 1717 to 1748. The young sovereign was not as docile as the two ministers had expected. He made an alliance with Nizam-ul-Mulk, viceroy of the Deccan, and with his aid assassinated Hussain Ali. Shortly afterward, in 1720, he succeeded in imprisoning Abdullah, and had him poisoned in 1722. Nizam-ul-Mulk refused the post of vizier and preferred to go back to the Deccan, where he set up a government in what was a virtually independent kingdom.

Muhammad Shah, young and remarkably handsome, led a life of pleasure, took an interest in the arts, and was a patron of musicians. Many songs now belonging to the great classical repertory are dedicated to him. He was, however, totally uninterested in state business. During his long reign, the empire disintegrated, province after province proclaiming its independence. The invasion by the shah of Persia, Nadir Shah, gave a terrible blow to the tottering empire of Delhi.

NADIR SHAH

Nadir Shah came from a modest family. His parents were clan chieftains living principally on brigandage. Raised among adventures, dangers, and privations, he was intelligent, shrewd, and intrepid. The Afghans had dethroned Shah Hussain, of the Safavid dynasty, in 1722. Nadir Shah helped Shah Tahmasp, Shah Hussain's son, to recover the throne in 1727. The new shah was incompetent and Nadir became, in practice, the real sovereign. He deposed Shah Tahmasp in 1732 and—since Shah Tahmasp's son and heir was dead—became the ruler of Iran.

The corrupt and decadent Mogul Empire was a tempting dish for any invader. India, with its legendary riches, excited the cupidity of all neighboring countries. The defense systems on the northwest side were in disarray, and appeals for aid from the governors of the frontier provinces met with no answer from the central government, split among factions snarling over the remainders of power. Nadir Shah began his march on India in 1738, on the pretext that Muhammad Shah had not kept his promises and had badly treated the Iranian ambassadors to Delhi. In 1739 Nadir took Ghazni, Kabul, and Lahore without difficulty, throwing the Punjab into total confusion.

Muhammad Shah and his drawing-room courtiers only started worrying when the Persian armies approached Delhi. The imperial army, assembled in haste, faced the Persians at Karnal, near Panipat, a few kilometers from Delhi. The Mogul troops were easily routed and the emperor, virtually a prisoner, sued for peace. Nadir the conqueror and the humiliated Muhammad entered Delhi together, and Nadir installed himself in Shah Jahan's palace. For a while everything went calmly, but rumors that Nadir was dead caused tumults among the people and many Persian soldiers were killed.

In a fury, Nadir ordered the massacre of all the inhabitants of Delhi. For a week, the Persian soldiers killed all the men they could seize, whether Hindu or Muslim. They led the women away into slavery and burned the houses. Nadir had the corn reserves sealed and guarded and sent detachments to pillage the villages, so as to starve any survivors. The chief nobles and merchants were tortured to obtain ransoms. After a week, Nadir put a halt to the massacre. He left a diminished throne to Muhammad Shah and departed, carrying away an immense treasure, including all the crown jewels together with the Koh-i-nur diamond, the peacock throne, and a famous illustrated manuscript on music written by order of Muhammad Shah. In addition—according to the account of Nadir's secretary—one hundred and fifty million gold rupees were taken, together with furnishings and precious articles, three hundred elephants, ten thousand horses, and the same number of camels. His soldiers too took with them an enormous booty. Persia annexed the provinces beyond the Indus (Sind, Kabul, and western Punjab).

Nadir Shah returned to Persia, but was assassinated in 1747. After his death, an Afghan chief, Ahmad Shah Abdali, succeeded in forging an independent kingdom in Afghanistan. He launched a series of raids on India, not for the purpose of conquest, but rather to affirm his own power and increase his treasury. An initial expedition in 1748 to the Punjab met with little success. A second expedition in 1750, however, allowed Ahmad to settle there permanently. He then seized Kashmir in 1751 and forced the son of Muhammad Shah to cede the territories to the west of Sirhind to him. In 1756 in the reign of Alangir II, Imad-ul-Mulk—the all-powerful vizier of Delhi—retook the Punjab and installed a governor there. Ahmad Shah Abdali invaded India again in November 1756, reaching Delhi in January 1757. The imperial city was once more pillaged.

In the years that followed, the Punjab was no more than a battlefield, where not only the Afghans and Moguls faced each other, but also the Jats, the Marathas, and the Sikhs. It was indeed at that time that the Sikhs managed to assert themselves as a major power in the Punjab. The last expedition of Ahmad Shah Abdali in 1767 was a stalemate. He had to withdraw hastily, having to deal with mutinies in his own army.

THE LAST "EMPERORS"

On the death of Muhammad Shah in 1748, his son Ahmad Shah succeeded him. A weak man, he was incapable of struggling with the forces that were disintegrating the empire, and it was soon reduced to the district surrounding the city of Delhi. Ahmad Shah was deposed in 1754 by his minister Ghazi-ud-din-Imad-ul-Mulk, who had his eyes put out. Imad-ul-Mulk then placed on the throne a great-grandson of Aurangzeb, the son of Jahandar Shah, Aziz-ud-din, who until then had lived in prison. He took the glorious title of *Alamgir*, which had been borne by Aurangzeb. He made enormous efforts to free himself of his powerful minister, but failed, and Imad-ul-Mulk had him executed. The successor of Aziz-ud-din, Shah Alam II, finally put himself under the protection of the English, who provided him with a pension up to his death in 1806. His son Akbar II lived at Delhi with the title of Emperor until 1837. After him, the last of the Moguls—Bahadur Shah—was deported by the English to Rangoon, where he died in 1862.

THE HINDU POLITICAL RENAISSANCE

The eighteenth century saw the awakening of the Hindu world against Muslim domination. This awakening did not, however, take the form of a restoration of traditional hierarchical society. Resistance to the Muslims was popular, and entire populations organized themselves to oppose Muslim tyranny. The peoples that played an active role were mainly the Rajputs, Sikhs, Jats, and Marathas.

A people of the desert, the Rajputs are first and foremost warriors. In the Hindu world, they symbolize all the ideals of chivalry, honor, and bravery. Their main states are those of Mewar (Udaipur), Marwar (Jodhpur) and Amber (Jaipur). Akbar managed to win their cooperation but Aurangzeb turned them into enemies of the Mogul Empire. After the death of the emperor, they began to coordinate their resistance, and Bahadur Shah, worried by the Sikh rising, did his utmost to make them every concession so as to obtain their cooperation, or at least their neutrality. Ajit Singh, ruler of Jaipur, was able to avoid direct conflict with the Moguls, and even gave one of his daughters in marriage to the Muslim emperor. Taking advantage of the party struggle at the Mogul court, the Rajput princes obtained important administrative posts for themselves. Ajit Singh was Governor of Ajmer and Gujarat. Under the reign of Muhammad Shah, Jai Singh II of Jaipur became Governor of Surat, then of Agra. The Rajputs thus controlled all the territory to the south of Delhi as far as the ports of Gujarat. The result of a shrewd policy, their position still remained dangerous, and cruel disillusionment was in store for them.

After the assassination of Guru Govinda by an Afghan in 1708, the Sikhs had found a head in the person of a certain Banda. He raised a ferocious insurrection against the Muslims, but was in the end captured and brought to Delhi, where he was put to death by being trampled on by elephants. The Sikhs had, however, become aware of their strength and unity. The principles clearly laid down by Guru Nanak and Guru Govinda had taken hold of the people's soul. Both peasant and worker, deeply attached to their faith, only awaited the right moment to take revenge. They made use of the period of disorder that followed Nadir Shah's invasion to increase their resources and develop their military potential. After the last invasion by Ahmad Shah Abdali, they took over effective control of the whole Punjab region, where they formed a majority.

The Jats were a popular warrior community, considered to be low-caste, and were thought to be of Scythian origin. Until the middle of the eighteenth century, they were not an organized group. Many Jat villages were scattered over a vast area to the south and east of Delhi. Their leaders were village headmen, and their society was strictly egalitarian. Up to then there had been no Jat state or Jat kings. They were regarded rather as robber bands and pillagers. Toward the end of Aurangzeb's reign, groups of Jats—under leaders such as Rajaram, Bhajja, and Churaman—launched pillaging raids in the area of Delhi and Agra, and became a force to be contended with among all those that faced them.

The scattered groups of Jats were united, with some difficulty, by a forceful and enterprising man, Badan Singh, the nephew of Churaman. Badan managed to extend his fief of Bharatpur and to establish his authority over all the districts of Agra and Mathura. He died in 1756. He adopted son and successor, Suraj Mal, a wise and clever man, extended Bharatpur's writ over the districts of Agra, Dholpur, Mainpuri, Hathras, Aligarh, Etawah, Meerut, Rohtak, Farrukhnagar, Mewat, Rewari, Gurgaon, and Mathura. By the time of his death in 1763, the Jats had become a very sizeable power.

In 1707 after the death of Aurangzeb, Azam Shah—on the advice of his shrewd minister Zulfiqar Khan—freed Shivaji II, better known by the name of Shahu, thinking thereby to provoke a dynastic crisis and dissension among the Marathas. This duly happened, but in the end Shahu was the victor, owing largely to the counsels of a Brahman called Balaji Visvanath. In 1713 Shahu appointed this Brahman as his *Peshwa*, or prime minister. The Peshwa gradually became the true head of state, while the ruler had a purely honorific role. The post of Peshwa became hereditary, thus creating a diarchy, a practice that seems to have given good results in India. Until recently, this was also the case in Nepal.

Balaji Visvanath was able to draw major advantages from the disorganization of the Mogul Empire. In 1714 he signed a treaty with the emperor's representative in the Deccan, by which Shahu took back all the territories that had belonged to Shivaji, as well as those that had since been conquered by the Marathas, and also annexed the provinces of Khandesh, Gondwana, and Berar. Most of the taxes levied in the Deccan were collected by Shahu, who, in exchange, had to provide fifteen thousand horsemen for the imperial army, pay a million rupees annually to the treasury, and ensure that order was maintained in the Deccan. This treaty clearly acknowledged the emperor's suzerainty and in this sense was contrary to the spirit of independence that had animated Shivaji. On the

other hand, it gave enormous practical advantages and the Marathas'
presence in Delhi as partners and allies could give them the chance to
seize the empire, should such a chance arise.

On the death of Balaji Visvanath, his son Baji Rao I succeeded him
as Peshwa. Baji Rao I launched a series of adventures northward, using,
as his order of the day, *Hindu-Pad-Padshahi*, "the Hindu Empire." He
invaded Malwa in 1723, everywhere supported by the minor princes and
local landowners. He managed to reduce the opposition he encountered
among the Maratha chiefs and, in 1731, signed a treaty with Nizam-ul-
Mulk, for the division of their spheres of influence.

Baji Rao allied himself with Jai Singh II of Amber and with the other
Rajput princes. In 1737 their armies threatened Delhi, but they avoided
any direct confrontation. The emperor summoned Nizam-ul-Mulk who,
forgetful of the treaty he had signed, organized defense against the
Marathas. The two armies met close to Bhopal. Nizam-ul-Mulk was
crushingly defeated. He had to sign a new treaty, acknowledging the
Marathas' complete sovereignty over Malwa and all the territory between
the rivers Narmada and Chambal, and promising payment of five million
rupees. The Maratha Empire thus saw its conquests recognized *de jure*.

Baji Rao I then attacked the Portuguese and took Salsette and Bassein
from them. He proposed a kind of national union with the Muslims to
resist the invasion of Nadir Shah, but died suddenly in 1740 at the age
of forty-two, before he could implement his plan.

His son, Balaji II, who was eighteen years old, succeeded him, but
found it very difficult to assert his authority over the various Maratha factions. He reorganized the army with the aim of modernization and, for the
purpose, engaged numerous mercenaries, depriving the army of its national
character. He also allowed his captains to make raids to pillage neighboring
states, whether Hindu or Muslim, ruining the Marathas' reputation, as
defenders of the Hindus, won by his father. The Marathas, however, continued to extend their empire. They fought the French, commanded by
Bussy, and made alliances with the English, commanded by Clive and
Watson. They annexed a part of Mogul territory in the Deccan, in particular the province of Bijapur and the fortress of Daulatabad.

In the north their expansion was considerable. They attacked Delhi in 1757, captured Sirhind and then Lahore in 1758. These expeditions did not, however, bring them any material advantage and lost them all support of whoever might have become their allies. When the Marathas decided to oppose the Afghan invasion led by Timur Shah, their forces were too scattered and their equipment insufficient to face the enemy. The two armies met close to Delhi, on the field of the historic Battle of Panipat, on 14 January 1761. The Afghan army comprised forty-five thousand soldiers, of whom half were Afghans and the others Indian allies. The Marathas were crushed, their generals killed, and thousands of their soldiers massacred. The Afghans took an enormous booty: fifty thousand horses, two hundred thousand head of cattle, five hundred elephants, thousands of camels, and great amounts of money. A merchant brought the Peshwa news of the disaster, in an enigmatic form: "Two pearls have dissolved, twenty-two pieces of gold have disappeared and none can count the number of silver and copper coins that have been lost." The Peshwa, who had caught tuberculosis, was to die a few months later.

After this battle, the Marathas' prestige slumped. However, the new Peshwa, Madhava Rao I, returned to the principles of Shivaji. Once the Afghans had left, the Marathas reorganized their forces. They reestablished the exiled emperor, Shah Alam II, on the throne of Delhi in 1789. The Maratha Mahadaji Sindhia became the virtual dictator of Delhi.

The mortal conflict between the Muslims and the Marathas had considerably weakened both parties. The influence of the Maratha chiefs at the diminished court at Delhi did not imply cooperation between the Hindu and Muslim masses, who now shared out northern India, and the English were to take advantage of the animosity and suspicion between the two communities. In actual fact, the Marathas represented the retaking of power by the Hindus and the end of Muslim domination. They thrice attempted to oppose the British invasion, but were finally beaten by the Anglo-Muslim alliance, and India lost its independence.

PART SIX

The Europeans in India

20

The Pioneers

THE PORTUGUESE

Since time immemorial, the sea route had served trade between India on the one side, and Africa and the Mediterranean countries on the other. Since the seventh century, sea trade had been in Arab hands. Their ships, coming from Egypt or Basra, joined up at the southern tip of Arabia, to the north of Socotra, and from there crossed the ocean to reach the ports of India. The expansion of the Turkish Empire closed both the land and sea routes between the merchants of Genoa and Venice and their Arab counterparts, and a new way had to be found. The Portuguese were the first to try out the long route around Africa. Bartholomeo Diaz doubled the Cape of Good Hope, which he called the Cape of Storms, in 1487. In 1498 Vasco da Gama discovered the new route to the Indies, crossing the ocean directly from the Mombasa region to the port of Calicut (Kozhikode in Kerala).

Vasco da Gama was very well received by the Zamorin, the Hindu King of Calicut, who allowed him to set up a trading post. Following him, in March 1500, Pedro Alvarez Cabral left Lisbon for India with thirteen vessels. The trade route with India was open to the Portuguese. Instead of being content with the related financial advantages, however, they soon sought to establish their hegemony over the eastern seas and began to molest the ships of other nations. This displeased the Zamorin, because the prosperity of Calicut mainly depended—and had long done so—on Arab merchants. The Portuguese then launched into political intrigue and made an alliance with the King of Cochin, who was the Zamorin's main rival.

Alfonso de Albuquerque arrived in India in 1503 at the head of a Portuguese squadron. In 1509 the King of Portugal appointed him "Governor of Portuguese business in India." In 1510 he took the rich port of Goa from the Sultanate of Bijapur and immediately set about fortifying the town and developing its commercial standing. To increase the population, he encouraged his soldiers to take Indian wives. His religious fanaticism and the persecutions he visited on both Muslims and Hindus soon caused him problems. Indian historians tell that, in the regions he annexed, Albuquerque had a cross and a stake raised; those inhabitants who would not abjure their religion and adopt Christianity were cruelly executed. At his death in 1515, Albuquerque had succeeded in assuring Portuguese naval dominion of the coasts of India.

His successors seized a good number of ports, settling at Diu, Daman, Salsette, Bassein, Chaul, and Bombay, as well as at San-Thomé, close to Madras, and at Hugli, in Bengal. Their authority also stretched over a considerable part of the island of Sri Lanka.

However, the Portuguese fairly rapidly lost their privileged position. Qasim Khan retook Hugli in the reign of Shah Jahan, and the Marathas retook Salsette and Bassein in 1739. In the end, the Portuguese only managed to keep Diu, Daman, and Goa. The causes of the decline of Portuguese influence were many. One was the dishonesty of their trading practices and their acts of piracy that alienated the Indian kings and their subjects. The discovery of Brazil oriented Portugal's colonial efforts in another direction. At the same time, the other European countries that followed them were redoubtable foes and would not recognize Portuguese claims to preeminence in the Indian Ocean, even though their claim had been confirmed by papal bull.

In 1600 the East India Company received a charter from the Queen of England, granting it a trading monopoly in the eastern seas. The Dutch government granted a charter in 1602 to the United Companies of the East Indies, assuring them exclusive trading rights, as well as the right to make war, sign treaties, and acquire territories and fortresses. The Danish arrived in 1616. The French Company of the East Indies, protected and encouraged by Colbert, received privileges from the King in 1664. A Flemish company was set up by the merchants of Ostend in 1722, and a Swedish company in 1731.

Innumerable conflicts ensued. The first was between the English and the Dutch, up to the latter's final defeat at the Battle of Bedara in 1759. The conflict between the English and the French was to last throughout the eighteenth century.

THE DUTCH

The Dutch, who were mostly interested in the profitable spice trade, had first directed their expeditions toward the main producers in the Indonesian archipelago—Sumatra, Java, and the Moluccan islands. In 1605 they took the island of Amboyna, lying between the Celebes and New Guinea, from the Portuguese. They seized Jakarta in Java in 1619 and built Batavia on the ruins of the ancient city. In 1641 they settled at Malacca, on the coast of Malaysia. They were not disinterested in India and its enormous resources, however, which brought them into direct conflict with the Portuguese and the English. The Dutch were also out for revenge against Catholic Spain—the enemy of their independence— and its ally, Portugal. With great ease they managed to seize most of the Portuguese possessions. They blockaded Goa in 1639 and by 1658 had seized Portugal's last possessions in Sri Lanka. Gradually, their trading interests led them to set up trading posts in India, some on the Gujarat coast and others on the eastern coast, as well as others inland. They soon had settlements in southern India, Orissa, Bengal, and Bihar. The most important were those set up at Pulicat in 1610, Surat in 1616, Chinsura in 1653, Cassimbazar, Barangor, and Cochin in 1663, and at Patna, Balasore, and Nagapatam in 1659.

Having succeeded in supplanting the Portuguese, the Dutch practically acquired a monopoly of the spice trade, which they kept throughout the seventeenth century. To this, they added trade in indigo, produced in central India, and in silk, textiles, rice, and opium from the Ganges valley. Furthermore, they took over the trade monopoly between India and Indonesia, which had greatly declined since the end of the Vijayanagar Empire.

The Dutch conflict with the English was strictly commercial, since both were seeking to establish a monopoly, and their keen rivalry lasted throughout the seventeenth century. In 1609 the Dutch negotiated a twenty-one year truce with Spain. Thus freed from the risk of a war in Europe, they could employ their maritime superiority against the British in the East, and succeeded in wresting from them the permanent control of Southeast Asia. An agreement was signed between London and The Hague in 1619, but fighting soon broke out again following the massacre of some Englishmen at Amboyna. Rivalry for commercial predominance in India lasted up to 1759, after which the Dutch left India to the English.

21

The British
East India Company

Francis Drake succeeded in making his voyage around the world in 1580. During the same period, the English defeated the Spanish Armada. England was now in a favorable position to launch itself into the Far Eastern adventure. In 1593 James Lancaster reached Kanyakumari, and went on as far as the island of Penang in Malaysia. In 1596 a fleet commanded by Benjamin Wood visited the eastern seas. In 1599 John Mildenhall, a London merchant, traveled to India overland and stayed in the East for seven years. In 1600 Queen Elizabeth granted the new East India Company its charter—a fifteen year trading monopoly with the East. The Company organized convoys of vessels, financed by subscribers who shared the profits.

The first of these voyages was to Sumatra, Java, and the Moluccas, with the intent of seizing a part of the spice trade. In 1608 the Company decided to establish trading posts in India and sent Captain Hawkins, who arrived at the court of Jahangir in 1609. The emperor favored the project and granted Hawkins the right to open a trading post at Surat, but the town's merchants objected. The English then took reprisals against vessels trading between Surat and the Red Sea ports. Thus, they defeated the Portuguese fleet. Finally, in 1613, Jahangir granted them the right to a permanent trading post at Surat.

With the Company's mediation, the King of England, James I, sent an ambassador to the Mogul court, with proposals for a commercial treaty. This ambassador, Sir Thomas Roe, was a pleasant person, elegant and cultivated. He was well received at court, where he stayed from 1615 to the end of 1618. He finally obtained permission to set up trading settlements in several regions of the empire. In 1619 the English had trading posts at Surat, Agra, Ahmedabad, and Broach. The general management was at Surat. The Company bought textiles and indigo.

The crowns of Spain and Portugal were united in 1580 and so remained until 1640. England had officially made peace with Spain in 1604, but remained in conflict with the Portuguese in the eastern seas. Having made an alliance with the shah of Persia, the English took Hormuz on the Persian Gulf from the Portuguese in 1622.

The *Treaty of Madrid* put an official end to Anglo-Portuguese rivalry in 1630. The head of the British trading post at Surat signed a convention with the Viceroy of Goa, guaranteeing that the interests of each would be respected. English rights to trade in the East were acknowledged by Portugal in a treaty signed in 1654. By another treaty signed in 1661, Charles II of England, who had received Bombay as part of the dowry of Catherine of Braganza, promised British support to the Portuguese against the Dutch. Indeed, Portuguese competition was no longer a danger, since they lacked any coherent organization.

In 1668 Charles II acquired the port of Bombay definitively, for an annual rent of ten pounds sterling. Bombay rapidly became the main center for English trade, and the central management of the East India Company was transferred there in 1687. In 1632 the sultan of Golconda granted the Company the right to trade in the ports of his kingdom, for a payment of five hundred pagodas per year. The English opened a trading post at Masulipatam. In 1639 Francis Day obtained the port of Madras from the King of Chandragiri, who had inherited the remains of the Vijayanagar Empire. Here the Company built a fort, bearing the name of Fort St. George, which became the center for its activities on the east coast. New settlements were soon set up in the delta of the River Mahanadi, and more especially in Bengal, Bihar, and Orissa.

The Company's fortunes had been multifarious during the first half of the seventeenth century, but that was to change with the charter granted to it by Cromwell in 1657. The Company's privileges were confirmed and extended, and a solid financial basis was established. The Company made use of this by changing its policy—which till then had been purely commercial—to one of territorial acquisition, taking advantage of the dissensions that were ruining the country.

After the pillage of Surat by the Marathas, the English organized themselves for defense against the Malabar pirates and from a military point of view. They came into conflict with the Mogul fleet, of which several vessels were seized. They finally made peace with an enfeebled Aurangzeb, however. After many vicissitudes, in 1698 they obtained territorial rights over the villages of Sutanuti, Kalikata (Calcutta), and Govindapur in Bengal, and built the fortress of Fort William. Juridically, Bombay was annexed by the English Crown. Madras had been given to the English, but still belonged to an Indian state. In Bengal British citizens remained subjects of the British Crown, although the Mogul Empire considered the British Government—which was high-handed with the Indians—merely as a princely landowner.

After the 1688 revolution in England, the Whigs withdrew the Company's exclusive rights. Rival companies were formed that, in the end, amalgamated with the East India Company, thus forming the "United Company of the Merchants of England for Trade with the East Indies." This Company retained its legal monopoly until 1793. In 1715 the Company obtained a charter from the Emperor Farrukhsiyar, ensuring its right to trade with all India, customs inspection exemption on payment of three thousand rupees annually, and permission to acquire territory. Company coins, struck in Bombay, became legal tender throughout the empire. Calcutta saw rapid development. In 1735 the town already numbered one hundred thousand inhabitants. The port's trading tonnage was ten thousand tons per year. In 1739 the English of Bombay signed a treaty of alliance with the Marathas. At Madras, they obtained considerable territory from the Nawab.

THE FRENCH

Although Henry IV and Richelieu understood the importance of trade and relations with Eastern lands, the French were the last to launch into competition and to secure trading bases in India and Southeast Asia. In 1664 Colbert took the initiative to encourage the setting up of the state-funded "Compagnie des Indes Orientales." The initial steps taken, however, were clumsy. The first expedition wasted time and energy by seeking to colonize Madagascar. In 1667 a second expedition, under the command of François Caron, assisted by a Persian named Marcara, reached India. The first trading post was set up by François Caron at Surat in 1668 and, in 1669, Marcara managed to obtain authorization from the sultan of Golconda to open a trading post at Masulipatam. In 1672, under the command of Admiral de la Haye, the French took San-Thomé, near Madras, but were driven out a year later by the combined forces of the Dutch and the sultan of Golconda. San-Thomé was occupied by the Dutch. In the meantime, in 1673, François Martin and Bellanger de Lespinay obtained from the Muslim governor of Valikondapuram the grant of a small village on the coast south of Madras. Such was the modest beginning of Pondicherry. François Martin, who was in charge of this settlement from 1674, showed the necessary courage, tact, and perseverance in developing the village and turning it into a major center. In 1674 the Nawab Shaista Khan of Bengal donated a small territory to the French on the Hugli River, where the famous trading post of Chandernagor was built between 1690 and 1692.

Supported by the English, the Dutch opposed French intrusion in India, making it difficult for the new arrivals. Pondicherry was taken by the Dutch in 1693, but given back to the French in 1697 by the *Treaty of Ryswick*. Martin took over once more and reestablished the prosperity of the territory that, when he died in 1706, had a population of forty thousand, whereas Calcutta numbered only twenty-two thousand in the same year. The French had to abandon their trading posts at Surat, Bantam, and Masulipatam. At Pondicherry, the governors who succeeded Martin—there were five up to 1720—were incapable of continuing his energetic policy and the company's resources dried up. In 1720 it was refounded with the name "Compagnie Permanente des Indes." Under two clever administrators, Lenoir and Dumas, its prosperity was reestablished.

In the meantime, the French occupied Mauritius in 1721. They annexed Mahé, on the Malabar Coast, in 1725, and Karikal, to the south of Pondicherry, in 1739. Their ambitions were, however, strictly commercial. The fortifications they built and the small armies they engaged had no aim other than to defend their trading posts against the English and Dutch. After 1742 this attitude changed. Dupleix dreamt of establishing a French empire in India, which put him into direct conflict with England.

22

Anglo-French Conflicts

The conflicts between the English and French for dominion over the Coromandel Coast lasted over twenty years. Although it was only a minor war on a military level, it was of great importance, since it decided which European power would have dominion over the Indian subcontinent. The conflicts among the various Indian princes had created a state of confusion and chaos in southeast India. The Indians were great ship builders, but had no war fleet, while the English and French positions on the coast largely depended on materials and arms arriving by sea. The success of both powers depended directly on their naval forces.

From 1740 to 1748, England and France were on opposite sides during the Austrian War of Succession, forcing the two companies, which had lived together fairly peacefully, to fight each other. Dupleix—who had become Governor of Pondicherry—did his best to negotiate with the English and avoid an armed conflict in India. The English refused, saying they had no power to control the movements of His Britannic Majesty's ships. The arrival of the fleet commanded by La Bourdonnais changed the balance of forces. The British fleet took refuge in Bengal, and the French besieged Madras by land and sea. Madras surrendered after a week.

Anwar-ud-din, the Nawab of the Karnataka country and the official protector of the foreign trading posts, demanded that the French evacuate Madras. On their refusal, he sent troops that, being badly disciplined, were easily dispersed by the French. The French position appeared highly favorable, but Dupleix and La Bourdonnais quarreled over the policy they should follow. A storm damaged the fleet and La Bourdonnais withdrew his ships from the Indian Ocean. Dupleix then sacked Madras, despite the promises he had made. In 1748 a strong squadron, commanded by Admiral Boscawen, was sent from England to besiege Pondicherry. The *Treaty of Aix-la-Chapelle* in 1748 put an end to the conflict and gave Madras back to the English.

The first conflict had demonstrated that victory belonged to the side that dominated the ocean. It was difficult for France to measure up to England in this field. Furthermore, the English had numerous bases in India and excellent harbors at Bombay and in Bengal, while the French had only their trading posts, built on the immense beaches of the Coromandel Coast, with no sheltered harbor. Their chances were thus minimal. Dupleix was not, however, a man to let himself be discouraged. He had observed at Madras how a small, well-disciplined European garrison could easily overcome much larger Indian armies. He undertook to assist certain Indian princes in their internal conflicts, confident that they would pay a decent price to have fate turn in their favor. Dupleix soon found favorable occasions. There were two claimants to the throne of the Nawab of Karnataka. A similar struggle engaged two factions for succession to the throne of the Deccan. The Nawab of the Karnataka country, Chanda Sahib—taken prisoner at Trichinopoly and dispossessed by the Marathas—had just been freed after seven years in exile and was trying to recover his family throne. He had joined Muzaffar Jang, the grandson of Nizam-ul-Mulk, and pretender to the throne of the Deccan. Dupleix made secret treaties with Chanda Sahib and with Muzaffar Jang, promising to help them both to triumph. French troops went as far as Trichinopoly, which they besieged. In recognition of his services, Muzaffar Jang appointed Dupleix Governor of all the territories of the Mogul Empire to the south of the River Krishna, and granted him full sovereignty over the territories around Pondicherry and on the coast of Orissa, including the famous trading post of Masulipatam. In exchange Dupleix placed his best officer, Bussy, at the disposal of Muzaffar Jang and Chanda Sahib, together with a French army that was, indeed, the best guarantee of influencing the court at Arcot.

Dupleix did not, however, succeed at Trichinopoly, still occupied by Muhammad Ali, Chanda Sahib's rival. The British seized the chance and the new British Governor, Saunders, placed his forces at Muhammad Ali's disposal. Although no state of war existed between their two countries, the English and French found themselves engaged in a deadly conflict, disguised as assistance to rival princes.

In order to gain time, Muhammad Ali started negotiations with Dupleix, but the latter did not understand the meaning of this until too late. The rulers of Mysore and Tanjore, as well as the Marathas, joined the English to bring help to Muhammad Ali. In the meantime, Robert Clive, who had just started serving in the English army at Madras, proposed to Governor Saunders that an attack on Arcot could create a diversion. Chanda Sahib, as could be expected, withdrew part of his troops from Trichinopoly in order to win back his capital. Clive was shut up in Arcot and heroically withstood a siege of fifty-three days, which the besiegers had to raise.

Law—the commanding general of the French troops at Trichinopoly—was worried by Clive's success, and decided to withdraw to the island of Shrirangam, in the midst of the Cauvery River. Encouraged by Clive, the English besieged the island. Dupleix sent reinforcements, but these were violently attacked by Clive's army and surrendered to the English on 9 June 1752. Three days later, Law and his troops were made prisoner. Chanda Sahib surrendered and was beheaded by the general commanding the troops at Tanjore. Dupleix's situation was becoming difficult. The stupidity and incompetence of his generals had lost him a vast enterprise that was on the verge of success. He was not discouraged, and by skilful diplomacy managed to win the Marathas over to his cause, as well as the king of Mysore, and to ensure the neutrality of the raja of Tanjore. At the end of 1752, he resumed military operations, which lasted with varying degrees of success throughout 1753. He had not given up the idea of retaking Trichinopoly, and his shrewd policy would probably have led to success.

His failure was due to the government of Louis XV. In France no one appreciated the clever strategy and greatness of Dupleix's plans, and there was worry over the cost of the operations and the reverses suffered by French troops. An inspector called Godeheu was sent out in August 1754. He immediately assumed full power and reversed Dupleix's policy. He signed a treaty with the English, by which the parties remained in possession of the territories they had occupied, and undertook not to intervene in the quarrels of Indian princes. France thus lost all the advantages won by Dupleix. Only Bussy, encouraged by Dupleix, managed to stay in the Deccan and obtained from the Nizam the revenue from several districts to maintain his army. If the French company—actually a governmental initiative—had received the support and understanding given by England to the work of Clive and the private firm that was the East India Company, it would not have been impossible to set up a French empire in India. Dupleix was recalled and ended his days in disgrace and oblivion.

The Anglo-French truce continued up to the Seven Years' War. Being on opposite sides, the French and English were once more almost forced to resume hostilities, toward the end of 1756. In the meantime, however, the relative advantages of the two countries had changed considerably. Contrary to their agreements with the Nawab of Bengal, the English had fortified Calcutta, and they supported the various pretenders and parties opposed to the king. When Nawab Alivardi died without a male heir in 1756, his successor was Siraj-ud-daulah, the son of his youngest daughter. This young man gave proof of great energy and took Calcutta. The British withdrew to their ships and made for Fulta.

Holwell, who was vice-governor at the time, claimed that one hundred and forty-six British prisoners had been shut up for the night in one narrow room, and that most of them had died of suffocation. This episode—known as the "Black Hole of Calcutta"—is, according to many historians, if not fictitious, at least grossly exaggerated. But it was frequently used thereafter to justify the massacres perpetrated by the British. Clive and Admiral Watson had gathered a strong army at Madras for the purpose of attacking the French and sent it to Bengal to retake Calcutta. They occupied the city without encountering much resistance. They also took advantage of the opportunity to seize the French trading post at Chandernagor.

The young Nawab—under the influence of his counselors, the banker Jagat Seth and the rich merchant Omchand—agreed to sign a treaty restoring to the English all their former privileges. But fearing that the Nawab would call on the French for aid, Clive fomented a coup d'état in order to replace him with someone more favorable to British interests. He chose Mir Jafar, one of the Nawab's generals. When Clive attacked the Nawab's army at the famous Battle of Plassey on 23 June 1757, the latter's troops refused to fight Mir Jafar and his accomplices and scattered. Siraj-ud-daulah fled to Murshidabad. He was captured and assassinated and Mir Jafar took power. In accordance with the treaty he had signed with Clive, he gave the British sovereignty over several rich districts of Bengal, known as the Twenty-Four Parganas, as well as a considerable sum of money. These events led to Britain's conquest of Bengal and, later on, of the whole of India.

In 1758 the British fleet returned from Bengal to Madras. The French received reinforcements under the command of the Comte de Lally. The naval forces, however, remained under the orders of d'Aché, a division of power that was once more to ruin the French enterprise. Lally was a skilled and enterprising soldier, but his haughty and brutal manners ill-disposed his men and collaborators. He attacked Fort St. David in May 1758, and the fortress surrendered on 2 June. He wished to strike a blow to the heart of British power by attacking Madras, but d'Aché and the French fleet—already beaten by the English—refused to cooperate. Lally then did his best to seize all the British outposts to the south, so that only Madras, Trichinopoly, and Chingleput still belonged to the English.

The French fleet had sailed. Lally waited until the monsoon forced the British fleet to move away from Madras that, like Pondicherry, has no harbor. The siege of Madras lasted too long, however, and the British fleet was able to return. Lally had to raise the siege hastily. This check practically decided the fate of the French in India. Lally had made the mistake of recalling Bussy from Hyderabad. Clive sent an army, commanded by Colonel Forde, who beat the French, occupied Rajahmundry and

Masulipatam, and signed a highly advantageous treaty for England with Nizam Salabat Jang. Further south, despite some successes, the French troops mutinied because their pay had been delayed too long. The English fleet commanded by Peacock inflicted a severe defeat on the ships of d'Aché, who had reappeared, only to leave India forever.

In October 1759 General Coote reached Madras with a strong contingent and on 22 January 1760 the French army was completely routed, close to Fort Wandiwash. Three months later, the French had lost everything in the south, except the fort of Genji and the small town of Pondicherry, which the English besieged in May 1760. Lally's efforts to obtain aid from Mysore had no positive result. He lacked money to maintain his army and—even when the town was surrounded by land and sea—was incapable of cooperating harmoniously with his officers and soldiers. Pondicherry was forced to surrender on 16 January 1761. The conquerors not only destroyed the fortifications, but almost the whole town. A little later, the English took Genji and Mahé, the last French possessions in India.

Like that of Dupleix, Lally's defeat was due to the company's defective organization, the lack of coordination, and, above all, the fact that Louis XV's government was incapable of estimating the importance of the stakes, and of supplying the enterprise with the necessary military or financial support. At the same time, the British position in Bengal gave them a solid and independent base for operations against the south of India, rendering the French position uncertain from the very beginning. The Battle of Plassey really decided the fate of the French in India. Lally was made prisoner and spent two years captive in England. In 1763 at the end of the Seven Years' War, he was allowed to return to France. This brave soldier—much less guilty of the disaster than the French government itself—was imprisoned in the Bastille and shamefully executed two years later.

The idea of conquering an Indian empire using Pondicherry—a small village on the southern part of the burning and semi-desert Coromandel Coast, with no natural harbor or defenses—as a base was in itself totally absurd, especially when the main adversary had as a base the rich territory of Bengal and the great port of Calcutta. After Pondicherry was restored to them, the French seem to have retained some kind of romantic attachment for this small town, isolated on a tropical beach, and have maintained there, down to our own time, institutions that would have been much more accessible if located closer to the major urban centers. This has certainly been prejudicial to French influence in India.

23

The Growth of British Power

TERRITORIAL ANNEXATIONS

The 1757 revolution in Bengal had installed as Nawab the man favored by the English—Mir Jafar—and had established their supremacy over the area. The territories over which they had received full sovereignty allowed them to maintain a properly equipped army. Their hated rivals, the French, had been eliminated. They had installed a Resident at the court of Mir Jafar and, although the latter was in theory the sovereign, in fact he depended on the English, and the control of affairs in Bengal was in the hands of Clive. In June 1758 the city council of Calcutta appointed Clive Governor of Bengal, a post that was legalized some months later by the Company.

Mir Jafar attempted to free himself from British tutelage by making an alliance with the Dutch, who brought a strong army from Java to their trading posts at Chinsura. Clive won at Bedara in November 1759, and left India in 1760. Shortly afterward, Miran, the Nawab's son, died. Holwell, who replaced Clive, forced Mir Jafar to abdicate and placed his nephew, Mir Kasim, on the throne. As a reward for his assistance, he received the provinces of Burdwan, Chittagong, and Midnapur.

Following disputes concerning the privileges of members of the Company, Mir Kasim tried to revolt. In 1763 he assembled an army and set up a confederation with several princes and the Emperor at Delhi, with a view to recovering the independence of Bengal.

This considerable and badly organized Indian army was defeated by Major Adam, and Mir Kasim fled, after killing all his English prisoners. The emperor, Shah Alam II, abandoned the confederation and made a separate peace.

Mir Jafar's son, Najm-ud-daulah, was placed on the throne of Bengal, on the express condition that all administrative powers would be in the hands of a minister appointed by the English. The government of Bengal was henceforth legally in Company hands. Clive returned as Governor of Bengal in 1765. He signed the *Treaty of Allahabad* with the emperor, reestablishing the Nawab of Oudh, but detaching Allahabad and giving it to the emperor. By *firmam*, the latter officially granted the sovereignty (*diwani*) of Bengal to the East India Company, on 12 August 1765. Clive then set about reorganizing the Company and the army, in which corruption had reached unimaginable proportions. He succeeded to a certain extent, but left India finally in 1767. Under his successors, oppression and corruption created poverty until then unknown in that rich province, causing many of the English to register their protests, but in vain. The arrival of Warren Hastings in 1771 as Governor of Bengal was to open a new chapter.

The Marathas had succeeded in virtually dominating both the court at Delhi and Shah Alam II. Unfortunately for them, the ferocious rivalry for the succession of the young Peshwa Madhava Rao I, who died in 1772, led the various factions to appeal to external allies, a fact of which the English immediately took advantage. After a series of conflicts and treaties, always denounced shortly afterward, the Government of Bombay managed to extend its territories and privileges, and Warren Hastings won an alliance with Mahadaji Sindhia of Gwalior. By the *Treaty of Salbai*, in 1782, the English made a peace with the Marathas that was to last for twenty years, allowing them to take care of their other enemies. Pitt's *India Act*, in 1784, ordered the Company not to interfere in Indian political affairs.

Mahadaji Sindhia—who had become the most important of the Maratha chiefs—observed the treaties scrupulously, employing a Savoyard, Benoît de Boigne, and various other European adventurers to modernize his army. He visited Delhi and took the feeble Shah Alam II completely in hand. Under cover of the latter's authority, he established Maratha supremacy in northern India. He was appointed Commander of the Imperial Army and made the emperor's delegate. He was "officially the slave, but in fact the severe patron of the unhappy Shah Alam, Emperor of Delhi." In 1792 Sindhia established his dominion over the Rajputs and Jats. He was on the point of taking over all the Maratha principalities when he died of fever at Pune in 1794, at the age of sixty-seven. The English, who viewed him as a redoubtable future enemy, greeted his death with relief.

Under the reign of a remarkably gifted Muslim adventurer called Hyder, who had supplanted its sovereign, Mysore had undergone considerable development, whereas southern India was disorganized by conflicts and Bengal by palace revolutions. The rebirth of Mysore's power disturbed the Marathas, the Nizam of Hyderabad, and the English. They formed a coalition against Mysore, but Hyder ably bought traitors from all parties. In the series of conflicts that took place between 1765 and 1782, alliances remained uncertain and considerable territory changed hands several times. Louis XVI sought to exploit this confusion to reestablish France's position in India. A squadron commanded by Admiral Suffren arrived at the beginning of 1782. A little later on, two thousand men under the command of du Chemin landed in India. Military operations came to a halt during the monsoon (July-August). Hyder was not to take up arms again, however. He died of cancer in December 1782.

His son, Tipu Sultan, who succeeded him, was no less enterprising and courageous than his father. He resumed the war against the English. In 1783 he managed to take prisoner the whole of the British high command at Bombay. Despite Warren Hastings' opposition, the new Governor General, Lord MacCartney, signed the *Treaty of Mangalore* with Tipu Sultan, restoring to each of the belligerents its territories and prisoners. Lord Cornwallis—who came to India as Governor General from 1786 to 1793—resumed hostilities, under the pretext that Tipu had annexed the state of Travancore, in the far south. He reformed the triple alliance with the Nizam and the Marathas and, after two years of war, from 1790 to 1792, Tipu was practically defeated, despite his skilful strategy. He had to sign the *Treaty of Seringapatam,* by which he lost more than half his territories, annexed by the Nizam, the Marathas, and the British, who took Malabar and Coorg. Tipu also had to pay the Company three million rupees and send two of his sons hostage to Cornwallis. A man of Tipu Sultan's character could not, however, resign himself to such humiliations. Seeking the support of the French, now Republicans, he registered as a member of the Jacobin Club, allowed a French lieutenant, Citizen Ripaud, to plant a tree of liberty at Seringapatam and to raise the flag of the Republic there. France sent him a few soldiers in 1798. Tipu also sent emissaries to Arabia, Constantinople, and Kabul.

None of this brought great results and Lord Cornwallis seized the pretext for an attack on Mysore. Tipu was defeated and killed at Seringapatam in May 1799. The members of his family were interned, first at Vellore, than at Calcutta. The British annexed some provinces and placed on the somewhat diminished throne of Mysore a young boy, a descendant of the ancient Hindu dynasty, with a considerable British contingent "for his protection." Mysore was in fact virtually annexed.

In theory, the Nizam of Hyderabad was merely the representative of the Emperor of Delhi. In fact, however, since the reign of Muhammad Shah, Hyderabad had been a practically independent state. Threatened by the Marathas and by the sultan of Mysore, the Nizam sought British support. The latter granted only meager aid and in exchange required the cession of Guntur. The Nizam then sought aid from the French in turn, and the most virulent Jacobins were welcome at his court. By means of a shrewd policy, however, Wellesley reached an agreement in 1822 by which the foreigners were eliminated and the British took over the state's defenses. The Nizam's troops were dismissed. This was to become a source of impoverishment, since the administration, bowing to foreign interest, no longer worked in the interest of its population. Furthermore, the former troops created a serious problem. "Imagine a country," remarked the Duke of Wellington, "where in each village there are twenty or thirty horsemen, dismissed from serving the state, who have no other means of existence than pillage. In such a country, there is neither law nor civil government. . . . None can farm the land unless he is protected by armed forces, stationed in his village. Such, in brief, is now the state of the Peshwa's and the Nizam's country."

The south of India suffered terribly as a result of the Anglo-French conflicts and was totally disorganized. The official ruler was the Nawab of Arcot, Muhammad Ali, a person of no character. He sold the administration of his lands to the English and lent enormous sums to various members of the Company, who thus made considerable fortunes. Lord Cornwallis attempted to put some order into the affairs of Madras, but without success. When Muhammad Ali died in 1795, his son Omdut-ul-Umara tried in vain to resist the exactions of the Company's members. An all-powerful class of persons interested in maintaining corruption had arisen, which opposed any measure attempting to reestablish order and justice.

When Omdut-ul-Umara died in 1801, Lord Wellesley declared that he had discovered at Seringapatam documents showing that the prince had betrayed his word. He placed on the throne one of the Nawab's nephews, and the Company took over the whole administration of the Karnataka country. After this, Wellesley also forced the rulers of Tanjore and Surat to leave all administrative powers to the Company. The annexation procedure employed at Surat, as in many states, was quite simple. After a military expedition, the English assumed the state's defenses, while the ruler saw to the civil administration. The sums demanded for defense, however, became so exorbitant that the ruler could not pay them and the British then dethroned him and simply annexed the country.

The British considerably extended their territories in the north of India. Warren Hastings took advantage of each conflict to demand enormous sums, exile the princes, levy punitive taxes, and seize the treasury. Gradually, Rohilkhand, at the foot of the Himalayas, and Oudh, with the cities of Allahabad and Cawnpore (modern Kanpur), had passed under British control. Disorder and corruption were rife everywhere. The most brutal exactions were perpetrated under the pretext of levying taxes. The many European adventurers made the disorder even worse. Numerous scandals were revealed to an indignant England when Hastings was recalled and judged by an English court. This did not stop Wellesley from continuing the same policy. He forced the Nawab of Oudh to cede to the Company the greater part of his lands and to suppress his army, which was replaced by Company troops.

The main obstacle to British power was still the Maratha Empire. Brave and enterprising, the Marathas lacked stable organization and cohesion. By means of a series of military operations and separate treaties with the various Maratha states, the British managed to dissolve their confederation between 1800 and 1818, and the Maratha Empire crumbled. British influence and authority spread over the country with surprising rapidity.

The Gurkhas, an indigenous tribe from the western Himalayas, had conquered Nepal in 1768, and gradually developed considerable military might. Blocked northward by the Chinese Empire, they sought to extend toward the southern plains and came into conflict with the English, who had occupied Gorakhpur, to the north of Benares. After a difficult war, the British forces defeated the Nepalese in February 1816, less than eighty kilometers from the capital, Kathmandu. Nepal was forced to sign a treaty ceding to the Company Garwal and Kumaon to the west, with the town of Almora, and the sites where the famous British hill stations were built such as Simla, Mussoorie, Ranikhet, and Nainital.

The rivalries between the feudal states of Rajputana and central India and the incursions of the Marathas had given rise to a state of instability and disorder, leading to the formation of considerable groups of marauders and pillagers. The Pindaris—a vast organization of brigand bands—had its center of activities in central India. Against them, Lord Hastings gathered a mighty expedition of one hundred and thirteen thousand men and three hundred cannon. Between 1817 and 1818 he exterminated them down to the last man. The Pathans too, taking advantage of the disorder, multiplied their highly profitable pillaging raids. The British managed to win over one of their leading chiefs, Amir Khan, whom they made Nawab of Tonk. This alliance allowed them to eliminate the Pathans' subversive activities without any conflict.

The Rajputs had lost much of their prestige and vitality, and Rajputana had without cease been prey to the aggressions of the Marathas, Pindaris, and Pathans. Ruined and disorganized, one after the other, the Rajput states signed treaties placing them under British protection. These treaties "of defensive alliance, perpetual friendship, protection, and subordinate cooperation" were signed by the Maharaja of Kotah in December 1817, of Udaipur in January 1818, of Bundi in February 1818, of Jaipur in April 1818. Jaisalmer signed in December 1818 and Sirohi in 1823. After the Rajput states, the minor principalities of central India signed similar treaties, sacrificing their independence in order to preserve a semblance of power.

Thus, at the end of the eighteenth and beginning of the nineteenth centuries, all the Indian states that had regained their independence with the decline of the Mogul Empire and could claim to play a role in the political life of India collapsed. The British became the only power capable of controlling the Indian subcontinent, from the Himalayas to Kanyakumari and from the Brahmaputra to the Sutlej. The Mogul Empire was now merely a fiction. The English had taken control of Delhi in 1803, and the emperor, Shah Alam II, received a rather modest pension from them. On his death in 1806, Lord Hastings requested his successor Akbar II to waive any ceremony that might "suggest that he exercised any authority over the Company's empire."

When Lord Hastings left India in 1823, one of his contemporaries, Prinsep, wrote, "The conflict that broke out on the establishment of British influence over the whole of India is of particular importance, since it will be the *last* that we shall ever have to put up with from the indigenous powers of India." For the security of their empire, however, the English still had to secure the eastern and western frontiers. Freed from French rivalry after the downfall of Napoleon, they soon had to deal with Russian expansionism in Asia.

The British Government of India started by attacking Burma. The Burmese had established their sway over the independent kingdoms of

Arakan in 1784, Manipur in 1813, and Assam in 1821–22. They had also seized the isle of Shahpuri, near Chittagong, that belonged to the Company. The British Governor General, Lord Almherst, declared war on Burma on 24 February 1824. It was an expensive and difficult war, in which the British were faced with a tough and highly organized Burmese resistance. The latter were, however, defeated. In 1826 they were forced to sign a treaty by which they had to pay a war indemnity of ten million rupees, cede the provinces of Arakan and Tenasserim, acknowledge the independence of Manipur, and accept a commercial treaty and the presence of a British Resident at the Burmese capital of Ava.

In 1837 the English dethroned King Hpagyidoa, replacing him with his brother Tharrawaddy. The latter, exasperated by British impudence, put up resistance, and was shut up as a madman. Despite his son and successor's efforts to avoid war, Commodore Lambert sent him unacceptable ultimatums, seized the town of Rangoon in 1852, then the port of Bassein. The British finally annexed the whole of lower Burma, leaving the ruler only a very diminished state, isolated from the sea and without any external contacts.

The Sikhs' efforts to win independence between 1708 and 1716 ended in disaster. Their leader, Banda, was tortured to death by the Moguls and the Sikhs became the target of constant persecution. The invasion by the shah of Persia, Nadir Shah, in 1739, and the repeated inroads of the Afghan Ahmad Shah Abdali from 1748 to 1752, weakened the Mogul Empire, allowing the Sikhs to recover and reorganize. They occupied Lahore in 1764 and founded an empire, which in 1773 stretched from Shahrampur to Attock and from Multan to Kangra and Jammu. The Sikhs were split into twelve clans, forming some sort of confraternities. The uniting of the Sikhs under a single monarchy was the work of Ranjit Singh.

On the death of his father, the twelve-year-old Ranjit Singh found himself the leader of one of the clans. He astutely provided important services for Zaman Shah of Kabul when the latter attacked northwest India. In exchange, Zaman Shah appointed Ranjit as Governor of Lahore. This allowed him to establish his supremacy over the other Sikh clans and then gradually to eliminate the Afghans, whose possessions he took over. The Sikhs' growing power and excellent organization soon began to worry the English. However, fearing an invasion by Napoleon's armies with the support of the Persians and Turks, they negotiated with the Sikhs. In 1809 they signed a treaty of "perpetual friendship" with Ranjit Singh, which limited his expansion but acknowledged his rights. Once the danger had passed, however, the English reconsidered their position. In the meantime, Ranjit Singh had taken Kangra in 1811, Attock in 1813, Multan in 1818, Kashmir in 1819, and Peshawar in 1824.

Fearful of Russian expansion, the Governor General Lord Bentinck counted on the Sikh state as an eventual bastion. Although the treaty of alliance was renewed in 1831, England opposed Ranjit Singh's designs on Afghanistan and Sind.

Ranjit Singh died in 1839 at the age of fifty-nine, and the powerful military monarchy that he had created did not last long. Internal dissension made the Sikh army uncontrollable. Fearing an attack by the British, whose preparations were clear to see, the Sikh army prepared for battle. Lord Hardinge declared war in 1845 and proclaimed that all the Sikh territories on the left bank of the River Sutlej were confiscated and annexed to the British territories. The Sikhs fought ferociously. They would have beaten the British army had it not been for the incompetence and defection of several of their chiefs. The losses on both sides were considerable. The Sikhs were finally defeated at Sobraon, on the River Sutlej, in January 1846. Their entrenched camps were taken by assault and a great number of Sikhs were massacred by the British soldiers. This victory rid the British Empire of "the most courageous and most resolute enemy that it had ever encountered in India."

The English occupied Lahore, and Lord Hardinge imposed a treaty on the Sikhs, by which he annexed all the territories east of the Sutlej and the mountain districts, including Kashmir, which he sold for one million pounds sterling to an official of the Court of Lahore, named Gulab Singh. This treaty was revised in December 1846 to ensure tighter British control over the remainder of the Sikh state. A revolt was not long in coming. It broke out, with Afghan assistance, in 1848. Taking as a pretext the murder of two officers at Multan, the British army, led by Lord Gough, attacked. After a terrible struggle, the Sikhs were finally crushed. As Malleson remarks, "there are no soldiers better than the Sikhs, but never was an army so badly commanded." The Sikhs laid down their arms in February 1849. Their Afghan allies were pursued as far as Kabul. Lord Dalhousie proclaimed the annexation of the Punjab on 30 March 1849, despite the British government's opposition.

The Afghans, under their capable ruler Dost Mohammed, sought British support against the Russians. But the British wished to depose the king and give his throne to the exiled sovereign, Shah Shuja, thus forcing Dost Mohammed to look to the Persians and Russians for aid. Lord Auckland assembled an army on the Indus, with a view to invading Afghanistan. The British occupied Kandahar in April 1834, took Ghazni by assault in July, and Kabul—evacuated by Dost Mohammed—in August. Shah Shuja was replaced on the throne of Kabul, without the slightest acclamation by the people. His entry into the city has been compared to a funeral. Dost Mohammed surrendered and was exiled to Calcutta. The British army had to stay in Afghanistan, however, to maintain Shah Shuja on the throne, costing the Government of India a considerable sum.

The Afghans mutinied in 1841, led by Akbar Khan, the son of Dost Mohammed. A great number of British officers and officials were assassinated or taken prisoner. The English had to negotiate and accepted withdrawal in January 1842. Sixteen thousand five hundred men and their families were forced to take the Peshawar road, despite the snow and cold. No one, however, could control the Afghan tribal snipers, hidden among the rocks. Only one wounded survivor reached Jalalabad to recount the disaster.

Shah Shuja was put to death and all the British troops withdrew from Afghan territory. To save face, the British sent a punitive expedition in August 1842; it reached Kabul, blew up the bazaar, and withdrew. Replaced on the throne, Dost Mohammed had then to be very friendly toward the English—as he was before—and oppose the Persians. The whole episode was senseless, but it cost the lives of more than twenty thousand persons and a considerable amount of money.

Between 1825 and 1858, the British annexed Sind, and then gradually imposed their administration on all the minor states, usually under the pretext of the bad conduct of public business. Earlier treaties were cancelled, but a certain number of states managed to retain their sovereign, at least in name, and an independent administration. The other states were incorporated into provinces administered directly by the English. India was therefore divided into two parts: the British provinces and the princely states, each governed by an Indian sovereign "assisted" by an English Resident.

THE 1857–1859 MUTINY

The extremely rapid expansion of British domination—imposing administrative and judicial concepts that differed greatly from the country's ancestral traditions—caused backlashes that were often violent. A series of revolts culminated in the great mutiny of 1857. The immediate causes of the mutiny were Lord Dalhousie's policy of annexing states, the repudiation of treaties, the expropriation of the great landowners, and, particularly, the planned expulsion of the last descendants of the Mogul emperors—a measure that shocked the Muslims—as well as the refusal to pay Nana Saheb, the son of Peshwa Baji Rao II, the pension granted to his father, which deeply upset the Hindus.

During the five years preceding the mutiny, a commission appointed by Lord Dalhousie confiscated more than twenty thousand major properties in the Deccan alone, reducing the nobles to poverty.

Missionary aggressiveness and the advantages granted to those who adopted the Christian religion, the abolition of certain customs—such as those forbidding widows to remarry, sati, and the practice of infanticide—caused great preoccupation in traditional circles. The latter were not interested in political matters, but rightly saw in English policy an attempt at cultural and religious colonialism that threatened India's own civilization. The British could not bring an army large enough to hold such a vast country. The key to the situation thus lay in the hands of the

Indian army at the service of the English, known as the Sepoy army. The introduction of the Enfield rifle, which had cartridges lubricated with beef or pork fat, thoroughly disgusted both Hindu and Muslim soldiers. The measure was highly significant of the absolute scorn felt by the British for Indian feelings.

The first signs of mutiny appeared at Barrackpore and Berhampore, in Bengal, at the outset of 1857, and were rapidly and cruelly repressed. In May 1857, however, the Indian soldiers at Meerut revolted, opened the prisons into which their fellows had been thrown, killed the European officers, and burned their houses. The next day, they rushed toward Delhi, massacring Europeans, and proclaimed Bahadur Shah II emperor of India.

Insurrections then took place almost everywhere, in Rajputana, central India, Benares, and Bihar. In many cases, and at Benares in particular, the British soldiers regained the upper hand and shot any mutineers they could seize. At Cawnpore, Nana Saheb—who had proclaimed himself Peshwa—managed to seize the fortress and its British garrison, and massacred all the occupants, including women and children. This, in particular, gave rise to violent vindictive fury among the English.

Many of the princes had, however, remained faithful to their British alliance. The south of India remained indifferent. It has been said that it was the Maharaja Sindhia of Gwalior who saved the English. With the troops that remained to them, the English attacked Delhi and retook the town after violent fighting. The emperor was arrested and deported to Burma. His children and grandchildren were put to death by Lieutenant Hodson, to whom they had been handed over. The imperial dynasty thus came to an end. According to the *Bombay Telegraph* at the time, "All the inhabitants found within the walls of the town when our troops entered were bayoneted on the spot. Their numbers were considerable, as you may imagine when I say that, in some houses, up to forty or fifty persons were hiding."

At Lucknow, the mutiny began on 30 May 1857, but the English garrison was able to hang on at the Residence until November, when troops arrived under the new Commander-in-Chief from England, Sir

Colin Campbell (later Lord Clyde), assisted by Jang Bahadur of Nepal, with his strong contingent of Gurkhas.

Badly coordinated, the insurgents gradually lost ground. One woman, the Rani of Jhansi, led a desperate struggle against the English and their allies in central India. She was killed in battle close to Gwalior on 17 June 1858. Little by little, the English regained control of the various provinces, where they exacted terrible vengeance. Nicholson demanded the legalization of "flogging to death, impalement and the stake" for the murderers of women and children at Delhi. Although Canning attempted to prevent the unleashing of indiscriminate reprisals against the innocent, the British took advantage of the circumstances to rid themselves of the cream of the Indian aristocracy. According to letters of the time, every day princes and ministers were tied to the mouth of cannon, in front of British officers calmly taking tea and laughing at the victims' contortions. This was followed by an incredible manhunt. British soldiers massacred and tortured any Indian who fell into their hands, their own servants, the villagers, sometimes the populations of entire towns. The crimes of the Indians have long been known, described by English historians, but of the incredible atrocities that followed, we have only the accounts of those who committed them.

According to the historian Kaye, "old men, women and children were sacrificed, as well as those guilty of rebellion. . . . They were burned alive in their villages.. . . Some of the English boasted in their letters that they had spared no one and that 'nigger-chasing' was a most amusing sport."

The mutiny came to an end owing to a lack of coordination between the various parties. It was first and foremost a mutiny by the army and the princes, but it only involved a part of India. In other regions the troops remained faithful to the English, while a certain number of princes—the only ones to survive—aided the British army. At the same time, the mutiny was an answer to the misgivings of a very ancient people whose traditions were threatened, along with their social life, their religion, and civilization. In the people's imagination, the Rani of Jhansi is still a symbol of Indian glory, of the virtues of a courageous people, proud of their culture. The British victory was to bring in its train the slow and perfidious destruction of one of the world's greatest civilizations—its philosophy, arts, science, and skills henceforth disparaged and discouraged. Although less rapid and less spectacular, for universal culture this event represents a disaster as great as the conquest of Greece, Egypt, and the south of the Mediterranean by the Islamized peoples of the Near East.

The savagery of the destruction and murder committed on both sides, during and after the mutiny, caused violent reactions in England. The administration of the Indian Empire was taken away from the Company and given to the Crown. An Act dated 2 August 1858 states that "henceforth India shall be governed, for the sovereign and in her name, by a Secretary of State assisted by a council of fifteen members." The Governor-General was replaced by a Viceroy. The charter—promulgated by Lord Canning on 1 November 1858 in the name of Queen Victoria—promised to respect the treaties signed with the princes and to take account of the former rights, usages, and customs of the peoples, granted an amnesty to all those who had not taken a direct part in the murder of British subjects, and gave assurance that in future the government would abstain from any intervention in the religious beliefs and rites of Indians. For civil servants, it also promised absolute equality among the empire's subjects, whatever their race or religion.

Such promises were, of course, only kept superficially. In fact, the feelings of hostility and inequality between Europeans and Indians, which had not previously existed, developed gradually, turning India into a real colony, where Europeans enjoyed immense privileges, constituting a "superior race." It was this attitude that, a century later, led to the nationalist movement and independence. Russel—then *The Times'* correspondent in India—wrote, "The revolts have created too much hatred and resentment between the two races for a mere change of government to be a remedy for the ills that affect India. . . . Many years will pass before the dark passions aroused by these disorders are spent. It may be that trust will never be reestablished. If that is the case, our domination over India can never be maintained except at the price of sufferings that are terrible to envisage."

INDIA AFTER THE MUTINY

The effect of the 1857 mutiny was profound, since the English kept themselves completely separate from the country's inhabitants. They had their own towns, clubs, and residential areas, and their contacts with Indians were purely administrative and authoritarian. The conception of the British Empire was expressed by Fitzjames Stephen, whom a modern English writer calls "the philosopher of the Indian Civil Service." In 1883 in defining the principles of British government, he described it as "essentially an absolute government, whose basis is not consent, but conquest. It does not represent indigenous concepts of life and government and will never do so, for then it would represent idolatry and barbarity. It represents a belligerent civilization, and nothing could be more dangerous than to have in its administration, at the head of a government founded on conquest—implying at all points the superiority of the conquering race, its concepts, institutions, and principles, and which has no other justification for its existence than this superiority—men who hesitate to assert themselves openly, uncompromisingly, with conviction, and who in some way seek to justify their position and refuse, for whatever reason, to maintain it."

An important aspect of British policy was to spread the English system of education and the English language as the sole basis for university teaching. Only English diplomas were recognized and could be used to obtain employment. The ancient centers of Hindu culture were gradually annihilated and only the private teaching of master to pupil managed to preserve the Sanskrit language and Indian philosophy among the Brahmans, who devoted themselves exclusively to their priestly functions.

The period during which India was governed directly by the British Crown can be divided into two parts: the imperialistic age, from 1858 to 1905; and the period of reforms, from 1905 to 1937. The administration of India was controlled by a Secretary of State in London, and the policy followed, particularly by the Foreign Ministry, was dictated by European interests.

Relations between England and Russia became a dominant factor in Indian policy. In 1844, during the visit of Nicholas I to London, he and Queen Victoria had laid the foundations for an agreement on central Asia, in view of which the emirates of Bukhara, Khiva, and Samarkand should constitute a buffer zone between the two empires. This friendly agreement was shattered by the Crimean War, when Russian expansion was checked in southeastern Europe and consequently turned toward central Asia. At the same time, the conquest of the Punjab and Sind had brought the British Empire to the mountains of Afghanistan, the only region separating Russian and British outposts. A long series of clashes of influence and military operations ensued, in which the English, Persians, and Russians had the upper hand successively, and in which the interests of the Afghans themselves were not even considered.

Taking advantage of the *Treaty of Berlin*—which regulated European questions and prevented the Russians, without prejudice to the advantages they had already acquired, from going to war with England—British troops invaded Afghanistan, occupying Kandahar and then Kabul. The Emir, Sher Ali, fled to Turkestan and was replaced by his nephew, Abdur Rahman, who had to let his foreign policy be dictated by England in exchange for an annual subsidy. Clashes between the English and the Russians were inevitable, after the annexation of Merv by the latter and their occupation of several Afghan districts. Gladstone skillfully managed to avoid an armed conflict. Finally, in 1886, a commission succeeded in marking out the Russo-Afghan border.

The turbulent tribes on the Indo-Afghan border were, however, a constant source of problems for the British administration, necessitating the building of strategic roads and the keeping of considerable garrisons in the region. In a letter to Lord Lansdowne in about 1890, the Emir Abdur Rahman warned the English of the risk they were running in annexing the northwestern regions. "If you should cut them (the hill tribes) out of my dominions, they will neither be of any use to you or to me. You will always be engaged in fighting or other trouble with them and they will always go on plundering. As long as your Government is strong and in peace, you will be able to keep them quiet by a strong hand, but if at any time a foreign enemy appear on the borders of India these frontier tribes will be your worst enemies."[1]

The English had already occupied Rangoon and the south of Burma. In the north, King Mindon of the ancient dynasty continued to reign at Mandalay, to which the capital had been transferred in 1857, where the English had a Resident. The French had annexed Cochin-China and Tonkin, and sought to extend their influence over the north of Burma. France signed a commercial treaty with Burma in 1885 and negotiated the opening of a bank and the building of a railway. Taking as a pretext a sentence condemning an English company to pay a considerable fine, British troops occupied Mandalay in 1885. The French refused to aid King Thibaw, Mindon's successor. After several years of guerrilla fighting, the whole of Burma was annexed as part of the Indian Empire, with Rangoon as its capital.

Queen Victoria's proclamation, "We do not desire to extend our actual territorial possessions," was in principle a guarantee for the integrity of the princely states. The Governor of India, however, reserved the right to intervene on two grounds, "the absence of a legitimate heir" and "bad administration by *indigenous* chiefs." This in fact allowed states to be annexed or new princes appointed whenever the imperial government so desired.

Thus it was that the Gaekwar of Baroda was deposed and a child— vaguely belonging to his family and educated at British schools—was placed on the throne. Similarly, Manipur was occupied and its ruler executed following the assassination of four British officers. A child was placed on the throne, and a British political agent took over the state's administration. At the same time, after fifty years of British administration, the state of Mysore was given back to its legitimate ruler in 1881.

By *Act of Parliament* in 1876, Queen Victoria took the title of "Empress of India." All the princely states consequently found that they had become part of the empire, and the Indian princes became the

---

1. In R. C. Majumdar, H. C. Raychaudhuri, and K. Datta, *An Advanced History of India* (London, 1965), 838.

Crown's vassals. No succession could occur without the approval of the governor general, who represented the sovereign. A declaration of Lord Hardinge's, after his intervention in the state of Hyderabad, expressed the British position.

> The right of the British Government to intervene in the internal affairs of Indian states is another instance of the consequences necessarily involved in the supremacy of the British Crown. The British Government have indeed shown again and again that they have no desire to exercise this right without grave reason. But the internal, no less than the external, security which the Ruling Princes enjoy is due ultimately to the protecting power of the British Government, and where imperial interests are concerned, or the general welfare of the people of a State is seriously and grievously affected by the action of its Government, it is with the Paramount Power that the ultimate responsibility of taking remedial action, if necessary, lies. The varying degrees of internal sovereignty which the Rulers enjoy are all subject to the due exercise by the Paramount Power of this responsibility.[2]

A decision of the British Government in 1858 placed real power in the hands of the "Secretary of State for Indian Affairs" in London. The secretary of state was assisted by a council, the Council of India, formed of eminent persons deemed to have a long experience in Indian affairs. Precise powers were granted to the council so that it could exercise control over the secretary of state, who reacted badly to any such control. By *Act of Parliament* in 1869, the council was deprived of most of its powers and became a mere consultative organ. The British Parliament knew nothing of Indian problems and had no interest in them. The secretary of state thus ended up taking all decisions and considered the viceroy as his agent. The setting up of a telegraph line in 1870 between India and England made London's control over Calcutta, the Indian capital, even closer.

The Government of India was composed of the governor general and

---

2. *Ibid.*, 846.

his executive council. No Indian took part. An *Act of 1861* had established the principles of administration. For practical reasons, the various activities were divided into "portfolios" entrusted to the various members of the council and to the provincial governments of Calcutta, Bombay, and Madras.

THE EMPIRE'S INDUSTRIAL MONOPOLY

The opening of the Suez Canal in 1869 had led to a considerable increase in trade. Indian exports grew from about five million two hundred thousand rupees in 1855 to nine hundred million in 1900, and six billion in 1928. The kind of exports had changed, however. Gradually, Britain had strangled Indian industry, whose finished products—and textiles in particular—were unique worldwide for their quality. Indian production was instead oriented toward semi-finished products to be utilized by British industry, such as jute, cotton, tea, and oil seeds. Cheap labor thus worked for England, while craftwork declined.

In the second half of the nineteenth century, a vast network of railways was created, monopolizing transport to the benefit of English companies. Telegraph lines were begun in 1851 and an efficient postal system was set up in 1854. Major industries were born, but were to a large extent paralyzed by the British who, in the case of textiles, for example, demanded free entry for products from Lancashire and imposed a heavy tax on the export of Indian textiles.

The End of the Empire
and Independence

NEW RELIGIOUS MOVEMENTS

A certain number of nationalist and religious movements sought to adapt the ancient culture to what they considered to be the requirements of the modern world. As a rule, it concerned the adaptation of Protestant ideas to the Hindu world, somewhat like the Sikh movement's adaptation of Muslim ideas.

The first of these movements was the *Brahma Samaj,* founded by the Rajah Rammohan Roy in Bengal in 1828. After his death, Devendranath Tagore, the poet's father, took over the movement. He preached an abstract monotheism and was against the cult of images. He recommended the recitation of the *Veda* texts, but was open to all castes, favored intercaste marriage (forbidden by Hindu law) and the remarriage of widows.

This movement was split by several schisms, following disagreement about the breadth of the social reforms to be envisaged, the education of women, and so on. Keshab Chandra Sen—who joined the movement in 1857—was excluded by Devendranath because of his hostility to Brahmans and to the Sanskrit language. He then formed a new sect, called the "Brahma Samaj of India." He extolled the practice of ecstatic community singing, called *sankirtana*. The worship of idols was replaced, however, by the adoration of religious leaders, and in particular of Keshab himself. The scandal caused by the marriage of Keshab's fourteen-year-old daughter to the maharaja of Cooch Bihar gave rise to a new schism. This led to the formation of the *Sadharana Brahma Samaj*, an organization that played an important role in supporting the government in its reforms aimed at imposing Anglo-Saxon Christian ethics on Hindu society.

A branch of the Brahma Samaj developed in Maratha country under the name of *Prarthana Samaj*. It did not consider itself a new religion, but as a reform movement within Hinduism. The members of this new sect busied themselves in particular with social reforms, under the direction of a judge, Mahadev Govinda Ranade, who also played a major role in the growth of the Indian National Congress.

The founder of *Arya Samaj*, Swami Dayanand Saraswati (1824–1883), was a scholar of Sanskrit training, who had had no English education. The basis of his reform was a return to the Vedas, considered as revealed texts implicitly containing all knowledge, including modern science. His interpretation of the Vedas is often fanciful and is contested by traditional scholars, as also by modern linguists. He too was strictly monotheistic and recommended the conversion of non-Hindus to Hinduism, using a rite that he called *shuddhi* (purification). His doctrine is expressed in his work *Satyartha Prakash*.

Ramakrishna (1836–1886) was a mystic, a holy man, almost illiterate, the priest at a temple near Calcutta. In the various religions, he saw only different forms of the same aspiration toward the divine. He rejected no form of cult and spoke to his disciples in mysterious parables. He lived and died almost unknown. The foremost of his disciples was Narendranath Dutta (1863–1902), later known as Swami Vivekananda. Having had an English education, he was invited in 1893 to the "Parliament of Religions" in Chicago, where the force of his personality and his eloquence created a strong impression. Vivekananda founded a religious order called the "Ramakrishna Mission," on the lines of a Christian order. His aim was to reform Hindu beliefs and society, taking from Hinduism what appeared to be of value in the light of modern

Western ideas, and rejecting the rest. The monks of the Ramakrishna order preach the unity of all religions, practice conversion, and devote themselves to social work, considered as an essential part of religious life. The teaching of the Ramakrishna Mission is far removed from the profound philosophy of Hinduism, of which the Ramakrishna monks are usually quite ignorant, preaching merely a kind of Westernized Vedanta, based on a few texts that they interpret in their own way.

The Hindus are, however, still thankful to Vivekananda, since he was one of the first to obtain from the Western world a certain respect for Hinduism on principle, however distorted his version may have been. This attitude makes one think of what it must mean to certain unrecognized musical cultures, misrepresented by folklore groups who distort and degrade them, yet at the same time cause their existence and eventually even their worth to be acknowledged.

The Theosophical Society was founded in the United States in 1875 by a Russian lady, Mrs. H. P. Blavatsky, and by an American, Colonel H. S. Olcott. They came to India in 1879, and settled at Adyar, near Madras, in 1886. The further remarkable developments of the Theosophical Society were largely due to an Englishwoman, Mrs. Annie Bessant, who became a member in 1889, settled in India in 1893, and was Chairman of the Society until her death in 1933.

The Theosophical Society constitutes an important turning in the attitude of certain Western circles toward Hindu culture. It is based on the fundamental recognition of Hindu religion, rites, and institutions as expressing one of the highest forms of human wisdom and thought. Right from the start, the Theosophical Society was associated with the various movements of Hindu Modernism which proclaimed the validity and even the superiority of Hindu concepts on the one hand, while doing their best to reform those institutions on the other. In her autobiography Mrs. Bessant wrote in 1893 that the action to pursue in India was above all to revitalize, strengthen, and put back the ancient religions in a place of honor. This would bring a new feeling of self-respect, pride in the past, faith in the future, and inevitably a renewal of patriotism, the start of the rebuilding of a nation. Mrs. Bessant founded a "Hindu School" at

Varanasi, which was to become a college and the starting point for the Hindu University, founded in 1915.

The Theosophical Society exercised a great influence on the reforms undertaken by the government and on the growing nationalist movement called the "Indian National Congress," of which Mrs. Bessant was one of the Chairpersons. The attraction that the East exercised on Mrs. Blavatsky and most of the other members of the Society was, however, of a more occult and magical nature—the "mysterious East." Thus, instead of serving as a bridge, the Theosophical Society was a major obstacle in the contacts of serious Westerners with Hindu philosophy and religion. The British Government, by way of disorganizing the real Hindu institutions, secretly supported the modernist sects and theosophy, while at the same time appearing to sympathize with the religious life of the country.

THE AWAKENING OF NATIONALISM

The English in India were no longer adventurers, more often than not interested in the country for the wrong reasons. They were now officials who—thanks to the Suez Canal and new travel facilities—remained in contact with their home country and returned there frequently. They brought their families and no longer had Indian mistresses. Living in separate reservations tended to isolate them from the country they administered; they had only professional contacts with India and its culture. Discrimination in employment remained almost absolute. The *Act of 1793*, by which no Indian could earn a salary higher than eight hundred rupees, had not been repealed. Whether they were men of letters or princes, it forbade Indians anything other than subordinate employment.

The system of competitive examination for important posts—on principle open to all Her Majesty's subjects—required a stay of at least two years at an English university before the age of twenty-one, and an examination entirely English both in language and subject matter, in which the Indians were naturally at a disadvantage. Only in 1879 did an ordinance require that a portion of not more than one sixth of the administration's officials be reserved for Indians.

In response to the on-going economic and political inequities, a great national movement arose, known as "The Indian National Congress" or just "Congress." It began to call for—and sometimes obtained—constitutional reforms. The Congress first demanded the setting up of provincial governments in states other than Bengal, Bombay, and Madras, and the extension of the councils to admit elected members, as well as wider powers for the councils, including in particular that of debating the budget and demanding information in the form of interpolations. Lord Dufferin advised the government in London to give way to these demands to a certain, even if very limited, extent. This led to the *Indian Councils Act of 1892*. For the Indians, this was the first step toward the possibility of making their voice heard in matters concerning their country's destiny.

A commission appointed by Lord Dufferin proposed to divide administrative posts into three categories: imperial, provincial, and subordinate. The first two categories were set aside for the British, while the last was left almost entirely to Indians. It was this system that remained in force, with some slight changes, up to independence. However, no administrative or commercial post was open to any Indian who had not received an English education. This led to a school and university system in which education had no connection with the country's own culture. This system was also in force in the French colonies. In India as elsewhere, it had disastrous results from a cultural point of view, tending to form a class of Indians whose allegiance to English culture was only superficial and who were almost entirely ignorant of their own. This class of superficial and pretentious individuals—despised by the Europeans as well as their fellow-citizens who had preserved their heritage of Indian culture—was to be, after the end of the colonial era, the source of almost all the difficulties that followed.

Indians sent to be educated in England absorbed the notions of democracy and patriotism that were the British political and social ideal in the nineteenth century. A great liberalist movement stirred British literature and politics and the same liberal attitude was seen in British proclamations concerning India. In 1858 Queen Victoria declared, "The same obligations that bind us to all our other subjects bind us equally to the natives of our Indian territories." This had all the more meaning in that the queen had granted a democratic constitution to Canada in 1848, an event followed by the emancipation of several colonies. The British in India, however, were not at all of that opinion. With few exceptions, they refused to admit Indians to other than minor posts in their administration.

Thus, when the Indians educated in England returned to India, imbued with Anglo-Saxon liberalism, they found their hopes frustrated, and turned to active agitation. This explains the character of the movement called the Indian National Congress. It was not a revolt of the Indian masses, princes, or scholars, but of an anglicized minority who found that they were refused equality outside England. The Congress—basing its politics on notions of democracy that were entirely foreign to India—wished to be a political and secular movement, open to all Indians, whatever their race, caste, or religion. Such idealism did not correspond to Indian realities and was to result in the tragic partition of India and, further, to the mistakes into which the government of independent India was to fall.

At the instigation of an Englishman, A. O. Hume, a certain number of Indians occupying major posts met in Bombay at the end of December 1885, under the leadership of a Bengali lawyer, W. C. Bonnerjea. This meeting was the origin and basis of the Indian National Congress. In his inaugural speech, Hume declared that the aim of the Congress was to allow all those who were working for the national cause to know each other personally, to discuss and decide on the political operations to be undertaken in the course of the year. He stated that the conference would indirectly form the core of a native parliament and, if properly managed, would constitute an irrefutable answer to the assertion that India was incapable of having representative institutions.

Up to the end of the nineteenth century, Congress merely criticized the government, but with moderation and dignity. It affirmed its loyalty to the Crown and its faith in the liberalism and sense of justice of the British statesmen. To begin with, the government was favorably disposed toward Congress, considering it a mine of information concerning the feelings of the population. This initial attitude was soon to change into suspicion. Congress then pursued a policy of constitutional agitation, both in England and in India, and occasionally managed to obtain from the British Parliament laws in favor of Indians. At the same time, the non-Indian nature of Congress ideology aroused hostility among wide sections of the population, including the Marathas, proud of their religious and political tradition, and the Muslims, who were not greatly interested in Western culture. The movements set up by Bal Gangadhar Tilak, a Maratha Brahman, and by Sir Syed Amad, the Muslim leader, were, however, still impregnated with Anglo-Saxon idealism. It would be a long time before authentically traditionalist Hindu and Muslim parties were to be seen.

During the early years of the twentieth century, as Indian nationalism was developing, the British Government's control over the Government of India was strongly reaffirmed. However, a 1909 reform allowed an Indian, Lord Sinha, to become a member of the Governor General's Executive Council for the first time and the legislative councils of the various provinces gradually included a few anglicized Indians. But the same reform facilitated conflict between Muslims and Hindus by instituting separate electorates for the two communities. The 1914–1918 war—in which considerable contingents of Indian troops took part—was the opportunity for the Indian nationalist movements to demand a greater share in the government.

GANDHI

At that time there appeared on the Indian scene an enigmatic character—shrewd and ascetic, ambitious and devout—one of those gurus who seem to exercise an incredible magnetism over the crowds and often lead them to disaster. This character was called Mohan Das Gandhi. A sentimental religiosity tied to a lack of scruples appears to favor the creation of personages who exercise this kind of magnetism over the masses. Gandhi had much in common with the gurus who, in our own time, fascinate so many otherwise reasonable people. Within a few years, Gandhi eclipsed all the other Congress leaders and became a kind of symbol of India.

Practically, it was with him alone that the British Government ultimately decided the future of India, in which independence came about in the most disastrous way imaginable, leading to the partitioning of the country, one of the greatest massacres in history, the elimination of the social system and traditional culture, the suppression of the princely caste, the genocide of primitive tribes, and the ruin of the artisan castes and their transformation into a miserable proletariat. All this was presented as progress. Hindu scholars looked upon Gandhi as a sort of Antichrist, and made thank-offerings when he was assassinated. But it was too late. While he was alive, none dared oppose his baneful influence. A great deal of time would have to pass before the victims of his charisma, in India as in the West, dared draw up the balance of his action.

In order to understand Gandhi's character, it must be remembered that he was a Bania, a member of the merchant caste. In India each caste has its own peculiar moral, intellectual, and religious concepts, making them a kind of sect. In the West the group that is mentally closest to the Indian merchants could be the Anglo-Saxon Quakers. The characteristics of the caste from which Gandhi came include extreme puritanism, the strictest vegetarianism, a total absence of metaphysical preoccupations and philosophical culture, offset by the grossest religious sentimentality, expressed by a Sunday school sort of art whose colored images are nowadays everywhere to be found. Charity is among the virtues that justify the merchant's avidity for gain, but not social justice. An icy puritanism masks dishonesty in all money and business matters. Wherever they may be, Indian merchants sooner or later end up owning everything.

His origins explain why this apparently ascetic person could always count on the unqualified support of major Indian capitalists such as the Birlas and the Tatas and why, at the same time, the social reforms he undertook were always to the advantage of the merchant middle class and landed proprietors. Caste solidarity played in his favor, whereas the Brahmanic and princely world regarded this fanatical Bania with distrust and occasionally with a certain disgust. The policy of the Congress Party, guided by this strange ascetic, led to the triumph of the merchant, industrial, and capitalist caste.

Mohan Das Gandhi (1869–1948) was the son of an official in the service of one of the minor princes of Kathiawar. He studied to be a lawyer in England, becoming a barrister in London. Clothed in the black frock coat and stiff collar of an English lawyer, he went to South Africa where he lead a movement demanding equal rights for Indians and Europeans. After a short term in the prisons of Pretoria, he arrived in India in 1914 and at once began to play a role in the political agitation that reigned during the First World War.

Gradually, Gandhi changed his character and appearance. The young revolutionary anglicized lawyer from South Africa was transformed into an Indian monk, half-naked and wearing rough homespun. It was claimed that this transformation was suggested to him by the Muslim leader and member of Congress, Mohammed Ali Jinnah. Gandhi's look of a Biblical prophet won the trust of the Indian masses and impressed the Westerners. His companions gave him the title of *Mahatma* (Great Soul). But he never convinced the elite of the traditional Hindu world, who considered him an impostor and a dangerous politician. Gandhi slowly took over the Congress Party, displacing the great moderate leaders, who had included Tilak, Lajpat Rai, S.N. Banerjee, Gokhale, and Annie Bessant. The little white cap adopted by the members of Congress was a copy of the prisoners' forage cap that Gandhi had worn in the prisons of South Africa.

The Turkish Empire was dismembered at the end of the 1914–1918 war and the sultan deposed. The sultan was the caliph of Muslim believers and his downfall made a profound impression on the Muslims of India. Great Britain was the principal beneficiary of the breaking up of the Turkish Empire and the humiliation suffered by the "Commander of the Faithful" exacerbated anti-British feeling among Indian Muslims. Gandhi took over the leadership of a movement in favor of the sultan. The All-India Khilafat Conference, presided over by Gandhi, threatened to launch a non-cooperation movement if Great Britain did not find a solution to the Turkish problem that was acceptable to Muslims. This allowed Gandhi to rally to the nationalist cause the Muslim masses, who until then had been very indifferent. On 20 August 1917, the secretary of state for India announced in the House of Commons that "The policy of His Majesty's Government, with which the Government of India is in complete accord, is to encourage the association and progressive development of independent institutions, with a view to establishing representative government in India, within the framework of the British Empire." However, the governor general retained exclusive authority over "reserved subjects," such as the police, justice and prisons, irrigation, forests, land revenues, and the inspection of industries. The Indians were disappointed by the English proposals and—under the leadership of Gandhi, who had just taken over Congress—a general strike (*hartal*) was decreed throughout the country in 1919. It completely paralyzed industry, administration, and transport.

In 1928 a commission chaired by Sir John Simon recommended the establishment of responsible government in the provinces. As a result, the British Government set up a conference in London, with the aim of establishing a project of constitutional reform for India. Gandhi took part in the second session, from September to November 1931. In 1935 the British Parliament voted a constitutional bill that was ultimately only partially implemented. It envisaged a federation of the provinces and princely states in which the governors would retain their powers of absolute veto. By July 1937 Congress had formed governments in most of the provinces. Guarantees were given to the princes, assuring them that the treaties that bound them to the Crown would not, without their agreement, be transferred to any new government of India, responsible to an Indian Parliament. These promises were not to be kept.

THE INDIAN NATIONAL CONGRESS

As we have already seen, the Congress was a non-religious political movement, mostly formed of Indians with an Anglo-Saxon education and ideology. To obtain the consent of the Indian masses, it needed some sort of religious cover. The reform movements, such as the Arya Samaj and Brahma Samaj, provided Congress with an alibi, allowing its leaders to attack their ancestral institutions, not on a purely political and social basis, but under the cover of a difference of religious opinion, a position that was perfectly acceptable to the Hindus.

Congress encouraged cultural organizations that took their inspiration from Anglo-Saxon idealism, picturesquely disguised in cheap Indian finery. The most important of these organizations was *Visvabharati*, a school created by Rabindranath Tagore at Santiniketan, in Bengal. Tagore was a disciple of Tolstoy, a friend of Romain Rolland, and a poet of astonishing versatility. His idealism and internationalism made him a very engaging character. The son of a religious reformer, he was profoundly hostile to all that Hinduism traditionally represented. But he did not trust Gandhi and withdrew from the Congress Party when Gandhi became its leader.

Another of these pseudo-traditional organizations was the ashram of Shri Aurobindo at Pondicherry. Aurobindo's religious syncretism provided a useful alibi for attacking traditional Hindu institutions. Congress governments everywhere encouraged the spread of education on an Anglo-Saxon model, disguised as Indian. The teaching of philosophy, the arts, and sciences that formed the prestigious cultural tradition of India was only able to survive thanks to the Brahmans who, without any government aid, continued to do their best to maintain India's cultural heritage. The official institutions teaching the Sanskrit culture and traditional sciences, like the Hindu University at Varanasi, organized their teaching according to Western methods, with very mediocre results.

Little by little, cultural and political movements were organized to defend the traditional culture, religion, and structure of Hindu society. The first was Hindu Mahasabha, whose aim was to counterbalance the influence of the Muslim League. Then, toward 1939—inspired by a Hindu monk of extraordinary culture and intelligence, Swami Karpatri—the Dharma Sangh cultural movement was born. It was followed in 1947 by a political movement, Jana Sangh, which has continued to oppose the Westernizing cultural policy of the Indian Government.

Utilizing British techniques, the Congress attacked these movements by trying to ridicule them, vastly exaggerating tales of untouchability, cow worship, and so on. Congress downplayed the existence and importance of the movements themselves. Thus, the Congress newspapers would devote a page to the visit of any party member to some town or other and would not even mention a meeting at which Dharma Sangh had gathered fifty thousand people. This policy was highly effective as far as foreign opinion was concerned. Since most of the Congress press was in the English language—whereas the traditionalist parties always employed Indian tongues—it was easy for Congress to present the Hindu parties as retrograde, fanatical, and ridiculous at the international level. Congress thus ensured that when independence was obtained, power would be transferred to itself, although it only represented a weak, anglicized minority. As the price of power, Gandhi accepted the partition of India, as useless as it was ill-fated. It was opposed by all moderate Hindus and Muslims who considered that since the British had to leave India in any case, it was useless to hasten it on and pay such a price.

In 1930 the Muslim poet Iqbal suggested that an independent state should be created in the northwest provinces. It was a Bengali Muslim, Chaudhuri Rahmat Ali, who at Cambridge invented the word *Pakistan* (which in Urdu means "Land of the Pure"), formed from the initials of the three provinces, Punjab, Kashmir, and Sind. When Britain declared that India was at war in 1939, the Congress refused to collaborate, but the Muslim League accepted, thus giving the Muslims an advantage during subsequent negotiations.

The princely states loyally supported England and India's resources and troops played an important role in Egypt against Rommel's army and in Burma against the Japanese. Indian losses were of the order of eighty thousand men, out of an army of about two million. Congress's condition for supporting the war effort was the formation of a national government, but in this they were not satisfied. In the meantime, in 1940, Mohammed Ali Jinnah, the Chairman of the Muslim League, challenged the notion of a democratic parliament based on a "head-count" and declared that the Muslims formed a separate nation. He officially demanded that India should be divided into two independent states.

In August 1942 Congress adopted a resolution recommending a

movement of non-cooperation and civil disobedience as widespread as possible. In a speech on the India question addressed to the Americans, Sir Stafford Cripps, Lord Privy Seal and Leader of the House of Commons, declared,

> Gandhi has demanded that we should quit India, which would leave the country the prey of religious divisions, without a government resting on a solid constitutional basis, and without an organized administration. No government conscious of its responsibilities could take such a measure, especially in the midst of a war. What is certain is that Gandhi's current threat—civil disobedience—aims at endangering yours and our war effort, and at providing the most important aid to our common enemies. It is possible that he may obtain mass civil disobedience, but it is our duty to insist that India remain a base where order and security reign. Whatever measures we may judge it necessary to take, we must take them fearlessly. We have offered to grant India an independent government when the war has been won. But for that, the Indians must not put spokes in our wheels.

Churchill sent Sir Stafford Cripps to India to propose dominion status after the cessation of hostilities if India's leaders cooperated in the country's defense. Gandhi compared this offer to a "blank cheque on a bankrupt bank." The Japanese had entered the war, and Indian sympathies were now on the side of the Axis. One of Congress's most brilliant leaders, Subhas Chandra Bose, had managed to escape from India in 1941. He contacted the Germans and was received by Hitler. He subsequently settled in Japan and, following an agreement with the Japanese, took charge of Indian prisoners who had fallen into the hands of the Japanese army. He used them to organize the Army of Free India (*Azad Hind Fauj*). He created a Government of Free India at Singapore in 1942 and his army advanced together with the Japanese to the borders of India, later surrendering to the British after Japan's defeat. Subhas Chandra Bose died in a plane crash.

On 8 August 1942 Congress adopted the "Quit India" motion and proclaimed a movement of civil disobedience. Many moderate Indians were, like the English, shocked at this stab in the back of an England that was defending itself so valiantly. This gesture, as little chivalrous as it was useless, was typical of Gandhi's mentality. Tagore—who had disassociated himself from Congress when Gandhi took over—was very opposed to it. Gandhi's refusal obliged the British to have recourse to repression. The Government outlawed Congress, imprisoned all its leaders and adopted severe measures of control. Nine hundred and forty persons were killed during the riots, six hundred and thirty wounded, sixty thousand arrested, and eighteen thousand detained without trial.

INDIA AND PAKISTAN

Hinduism is not a religion, in the generally accepted meaning of the word. In Hinduism there are no prophets who have fixed once and for all the "truths" that must be believed, or unalterable rules of conduct common for all. Hinduism is a philosophy, a way of thinking, which penetrates and coordinates all aspects of life and seeks to harmonize it with an infinitely diversified world whose fundamental causes are beyond the grasp of humankind.

Even among the less sophisticated social classes, toleration is seen as a basic virtue. Each seeks to do his best, according to his capacity, but none can know the path another must follow to attain the divine and self-realization. All human beings are different and none can judge the mysterious intentions of the gods, by whose will one person is born rich, handsome, intelligent, or strong, and another poor, ugly, stupid, or sickly. The violence, excessive assurance, unconsidered dogmatism, and proselytism of Muslims and Christians are to Hindus naïve and impious attitudes. What madman can claim to know the secret intentions of the gods?

This is why Hindu conversions to Islam and Christianity have been rare and occur only among the lower social classes, due to force, interest, or the need to survive. Such conversions as often as not are merely superficial. Many of India's Muslims are vegetarians, observe the Hindu rites of purification, worship Kali, the goddess of death, and sing about the loves of Krishna. Most of them are Shiites, like the Persians. They are inclined to mysticism, and their conception of Islam is very different from that of the puritan and aggressive Sunnis. In India Sunni Muslims are mostly foreigners, those who came with the armies of Arab, Turkish, or Mongol invaders. They formed the administrative class around the emperors, but their numbers were never very great.

Trade and industry have always been in Hindu hands. The Muslim conquerors were merely soldiers forming a kind of warrior elite, whereas the converted Indians belonged to the artisan classes. A very large number of the less favored classes had been forcefully converted to Islam and formed a very numerous Muslim artisan and peasant proletariat. They provided servile labor and, at the time of the partition, massacred the Hindus, who were the commercial, land-owning, and intellectual class. For them, it was a movement of social and economic, rather than religious, demands, not without some analogy to anti-Semitism.

For the Hindus, Muslims simply belonged to a different caste, and could live as they saw fit, so long as they did not interfere with the customs of other castes. Many Hindus appreciated the extreme Persian courtesy that had been preserved among cultivated Muslims. In the nineteenth and twentieth centuries, a great number of Indian poets and musicians were Muslims, applauded and honored by the whole people.

The political maneuvers that made it possible to set these two overlapping communities against each other had been long prepared by the British with a view to the partition of India, as a way for Britain to retain control over the subcontinent when independence seemed inevitable. Quite a number of English administrators who opposed this Machiavellian plan were removed over the years. Mohammed Ali Jinnah was then encouraged to set up a "Muslim League," formed of the most aggressive Sunni elements. The Muslim population as a whole let the League do what they wanted, rather as the Hindus did with Congress. Very likely encouraged by the British secret service and with the aim of creating an irreversible situation, in 1946 Jinnah declared a "day of direct action." On all sides, the Muslims attacked the Hindus, causing violent reactions. At Calcutta alone, there were over 4000 dead on the first day, followed almost everywhere by similar operations. After the cunningly managed riots, the two communities were equally worried. Worry mounted among peoples who had lived side by side for generations, in the same villages, the same towns, the same districts.

Taking as a pretext the riots it had itself organized, the British Government proposed a partition of India between a Muslim Pakistan and a Hindu India (*Bharat*). This was accepted by both the Muslim League and by Congress, despite the opposition of all moderate elements, both Hindu and Muslim. Partition was proclaimed on 3 June 1947 and Sind, Baluchistan, the Northwest Province, western Punjab, and eastern Bengal were ceded to Pakistan. The absurd creation of Pakistan as two regions separated by 2000 kilometers of Indian territory was to be solved later on by the secession of Bengal and the proclamation of an independent Bangladesh.

Pakistan was thus formed of populations with very different languages and customs. Baluchistan spoke both Persian and an ancient Dravidian language, Brahui. Sind and Punjab spoke Urdu, (a Persianized variety of Hindi). Bengal spoke Bengali. The turbulent tribes of the northern frontiers spoke Pushtu, like their Afghan neighbors, and claimed their own independence.

INDEPENDENCE

Lord Wavell, viceroy of India from October 1943, was a firm and moderate man. He succeeded in reestablishing order and creating favorable conditions for the eventual transfer of power. Starting in 1946, the British sent a series of missions to India to prepare a constitution. On 2 September 1946, Jawaharlal Nehru and his colleagues, just out of prison, agreed to become members of the viceroy's Executive Council.

In the meantime, the Labor Party had come to power in Britain and the Attlee government—with the unconsidered impatience that often characterizes socialist ideologues—announced in February 1947 the British decision to quit India in June 1948. Such haste made negotiations particularly difficult and encouraged blackmail. The Muslim intelligentsia who had dominated India under the Mogul Empire were now a minority. They demanded a special status and guarantees that Congress refused in the name of its democratic principles. Such intransigence gave Jinnah the chance to demand the division of India into separate states, Hindu or Muslim dominated. Lord Mountbatten was sent to India to organize the takeover of power. He took office as viceroy on 24 March 1947.

Under pressure to conclude, Mountbatten talked only with the leaders of Congress and the Muslim League, thus giving inordinate importance to the two parties to whose creation the British had contributed. He totally ignored the other political movements, the Hindu parties, the Marathas, the ministers of the princely states, whether Hindu or Muslim, the Dravidians, and the tribes.

Mountbatten wished to negotiate solely with the three lawyers of the London bar, namely Gandhi, Nehru, and Jinnah. The fate of India was decided among "the right kind of people" at drawing room conversations in which Lady Mountbatten took an active part. Mountbatten, pressed by time—a circumstance that favored Jinnah's claims—imposed the partition of India. He organized the transfer of power to Congress and the Muslim League, who in no way represented the people as a whole. Their only legitimization was conferred by Britain in choosing them as interlocutors. Indeed, the Muslim League was an artificial party, with neither structures nor members, created from scratch by Mohammed Ali Jinnah after his break with the Congress Party. The Congress Party itself was a non-confessional and anti-traditionalist revolutionary party. It was monstrous to consider that it represented the Hindus, when the highly organized Hindu parties like the Jana Sangh and Rashtriya Swayam Sevak Sangh had been totally ignored.

The partition of India was decided in abstract, on paper, without sufficient preparation. On 3 June 1947—less than three months after his arrival in an India with whose problems he was not familiar—Lord Mountbatten launched a proclamation on how power would be transferred to the Indians. The proclamation indicated that not only the provinces but also the districts with a Muslim majority, could, if they desired, form a separate dominion. This was to lead to the partition of Bengal and the Punjab.

Despite serious dissension, the Congress Party and the Muslim League accepted this offer in the end, against the will of all the other parties. On 16 August 1947 India and Pakistan were declared independent, within the framework of the British Commonwealth. Lord Mountbatten was appointed Governor General of India, and Mohammed Ali Jinnah was appointed Governor General of Pakistan.

Except for a few regions on the Afghan border, there was no region in India in which the two communities were not present. The country was divided according to the percentage of the population. Regions with over fifty percent Muslims were declared Muslim and given to Pakistan. Everything depended, naturally, on how the regions were drawn up. In Bengal, where the two populations had more or less equal numbers, it would have sufficed to take the province as a whole for it to remain with India. By dividing Bengal into districts and leaving aside the enormous city of Calcutta, with its large Hindu majority, an East Pakistan was created out of the rural areas, which was an absurdity. It later proclaimed its own independence in 1971 under the name of Bangladesh.

Furthermore, by placing India and Pakistan on the same footing, Britain divided the subcontinent between the secular multi-religious state of India, in which citizens' rights were defined by modern laws, and the theocratic state of Pakistan, where only Koranic law was allowed, which recognized no rights of non-Muslims and made their murder a virtue. The Hindu parties were never consulted, since Nehru, an agnostic, and Gandhi, an enlightened reformer, in no way represented the Hindu population. Gandhi's disguise as a holy man was a carefully used mask to make the outside world believe he represented the Hindus.

Over half the Muslims remained in India. On the other hand, the Hindus in Pakistan were despoiled, massacred, deprived of their civil rights and protection. The mass of the survivors abandoned their homes, lands, and villages in an exodus that was one of the most frightening of modern times, and has not yet been completed. Millions of wretches took refuge in an already over-populated India. Many died of starvation and poverty in the improvised camps or on the streets of Calcutta, transformed into a "court of miracles." The massacres and exchanges of those populations who survived the partition were terrifying. A conservative estimate made by Judge G. D. Khosla (*Stern Reckoning*, page 299) counted five hundred thousand dead and ten and a half million displaced persons.

When the tension created by the refugees threatened to cause a massacre of the Muslims remaining in India, Gandhi—who had only reluctantly signed the partition agreement and had left in an attempt to calm the agitation in Bengal—returned to Delhi to defend the Muslims threatened with reprisals and to demand that a part of the monetary reserves should be made over to Pakistan. On 20 January 1948 he was assassinated while taking part in a prayer meeting in New Delhi. The main reason behind his assassination by a young Brahman belonging to the orthodox party was the dismay caused by Gandhi's hostility toward the traditional Hindu institutions, deemed much more pernicious than previous British indifference. Another reason was Gandhi's over-conciliatory attitude toward the Muslims, despite the terrible massacres that had preceded and followed the partition of India. Gandhi preached that cooperation could be won by love and disinterest, whereas the Muslims of both India and Pakistan were shouting everywhere, "We have had Pakistan for a song; Delhi will cost us a battle!" Publication of the murderer's plea in court to explain his gesture was forbidden in India. Gandhi's death was celebrated with thanksgiving services in many Hindu cities. It is difficult to say what India might have been had Gandhi lived. His prestige was great. He was equally opposed to the political structures of traditional India as to the industrialization of the country. All his disciples had to spin and weave their own garments. His egalitarianism, in a country with such diverse races and cultures, was impracticable. It appears that, despite their statements, certain Congress leaders were rather relieved to be free from the old dreamer.

While India kept the main industrial hubs and ninety-five percent of the hydroelectric power stations, Pakistan's only important city was

Lahore. Like Dacca, Karachi was only a small regional center. Furthermore, the Hindus that took refuge in India were all from the professional and commercial classes, as well as artisans, whereas the Muslims who left India for Pakistan were mostly peasant laborers. Pakistan was forced to employ a large number of former British officials to run its administration. Though it possesses some mining resources, cadres and organization have continued to be lacking and literacy remains very low.

On both a human and a political level, the partition of India was a mistake made by the last British colonizers. It gave the Middle East an unstable state—Pakistan—without any economic, industrial, or cultural superstructures. At the same time, it burdened India with an enormous weight to add to the already serious problems that were overwhelming it. The balance of the operation was, however, to be paid by the West.

India, whose former frontiers had been beyond Afghanistan, had—with the loss of "the Land of the Seven Rivers" (the Indus Valley)—lost the historical center of its civilization. At the very moment when the Muslim invaders appeared to have abandoned their virulence and to have become gradually assimilated with the other peoples of India, the European conqueror, before returning home, delivered the very cradle of the Hindu world up to their fanaticism.

The princely states found themselves in a difficult position. The British Crown could not maintain its suzerainty and this could not be transferred to the governments of India and Pakistan. Some states accepted the principle of an Indian union, in which the states' internal administration would remain independent. Other states wanted to proclaim their independence. This was unacceptable to the Congress Government. Most of the states were gathered into a union and their maharajas dispossessed. Two problems remained: that of Hyderabad, in the center of India, with a Muslim sovereign, but where the majority of the population was Hindu; and Kashmir, with a Hindu sovereign and a Muslim majority. After the Nizam of Hyderabad threatened to join with Pakistan, Sardar Patel—who had become Minister of the Interior—dispatched the Indian army to invade the state and imprison the Prime

Minister. The Nizam was forced to sign a Deed of Annexation on 26 January 1950 and his states were divided up.

As a frontier state between India, Pakistan, Afghanistan, and Tibet, Kashmir posed a more delicate problem. Armed bands from Pakistan occupied a part of Kashmir. The maharaja immediately signed the *Deed of Union* with India on 26 October 1947, and Indian troops were flown in starting from the day after. The question is still unsolved. Indian and Pakistani troops came face to face and since then have maintained their positions. Pakistan continues to occupy a part of Kashmir. The problem has been pending before the United Nations Security Council since 1948. The country remains divided between two armies of occupation.

After the death of Gandhi, power lay in the hands of two men. One was the Prime Minister, Nehru, a socialist of aristocratic origins. The other was Sardar Vallabhai Patel, Deputy Prime Minister and Minister of the Interior, an energetic and conservative man of plebeian origin who was trusted by the industrial and land-owning class as well as by the Hindu traditionalists. He had succeeded in integrating the princely states, had annexed Hyderabad, and had growing influence. He was the only person who could have found a compromise between the values of traditional society and modernism. Unfortunately, he was to die in 1950, leaving Nehru as the sole master of India.

PART SEVEN

India after Independence

25
Congress and the Nehru "Dynasty"

NEHRU

Jawaharlal Nehru—who became the dominant figure of the new India—was the perfect replica of a certain kind of Englishman, courteous, elegant, with a hint of affectation. He often employed the expression "continental people," in speaking of the French or Italians, with benevolent and amused superiority. He despised non-anglicized Indians and had but a very superficial and restricted acquaintance with Indian culture, acquired solely through works in the English language. He spoke Hindi and Urdu badly, somewhat like a British non-commissioned officer. By taste and habit, Nehru was a Westerner, a layman who refused to consider himself a Hindu and who rejected all the values of traditional society.

"Nehru's outlook was essentially that of a democratic socialist of the nineteen-thirties, [but . . . he rejected] Gandhi's belief in village democracies loosely knit in a non-industrial society because he believed that the introduction of modern mechanized industry was the only way by which [eliminating poverty] could be done."[1]

"Nehru is an aristocrat by birth and by culture, a Brahman, the son

1. Percival Spear, *A History of India* (London, 1965–1970), 246.

of a great westernised lawyer, educated at Harrow and Cambridge, he has never left the peaks. . . . Nehru is impulsive and from certain points of view a romantic, with charm and goodness and simple tastes, although he is sensitive to the aesthetic side. . . . His explosions of rage are famous."[2] Nehru was first and foremost an absolute autocrat.

The Hindus, who by and large had supported Congress in its fight for independence, believed that the Anglo-Saxon inspired modernist ideology of the Congress leaders was a political arm used to justify independence in Western eyes. They thought that once independence had been won, Congress would revise its principles and reestablish respect for Sanskrit culture, along with the religious and social institutions that are the basis of Indian civilization. This was not to be so. The minority—who were the Congress leaders—were far too anglicized and their level was too mediocre to be able to reconsider the value of what they had learned, as any Englishmen of culture could have done. Few things changed in the administration, except the color of the skin of the new directors, who were often none other than the underlings of the former regime occupying their master's place.

A new Constitution was enacted by a Constituent Assembly according to Nehru's ideas. This new Constitution, wholly inspired by Western models, in conformity with European ethical and political conceptions, abolished all the traditional institutions. Based on universal suffrage and the absolute equality of all individuals, it suppressed in one fell swoop the guarantees and protections enjoyed by the various ethnic and religious groups and corporations. It was just such egalitarian intransigence that had led the Muslim minority to demand the partition of Indian territory. The other minorities were henceforth defenseless in the face of the exactions of the merchant bourgeoisie.

The Constitution made India a republic within the Commonwealth. Gandhi's non-violence, which had served his anti-British policy, was quickly forgotten. Nehru used the military to annex Goa and Portugal's Indian territories in 1961. France preferred to withdraw voluntarily from

---

2. Jacques Pouchpadass, *L'Inde au XXe Siècle* (Paris, 1975), 243.

its trading posts and Pondicherry was integrated with India in 1956.

Desirous of playing a central role among Asian countries, Nehru was the initiator of the group of non-aligned countries. Like many men of the left at the time, Nehru considered Marxism as an ideal, even if he did not approve of its application within the Soviet Union. Despite border conflicts, he sought a rapprochement with Communist China. Zhou Enlai was received in Delhi with great honor. India did not even lift a hand when China occupied Tibet. As a result of the Tibetan revolt, crushed by the Chinese in 1959, the Dalai Lama fled to India with a following of 13,000 Tibetans, displeasing the Chinese. At the same time, the Chinese were building a motorway over part of the Tibetan plateau that was theoretically under Indian sovereignty. A series of incidents finally led to a conflict. In October 1962 China attacked India in Assam and Ladakh. The Indian troops were routed. After a short occupation, however, the Chinese withdrew to their former position.

Nehru then found himself facing a serious economic crisis. Currency reserves were exhausted. Agricultural stagnation turned to penury, which caused rioting at the outset of 1964. Nehru died shortly afterward, on 27 May 1964. He left most of his enterprises unachieved, his efforts at modernization had above all served to develop a middle class, with no advantage for the population at large.

CONGRESS LEADERS AFTER NEHRU

Lal Bahadur Shastri—a modest and relatively unobtrusive man who had been a member of Congress since the beginning—was designated as Nehru's successor. He soon had serious problems to tackle, particularly in the south, when Hindi was proclaimed the national language in 1965, despite the opposition of the Dravidian speaking peoples. He had then to face a war with Pakistan as a result of territorial clashes in Sind. The Indian army beat off the Pakistanis and even managed to threaten Lahore. A peace conference was organized by the Soviet Union at Tashkent. Lal Bahadur Shastri died tragically a few hours after signing the peace agreement.

The Congress refused to accept as his successor Morarji Desai, who represented the conservative wing of the party. Instead they chose Indira Gandhi, Nehru's daughter, as Prime Minister, although they forced Desai on her as Deputy Prime Minister and Minister of Finance. This nomination was in principle a temporary one, aiming to direct Congress affairs up to the elections of 1967.

INDIRA GANDHI

The daughter of Jawaharlal Nehru, Indira was brought up in Switzerland and England and attended Rabindranath Tagore's whimsical school at Santiniketan for some time. To the great scandal of her family, she made a love marriage (out of caste) when still very young, with a Parsi, Firoze Gandhi (no relation to the Mahatma), with whom she had two children. Her husband was soon left aside, however, since Indira lived in the shadow of her father, whose faithful collaborator she was and toward whom she bore limitless admiration.

Indira Gandhi was cold and authoritarian. Living in the midst of the rich anglicized bourgeoisie of New Delhi, she knew nothing about Indian culture and displayed a profound scorn for traditional institutions. Her interests were essentially political and she was not without skill. Immediately after being chosen as Prime Minister, Indira launched on a "progressive" policy and nationalized the fourteen private banks. The rupee was considerably devalued and Morarji Desai was forced to resign.

At the general election in February 1967, Congress lost 80 seats, while retaining a slight majority. The Congress then split into two branches: one conservative, known as "Organization Congress," and the other, which supported Mrs. Gandhi and was in power, called "Ruling Congress." The split obliged the Ruling Congress branch to call on the support of the parties of the left. At Madras, the Dravidian party D.M.K. won a majority. In Madhya Pradesh and Uttar Pradesh, the Hindu Jana Sangh won, in Gujarat the conservative Svatantra, and in Kerala, the communists. Unstable coalition governments were formed everywhere.

The general election of 1971 turned in the Congress Party's favor, thus supporting Indira and establishing her firmly as her father's successor.

Congress remained split, however, between an ideological wing and a governmental wing preaching authoritarian socialism. Taking up her father's rather vague socialistic ideas, Indira signed a mutual aid treaty with the Soviet Union, placing India in the Russian sphere of influence. Laws made to favor the needy classes succeeded only in attracting the peasant masses to the great cities, where they form a wretched proletariat.

THE BIRTH OF BANGLADESH

Besides having a slight Muslim majority at the time of the partition, East Pakistan (East Bengal) had nothing in common with West Pakistan, the Punjab. The two parts of the new state of Pakistan, separated by two thousand kilometers of Indian territory, did not even speak the same language. The Bengalis found it difficult to submit to the domination of the Arabized Muslims of the Punjab. An autonomist movement developed in Bengal, and its leader—Sheikh Mujibur Rahman, who favored improving relations with India—was elected with an overwhelming majority at the Pakistani National Assembly. On 25 March 1971, the Pakistani Government had him arrested, outlawed the autonomist movement, and ferociously repressed a revolt in Bengal. The result was a new exodus to India of about seven million Hindus and two million Bengali Muslims, causing terrible problems in West Bengal, once more invaded by starving refugees. Indira Gandhi launched an appeal for aid to the West that went unanswered. In the end, she obtained support from the Soviet Union.

Guerrilla warfare came into being in East Bengal, where the Mukhti Bahini (army of liberation), aided by India, paralyzed the administration. The Pakistani Government bombarded India's airports on 6 December 1971. This was the signal for an Indo-Pakistani war that lasted twelve days. The Indian army occupied East Pakistan and the Pakistani Bengali army was captured. From the outbreak of hostilities, India had recognized the independence of a new state called Bangladesh. Russia gave its assent, while China remained enigmatic. The Americans, irritated by the break-up of their policy of an Indo-Pakistani balance, were in the end resigned to the fact.

India in 1983

India withdrew its troops and was able to repatriate most of the refugees. Indira Gandhi visited Dacca, the new capital of Bangladesh, and signed a friendship agreement with Sheikh Mujibur Rahman. In June 1972 a summit meeting at Simla between Mrs. Gandhi and Z. A. Bhutto, the Prime Minister of Pakistan, led to an agreement for the mutual withdrawal of troops and repatriation of 93,000 Pakistani soldiers captured by the Indians.

The period of euphoria that followed the birth of Bangladesh was not to last long. As in other countries lacking solid social and economic structures, a series of military coups d'état have led to tyrannical methods of government, and brought the country to bankruptcy, thus making it clear that the division of Bengal on a religious basis was, and continues to be, an unbelievable absurdity.

East Bengal—present-day Bangladesh—essentially comprises the deltas of two immense rivers, the Ganges and the Brahmaputra, which join at that point. It is formed of small islands, separated by unstable watercourses and canals, and is subject to perpetual flooding. It is also periodically visited by typhoons. Bangladesh produces mostly rice and jute on scattered patches of land. All the industrial and commercial organizations that utilized Bengali goods are in the region of Calcutta, part of India. Furthermore, Bangladesh is surrounded on all sides by territories belonging to the Indian Union, Assam in particular, which is a great tea producer and now communicates with the rest of India by means of a narrow corridor. A population of poor peasants with an aberrant demographic growth makes Bangladesh a non-viable state, one that can only survive thanks to international aid and loans. In 1979 the population was 87 million with a territory of 142,800 square kilometers.

THE JANA SANGH

Her military successes against Pakistan confirmed Indira Gandhi's popularity. A new agricultural plan established in 1970 brought about a spectacular improvement in rice production, but nothing managed to slow a population increase of over twelve million every year. India devoured its prosperity by producing too many mouths to feed. In 1975 the lack of foodstuffs, together with the increase in the price of oil, inflation, and corruption, led to revolt. Indira Gandhi imposed a "State of Emergency" and had the opposition leaders arrested. In 1977 the State of Emergency came to an end and elections were held. Indira Gandhi lost her majority to a coalition calling itself the "*Janata* (Peoples) Party." This coalition was formed mainly of the Jana Sangh (the Hindu orthodox party), supported by the Rashtriya Swayam Sevak Sangh (the paramilitary Maratha organization), the Bharatiya Lok Dal (the peasants' party founded in 1967 by the vigorous seventy-year-old Chandra Singh of Uttar Pradesh), as well as by Svatantra (the party of the pro-American landed proprietors led by Morarji Desai, the intransigent and austere conservative former Prime Minister of Bombay), and lastly by the socialist party of the old leader Jai Prakash Narayana.

Such a patchwork coalition could not govern effectively. Indeed, in 1977 it had been the Jana Sangh, representing the majority of the electorate, that had overthrown Indira Gandhi's government, but its alliance with the Socialist Party—which opposed the Congress for different reasons—could not work. Lacking any authoritative leader capable of taking radical measures and eliminating its own allies, the Jana Sangh could not succeed.

If too many concessions are made to socialist ideas, conservative parties lose the trust of their electorate without gaining the sympathies of the left. Jana Sangh's problem was that it was a movement organized by Brahmans and sannyasins, by priests and monks, based on principles of religion and culture, but lacking any feeling for political amorality.

The new government was incapable of taking effective measures and Indira Gandhi returned to power in 1980. Her efforts to introduce her elder son Sanjay into political life and thus in some way assure the dynastic succession did not meet with success. Sanjay embarked on a campaign to sterilize the villagers, which made him very unpopular, and he was also implicated in an industrial and financial scandal. He died on 23 June 1980 in an accident in his private airplane, which he was piloting himself.

THE DEATH OF INDIRA GANDHI

After returning to power in 1980, Indira Gandhi had to face numerous social problems that she attempted to resolve in a highly authoritarian manner. Many Muslim Bengalis, fleeing from the endemic famine of Bangladesh, invaded the northeastern provinces, and particularly the rich province of Assam, causing hostile reactions among the animist and Hindu population. When the central power wished to grant the émigrés the status of residents and the right to vote, a violent revolt and several massacres took place. Indira did not hesitate to employ the army, giving rise to many victims.

In the Andhra country to the southeast, Indira took advantage of the ill health of Rama Rao, the local Prime Minister, who was very popular and belonged to the Hindu opposition. She had him removed and replaced by a man of her own choice. In Kashmir, she likewise removed the Muslim Prime Minister, Farook Abdullah, a very moderate man, whom she suspected of connivance with Pakistan. The Soviet Union occupied Afghanistan, creating serious problems for Pakistan, which found itself squashed between a Soviet Afghanistan and an India allied to the Russians.

In opposition to a project to redistribute the waters of the rivers that irrigate the fertile plains of the Punjab, India's granary, a strong move-ment arose among the Sikh communities that form the vast majority of the Punjab's population. A fanatical religious leader, Jarnail Singh Bhindranwale, began an independence campaign for the Punjab, secretly supported by Pakistan. After several clashes, Indira ordered the occupa-tion of the Sikhs' sacred temple at Amritsar by the Indian army. Bhindranwale was killed and his partisans massacred. There were a great many deaths on both sides.

On 30 October 1984, Indira was assassinated in her garden by a Sikh commando belonging to her personal guard. For several days, a massacre of Sikhs ensued, led by self-styled Hindus who appear to have been agents provocateurs. The Hindus certainly had little sympathy for Indira Gandhi. Sikhs occupied very high positions in the administration and the army. The President of the Indian Republic was a Sikh. It was owing to the moderation of the Sikh and Hindu leaders that the conflict could be contained.

Indira's second son, Rajiv, had given up his job as a pilot in order to assist his mother in politics after the death of his elder brother. To avoid a power vacuum at a critical moment, the members of Congress present in Delhi at once appointed him Prime Minister, thus creating a kind of dynastic succession.

Rajiv is a moderate. The son of a Parsi, raised in England and married to an Italian, he is in fact a foreigner. He may have a more positive vision than Nehru and Indira of the cultural values of traditional India, which have nowadays found a place in Western culture that they lacked a few decades ago. It is on his wisdom and moderation that the unity of India henceforth depends, if he manages to stay in power.

26

Pakistan

From the outset, Pakistan's main problem was to find a raison d'être that could be expressed in a constitution acceptable to its inhabitants as a whole. In 1947 it was set up as a republic under the aegis of the British Crown, but possessed no administrative or political structure other than the goodwill of Mohammed Ali Jinnah.

A first Constituent Assembly was called in 1950, but could not come to an agreement. The religious authorities found that the draft did not conform to Koranic law. A Constitution was finally accepted in 1956, replaced by another in 1962, changed again in 1969, and yet again in 1973.

Mohammed Ali Jinnah, Pakistan's founder and first Governor General, died of tuberculosis in 1948. He was succeeded by one of his faithful collaborators, Liakat Ali Khan, who was assassinated in 1951. Jinnah's death left Pakistan in dire straits. It was he who had invented this toy, which in no way matched the desires of the peoples gathered together against their will, whose differences were more violent than those that separated them from other Indians. The Muslims had governed India for three centuries and felt at home there. It took political intrigue to persuade them that they were a threatened minority.

Sheikh Abdullah, the Muslim leader of Kashmir, and very close to Nehru, had remained in India. Abdul Ghaffer Khan, the Pathan chief of the northwest, was a faithful disciple of Gandhi's. Sheikh Mujibur

Rahman sought India's support and the reunification of Bengal. The President of the Indian Congress Party, Abul Kalam Azad, was a Muslim. The tribes of Baluchistan wanted first and foremost to maintain their autonomy. After the initial moment of exaltation had passed, everyone was wondering what he or she could do in Pakistan. Almost all the Muslim artists and musicians returned to India.

The Muslim League lost power in Bengal in 1954 and in West Pakistan in 1956. Unity disintegrated; corruption and the abuse of power spread throughout the administrative staff. In 1958 the commander-in-chief of the armed forces, Mohammad Ayub Khan, seized power. He suspended the Constitution, abolished political parties and placed the military in all administrative posts. The capital was moved northward to a new city called Islamabad. A political system known as "basic democracy" was started in 1960. The people elected village councils, then provincial councils, up to the National Council. Government representatives took an ex–officio part on all the councils.

The National Council, thus elected, appointed Ayub Khan as President for twenty-five years. Ayub Khan did his best to reestablish the political parties starting from 1962, but the problems of Bengal and general discontent led to riots and he had to resign in 1969. The commander-in-chief of the army, Mohammad Yahya Khan, then took power and called for new elections with a view to forming a new Constituent Assembly. The Awami League of Bengal (East Pakistan) won 162 seats and the People's Party of Zulfikar Ali Bhutto, who opposed Yahya Khan, won 81 of the 138 seats for West Pakistan. The Assembly never sat, since Yahya Khan rejected the conditions of the Awami League that—under the leadership of Sheikh Mujibur Rahman—demanded the independence of East Pakistan. A liberation army was formed in Bengal and undertook widespread guerrilla action. The consequent repression, lasting eight months, was very severe, until India's intervention caused the Pakistani army to surrender. Yahya Khan then resigned.

Zulfikar Ali Bhutto, as leader of the main political grouping, became the master of the new Pakistan, now reduced to its western provinces, and comprising a semi-desert country of 800,000 square kilometers with a

population of 80 million. Bhutto was the first Pakistani leader to be dem-
ocratically elected. He was a skilled politician, arrogant, and without
scruples. He negotiated with India for the return of his army taken prisoner and for the return of some 10,000 square kilometers of territory
occupied by the Indian army. In 1972 Pakistan withdrew from the
British Commonwealth in protest against Britain's recognition of
Bangladesh.

On the home front, Bhutto attacked the rich industrialists. Twenty-
two families shared all the industries among themselves. He also dismissed 12,000 officials accused of corruption and a considerable number
of upper army officers. He also set up a paramilitary organization, the
"Federal Security Forces," that he employed to harass his adversaries.
Whoever criticized his government was beaten and thrown into prison.
As a result of his authoritarian methods, Bhutto gradually lost the sup-
port of his partisans, particularly that of the intellectuals and students.
Government authority was soon threatened by guerrilla movements in
Baluchistan and, more especially, in the Northwest Province, on the
Afghan frontier.

Although the elections to the provincial assemblies in March 1977
appeared to go in Bhutto's favor, they were followed by disturbances on
the pretext that the results had been falsified. Bhutto appealed to the
army and imposed martial law. The military leaders, however, judging
that he had lost popular support, had him arrested and installed General
Mohammad Zia al-Haq as Administrator General. In March 1978
Bhutto was condemned to death for conspiracy. He was hanged in April
1979.

Mohammad Zia took the title of President in September 1978. He
emphasized the Islamic character of his government and established
severe punishments for anyone sinning against Koranic law. He strengthened ties with other Muslim countries of the Middle East and Africa,
who provided him with considerable financial aid. The promised elections were postponed indefinitely.

An artificial country without traditions or unity, Pakistan's only
cohesive element is religion. It can only perpetuate itself as a theocratic

and military state, based on an inquisition and the severity of Koranic law. The West appears not to understand that this return to a medieval concept is by nature incompatible with modern notions of freedom, democracy, and the rights of man. Pakistan can only keep going as an armed camp and can never become a peaceful state.

Pakistan's foreign policy is thus essentially dictated by military objectives, whence its efforts at an alliance with China and the creation of the Karakorum road that—running through passes more than 5000 meters high—opened the gate to Chinese armies coming from Sinkiang toward the Indus Valley, thus forcing India to a rapprochement with the Soviet Union.

According to the British concept, the creation of Pakistan was to be a source of perpetual conflict for the Indian subcontinent, thus maintaining England's power as arbitrator. It was, in fact, a grave political mistake.

The creation of small Islamic states serving as buffers between Russia and India had begun with the Emirate of Bukhara, followed by the creation of Afghanistan and, lastly, of Pakistan. Such states could only be a temptation for the expansionism of the Russian Empire. The situation of Afghanistan today would be different if there were a powerful and united India on its southern border, with an interest in maintaining its independence.

27

National Challenges

SOCIAL AND ECONOMIC PROBLEMS

Since independence, India has had to face a series of problems. Some are common to those of other nations, while others are peculiar to India itself. Such problems are mainly economic, ecological, demographic, cultural, linguistic, social, and religious, without mentioning frontier wars and internal revolutions. India is a country of prodigious wealth. It has every kind of climate, from the burning desert of Thar to the Assam region with the heaviest rainfall in the world, from the fertile Ganges plains to the summits of the Himalayas and the tropical hills of the Nilgiri. It possesses considerable mineral resources and produces an abundance of wheat, rice, tea, coffee, bananas, mangoes, apples, lemons, and maize. The number of vegetable and animal species in India is unrivalled anywhere in the world, while the variety of birds is comparable only to South America. Covering two percent of the world's landmass, India shelters five percent of its known living species.

How could such an El Dorado, whose fabulous riches had always been the envy of other nations of the world, now find itself among the less favored countries? Its exploitation during the colonial period clearly played a part. Since independence, however, the situation has degenerated catastrophically, despite spectacular technical developments, including the atomic bomb and the accompanying triumphant declarations by the government.

The worsening of the situation seems partly due to the second degree colonialism exercised by an indigenous foreign–educated minority, whose will to reform tends to destroy a traditional and workable society by attempting to replace it with a society on a foreign model that does not correspond to the people's way of life. The socialist bourgeoisie that took power in India was against the caste hierarchy, against the moderating power of the poor but powerful learned Brahman priests, and against the power of the princes who, although rich, were imbued with chivalrous principles and were protectors of the people. At the same time, they were also against the corporations that guaranteed the cultural and moral structures and the dignity and defense of the artisan classes.

Wherever it may be, it is difficult to establish the limits between what is called socialism and state capitalism. The socialist state is a formidable machine for pumping the products of a nation's work and its riches under the pretext of redistributing them equitably. It can only function properly under conditions of absolute authoritarianism. Money power that knows how to mix with socialist terminology can acquire considerable hidden force. It is not without reason that the major Indian capitalists have, since its beginning, always supported the policy of the Congress Party that—by breaking down social barriers and group privilege—has allowed them to extend their power over all classes of society.

Mention must also be made of the major banks that have been nationalized. "The public sector now embraces seventeen branches of industry. . . . This policy has in reality favored private capital to the extent to which it creates, at state expense, the bases of the most rapid industrial expansion. . . . In sharing out the rewards of this expansion, India's main capitalist groups and in particular the principal managing agents that have grown up between the two wars (Tata, Birla) have taken the lion's share."[1]

---

1. *Ibid.*, 172–173.

Nationalization, the prohibition on transferring profits abroad, as well as excessive taxes, like those of England, had first and foremost caused all foreign capital to flee. The terms offered to foreign investors have, however, been further liberalized.

According to Narottam Shah—director of the Center for Monitoring the Indian Economy—during the thirty years following independence, India's exports declined from 2.2 percent to 0.4 percent, or over eight billion dollars. India became increasingly dependent on the Soviet Union, to which its 1980–81 exports were valued at eleven and a half million rupees, versus only eight and a half million to the United States.

In 1981 the black market was estimated to be as much as fifty percent of the domestic market. According to official statistics, between 1951 and 1961, domestic income increased by forty-two percent and consumption by sixteen percent. However, the "growth in domestic income has only benefited the more favored classes."[2] Eighty-five percent of the electorate is illiterate and in a condition of semistarvation. In 1972 half the population lived on the equivalent of US$7.20 per month. Despite successive devaluations of the rupee—the first, in 1965, of fifty percent—inflation continues to grow. The population increase is frightening, while resources diminish. A campaign for the (often forced) sterilization of men was a failure and caused violent reactions. Of a population of 700 million, seventy percent are employed in agriculture on properties so small that they hardly suffice to feed a single family. The suppression of large estates and redistribution of the land to the peasants without any adequate funding system has placed the rural population in the clutches of wandering moneylenders. It has led to an exodus toward the cities, creating a wretched proletariat exploited at low cost by an extremely rich industrial class tied to the government.

A plan established in 1951 in favor of agriculture—using new varieties and modern fertilizers on the former farm estates confiscated by the state—enjoyed a certain success and production is said to have increased by twenty-five percent in five years. This, however, brought no profit to

2. *Ibid.*, 74.

the peasant, who had now become a farm worker. At an ecological level, excessive deforestation has produced periods of drought and unprecedented flooding. Seventy percent of the water available today is polluted, the air is polluted, and epidemics are uncontrollable.

The sorcerer's apprentices who have installed themselves comfortably in the seats of the British officials in New Delhi form a tiny oligarchy totally estranged from the culture of India and incapable of mastering the economic and social forces they have unleashed.

Continuing British policy, the new masters of India only recognize the Anglo-Saxon kind of "education." All forms of traditional education are considered non-existent and lead to no kind of employment. The schools and universities produce a growing number of young graduates who no longer belong to Hindu society, but only to the pseudo-society of bureaucrats with anglicized habits. Statistics classifying the majority of the population as illiterate take only modern education into account. A villager knowing no English who has become a lift-boy in Calcutta may well be a poor Brahman who reads the Upanishads in Sanskrit while waiting for his customers. But he is classified among the illiterate.

Nehru wanted to create a new society on the ruins of the old. Every institution and all the reciprocal guarantees of the latter were declared to be null and void. This new society, however, very soon found itself divided into a very rich class with a Western education, a poorly paid middle class with a modern education (engineers, teachers, physicians, etc.), and the enormous mass of the people, totally bewildered, living below the poverty line and making up half the population.

India's intellectual capital is today oriented toward the training of electronic specialists, atomic engineers, and biologists who have hardly any hope other than emigration.

THE FATE OF THE TRIBES

The policy of annexation and social leveling, more theoretical than actual, followed first by Nehru and then by Indira, had tragic consequences for the peasants, but even more so for the tribes, the Adivasis, those first inhabitants of the Indian subcontinent whose way of living, territories, and independence had been respected by Hindu society for thousands of years.

After a few attempts at assimilation, the British Government had adopted an attitude of non-interference toward what it called "the scheduled tribes." This allowed the Adivasis to keep their beliefs and way of living. According to the census of 1976, the Adivasis, grouped in democratic tribes, numbered about forty-one million, almost one tenth of India's population. They had always lived in a state of practical self-sufficiency. "The Adivasi felt wonderfully at ease in the jungle, where he knew the plants and their uses, the habits of the animals. He excelled in building a home, in wielding a hatchet, fashioning tools, sculpting, and weaving his clothes."[3]

For Nehru, "the Adivasis were not a separate racial and cultural group, but only one of the communities, composing with others the backward classes of Indian society."[4] Nehru established a five-point plan, the Panch Shila, for their development, which meant, in fact, their extermination.

Considering the Adivasis as merely backward classes, the Indian authorities sent them educators and missionaries, but also opened their territories to land speculators, money lenders, and vendors of alcoholic drinks, who appropriated the land and ruined the populations, leading to revolts, which have been ferociously repressed.

A city child is as incapable of surviving in the forest as a tribal child is of defending himself in the jungle of industrial society. Refusal to recognize the different aptitudes of the various ethnic groups easily leads to what can be termed democratic slavery—the employment of groups of people, hereditarily less adapted, as servile labor exploited cheaply for the roughest kind of jobs in an urban environment. Thus, the Adivasis, dispossessed of their lands, persecuted by the moneylenders, are forced to serve in the mines and other enterprises for starvation wages and have been rapidly decimated.

---

3. B. D. Sharma, *Tribal Development* (Bhopal, 1978).

4. Ghurie, "The Aborigines So-Called and their Future," in Gerard Busquet and Christian Delacampagne, *Les Aborigènes de l'Inde* (Paris, 1981), 220.

In the Mizo Hills, located between Bangladesh and Burma, the Mizos have been at war since 1959 with the Government of India, which has imposed a night-long curfew for seven years (breach of which can be punished by five years' imprisonment). Agricultural production has been reduced to starve the population. Many have died of hunger. Ladenga, the Mizos' chief, who had received a safe-conduct for negotiations, has been imprisoned. At Chhota Nagpur, in south Bihar, efforts to organize an independent state, Jharkhand, have failed, and the country is now occupied by industry, particularly in the region of Ranchi. Over 600,000 Adivasis have been displaced, "the Adivasi villages are attacked, the peasants beaten and imprisoned under the slightest pretext, their goods pillaged and destroyed."[5] In the Naga country, the Nehru government sent detachments of police, starting from 1953. Since the Sino-Indian conflict in 1962, an independence movement led by a chief called Phizo has received Chinese aid and has even set up a government in exile. "As foreseeable, India's annexation policy has ended in the creation of an All Naga Land Communist Party."[6] "Is it astonishing that these Adivasis, living in such penury, economically exploited, brutalised by the police, unable to win their case with a corrupt administration, should be sensitive to the arguments of Communist leaders who preach violence to them?"[7] In India, under the hypocritical cover of helping "backward" peoples toward progress, we are seeing the exploitation and genocide of populations without any economic or social problems, while at international assemblies India's representatives accuse other countries of colonialism.

THE FUTURE OF INDIA

With its seven hundred and twelve million inhabitants (1982 census), India is one of the largest countries in what is called the Third World. Today, after the end of the colonial era, it is faced with a difficult choice.

---

5. Gerard Busquet and Christian Delacampagne, *Les Aborigènes de l'Inde* (Paris, 1981), 202.

6. *Ibid.*, 192.

7. *Ibid.*, 203.

Modern technical progress—although its point of departure took place in certain European countries—is a general phenomenon, connected to no particular religion or civilization. It would be absurd to believe that the religious, moral, and social principles established by prehistoric Hebrew prophets are a better basis for the development of modern technology than those of Hindu or Buddhist philosophers and legislators.

Japan has clearly demonstrated that although the development of a modern technological civilization required an adaptation of ancient Shinto and Buddhist concepts—similar moreover to the adaptation that the Christian world has had to make—this did not entail the abolition of the values of an ancient culture, or of its social, ethical, and aesthetic traditions. In countries like India, where traditional civilization has been disorganized, scoffed at, and ignored, the choice is much more difficult. Traditionalists would like to reject the modern world as a whole, believing that it is tied to a foreign and hostile civilization. Modernists want to reject as a whole all tradition—which according to them slows down technical development—and seek total integration with a Western society in which they take part only superficially. Thus they tend to transform their country into a sort of suburb of the West, lacking cultural vitality and social cohesion. Since public education on a national scale has been systematically destroyed, leaders with an English education no longer have any access to it and have to content themselves with vague notions of Indian culture. Subconsciously, they take up their former masters' partial judgement on their own institutions.

Thanks to its cellular society, India has managed to preserve most of its institutions, knowledge, philosophy, and arts. The puppets of New Delhi, whatever efforts they make, will change none of it. Hindu institutions are too human, too evolved, too ancient, and concern a population that is too enormous, not to survive cultural revolutions, invasions, governments, or changes of the times. These very institutions have allowed India to maintain its identity throughout thousands of years, while other civilizations of antiquity have been swept away by successive invasions and revolutions. But to reckon up the balance of the institutions, knowledge, and technologies in such a vast and so diversified an area would be a considerable undertaking. Each caste, each ethnic group has its own customary law, its rites, arts, beliefs, festivals, and its marriage or inheritance system. Any effort to standardize or reform such complex institutions, representing thousands of years of civilization and experience, would require a long and thorough study. The ignorance of India's new masters is often amazing. The Indian Parliament passed a law authorizing divorce (forbidden to Brahmans), apparently without being aware that divorce was already legal and practiced according to customary law by ninety-five percent of India's inhabitants.

Is there any solution for India? By abolishing the often cruel rules and prohibitions that had maintained a demographic balance for centuries, an infinitely crueler generalized misery has arisen, destroying the civic virtues and group solidarity that gave life meaning, destroying to a great extent the oases of culture that show the value of a civilization. The efforts—inspired by Western social concepts, whether capitalist or Marxist—to replace the coherent and effective corporations that give pride to their members with unions that are immediately politicized and manipulated create only difficulties and produce a discontented and disoriented working class.

The destruction of the princely states created a vacuum that will be difficult to fill. Although these states had often been weakened and had degenerated, the princes had maintained the social and political structures and principles of government that characterized the Hindu world. Great ministers had shown how this society can adapt itself without trauma to the developments of the industrial age. Industries, mines, transport, hospitals, and agriculture were all far more up to date in the princely states than in British India. The political tradition of India, tied to the warrior and princely caste that embraces and protects religious tradition, is essentially realistic and often Machiavellian. It remains outside the sentimental, mystical, and moral aspects of religious tradition.

Only the Marathas—the realistic warrior folk who had almost succeeded in liberating India from the Muslim yoke—might one day reestablish political and religious balance in an India that is both modern and respectful of its cultural tradition, as was the wish of Tilak, eliminated by Gandhi.

This most ancient and longest lasting of civilizations could contribute much to the modern world if it managed to regain its balance after a millennium of first Muslim, then European domination. Unfortunately, Western countries are very badly informed about the realities of Indian politics. All the Congress government has to do is to favor alternately one of the super-powers in order to obtain the support with which it can crush the traditionalist majority. The break-up of the human ecology system, as well as vegetable and animal ecology, is—here as elsewhere—an endless tangle, to which the only resolution that can be forecast is catastrophic.

India's destiny, like that of the rest of the modern world, is not promising. What is important for the future is that India is able to preserve somewhere, in hidden pockets, just as she has done in the past, the secrets of her ancestral knowledge, from which new civilizations can one day arise. At certain levels, however, a few truly Indian cultural values can be recognized. India's pure classic music has once more found a prime position, also aided by its success outside India. Every year in the West, "new" medicines appear, which are in reality very ancient medicines from India's immense pharmacopeia, lending a certain prestige to the schools of Ayurvedic medicine. Western countries tend to use religion and missionaries less and less as a means of establishing their political and commercial influence. On the contrary, the powerful trend among young Westerners toward the thought, philosophy, and wisdom of India— although superficial and childish and as often as not on the wrong track—has made quite an impression on Indian leaders. They may finally perceive the existence of their great scholars, the possessors of knowledge that is thousands of years old, who nowadays survive in the dark and in poverty.

Editor's Note:
Subsequent Developments
(1983–2002)

Indian history in the two decades since the author's concluding remarks has seen several significant developments. The population now exceeds 1 billion, with India second only to China in population, and the population density of some areas growing at a disturbing pace. However, with strong government support, family planning is on the rise and the annual population growth rate has dropped to 1.85 percent. Literacy has been steadily improving, having reached 65 percent by the end of the twentieth century. Access to education has also improved, and the status and prevalence of courses and institutions that teach traditional knowledge, such as ayurveda and yoga, have increased both within India and abroad.

Although Indian politics have continued to be turbulent, India has remained the world's largest democracy, with a highly vocal free press. Rajiv Gandhi served as Prime Minister from 1984 to 1989. His leadership fostered economic development, furthering the liberalization of policies regarding foreign investment and imports, a direction still being pursued by the government. Computer and other high technology industries have flourished. Trade with the United States and other trading partners like Hong Kong, the United Kingdom, Japan, Germany, and Saudi Arabia has also increased.

Accordingly, the middle class has grown dramatically both in prosperity and percentage of population. The poor still outnumber the middle class three to one, however, and are taunted by the media display of material comforts still unthinkable for them. Rising prices have also had a crushing impact on the lowest paid workers, rural poverty is extreme, and the status of women in most of India is woeful, as demonstrated by a skewed gender ratio (the 2001 census lists the ratio of females to males as 933 females to every 1000 males). This ratio results from the practice of selectivly aborting of female fetuses in India, coupled with poorer nutrition and less access to medical care for female children and women than for males. The average literacy rate of women that is far less than that of males as well (54 percent compared to 76 percent). Although India has become one of the world's major food exporters, half of her children are malnourished. The frustration of the poor manifests itself in frequent anti-government strikes and riots, as well as in nationalist and separatist movements.

In 1987 Rajiv Gandhi authorized military intervention in the intercommunal conflict in Sri Lanka, in response to the influx of Tamil refugees and resulting agitation in Tamilnadu. The Indian army—sent as a peace-keeping force—became a target for both sides as the conflict became increasingly vicious. It was withdrawn in 1989.

As was his mother, Rajiv was assassinated—in May of 1991 while on an electoral tour near Madras—even though he was no longer serving as Prime Minister. Several terrorist groups were active in the country at the time, including those connected with secessionist movements in Assam and Uttar Pradesh. However, investigation confirmed that his assassination was carried out by terrorists belonging to the Liberation Tigers of Tamil Eelam (LTTE), who were angry that India under his leadership did not support their struggle for a separate Tamil state in Sri Lanka.

Although the Congress Party continued in power under Prime Minister P. V. Narasimha Rao (1991–1996), its electoral standing waned until the Hindu nationalist party—the Bharatiya Janata Party (BJP)—took the lead in the 1996 elections. The rise in popularity of the BJP and its advocacy of a Hindu rather than secular nation was fueled by the frustrations of the poor combined with growing concerns about the erosion of traditional values in the face of modern global influences.

Although the BJP—largely due to its extremist stances—at first had difficulty forging a stable coalition government, it has been in power since 1998, with A.B. Vajpayee serving as Prime Minister. Tainted by scandal, Congress has been unable to regain power despite the intense campaign efforts of Rajiv's widow, Sonia Gandhi. Nuclear tests conducted in 1998 stimulated a groundswell of support for the BJP, but its popularity has significantly decreased since then. The BJP's willingness to exploit religious fervor to restore its sagging popularity has contributed to a climate in which religious violence erupts periodically, as in Gujarat in February of 2002.

Pakistan continues to be an unstable and antagonistic neighbor, its government prone to military seizures of power. In 1998 Pakistan and India both conducted nuclear tests, provoking widespread condemnation and international sanctions. Friction over the status of Kashmir—exacerbated by the influx of Islamic terrorists from Afghanistan in the wake of the U.S. government's 2001–2002 "war on terrorism"—teeters on the brink of all-out war.

The demise of the Soviet Union has not had a severe impact on India, which still enjoys close links with Moscow. At the same time, relations with China are steadily improving and the two governments have signed a major trade agreement. Refugees, both political/religious and economic, continue to pour into Bengal from Bangladesh.

The traditional arts and crafts of India have enjoyed a renaissance in the last two decades of the twentieth century, in response to growing interest within India and internationally. In 1985 the governments of India and the United States cooperated in presenting a "Festival of India" to U.S. audiences. Growing numbers of Indian authors writing in English or in translation are also appreciated by a worldwide audience.

Another interesting development is that volunteer groups dedicated to the preservation of what little remains of the natural environment in India are growing in number and influence. Consciousness about environmental destruction and its far-reaching impacts is spreading among the population at the same time as global and local economic pressures raise further threats.

Chronological Table

INDIA		EUROPE, MIDDLE EAST, FAR EAST	
30000 B.C.E.	Proto-Australoids (Nishadas) speaking Munda languages	30000	Beginning of Magdalenian art
10000	A dolichocephalic people speaking Dravidian languages is superposed on the Nishadas	15000	Lascaux, Altamira (paintings)
9990	Beginning of the first Sangam, tradition of Dravidian poets (trad.)		
6000	Beginnings of Shaivism (trad.) Foundation of Kashi (Varanasi) (trad.)		
5550	End of the first Sangam of the Dravidian poets (trad.) Madura (Madurai) drowned by the sea (trad.)		
		5000	Start of the Chogha Mish civilization in Iran (lasting until 3000)
		4500	Beginnings of the urban civilizations whose remains have been found (bricks, metals, wheels, sailboats)
4000?	Rishabha founds the Jain religion (trad.)		
4000	Dravidian exodus westward (?)	4000	First Sumerian documents (Dravidian-type language)
		4000	Start of the Egyptian civilization (Gangetic-type skulls)
		4000	The ancestors of the Minoans arrive in Crete from Asia
3400	Amri (Indus Valley) civilization, Mesopotamian-type pottery in Baluchistan		

Note: Dates derived from traditional sources are indicated by: (trad.)

INDIA		EUROPE, MIDDLE EAST, FAR EAST	
3300	First *Rig Veda* hymns (trad.)	3300	First written Sumerian documents (Ur, Lagash, Eridu) Indian Amazonite found at Ur
3200	First Aryan penetration into northwest India (Gandhara) (trad.)	3200	Start of first Egyptian dynasty, first archaeological documents in Crete, first Egyptian writing
3102	Mahabharata War (trad.) (Aryan defeat), beginning of Kali Yuga (trad.)		
3100	Arishkanemi, 22nd Jain prophet (trad.)	3000	Fo Hi, first Emperor of China (Shaivite symbols)
		3000	Copper used in Persia
		2800–1800	First Minoan civilization in Crete
		2780–2720	Third dynasty in Egypt, beginning of the Old Kingdom
2700	Indus seals found at Kish and Bahrain	2400	Sargon, foundation of Akkad, invasion of Cyprus
		2300	First Babylonian dynasty
2200	Indian cotton exported to Babylon, evidence of sea trade between India and the Middle East		
		2150	Ur-Nammu establishes the supremacy of Ur over the Sumerian cities
		2100	Beginning of the Egyptian Middle Kingdom
		2025	Ur destroyed by the Amorites and Elamites
2000	Iranian pottery found in the Ganges Valley	2000	Palace of Knossos in Crete, appearance of the horse in Asia Minor
1900	New Aryan invasions of India (trad.)	1900	Hittite invasion of Asia Minor, foundation of Boghazköy, foundation of Troy, arrival of blond Greek-speaking Achaeans in Greece
1850	End of the second Sangam of Dravidian poets (trad.)		
1800	Vedic literature of the *Brahmanas* (trad.)	1800	Birth of Abraham at Ur
1800	Separation of the Aryan and Iranian tribes	1800–1550	Second Minoan civilization in Crete
		1792	Reign of Hammurabi, development of Babylon
		1555	Beginning of Egyptian New Kingdom
		1550	End of second Minoan civilization
		1500	Beginnings of civilization in Europe, iron used by the Hittites

INDIA	EUROPE, MIDDLE EAST, FAR EAST
1400 Aryan kings in western Asia	1400 Existence of Jerusalem; inscriptions of the Mittani kings at Boghazköy; the Armenians discover an economical process for iron; Knossos invaded by the Mycenaeans; Hebrew tribes are still nomadic
1380 The Assyrians dominate the upper Tigris Valley	
1375 Aryan gods worshipped at Mittani	
	1350 Death of Tut Ankh Amon (end of the 18th dynasty)
1300 The Aryans dominate the northwest as far as the River Saraswati	1300 Babylon taken by the Semitic Assyrians
1275 Victory of Ramses II over the Hittites	
1200 Transcription of the Vedic hymns	1200 Etruscans in Lydia mentioned by the Egyptians
1190 Siege of Troy by the Mycenaeans	
1100 The Aryans occupy the whole of the Punjab	1100 Start of the Iron Age in Greece
	1100 Dorian invasion destroys the Mycenaeans; the Hittites are driven out of Asia Minor; Egypt is defeated by the Libyans and Nubians
1050 The Aryans extend their dominion over the Ganges Valley (trad.)	
	1025 Saul, first king of the Hebrews
	1010–970 David
1000 The Aryans penetrate Gujarat	
1000 The Vedic literature of the *Sutras* (trad.)	
	970–933 Solomon, who imports ivory, monkeys, and peacocks from south India
900 Brahmi (Phoenician) writing is adopted in India	900 The Etruscans, driven out of Lydia, arrive in Italy
	900–800 Homer
817 Birth of Parshvadeva (23rd Jain prophet)	
800 Major trade between India and Babylon	800 Foundation of Carthage by the Phoenicians
778 Death of Parshvadeva; Vedic literature (*Brahmanas*) (according to modern historians)	
750 The Aryans extend their dominion over the Ganges Valley (according to modern historians)	
642–320 Shishunaga-Nanda period	

INDIA	EUROPE, MIDDLE EAST, FAR EAST
	612 Niniveh, the Assyrian capital, taken by the Babylonians, Medes, and Scyths
600 Vedic literature, period of the *Sutra*s (according to modern historians) Kharoshthi (Aramaic) writing appears in India	
	597 Nebuchadnezzar (of Babylon) leads the Hebrews into captivity; Teak from Malabar found in Babylon
563–483 Siddhartha Gautama Buddha	
559–468 Mahavira (24th Jain prophet)	
	558–530 Cyrus, King of Persia
	549–468 Hecataeus of Miletus
525–500 Bimbisara, King of Magadha	525 Cambyses, King of Persia, conquers Egypt
	522–486 Darius I, King of Persia; the Achaemenid Empire stretches from India to Greece
520 The Indus annexed by the Persians	
517 The expedition of Skylax	
500–475 Ajatashatru, King of Magadha	
500 The grammarian Panini	
	490 Battle of Plataea (the Greeks repel Darius's invasion)
	486–465 Xerxes, King of Persia
	480 Athens destroyed by Xerxes; many Buddhist philosophers and monks visit Greece and Egypt
425–325 The Nanda Dynasty	
416 *Indika* by Ktesias	
356–323 Alexander	
326 Alexander invades India	
325 Alexander leaves India	
325 Chandragupta Maurya seizes the throne of Magadha	
325–184 The Maurya Dynasty	
321–297 Chandragupta	312–280 Seleucus Nicator, King of Syria
305 Alliance between Seleucus and Chandragupta	
300 Megasthenes at Chandragupta's court	
300 *Artha Shastra* by Kautilya	
	286–247 Antiochus II Theos, King of Syria
	285–247 Ptolemy Philadelphus, King of Egypt

INDIA	EUROPE, MIDDLE EAST, FAR EAST
274–237 Reign of Ashoka	
220 Establishment of Andhra power Kharavela, King of Kalinga	
206 Expedition of Antiochus III, King of Syria, to India	
200 First frescoes at Ajanta	
187–175 The Shunga Dynasty	
	171–138 Mithridates I, King of Parthia
165 Yueh Chi defeated by the Huns	
165 Plato, King of Bactria	
151 Death of Pushyamitra	
150 *Mahabhashya* by Patanjali	
	138–128 Phraades II, King of Parthia
	138 Conflict between Parthians and Scythians in Iran
	135 The Scythians invade Bactria
	128–123 Artabanus I, King of Parthia
	123–88 Mithridates II, King of Parthia
100 Intense trade with Rome	
78 Manes, first Scythian king in India	
75 Start of the Kanva Dynasty; Scythian supremacy over the Punjab	
50 End of the third Sangam of the Tamil poets (trad.)	
30 End of the last Greek kingdom	
25 Expedition sent by Augustus to check the sea route to India	
26–20 Indian embassy to Augustus; Establishment of the Satavahana dynasty (Andhra)	
	22 Augustus's embassy to King Pandion (South India)
1 C.E. Sanchi *stupa*	1 Birth of Jesus Christ
48 The Yueh Chi Kushanas occupy Gandhara	
	50 Beginnings of the Hinduization of southeast Asia
	70 *Periplus of the Erythraean Sea* Destruction of the temple at Jerusalem
78 Beginning of the Shaka (Scythian) era	
	80 Building of the Colosseum
90 Baalbek	
98–117 Trajan	
100 Indian embassy to Trajan	

INDIA	EUROPE, MIDDLE EAST, FAR EAST
117–138 Hadrian	
120–380 Scythian domination over western India	120 Considerable Indian colony at Alexandria
120 Amaravati *stupa* Indian embassy to Hadrian	
	138–161 Antoninus Pius
140 Ptolemy's *Geography*	
144? Accession of Kanishka; Greco-Buddhist art; Mathura sculptures	
150 Indian embassy to Antoninus Pius	
	160 Arrival of first Buddhist monks in China
162? Death of Kanishka	
	200 Palmyra, Roman colony
212 Baths of Caracalla; the Franks settle on the Rhine	
220 Indian embassy to Heliogabalus	
	225 Accession of the Sassanid Dynasty (Persia)
270–275 Aurelian	
273 Indian embassy to Aurelian	
300 Accession of the Gupta Dynasty	
319–330 Chandragupta	323–353 Constantine
330–380 Samudragupta	330 Foundation of Constantinople
340 Indian embassy to Constantine	
362 Indian embassy to Julian	
380 End of the Shaka (Scythian) Empire	
380–415 Vikramaditya	
399–414 Journey of Fa Hsien; Kalidasa	
400 The Huns settle in Gandhara Ajanta frescoes	
450–650 Sri Lanka frescoes; Aihole temples	451 Defeat of Attila
	481–511 Clovis
500 Deogarh temple; The Huns invade Rajputana, Punjab, and Kashmir	527–565 Justinian
530 Indian embassy to Justinian	531 Chosroes I, King of Persia
550 End of the Gupta Empire	
570 Development of the Pallava Dynasty	
	590–604 Gregory the Great
606–647 Harsha	
	618 Accession of the Tang Dynasty (China)
622 Start of the Hegira	
629–645 Journey of Hiuen Tsang	

INDIA	EUROPE, MIDDLE EAST, FAR EAST
650–663 The Arabs occupy Herat and Kabul	
700 The Pala Dynasty in Bengal	
	711 The Arabs in Spain The Nara Buddha in Japan
712 The Arabs invade Sind	
725 Vijayeshvara temple at Pattadakal	
731 Yashovarman embassy to China	
733 Charles Martel halts the Arab invasion at Poitiers	
751–768 Pépin le Bref	
768–814 Charlemagne	
778 Java; Borobudur	
790 Euclid is translated into Arabic	
794 Kyoto becomes Japan's capital	
788–820 Shankara, exponent of non-dualist philosophy (Advaita)	
800 Kailasa temple at Ellora	800 The Turks occupy Turfan
809 Death of Haroun al-Rashid	
816 The Pratiharas take Kanauj	
	820 Start of the Norman invasions
840–890 Bhoja	
850 Mukteshvara temple at Bhubaneshwar	864 Foundation of Kiev
885 The Normans besiege Paris	
900 End of the Pallava Dynasty	
	901 Sicily conquered by the Arabs
907–1251 Chola Empire	
	936 The Hungarians invade Europe
954 Khajuraho (Lakshmana temple)	
	962 Otto I the Great founds the Germanic Holy Roman Empire
987 Accession of the Capetians	
987–996 Hughes Capet	
998–1030 Mahmud of Ghazni	
1000 Khajuraho (Mahadeva temple); Bhubaneshwar (Lingaraja temple)	
1005 Muslim occupation of the Punjab by Mahmud of Ghazni	
	1010 Sicily conquered by Norman knights
1014 Destruction of the Mathura temple	
1018 Sack of Kanauj; Mahmud of Ghazni occupies the eastern side of the Ganges basin	
1020 Tanjore temple	

INDIA	EUROPE, MIDDLE EAST, FAR EAST
	1037 Death of Avicenna
1055–1113 Ramanuja defines qualified non-dualist philosophy (Vishishtadvaita)	
	1065 Chanson de Roland
	1066 Conquest of England by William of Normandy
	1078 Jerusalem taken by the Turks
	1095 St. Mark's in Venice
	1099 Jerusalem taken by the crusaders
	1100 Angkor Wat
	1162–1227 Genghis Khan
	1163 Notre-Dame in Paris
	1180 Angkor Thom
	1182–1226 St. Francis of Assisi
1186 Muhammad of Ghour, Lord of Ghazni	
1192–1196 Northern India conquered by Muhammad of Ghour	
	1198 Death of Averrhoes
1202 Varanasi taken by the Muslims	
	1209–1229 The Albigensian Crusade
1210–1236 Iltutmish, Sultan of Delhi	
	1215 Peking taken by Genghis Khan
1220–1230 Building of Qutb Minar	
1221 Arrival of the Mongols, led by Genghis Khan	1226–1270 St. Louis
	1236 *Roman de la Rose*
1240 Lahore ravaged by Mongols	1243 Sainte-Chapelle
1250 Konark	
1266 Balban, Sultan of Delhi	1266–1337 Giotto
	1266–1274 St. Thomas Aquinas
	Introduction of Islam in Indonesia
	1271–1295 Journey of Marco Polo
1287 Death of Balban	1285–1314 Philippe le Bel
1290 Firuz founds the Khalji Dynasty	
	1291 Start of the Swiss Confederation
1296 Ala-ud-din, Sultan of Delhi	
1308–1326 Muslim conquest of the Deccan and south India	
1320 Ghiyas-ud-din founds the Tughluq Dynasty	
	1320–1388 Hafiz, Persian poet
	1321 Death of Dante

INDIA	EUROPE, MIDDLE EAST, FAR EAST
1336 Foundation of the Kingdom of Vijayanagar	
	1337 Start of the Hundred Years' War
	1363–1405 Timur (Tamerlane)
	1368–1644 Ming Dynasty at Peking
1369 Timur (Tamerlane) accedes to the throne of Samarkand	
1374 Vijayanagar embassy to China	
1380–1420 Kabir	
	1386 Timur takes Isfahan, Shiraz, Baghdad
	1387–1455 Fra Angelico
1398 Timur invades India and takes Delhi	
	1429 Joan of Arc at Orleans
	1430–1470 François Villon
	1447–1501 Botticelli
	1450 Guttenberg
	1452–1519 Leonardo da Vinci
	1453 End of the Hundred Years' War, Constantinople taken by the Mongol-Turks
	1461–1483 Louis XI
1498 Vasco da Gama arrives in India	
	1500–1524 Ismail Safavi founds the Safavid Empire in Persia
1504 Babur takes Kabul	
1510 Albuquerque seizes Goa	
	1515–1547 François I
	1520–1566 Suleiman the Magnificent adds southeastern Europe to the Turkish Empire
1524 Babur occupies Lahore	
1525 Battle of Panipat; Babur occupies Delhi	
1526–1530 The Mongol-Turks subdue the Afghans and Rajputs	
1530 Death of Babur; accession of Humayun	
1538 Death of Guru Nanak	
1545 Death of Sher Shah	
1556 Death of Humayun	1558–1603 Elizabeth I
1556–1605 Reign of Akbar	1564–1616 Shakespeare
1565 Vijayanagar destroyed by the Muslims	
	1586 Execution of Mary Stuart
	1589–1610 Henry IV

INDIA	EUROPE, MIDDLE EAST, FAR EAST
1600 Creation of the East India Company	
1605–1627 Jahangir	
	1610–1643 Louis XIII
1616 Arrival of the Danes	
1628–1658 Shah Jahan	
1630–1680 Shivaji	
	1630–1685 Charles II
	1630 Treaty of Madrid
	1643–1715 Louis XIV
	1653–1658 Cromwell
1658 The Dutch take Sri Lanka	
1658–1707 Aurangzeb	
1664 Foundation of the Compagnie française des Indes orientales	1664–1716 Colbert
1673 The French acquire Pondicherry	
1690 Building of Chandernagor	
1698 The English found Calcutta and annex Bombay	
	1713 Treaty of Utrecht
	1715–1774 Louis XV
1725 Mahé annexed by the French	
1739 Nadir Shah takes Delhi	
1740–1754 Dupleix, Governor of Pondicherry	1740–1748 The War of the Austrian Succession
	1763 Treaty of Paris
1765 The English acquire full sovereignty over Bengal	
1772 Warren Hastings, Governor of Bengal	
	1774–1792 Louis XVI
1782–1799 Tipu Sultan	
	1804–1814 Napoleon I
1806 Death of Shah Alam II	
	1814–1824 Louis XVIII
	1837–1901 Victoria
1842 British army destroyed by the Afghans at the Khyber Pass	
1844 Anglo-Russian Treaty	
	1848 Second Republic
1849 Annexation of the Punjab	
1852 Annexation of Burma	1852 Napoleon III
1857–1859 Indian Mutiny	
	1871 Third Republic
1876 Victoria becomes Empress of India	
1880 Creation of the Indian National Congress	

INDIA	EUROPE, MIDDLE EAST, FAR EAST
1947 Declaration of Independence of India and Pakistan	
1948 Death of Gandhi	
1948 Death of Jinnah	
	1951 Chinese invasion of Tibet
1964 Death of Nehru	
	1973 End of Vietnam War
1965 Indira Gandhi, Prime Minister	
1971 Independence of Bangladesh	
	1979 The Shah leaves Iran
1980 Indira Gandhi returns to power	1980 Russian invasion of Afghanistan

Bibliography

Adigal, Ilango. *Le Roman de l'Anneau (Shilappadikaram)*. Translated from the Tamil by Alain Daniélou and R. S. Desikan. second edition. Paris, 1981.

Agrawala, Vasudeva S. *India as Known to Panini*. Varanasi-Benares, 1963.

———. *Matsya Purana—A Study*. Varanasi, 1963.

———. *Vamana Purana—A Study*. Varanasi, 1964.

Antonova, K., Bongard-Levine, and Kotvski G. *Histoire de l'Inde*. Moscow, 1979.

Arrian. *L'Inde*. Translated by Pierre Chantraine. Paris, 1927.

———. *Anabasis of Alexander*. English translation by J. W. McCrindle. Edited by R. C. Majumdar in *The Classical Accounts of India*. Calcutta, 1960.

Banerjea, G. N. *Hellenism in Ancient India*. Delhi, 1961.

Banerji, R. D. *Prehistoric Ancient and Hindu India*. Bombay, 1942.

Barton, George A. *Semitic and Hamitic Origins Social and Religious*. Philadelphia, 1934.

Bary, Wm. Theodore de. *Sources of Indian Tradition*. New York, 1966.

Bhalchandra, Shantaram. *History of Jaina Monachism*. Poona, 1956.

Bhandarkar, D. R. *Carmichael Lectures*. Oxford, 1921.

Bhowmick, P. K. *The Lodhas of West Bengal*. Calcutta, 1963.

Bory, J. B., Cook, S. A., and Adcock, F. E. *The Cambridge Ancient History*. Cambridge, 1964.

———. *Bulletin of the Institute of Traditional Cultures-Madras*. Madras.

———. *The Cambridge History of India*. 6 vols. Indian Edition. Delhi, 1963.

Busquet, Gèrard, and Delacampagne, Christian. *Les Aborigènes de l'Inde*. Paris, 1981.

Chattopadhyaya, Sudhakar. *Early History of North India.* Calcutta, 1958.

———. *Chronology of Gujarat.* Baroda, 1960.

Cœdes, G. *Les Etats Hindouisés d'Indochine et de l'Indonésie.* Paris, 1948.

Collins, Larry, and Lapierre, Dominique. *Cette nuit la liberté.* Paris, 1975.

Coomaraswamy, Ananda K. *History of Indian and Indonesian Art.* London, 1927.

Cunningham, Sir Alexander. *Ancient Geography of India.* Calcutta, 1924.

Dani, Ahmad Hasan. *Prehistory and Protohistory of Eastern India.* Calcutta, 1960.

Daniélou, Alain. *Shiva and Dionysus.* Vermont, 1984.

Dubois, Abbé J.A. *Hindu Manners and Customs.* third edition. Oxford, 1928.

Dumont, L. *Homo Hierarchicus, Essai Sur Le Système Des Castes.* Paris, 1966.

Edwardes, Michael. *A History of India.* Bombay, 1961.

Etienne, G. *Les Chances de l'Inde.* second edition. Paris, 1973.

Fa Hsien. *The Travels of Fa Hsien, A.D. 399-414.* Translated by H. A. Giles. London, 1923–1959.

Fischer, Louis. *The Life of Mahatma Gandhi.* London, 1951.

Frankfort, H. "The Indus Civilization and the Near East." *Annual Bibliography of Indian Archaeology.* Leyden.

Gokhale, B. G. *Ancient India.* Bombay, 1942.

Ghurie, "The Aborigines So-Called and Their Future." In Busquet, Gèrard and Delacampagne, Christian. *Les Aborigènes de l'Inde.* Paris, 1981.

Gyani, S. D. *Agni Purana, A Study.* Varanasi, 1964.

Hall, H.R. *The Ancient History of the Near East.* London, 1913.

Hastings, James, and Gray, Louis A. *Encyclopaedia of Religion and Ethics.* 12 vols. Edinburgh, 1953-59.

Hazra, R.C. *Studies in the Upapuranas.* Calcutta, 1963.

Heury, R. *Les Sommaires de Photius, (Crésias, la Perse, l'Inde).* Bruxelles, 1947.

Heras, S. J., *Studies in Proto-Indo-Mediterranean Culture.* Bombay, 1953.

———. *The History of India as Told by Its Own Historians,* the Posthumous Papers of the Late Sir H. M. Elliot. Calcutta, 1867.

Hiuen Tsang. *Travels.* English translation by Samuel Beal. London, 1884. Reproduced in *Chinese Accounts of India.* Calcutta, 1963.

Hultzsch, ed. *Corpus Inscriptionem Indicarum.* Oxford, 1925.

Jaisabhoi, R. A. *Foreign Influence in Ancient India*. Bombay, 1963.

——. *Journal of The Royal Asiatic Society*. London, 1898.

Karmarkar, A. P. *Cultural History of Karnataka*. Dharwar, 1947.

Kautilya. *Kautilya's Arthasastra*. English translation by H. Shamasastry. Mysore, 1929.

Khosla, G. D. *Stern Reckoning*. New Delhi, 1950.

Law, Bimala Charana. *India as Described in Early Texts of Buddhism and Jainism*. London, 1941.

Leemans, W. F. *Foreign Trade in the Old Babylonian Period*. Leyden, 1928.

Macdonell, A. A. *India's Past*. London, 1956.

——. *Mahabharata (The)* In Sanskrit. 9 vols. Benares, 1940.

Geiger, W., ed. *Mahavamsha*. Translated by W. Geiger. London, 1908–1912.

Majumdar, R. C. *Ancient India*. Delhi, 1964.

——. *The Classical Accounts of India*. Calcutta, 1960.

——. *History of the Freedom Movement in India*. 3 vols. Calcutta, 1962–63.

Majumdar, R. C., and Pulasker, A. D. *The History and Culture of the Indian People*. Bombay, 1951–1965.

Majumdar, R. C., Raychaudhuri, H. C., and Datta, K. *An Advanced History of India*. London, 1965.

Marshall, Sir John. *Mohenjo Daro and the Indus Civilization*. 13 vols. London, 1931.

McCrindle, J. W. *Ancient India as Described by Megasthenes and Arrian*. London 1877. Calcutta, 1960.

——. *Ancient India as Described by Ptolemy*. Bombay, 1885. Calcutta, 1927.

Megasthenes. *Indika*. Fragments gathered by Dr. Schanbeck and translated by J. W. McCrindle. In *Ancient India as Described by Megasthenes and Arrian*. London, 1877. Calcutta, 1960.

Metcalf, T. R. *Modern India*. London, 1971.

Mittal, Amar Chand. *An Early History of Orissa*. Benares, 1957.

Mookerjee, R. K. *Chandragupta Maurya and His Time*. Madras, 1943.

——. *The Gupta Empire*. Bombay, 1959.

Mortimer Wheeler, Sir R. E. "The Civilization of the Indus." *Antiquity*. XXXII. 1958.

Mukerjee, L. *History of India*. Calcutta, 1938.

Munshi, K. M. *The Age of Imperial Unity*. Bombay, 1951. Also in *The History and Culture of the Indian People*. Bombay, 1960.

Murthy, Dr. H. Y. Sreenivasa. *History of Ancient India*. Pathsala-Assam, 1963.

Narain, A. K. *The Indo-Greeks*. Oxford, 1957.

Nehru, Jawaharlal. *Autobiography*. London, 1936.

Panikkar, K. M. *Survey of Indian History*. London, 1960.

Pargiter, F. E. *Ancient Indian Historical Tradition*. Delhi, 1922.

———. *Purana Text of the Dynasties of the Kali Age*. Varanasi, 1913.

Patanjali. *Mahabhashya*. In Sanskrit. Edited by Sadaranjan Roy Vidyavinod. Calcutta, 1926.

Pathak, Vishuddhanand. *History of Kosala*. Delhi, 1963.

Pouchpadass, Jacques. *L'Inde au XXe Siècle*. Paris, 1975.

Philips, C. H. *East India Company*. second edition. London, 1962.

Prasada, Durga, ed. *Rajatarangini*. English translation by R. S. Pandit. Allahabad, 1935.

Premi, Nathuram. *Jaina Sahitya aur Ithihasa*. In Hindi. Bombay, 1942.

Priaulx, Osmond de Beauvoir. *The Indian Travels of Apollonius of Tyana and the Indian Embassies to Rome*. London, 1873.

Puri, Baijnath. *India in Classical Greek Writings*. Ahmedabad, 1963.

Radhakrishnan, Sarvapalli. *Eastern Religion and Western Thought*. London, 1940.

Ragozin, Zanaide A. *Vedic India*. Delhi, 1961.

Rajaram, Devendrakumar. *Cultural History from the Vayu Purana*. Poona, 1946.

Rawlinson, H. C. *Indian Historical Studies*. London, 1913.

———. *Intercourse Between India and The Western World*. Cambridge, 1916.

Renou, Louis, and Filliozat, Jean. *L'Inde Classique*. Paris, 1953.

Rhys-Davids, T.W. *Buddhist India*. London, 1903. Calcutta, 1950.

Saletore, Bhaskar Anand. *Ancient Karnataka*. Poona, 1936-44.

Sankalia, H. D. *Prehistory and Protohistory of India and Pakistan*. Bombay, 1962.

Sastri, Nilakanta K. A. *The Age of the Nandas and Mauryas*. Benares, 1952.

———. *Early History of the Deccan*. Calcutta, 1960.

———. *The History and Culture of the Tamils*. Calcutta, 1964.

Scharma, B. D. *Tribal Development*. Bhopal, 1978.

Schröder. *Pythagoras und die Inder*. Leipzig, 1884.

Sen, Amulyachandra. *Ashoka's Edicts*. Calcutta, 1956.

Sen, S. P. *French in India*. Calcutta, 1958.

Sharma, B. D. *Tribal Development*. Bhopal, 1978.

Sharma, Ram Sharan. *Sudras in Ancient India*. Delhi, 1958.

Smith, V. A. *Early History of India*. Oxford, 1924.

———. *Oxford History of India*. Oxford, 1958.

Spear, Percival. *History of India*. London, 1965–70.

Suryavanshi, Bhagwansingh. *The Abhiras, their History and Culture*. Baroda, 1962.

Tampimuttu, E. L. *Dravida*. Madras, 1945.

Tilak, Lokamanya. *The Antic Home of the Vedas*. Poona, 1925.

Toynbee, Arnold J. *Between Oxus and Jumna*. London, 1961.

Tripathi, R. S. *History of Ancient India*. Delhi, 1942.

Upadhyaya, Baladeva. *Bharatiya Darshana*. In Hindi. Benares, 1942.

Upadhyaya, Bhagwat Saran. *India in Kalidasa*. Allahabad, 1947.

Vatsyayana. *Kamasutra*. With commentary by Yashodhara. In Sanskrit. Benares, 1929.

———. *Vishnu Purana*. In Sanskrit with commentary in Hindi. Gorakhpur, 1936.

Verrier, Elwin. *The Aboriginals*. Oxford, 1944.

Vishakhadatta. *Mudra Rakshasa*. Edited by R.S. Walimbe. Poona, 1948.

Wheeler, James Talboys. *Ancient and Hindu India*. Calcutta, 1961.

Wilson, H. H. *The Vishnu Purana*. Calcutta, 1961.

Woodcock, George. *The Greeks in India*. London, 1966.

Xenophon. *Anabasis*. Translated by Rex Warner. Edinburgh, 1949.

Index